Getting It Wrong

ALSO BY W. JOSEPH CAMPBELL

Getting It Wrong

*Debunking the Greatest Myths
in American Journalism*

Second Edition

W. Joseph Campbell

UNIVERSITY OF CALIFORNIA PRESS

University of California Press, one of the most
distinguished university presses in the United States,
enriches lives around the world by advancing scholarship
in the humanities, social sciences, and natural sciences. Its
activities are supported by the UC Press Foundation and
by philanthropic contributions from individuals and
institutions. For more information, visit www.ucpress.edu.

University of California Press
Oakland, California

Library of Congress Cataloging-in-Publication Data

Names: Campbell, W. Joseph, author.
Title: Getting it wrong : debunking the greatest myths in
American journalism / W. Joseph Campbell.
Description: Second edition. | Oakland, California :
University of California Press, [2017] | Originally
published: 2010. | Includes bibliographical references
and index.
Identifiers: LCCN 2016028742 (print) | LCCN 2016030205
(ebook) | ISBN 9780520291270 (cloth : alk. paper) |
ISBN 9780520291294 (pbk. : alk. paper) |
ISBN 9780520965119 (Epub)
Subjects: LCSH: Journalistic ethics—United States—
History—20th century. | Journalism—Objectivity—
United States—History—20th century. | Press and
politics—United States—History—20th century. |
Sensationalism in journalism—United States—
History—20th century. | Journalism—Social aspects—
United States—History—20th century.
Classification: LCC PN4756 .C36 2017 (print) | LCC PN4756
(ebook) | DDC 174/.9097—dc23
LC record available at https://lccn.loc.gov/2016028742

25   24   23   22   21   20   19   18   17
10   9   8   7   6   5   4   3   2   1

To the memory of Verne E. Edwards Jr.,
journalism educator

Contents

Illustrations

Preface to the Second Edition

In the early years of his vice presidency, Joe Biden went to Moscow and repeated the heroic-journalist trope of Watergate. He told a university audience in a speech that "it was a newspaper, not the FBI, or the Justice Department, it was a newspaper—the *Washington Post*—that brought down a President for illegal actions."[1]

Biden was referring to the fall of President Richard M. Nixon in August 1974 and, in doing so, invoked the popular media myth that the *Post*'s reporting of the Watergate scandal had uncovered the crimes that forced the president's resignation. The claim is exaggerated and extravagant, but it resonates across the political spectrum. Rush Limbaugh, the combative conservative talk-radio host, has likewise indulged in the heroic-journalist myth. He declared on his program in 2013 that the *Post*'s Watergate reporting "destroyed the Nixon presidency."[2] On a show a few days before that, Limbaugh referred to one of the *Post*'s Watergate reporters, Bob Woodward, and declared: "Woodward brought down Nixon."[3]

It's an interpretation that not even Woodward embraces. As he once said on the PBS program *Frontline,* "The mythologizing of our role in Watergate has gone to the point of absurdity, where journalists write . . . that I, single-handedly, brought down Richard Nixon. Totally absurd."[4] Still, the heroic-journalist trope lives on as the dominant narrative of Watergate, as easily understood shorthand about the outcome of a scandal that was formidable in its complexity.

The heroic-journalist trope cited by Biden and Limbaugh demonstrates the broad, bipartisan appeal of media-driven myths. And it is suggestive of how luminaries—authors, entertainers, and social critics, as well as politicians and talk show hosts—not infrequently give expression and amplification to "media myths," those tall tales about journalists and the news media that masquerade as fact. The roster of well-known personalities who have done so in recent years is not short. And the upshot is not trivial: prominent people retelling media myths ensures that the content will reach wide audiences, which, in turn, makes the myths all the more difficult to uproot. Such contributions to the diffusion of media myths have become better recognized, and better documented, in the years following publication of the first edition of *Getting It Wrong* in 2010.

Since then, for example, the popular storyteller and humorist Garrison Keillor has told listeners of *The Writer's Almanac,* his podcast that airs on NPR, about the hoary tale of William Randolph Hearst and his vow to "furnish the war" with Spain. The occasion for Keillor's treating the myth was the 152nd anniversary, in 2015, of Hearst's birth.[5]

The alleged vow meshes well with the misleading and superficial image of Hearst as warmonger, as an unscrupulous media mogul who fomented armed conflict between the United States and Spain in 1898. That he did is another media myth—one repeated by Juan Williams, a political commentator for the Fox News Channel, in his 2011 book, *Muzzled: The Assault on Honest Debate.* Williams wrote that Hearst and his leading newspaper competitor, Joseph Pulitzer, "became infamous for starting a real war. They whipped up so much anger at Spain . . . that they incited the United States to go to war with Spain in the Spanish-American War."[6] No, they didn't: serious historians of the Spanish-American War period reject that interpretation, and for good reason. The diplomatic impasse that gave rise to war with Spain had little to do with newspaper reporting and was far beyond the ability of Hearst or Pulitzer to control, let alone much influence.[7]

Other instances of celebrities giving media myths their imprimatur are not hard to find. In an online commentary written for the *New York Times* in 2015, former television talk show host Dick Cavett invoked the mythical "Cronkite Moment" of 1968, which has it that Walter Cronkite's pessimistic, on-air assessment about the conflict in Vietnam led President Lyndon B. Johnson to alter his war policy. Cronkite then was the anchorman of CBS News. "At long, long last the war was ended," Cavett wrote. "Not by a president or a Congress or by the protesters.

Someone said it was the only war in history ever ended by a journalist. 'The Most Trusted Man in America,' Walter Cronkite, not always a critic of the war, went to see the damage of the Tet offensive [in 1968], came back, and said on his news broadcast that we had to get out. The beleaguered Lyndon Johnson's reported reaction: 'If I've lost Cronkite, I've lost Middle America.'"[8]

In 2015, Robert Reich, a former U.S. labor secretary, referred to the television program in which Edward R. Murrow supposedly unmasked Senator Joseph R. McCarthy and his red-baiting tactics. "In the 1950s," Reich wrote in a commentary, "the eminent commentator Edward R. Murrow "revealed Wisconsin Sen. Joe McCarthy to be a dangerous incendiary, thereby helping end McCarthy's communist witch hunts."[9] McCarthy, though, had been recognized as "a dangerous incendiary" long before Murrow's program was broadcast in March 1954.

And so it goes: prominent people, in their statements and their writings, propel dubious tales about the media. Their doing so has been slapdash, undoubtedly unintentional, and naïve. Even so, the effect has been to send media myths further into the popular consciousness.

The years since the first edition of *Getting It Wrong* was published also have brought frequent reminders of just how close to the surface media myths exist, how easy they are to summon, and how resistant to repudiation they can be. All that is required, sometimes, is a passing anniversary or the death of a celebrated journalist to unleash a surge of myth-telling. The seventy-fifth anniversary of the *War of the Worlds* radio performance in October 1938 was such an occasion. The anniversary was accompanied by reminders of how the dramatization, which told of Martians invading New Jersey and New York, supposedly sent waves of panic swarming across America.[10] On the eve of the anniversary in 2013, PBS aired an hour-long documentary promoting the notion that the *War of the Worlds* radio show scared many Americans out of their wits. But in fact there is no evidence that such reactions were anything more than isolated, anecdotal, and rare.

The death in 2014 of Ben Bradlee, the executive editor at the *Washington Post* during the Watergate period, set off an outpouring of claims that, under Bradlee's supervision, the newspaper had taken down Nixon. *USA Today*, for example, declared that Bradlee "led" the *Post*'s "Watergate coverage that brought down the Nixon administration."[11] The London *Independent* newspaper said in its obituary about Bradlee that the *Post*'s reporting "eventually brought down President Richard Nixon."[12] Few journalists recalled Bradlee's more modest interpretation:

It "must be remembered," he said in 1997, "that Nixon got Nixon. The *Post* didn't get Nixon."[13] Bradlee was referring to Nixon's secret audio tapes that revealed the president's complicity in attempting to conceal the crimes of Watergate. The incriminating content of the tapes made his resignation inevitable.

For journalists, these myths are very seductive: they place the news media at the epicenter of vital and decisive moments of the past, they tell of journalistic bravado and triumph, and they offer memorable if simplistic narratives that are central to journalism's amour propre. They also encourage an assumption that, disruption and retrenchment in their field notwithstanding, journalists can be moved to such heights again. Remembering and repeating these romanticized tales is perhaps understandable in that they bring some measure of reassurance to a battered profession.

As such, there is little incentive for journalists to revisit and discard those narratives or explain how they came to be. What is known as "motivated blindness"[14]—the inclination to overlook or ignore information that runs counter to one's interests—helps account for the persistence of media myths. But debunking myths is crucial, as doing so forces a sharper and more sophisticated understanding of journalism, its legacies, and its place in contemporary culture. If our understanding of the news media is to be perceptive and astute, then it is important to get beyond the myths and the distortions they present. There is, after all, scant value in standing idly by while the past is romanticized and misrepresented.

The universe of media myths was by no means confined to the ten myths examined and dismantled in the first edition of *Getting It Wrong*. This edition presents three new chapters that discuss the following topics: the popular notion that television viewers and radio listeners differed sharply as to who won the first televised presidential debate in 1960 between Richard Nixon and John F. Kennedy; the famous *Napalm Girl* photograph of the late Vietnam War period and the several myths attached to that powerful and provocative image; and the phenomenon of bogus quotations—some of which could be media myths in the making—and the impressive velocity and circulation they reach, thanks to the Internet and social media. These chapters thus extend the examination of media myths to realms of the image and the digital world. And they signal anew that the work of debunking is never over.

Acknowledgments

In late summer 2005, Reed Malcolm, a senior editor at the University of California Press, asked me by email whether I had ever thought of writing "a sort of 'great myths in journalism' book." He had found references online to my earlier works, which debunked well-known tales of the yellow press period in late-nineteenth-century American journalism. Reed said he had in mind a readable book "geared for a general audience." His query was astonishingly coincidental. At the time, I was completing a book about 1897, a decisive year in American journalism. And I was contemplating as my next project a detailed look at media myths—stories about or by the news media that are widely believed and often retold but which, upon scrutiny, prove to be apocryphal or wildly exaggerated. Reed's inquiry dovetailed remarkably with my research plans.

So began a collaboration that has resulted in two editions of *Getting It Wrong*. Throughout, Reed and his colleagues at the press have been unfailingly courteous, helpful, and professional. Both editions of the book have benefited from Reed's enthusiasm and from the thoughtfulness of his associates, Kalicia Pivirotto and Stacey Eisenstark.

Kate Warne and Dore Brown did outstanding work in production phases of the respective editions. They were a delight to work with.

I am in the debt of many people for their contributions to this work. Graduate research assistants at American University devoted significant time, energy, and attention to the project. I thank them all: Andrew Knapp, James Doubek, Mahafreen Mistry, Mark Syp, and Ryan Sibley.

Ruxandra Giura, a talented digital journalist, extended invaluable assistance on this and other projects. I am grateful for her help, especially in the preparation of many of the photographs that appear on these pages.

I also am indebted to John Watson, a faculty colleague at American, for helping to make sure that I completed draft chapters in a timely manner. Other faculty colleagues—including Jeff Rutenbeck, Larry Kirkman, Kathryn Montgomery, Rodger Streitmatter, John Doolittle, and Amy Eisman—were generous with their support and suggestions.

A great deal of research on this book was conducted at the Newspaper and Current Periodical Reading Room of the Library of Congress, a marvelous place where Georgia Higley, Travis Westly, and their staffs provided enthusiastic and tireless support.

I am very grateful to my friends and colleagues of the American Journalism Historians Association, including Michael Sweeney, Fred Blevens, and Tamara Baldwin, for a grant that helped finance research trips to places as diverse as New York City, Atlantic City, and Grover's Mill, New Jersey.

Wally Eberhard, one of the eminent scholars in American journalism history, offered important suggestions. So did Don Ross, formerly of the Newseum. I appreciated the insights they shared. Rick Mastroiani of the Freedom Forum library was invariably welcoming and accommodating on my visits. Lee Ann Potter of the National Archives and Records Administration was generous in making available a front-page image pertaining to the famous *War of the Worlds* radio broadcast of October 1938. Harlen Makemson of Elon University shared thoughtful suggestions about the chapter on *The War of the Worlds*. Washington journalist Carl M. Cannon offered interesting insights about bogus quotations propelled by social media.

Special thanks go to Richard Pyle, a former Saigon bureau chief and veteran correspondent for the Associated Press, and Hal Buell, formerly the news agency's executive news photo editor, for their suggestions and insights about the *Napalm Girl* photograph. Valerie Komor, director of the AP corporate archives, was quite helpful and generous with her time. Matt Lutts of AP images was most helpful, too.

My thanks also go to Paul Merkoski, formerly the editor of the *Press* of Atlantic City. He offered important suggestions on the book's bra-burning chapter. Paul and the multimedia editor at *Press*, Vernon Ogrodnek, made available the image of the demonstration on the Atlantic City boardwalk in September 1968. The bra-burning chapter also benefited from the recollections of Jon Katz and Jack Boucher, both of whom were generous with their time. Heather Halpin Perez of the Atlantic City Free Public Library was very helpful, too. Tyler Abell shared with me important insights about his stepfather, Drew Pearson.

My very good friend Hugh D. Pace was always eager to talk about media-driven myths and offered several interesting suggestions.

My wife, Ann-Marie C. Regan, deserves a special note of thanks. She was patient and accommodating as this book was researched, written, and revised.

Inevitably, writing a book that debunks media myths causes a bit of looking over one's shoulder. If errors appear in this work, they are mine alone.

Introduction

Media myths aren't harmless. They can scare people,
reinforce their biases and become tools of manipulation.
—Rene Denfeld, "Hoodwinked," *Sunday* [Portland]
Oregonian (March 10, 2002): E1

The *New York Sun* was one of the great names in American journalism. It was a newspaper that first appeared in 1833, in the vanguard of dailies that sold for a penny. For many years, it was edited by Charles A. Dana, a prickly force in nineteenth-century journalism who taunted rival editors in print while cultivating the *Sun*'s reputation as a writer's newspaper.

The *Sun*'s most notable and lasting contribution was its famous "Is There a Santa Claus?" editorial, a paean to childhood and the Christmas spirit that featured the often-quoted passage, "Yes, Virginia, there is a Santa Claus." The *Sun* published the editorial in 1897, and it has long since become a classic—the best-known and most reprinted editorial in journalism history.

The *Sun* was never the richest of newspapers, and in 1950 it was absorbed by a stronger rival, anticipating the decline and disappearance of many afternoon newspapers in urban America. The *Sun* was reborn in 2002 as a feisty, literate, conservative daily—the first entry in New York newspaper journalism in many years. The new *Sun* won a small but loyal readership that allowed it to hold on for six years. But losses of $1 million a month[1] proved crushing, and in September 2008, the *Sun* folded a second time.

About two months before it went dark, the *Sun* offered readers a double dose of media-driven myth, in an article that touched on the influence network television once exerted. To back up that claim, the *Sun* cited two moments hallowed in broadcast journalism.[2] One was an episode of Edward R. Murrow's legendary *See It Now* program that aired in March 1954, in which he took on the dreaded and powerful U.S. senator Joseph R. McCarthy. The other was Walter Cronkite's special report on CBS in February 1968, in which the respected network anchorman declared that U.S. forces in Vietnam were mired in a stalemate. Murrow's program supposedly led to the downfall of McCarthy and put an end to the senator's communists-in-government witch hunt. Cronkite's assessment supposedly forced President Lyndon Johnson to recognize that the American war effort in Vietnam was doomed. "If I've lost Cronkite," the president purportedly said, "I've lost Middle America."

Both anecdotes are well known and even cherished in American journalism. They almost always are invoked in the way the *Sun* presented them, as telling examples of media power, of journalists at their courageous best. Memorable though they may be, both anecdotes are misleading: neither the Murrow program nor the Cronkite report produced the outcomes so frequently associated with them. Both anecdotes are media-driven myths—dubious, fanciful, and apocryphal stories about or by the news media that are often retold and widely believed. Media-driven myths are tales of doubtful authenticity, false or improbable claims masquerading as factual. In a way, they are the junk food of journalism—alluring and delicious, perhaps, but not especially wholesome or nourishing.

The Murrow-McCarthy and Cronkite-Johnson anecdotes are two of the media-driven myths examined and dismantled on these pages. The others, in chronological order, are:

- **Remington-Hearst:** William Randolph Hearst famously vowed to "furnish the war" with Spain in a telegraphic exchange with Frederic Remington, an artist on assignment in Cuba in January 1897 for Hearst's *New York Journal.*

- *The War of the Worlds:* The radio adaptation of H. G. Wells's science fiction work threw Americans into panic and hysteria in late October 1938.

- **The first Kennedy-Nixon debate:** Television viewers and radio listeners differed sharply about the outcome of the debate between U.S. presidential candidates in September 1960.

- **The Bay of Pigs invasion:** The *New York Times*, at the request of President John F. Kennedy, censored its reporting about preparations for the ill-fated Bay of Pigs invasion of Cuba in April 1961.

- **Bra burning:** The women's liberation protest on the Atlantic City boardwalk in September 1968 gave rise to flamboyant bra burnings by militant feminists.

- *Napalm Girl:* The famous photograph of terrorized Vietnamese children fleeing an errant napalm attack on their village in 1972 hastened the end of the Vietnam War.

- **Watergate:** The tireless investigative work of two young, aggressive reporters for the *Washington Post* brought down the corrupt presidency of Richard M. Nixon.

- **Crack babies:** Children born to women who took cocaine during pregnancy were fated to become what journalists called a "bio-underclass."

- **Jessica Lynch:** A nineteen-year-old U.S. Army supply clerk fought like a female Rambo in an ambush during the early days of the Iraq War in 2003, news reports of which propelled her to hero status.

- **Hurricane Katrina:** The news coverage of the hurricane's destructive sweep through New Orleans was superlative, a fine moment for American journalism amid its decade of retrenchment and despair.

- **Counterfeit quotations:** The accelerant properties of the Internet and social media allow bogus quotations to circulate at light speed and insinuate their way into popular consciousness as embryonic media myths.

Only indirectly can media-driven myths be likened to "myths" in the classic sense—stories passed along from generation to generation about archetypes and heroes whose conduct offers timeless lessons and helps make sense of baffling and unsettling phenomena.[3] For purposes of this study, media-driven myths are dubious or apocryphal tales connoting or conjuring pseudo-reality, tales that often promote misleading interpretations of media power and influence. Given the centrality of some of these stories in American journalism, media myths also may be thought of as misleading "consensus narratives"—anecdotes and legends that are found at the heart of a profession's culture and are readily recalled.[4]

The objective in confronting media-driven myths is not to apply ex post facto judgments and excoriate the news media for failings past. The news media are scorned routinely enough as it is. Rather, this study aligns itself with a central objective of news gathering—that of seeking to get it right, of setting the record straight by offering searching reappraisals of some of the best-known stories journalism tells about itself. Given that truth seeking is such a widely shared and animating value in American journalism, it is a bit odd that so little effort has been made over the years to revisit, scrutinize, and attempt to verify these stories. But then, journalism seldom is seriously introspective or very mindful of its history. It usually proceeds with little more than a nod to its past.

As this work makes clear, media-driven myths are neither trivial nor innocuous. They can and do have adverse consequences. Notably, they tend to distort understanding of the role and function of journalism in American society, conferring on the news media far more power and influence than they necessarily wield. Media myths often emerge from an eagerness to find influence and lasting significance in what journalists do, and they tend to give credit where credit is not entirely due. The heroic-journalist myth of Watergate is a telling example. The myth holds that the reporting of Bob Woodward and Carl Bernstein in the *Washington Post* brought down Richard Nixon. In reality, the *Post* and other news organizations were marginal factors in unraveling the Watergate scandal. Nixon's fall was the consequence of his criminal conduct, which was exposed in the convergence of many forces, newspaper reporting being among the least decisive. So media myths can be self-flattering, offering heroes like Woodward and Bernstein to a profession more accustomed to criticism than applause.

Media myths also tend to minimize or negate complexity in historical events and present simplistic and misleading interpretations instead. Edward Murrow no more took down Joseph McCarthy than Walter Cronkite swayed public opinion about the war in Vietnam. Yet those and other media myths endure, in part, because they are reductive: they offer unambiguous, easily remembered explanations of complex historic events. Similarly, media myths invite indulgence in the "golden age fallacy," the flawed but enticing belief that there really was a time when journalism and its practitioners were respected and inspiring—the time, say, of Murrow and Cronkite or Woodward and Bernstein. Confronting media myths discourages the tendency to regard prominent journalists in extreme terms—as heroes or villains. Piercing the myths surrounding Murrow and Cronkite renders them less Olympian and less remote. Similarly, debunking the myth about Hearst and his purported vow to "furnish the war" with Spain makes him seem less demonic and less manipulative.

Another hazard of media myths lies in their capacity to feed stereotypes. The misleading if euphonic epithet "bra burning" emerged from a demonstration on the Atlantic City boardwalk in 1968 to become a shorthand way of denigrating the emergent feminist movement and dismissing it as trivial and even a bit odd. The widely misreported pandemic of "crack babies" in the late 1980s and early 1990s seemed to confirm the worst pathologies associated with inner-city poor people. The highly exaggerated news reports of nightmarish violence and wanton criminality in New Orleans following Hurricane Katrina's landfall in 2005 defamed a battered city and impugned its residents at a time of their deep despair.

Media myths, moreover, can blur lines of responsibility and deflect blame away from makers and sponsors of flawed public policy. Had the *New York Times* told all it knew about the pending Bay of Pigs invasion of Cuba, the administration of President John F. Kennedy likely would not have gone ahead with the expedition, thus sparing the country a stunning foreign policy reversal. Or so the media myth has it. In the final analysis, of course, it was Kennedy, not American journalists, who gave the go-ahead in April 1961, sending a brigade of Cuban exiles to a disastrous rendezvous in the swamps of southwestern Cuba.

Because it takes on some of the most treasured stories in American journalism, this book has a provocative edge. It could not be otherwise. This study is empirically based but recognizes that the effort to debunk myths may produce paradoxical, even counterintuitive effects. A small body of social science research suggests that the process of debunking can have the indirect and wholly unintended effect of perpetuating and extending the myth under scrutiny. Debunking invariably requires that the essence of the myth be repeated, which in some cases can *reinforce* rather than discredit the erroneous claim or belief, making it more resilient, not less.[5] Other research suggests that preliminary news accounts can leave unshakable impressions, even when those reports are subsequently disproved.[6] This curious reluctance to jettison unfounded beliefs may help explain why Jessica Lynch, the Army private inaccurately described as having fought Iraqi attackers until her ammunition ran out, was years later still thought of in some quarters as the first American hero of the Iraq War.[7]

So some myths addressed here may prove resistant to debunking. They may still be widely believed despite the contrary evidence marshaled against them. The most resilient myths may be those that can be distilled to a catchy, pithy phrase like "If I've lost Cronkite, I've lost

Middle America." Such quotations are neat, tidy, and easily remembered. Cinematic treatments influence how historical events are collectively remembered and can harden media-driven myths against debunking. The motion picture *All the President's Men,* which cast Robert Redford and Dustin Hoffman in the lead roles of *Washington Post* reporters Woodward and Bernstein, helped ensure that the journalists and their newspaper would be regarded as central to cracking the Watergate scandal. There is more than a kernel of truth in the observation that "historical lies are nearly impossible to correct once movies and television have given them credibility."[8]

But even if some media-driven myths confronted here survive debunking and retain their appeal, the effort to dismantle them is certainly worthy, if only to insist on a demarcation between fact and fiction. In this sense, it is hard to quarrel with the high-minded observation offered by Max Frankel, formerly the executive editor of the *New York Times,* who wrote that it is "unforgivably wrong to give fanciful stories the luster of fact, or to use facts to let fictions parade as truths."[9]

Debunking myths need not be an entirely somber and solemn enterprise, given mostly to brow-furrowing intensity. Debunking can be an entertaining and even faintly mischievous pursuit: witness the popularity in recent years of television programs such as *History Detectives* on PBS and *Mythbusters* on Discovery Channel. The shows sought, respectively, to pierce modest historical mysteries and to apply pyrotechnics and scientific analysis in sorting out rumors, legends, and other phenomena.[10] While they offered more than a hint of contrivance, the shows were aimed at popular audiences, suggesting broad interest in identifying and dismantling myths and urban legends.

The media-driven myths considered here have never before been examined in a single volume. The only remotely similar study is Edward Jay Epstein's fine 1975 work, *Between Fact and Fiction: The Problem of Journalism,* which includes chapters challenging whether the news media were central and decisive to the outcomes of the war in Vietnam and the Watergate scandal. Some media-driven myths taken up in these pages have been considered discretely, as book chapters and journal or magazine articles. For example, in his richly titled work on panics and mass delusions—*Little Green Men, Meowing Nuns and Head-Hunting Panics*—Robert Bartholomew raised doubts about the extent of hysteria caused by the *War of the Worlds* radio dramatization. So did Michael Socolow in an essay published on the seventieth anniversary of the famous program.[11] David Vancil and Sue D. Pendell challenged in impressive fashion in 1987 the deeply engrained notion that television viewers and radio listeners had sharply differing interpretations about the outcome of the first Kennedy-Nixon presidential debate in 1960.[12] The historian David Culbert, in assessing Lyndon Johnson's relations with the news media, posed searching questions about the legendary Cronkite-Johnson anecdote.[13] Mariah Blake, in an article in *Columbia Journalism Review,* aptly described the "crack-baby" scourge as "a media myth built on wobbly, outdated science."[14] Brian Thevenot of the *New Orleans Times-Picayune* wrote critical and revealing assessments of the erroneous reporting that characterized the aftermath of Hurricane Katrina.[15]

But it would be misleading and quite mistaken to regard this study as a rehash of the work and findings of others. This study draws on secondary sources, and goes well beyond them, to present fresh insights and interpretations that are buttressed by considerable archival research. It draws on previously neglected sources, such as coverage in the Atlantic City newspaper of the protest at the 1968 Miss America pageant. That newspaper's report said that bras *were* set afire during the protest, offering a long-overlooked contemporaneous challenge to the many and insistent denials of the protest's organizers. Also scrutinized was the report of a select committee of the U.S. House of Representatives that investigated Hurricane Katrina's aftermath. The panel's hefty study included detailed discussions about the consequences of the seriously flawed news coverage of the disaster—passages that the American media almost entirely ignored.

The vast collection of newspapers on microfilm at the Library of Congress is a resource unrivaled in the United States. Close reading there of leading U.S. newspapers published in the days after *The War of Worlds* broadcast in 1938 found little evidence that the radio show set off panic and hysteria throughout the country, as legend has it. Those accounts pointed to a little-recognized source of fright that night: agitated but well-intentioned people, acting with an incomplete understanding about the broadcast's content, who set out on their own to alert others to the supposed calamity. They entered churches, theaters, cinemas, and taverns, shouting that the United States was under attack or that the end of the world was near. Their disparate, uncoordinated, and self-motivated actions had the evanescent effect of spreading fear to untold thousands of people who had heard not a single moment of the broadcast.

Decades-old polling data also lent invaluable insight and detail to this study. Public opinion surveys conducted in late 1953 and early

1954 showed that Joseph McCarthy's favorable ratings had begun to slide well before Murrow took to the air with his celebrated program about the demagogic senator. Similarly, polls taken in 1967 showed that popular sentiment began turning against the war in Vietnam months before the Cronkite program that supposedly had such a decisive effect on Lyndon Johnson and American public opinion.

Visits were paid to several venues related to media mythmaking. These included Grovers Mill, the New Jersey hamlet that was ground zero for the Martian invasion in the *War of the Worlds* dramatization; the boardwalk at Atlantic City, the site of the protest that gave rise to the "bra burning" epithet; and the hushed, exclusive Sulgrave Club in Washington, DC, where, in December 1950, McCarthy slapped, kneed, or punched Drew Pearson, the muckraking columnist who dogged him the most. Also visited was Key West, from where Frederic Remington and Richard Harding Davis set out in 1897 on an assignment to Cuba that gave rise to the tale about Hearst's vow to "furnish the war" with Spain—the media-driven myth that is the subject of this study's opening chapter. It should be noted that the author has previously addressed the famous Hearstian vow, in a study about the yellow press period in fin de siècle American journalism.[16] The chapter here presents fresh evidence that the vow was never made and examines how, when, and why that media myth took hold.

"I'll Furnish the War"

The Making of a Media Myth

You furnish the pictures, and I'll furnish the war.

—Attributed to William Randolph Hearst in James
Creelman, *On the Great Highway: The Wanderings
and Adventures of a Special Correspondent* (Boston:
Lothrop, 1901), 178

As America prepared for war with Iraq in the early years of the twenty-first century, commentators at opposite ends of the political spectrum turned to what may be the most famous anecdote in American journalism to describe how poorly U.S. media were reporting the run-up to the conflict. The anecdote is more than one hundred years old and tells of the purported exchange of telegrams between William Randolph Hearst, the activist young publisher of the *New York Journal*, and Frederic Remington, the famous painter and sculptor of scenes of the American West. Hearst engaged Remington's services for a month in December 1896 and sent him to Cuba to draw sketches of the rebellion then raging against Spain's colonial rule. The Cuban rebellion gave rise in 1898 to the Spanish-American War, in which the United States wrested control of Cuba, Puerto Rico, Guam, and the Philippines.

After only a few days in Cuba in January 1897, Remington purportedly sent a cable to Hearst in New York, stating: "Everything is quiet. There is no trouble here. There will be no war. I wish to return." In reply, Hearst supposedly told the artist, "Please remain. You furnish the pictures, and I'll furnish the war."[1]

Hearst's famous vow to "furnish the war" has achieved unique status as an adaptable, hardy, all-purpose anecdote, useful in illustrating any number of media sins and shortcomings. It has been invoked to illustrate the media's willingness to compromise impartiality, promote political agendas, and indulge in sensationalism. It has been used, more broadly, to suggest the media's capacity to inject malign influence into international affairs.

As debate intensified in the United States about the prospect of war in Iraq, the conservative columnist Charles Krauthammer invoked Hearst's "furnish the war" vow to condemn Iraq-related coverage in the *New York Times*. The unbroken flow of antiwar reporting and editorializing in the *Times*, Krauthammer claimed, was so extreme and egregious as to invite comparison to Hearst's agitation for war with Spain in the late 1890s.[2] A few months later, the editors of the liberal magazine *American Prospect* also turned to "I'll furnish the war" and claimed that Hearst "was a pacifist compared with the editors of the *Wall Street Journal*'s editorial page, who are not only fomenting a war with Iraq but also helping to orchestrate it."[3]

Although its appeal is timeless and its versatility impressive, the anecdote about Hearst's vow and his exchange with Remington is a media-driven myth. It is perhaps the hardiest myth in American journalism, having lived on despite concerted attempts to discredit and dismantle it.[4] The Remington-Hearst anecdote is often cited and widely believed. In most retellings, Hearst is said to have made good on his promise,[5] and war with Spain "was duly provided."[6] As such, the Spanish-American War has been termed "Mr. Hearst's War."[7] But the factors explaining why the United States went to war with Spain in 1898 are far more profound and complex than the supposed manipulative powers of Hearst and his newspapers.[8]

Like many media-driven myths, the Hearst anecdote is succinct, savory, and easily remembered. It is almost too good *not* to be true. Not surprisingly, Hearst's vow to "furnish the war" has made its way into countless textbooks of journalism.[9] It has figured in innumerable discussions about Hearst and about the news media and war.[10] It has been repeated over the years by no small number of journalists, scholars,[11] and critics of the news media, such as Ben Bagdikian, Helen Thomas, Nicholas Lemann, Evan Thomas, and David Halberstam.[12]

Interestingly, the anecdote lives on despite a nearly complete absence of supporting documentation. It lives on even though telegrams supposedly exchanged by Remington and Hearst have never turned up. It lives on even though Hearst denied ever sending such a message. It lives on despite an irreconcilable internal inconsistency: it would have been absurd for Hearst to vow to "furnish the war" because war—specifically, the Cuban rebellion against Spain's colonial rule—was the very reason Hearst sent

Remington to Cuba in the first place. Anyone reading U.S. newspapers in early 1897 would have been well aware that Cuba was a theater of a nasty war. By then, the Cuban rebellion had reached islandwide proportions, and not a single province had been pacified by Spain's armed forces.[13]

The origins of the "furnish the war" anecdote are modest and more than a little murky. The story first appeared as a brief passage in *On the Great Highway: The Wanderings and Adventures of a Special Correspondent,* a slim memoir by James Creelman, a portly, bearded, cigar-chomping, Canadian-born journalist prone to pomposity and exaggeration. Creelman relished making himself the hero of his own reporting, a preference that quickly becomes clear in *On the Great Highway.* In the book's preface, Creelman said he sought to illuminate "the part which the press is rapidly assuming in human affairs, not only as historian and commentator but as a direct and active agent." Figuring prominently in *On the Great Highway* are accounts of Creelman's meetings and interviews with Leo Tolstoy, Sitting Bull, and Pope Leo XIII. "The frequent introduction of the author's personality," Creelman wrote, "is a necessary means of reminding the reader that he is receiving the testimony of an eyewitness."[14]

On the Great Highway was favorably received by critics when it appeared in the autumn of 1901.[15] Few reviewers, however, noted or commented on the passage reporting the supposed Remington-Hearst exchange. Hearst's *Journal* in November 1901 devoted two pages to lengthy excerpts from *On the Great Highway.*[16] But the passage about Hearst's vowing to "furnish the war" was not included in the selection. It also is noteworthy that Creelman invoked the Remington-Hearst exchange not as a rebuke but as a compliment, to *commend* Hearst and the activist, anticipatory "yellow journalism" that he had pioneered in New York City. Creelman wrote:

> Some time before the destruction of the battleship *Maine* in the harbor of Havana, the *New York Journal* sent Frederic Remington, the distinguished artist, to Cuba. He was instructed to remain there until the war began; for "yellow journalism" was alert and had an eye for the future.
> Presently Mr. Remington sent this telegram from Havana: "W.R. HEARST, *New York Journal,* N.Y.: Everything is quiet. There is no trouble here. There will be no war. I wish to return. REMINGTON."
> This was the reply: "REMINGTON, HAVANA: Please remain. You furnish the pictures, and I'll furnish the war. W.R. HEARST."

And Hearst was as good as his word, Creelman declared.[17]

If such an exchange had taken place, it would have been in January 1897, the only time Remington was in Cuba before the *Maine*'s destruction in February 1898. Remington had been hired by Hearst for a month and not, as Creelman wrote, for an indefinite period "until the war began."[18] Moreover, Creelman had no firsthand knowledge about the purported Remington-Hearst exchange. Creelman in early 1897 was neither in Cuba nor in New York. He was in Europe, as the *Journal's* "special commissioner" on the Continent. This means someone would had to have told him about the exchange, or that he invented the anecdote from whole cloth. In any case, Creelman never explained how he learned about the anecdote.

Although Remington apparently never spoke publicly about the purported exchange with Hearst, the artist's conduct, correspondence, and recollections of the assignment to Cuba all belie Creelman's account. According to Creelman, Hearst instructed Remington to "please remain" in Cuba. But Remington did nothing of the sort. After just six days in Cuba, on January 16, 1897, the artist left Havana aboard the *Seneca,* a New York–bound steamer that carried six other passengers.[19] The *Seneca* reached New York four days later, and soon afterward Remington's sketches began appearing in Hearst's *Journal.* The work was given prominent display. The newspaper's headlines hailed Remington as a "gifted artist"[20]—hardly an accolade that Hearst would have extended to someone in his employ who had brazenly disregarded instructions to remain on the scene. Far from being irritated and displeased with Remington, Hearst was delighted with his work. He recalled years later that Remington and Richard Harding Davis, the celebrated writer who traveled to Cuba with the artist, "did their work admirably and aroused much indignation among Americans" about Spanish rule of the island.[21]

For his part, Remington chafed about how poorly his sketches were reproduced in the *Journal.*[22] Although they hardly were his best work, the sketches serve to impugn Creelman's account that Remington had found "everything . . . quiet" in Cuba. The sketches depict unmistakable (if unremarkable) scenes of a rebellion—a scouting party of Spanish cavalry with rifles at the ready; a cluster of Cuban noncombatants trussed and bound and being herded into Spanish lines; a scruffy Cuban rebel kneeling to fire at a small Spanish fort; a knot of Spanish soldiers dressing a comrade's leg wound. The sketches appeared beneath headlines such as "Cuban War Sketches Gathered in the Field by Frederic Remington" and "Frederic Remington Sketches a Familiar Incident of the Cuban War."[23] Accompanying the sketch of the captive noncombatants was a caption in which Remington said the treatment of Cuban women by irregulars allied with the Spanish was nothing short of "unspeakable." And "as for the men captured by them alive," Remington's caption said, "the blood curdles in my veins as I think of the atrocity, the cruelty, practiced on these helpless victims."[24]

Following his return to New York, Remington wrote a letter to the *Journal*'s keenest rival, the New York *World,* in which he disparaged the Spanish regime as a "woman-killing outfit down there in Cuba."[25] In 1899, Remington recalled the assignment to Cuba in a short magazine article that further challenges Creelman's account. Remington wrote: "I saw ill-clad, ill-fed Spanish soldiers bring their dead and wounded into" Havana, "dragging slowly along in ragged columns. I saw scarred Cubans with their arms bound stiffly behind them being marched to the Cabanas," a grim fortress overlooking the Havana harbor. The countryside, Remington said, "was a pall of smoke" from homes of Cubans that had been set afire.[26]

Remington's sketches and correspondence thus leave no doubt that he had seen a good deal of war-related disruption in Cuba. The island during his brief visit was anything but "quiet." Still, it remains something of a mystery why Remington never publicly addressed Creelman's anecdote, an unflattering anecdote that certainly cast the artist as timid, ineffective, and feckless. And Remington presumably had opportunities to confront Creelman. He lived until the day after Christmas in 1909, eight years after publication of *On the Great Highway.* Perhaps Remington kept his silence because the anecdote had not yet become widely known or infamous in the first years of the twentieth century. As noted, Creelman intended the anecdote as a compliment—a tribute to Hearst and his aggressive style of yellow journalism.

Although Creelman again recounted the Remington-Hearst exchange in 1906 in a magazine profile of Hearst,[27] the anecdote stirred little public controversy until 1907, when a correspondent for the *Times* of London mentioned it in a dispatch from New York. The correspondent wrote: "Is the Press of the United States going insane? . . . A letter from William Randolph Hearst is in existence and was printed in a magazine not long ago. It was to an artist he had sent to Cuba, and who reported no likelihood of war. 'You provide the pictures,' he wrote, 'I'll provide the war.'"[28]

The *Times*'s article was the first to give the Remington-Hearst anecdote an unflattering interpretation. It was an interpretation that stirred Hearst to anger. In a letter to the *Times,* he dismissed as "frankly false" and "ingeniously idiotic" the claim that "there was a letter in existence

FIGURE 1. Frederick Remington's sketches for the *New York Journal* made clear that he had seen a good deal of war-related upheaval during his brief stay in Cuba. Among other drawings, Remington illustrated Richard Harding Davis's report about the firing-squad execution of a twenty-year-old Cuban insurgent, published February 2, 1897. [*Library of Congress*]

from Mr. W. R. Hearst in which Mr. Hearst said to a correspondent in Cuba: 'You provide the pictures and I will provide the war,' and the intimation that Mr. Hearst was chiefly responsible for the Spanish war. This kind of clotted nonsense," Hearst declared, "could only be generally circulated and generally believed in England, where newspapers claiming to be conservative and reliable are the most utterly untrustworthy of any on earth. In apology for these newspapers it may be said that their untrustworthiness is not always due to intention but more frequently to ignorance and prejudice."[29]

The controversy soon sputtered out, and the unflattering interpretation of Creelman's anecdote was largely forgotten for years until it was resuscitated in the 1930s. At that time, public opinion was running strongly against Hearst and his newspapers. The media baron turned seventy in 1933 and seemed more roundly disliked and distrusted than ever. His anticommunist advocacy had become strident and harsh. His newspapers solicited essays from the likes of Hitler and Mussolini[30] while campaigning viciously against Franklin D. Roosevelt, likening the president to a communist dupe. In the 1936 election campaign, Hearst's newspapers characterized Roosevelt as Moscow's candidate for president.[31]

Americans then were deserting the Hearst newspapers. Given a choice between the publisher and the president, readers exiled Hearst newspapers from their homes, David Nasaw, Hearst's leading biographer, has written. By the late summer of 1936, unflattering characterizations of Hearst were etched so deeply in the nation's psyche, Nasaw wrote, "that Roosevelt and his advisers recognized that the worst thing that could be said of [the Republican presidential candidate] Alfred Landon was that he was supported by Hearst."[32]

Against this backdrop, the Remington-Hearst anecdote reemerged and took on a permanently sinister cast. Notably, the anecdote appeared in several works in the 1930s that identified the press as an active agent in bringing about the Spanish-American War. Among these works was Joseph E. Wisan's *The Cuban Crisis as Reflected in the New York Press (1895–1898)*, which influenced a generation of scholarship on the press and the Spanish-American War. Wisan argued that the "principal cause of our war with Spain was the public demand for it, a demand too powerful for effective resistance by the business and financial leaders of the nation or by President McKinley. For the creation of the public state of mind, the press was largely responsible."[33]

Wisan wrote that the "most widely circulated of the newspapers," such as Hearst's *Journal,* "were the least honestly objective in the reporting of news and in the presentation of editorial opinion. . . . Hearst's famous reply to the artist Remington's complaint that there was no war in Cuba— 'You furnish the pictures; I'll furnish the war,'—well illustrates the degree of objectivity that prevailed."[34]

Other works of the time helped revive the anecdote. A year before Wisan's book appeared, Willis J. Abbot, a former editor at Hearst's *Journal,* brought out *Watching the World Go By,* a memoir that invoked the supposed Remington-Hearst exchange.[35] John Dos Passos cited it in his 1936 novel, *The Big Money.*[36] Ferdinand Lundberg, the most unforgiving of Hearst's several biographers, cited Creelman's account of "furnish the war" in *Imperial Hearst,* a slim and truculent polemic that appeared in 1936. Lundberg erroneously suggested that Creelman had accompanied Remington to Florida.[37]

What firmly and finally pressed Hearst's purported vow to "furnish the war" into the public's consciousness was *Citizen Kane,* the 1941 motion picture based loosely on Hearst's life and times. *Kane* was not a commercial success, in part because of Hearst's attempts to block its release,[38] but the film is consistently ranked by critics as among the finest ever made.[39] A scene early in the film shows Charles Foster Kane, the reckless newspaper tycoon who invites comparisons to Hearst, at his desk, quarreling with his former guardian. They are interrupted by Kane's business manager, Mr. Bernstein, who reports that a cable has just arrived from a correspondent in Cuba. Bernstein reads the contents, and Kane, superbly played by Orson Welles, dictates a reply that paraphrases Hearst's purported vow. "You provide the prose poems," Kane says, "and I'll provide the war." Bernstein congratulates Kane on a splendid and witty reply. Saying he rather likes it himself, Kane tells Bernstein to send it off immediately.

The Remington-Hearst anecdote thus had become something far removed from the compliment Creelman intended in *On the Great Highway.* It had taken on an unflattering and threatening tone. Hearst's toxic personality made the malevolent interpretation seem plausible. The cinematic treatment of *Citizen Kane* made it vivid and enduring.

REMINGTON WAS ASKED TO LEAVE

As we have seen, Remington's contemporaneous writings impugn Creelman's anecdote. So, too, does the correspondence of Richard Harding Davis, the dashing if self-absorbed author and playwright whom Remington accompanied on the assignment to Cuba. In early 1897,

Davis was burnishing his credentials as a war correspondent. And he commanded top dollar: Hearst paid him $3,000 for a month-long assignment in Cuba.[40]

The plans mapped with Hearst's editors were to take Davis and Remington to Cuba surreptitiously, aboard the *Vamoose,* a high-speed steam yacht that Hearst had chartered. The *Vamoose* was to deposit Davis, Remington, and a couple of Cuban guides in Santa Clara Province. From there, they would travel to the camp of the Cuban rebel leader, Máximo Gómez.[41] But the trip almost did not take place.

Davis and Remington met the *Vamoose* at Key West, as planned, in late December 1896. At first, the weather was too unfavorable to hazard a crossing of the Straits of Florida to Cuba. Then the captain balked at making the run over Christmas. Finally, when all seemed ready, the *Vamoose* proved unseaworthy. Twenty miles out of Key West, the crew refused to go on. The *Vamoose* turned back, and Davis stretched out on the deck and cried.[42] Exasperated by the bungled plans, Davis declared, "I am done with [J]ournal forever."[43]

In all, Davis and Remington spent three weeks in Key West awaiting passage to Cuba. Davis fumed about the time wasted and insisted on a thousand-dollar advance payment from the *Journal* "because of the delay over the *Vamoose.*"[44] "Wait," he seethed, "is all we do and that is my life at Key West. I get up and half dress and take a plunge in the bay and then dress fully and have a greasy breakfast and then light a huge Key West cigar price three cents and sit on the hotel porch with my feet on a rail. Nothing happens after that except getting one's boots polished."[45] Remington, whom Davis called "a large blundering bear,"[46] was frustrated, too, and thought about aborting the assignment to return to New York. But Remington "gave up on the idea . . . as soon as he found I would not do so," Davis wrote.[47]

Fed up with waiting for Hearst to send a vessel more seaworthy than the *Vamoose,* Davis and Remington abandoned plans to enter Cuba by stealth and booked passage on a scheduled passenger steamer to Havana. "Davis proposed that, since we could not get in the coal-cellar window, we had best go around and knock at the front door," Remington recalled. "I should never have dreamed of such a thing, but Davis has the true newspaper impudence."[48] They arrived January 9, 1897. Davis wrote to his mother that it was a great relief to reach Cuba "after the annoyances and disappointments of those days at Key West. I cannot tell you what we will do but we are both anxious to pull a sort of success out of a failure, if we can. . . . Had we not wanted to go [to Cuba] so much neither of us would have put up with the way we have been treated" by Hearst and the *New York Journal*.[49]

If Hearst had vowed to "furnish the war" in an exchange of cables with Remington, it would have occurred while Davis was in Cuba. Had Davis known about it, there is little reason to believe he would have kept quiet. His loathing for Hearst would have inspired Davis to direct wide attention to the "furnish the war" telegram, had it been sent. But in his extensive correspondence from Cuba, Davis did not mention an exchange between Remington and Hearst. None of Davis's letters from Cuba suggest that the artist wanted to return to the United States on the pretext that "everything is quiet." Instead, Davis offered three related reasons for Remington's departure. In a letter that Remington carried with him to mail in the United States (a letter the artist may have read en route), Davis said: "Remington has all the material he needs for sketches and for illustrating my stories so he is going home. I will go on further as I have not yet seen much that is interesting or new." Davis added that *he* had asked Remington to leave, "as it left me freer."[50]

In another letter, written the same day and mailed from Cuba—a letter that Remington probably did not see—Davis rejoiced at the artist's departure. "I am as relieved at getting old Remington to go as though I had won $5000," Davis wrote. "He was a splendid fellow but a perfect kid and had to be humored and petted all the time." Davis confided that he "was very glad" that Remington had left, "for he kept me back all the time and I can do twice as much in half the time. He always wanted to talk it over and that had to be done in the nearest or the most distant cafe, and it always took him fifteen minutes before he got his cocktails to suit him. He always did as I wanted [in] the end but I am not used to giving reasons or traveling in pairs."[51] Davis gave a related explanation for Remington's departure in another letter written in January 1897. In it, he said Remington left because he was too frightened to try to cross Spanish lines and attempt to meet up with the rebels under Gómez. "Remington got scared and backed out much to my relief and I went on and tried to cross the lines," but without success, Davis wrote.[52]

Moreover, Davis's correspondence and his dispatches to the *Journal* described considerable upheaval in Cuba. "There is war here and no mistake," Davis wrote the day Remington left to return to the United States, "and all the people in the field have been ordered in to the fortified towns where they are starving and dying of disease."[53] His correspondence contained graphic descriptions of what he called the grim process "of extermination and ruin" in Cuba. "The insurgents began

FIGURE 2. Remington and Richard Harding Davis traveled to Cuba in early 1897 on assignment for Hearst's *New York Journal*. The trip gave rise to the myth about Hearst's vow to "furnish the war" with Spain. [*Library of Congress*]

first by destroying the sugar mills some of which were worth millions of dollars in machinery, and now the Spaniards are burning the houses of the people and hoarding them in around the towns to starve out the insurgents and to leave them without shelter or places for food or to hide the wounded," Davis wrote. "So all day long, wherever you look you see great heavy columns of smoke rising into the beautiful sky above the magnificent palms."[54]

Davis's correspondence thus represents a powerful and contemporaneous challenge to Creelman's anecdote. There is a small chance, however, that Davis was unaware of the purported exchange of telegrams between Remington and Hearst. Had it occurred, the exchange would have taken place late on January 15, 1897, after Remington had left Davis in Matanzas to return to Havana, or in the morning or early afternoon of January 16, 1897, before Remington left Havana for New York aboard the *Seneca*. In such a scenario, Davis would not have known about an exchange between Remington and Hearst.

But such a scenario does not explain how Hearst's arrogant vow would have cleared the rigid censorship that Spanish authorities had imposed on international cable traffic from Havana.[55] The U.S. consul-general in Cuba, Fitzhugh Lee, reported in February 1897 that the "Spanish censor permits nothing to go out except formally [official traffic] to Spain & whenever you see a dispatch in newspapers dated Habana it is shaped to pass the censor."[56] The restrictions were so imposing that the trade journal *Fourth Estate* declared in mid-February 1897, "The power of the press has been paralyzed by the Spanish censorship."[57] The *New York Tribune* reported in mid-January 1897 that, inside Cuba, "censorship is more rigorous than ever. The publication of news on the burning of cane-fields, farms, estates, etc., known to be occurring daily in the western provinces, especially Havana and Matanzas, is prohibited."[58]

So there was no chance that telegrams such as those Creelman described would have flowed freely between Remington in Havana and Hearst in New York. Spanish control of the cable traffic in Havana was too vigilant and severe to have allowed such an exchange to go unnoticed and unremarked upon. A vow such as Hearst's to "furnish the war" surely would have been intercepted and publicized by Spanish authorities as a clear-cut example of Yankee meddling in Cuba.

A TASTE FOR HYPERBOLE

Creelman's documented fondness for overstatement and hyperbole stands as further reason to doubt that Hearst ever vowed "to furnish the war." It is indeed ironic that what may be American journalism's best-known anecdote owes its existence to the undocumented ruminations of an absentee and notoriously unreliable journalist whom contemporaries derided for his pomposity and extreme self-regard.

FIGURE 3. James Creelman was a widely traveled, cigar-chomping correspondent who had a keen taste for hyperbole and a fondness for overstatement. He often took a starring role in his own dispatches. [Fourth Estate/*Newseum*]

Creelman had a far-flung foreign and domestic career in journalism, writing for James Gordon Bennett's *New York Herald,* Joseph Pulitzer's *New York World,* and Hearst's *Journal.* Among Creelman's specialties was interviewing prominent figures of the day. Invariably, these interviews seemed more about Creelman than his subjects. An editor at Hearst's *Journal* recalled that Creelman would "put so much of himself into an interview or story that the real subject of the article was utterly obscured."[59] After the *Journal* published Creelman's interview with the union leader Eugene V. Debs in 1897, a columnist for the trade publication *Journalist* observed, "Creelman talks a hundred fifty words to ten from Debs. What an ass that Creelman is, and I have often wondered whether Hearst supposes that anybody is fooled by his platitudinous nonsense."[60]

Creelman was something of an anomaly in American journalism of the late nineteenth century. He was more a polemicist than a reporter. He routinely called attention to himself at a time when nearly all American journalists labored obscurely, rarely even receiving a byline to recognize their work. Few ever became prominent. The ethos of fin-de-siècle American journalism was that a reporter had to "sink his personality out of sight and merge his very identity in that of his paper. . . . Every newspaper has a policy, determined by the editor-in-chief, and it is the reporter's duty to hew the line that has been stretched for him. Nobody cares what his private opinions may be upon matters political or things critical."[61] But there was to be none of that for Creelman. Hearst and, to a lesser extent, Pulitzer indulged Creelman's self-importance[62]—and usually looked the other way when he traded in hyperbole.

A notable example came in 1894, when Creelman filed reports to the *World* describing how Japanese soldiers had massacred and mutilated Chinese civilians while overrunning Port Arthur, now known as Lüshun, a city at the tip of Liaodong Peninsula. So complete was the slaughter, wrote Creelman, that the only Chinese left alive were those who formed burial parties.[63] Creelman's atrocity report was dismissed by the *New York Tribune* as "reckless sensationalism." The *Tribune* declared that the details Creelman related were "so untrue that to call them wild exaggerations would be gross flattery."[64] Nonetheless, Creelman's report stirred something of an uproar in the United States[65] and the U.S. minister to Japan, Edwin Dun, was ordered to investigate. Dun interviewed Creelman as well as American, French, and Japanese military officials and, in a report to the U.S. State Department, concluded that "the account sent to 'The World' by Mr. Creelman is sensational in the extreme and a gross exaggeration of what occurred."[66]

The rebuke dogged Creelman for years. "Port Arthur Creelman" became a sneering epithet, one favored by the gossip columnist for the *Journalist,* who relished poking at Creelman's outsized ego.[67] Creelman, though, was hardly chastened. In *On the Great Highway,* he resurrected his account of atrocities at Port Arthur, writing that "the Japanese killed everything they saw. Unarmed men, kneeling in the streets and begging for life, were shot, bayoneted, or beheaded. The town was sacked from end to end, and the inhabitants were butchered in their own houses."[68]

Creelman described similarly gory scenes in dispatches to the *World* from Cuba in 1896. Spanish atrocities, he claimed, were commonplace. "The horrors of a barbarous struggle for the extermination of the native population are witnessed in all parts of the country," Creelman wrote. "Blood on the roadsides, blood in the field, blood on the doorsteps: blood, blood, blood! The old, the young, the weak, the crippled—all are butchered without mercy. There is scarcely a hamlet that has not witnessed the dreadful work."[69] Given the predominantly hit-and-run guerrilla nature of the Cuban rebellion, extensive bloodshed of the kind Creelman recounted was rare.[70] In any event, his exaggerated reports about conditions in Cuba prompted Spanish authorities to order him expelled.[71]

Cuba was the theater of another of Creelman's self-starring exploits in July 1898, during the Spanish-American War. This time, Creelman claimed to have single-handedly captured a Spanish blockhouse, or stone fort, near the end of a vicious, day-long battle at El Caney, a town on the San Juan heights above Santiago de Cuba. The blockhouse was protected on three sides by a deep trench from which Spanish defenders laid down withering fire, holding off successive assaults by American troops and thwarting their plans to advance on Santiago, Cuba's second-largest city.

In a first-person account published a few months after the battle at El Caney, Creelman wrote that the Spanish troops offered no resistance as he walked up the hill late in the afternoon. He entered their battered fortress and demanded their surrender: "I went up to the officer [in command], and looking him straight in the eye, said in French: 'You are my prisoner.' He threw up his hands and said, 'Do with me as you please.' Do you know at that moment I got a sneaking idea into my head that a soldier's work was about the easiest thing I had ever struck; but I found out my mistake later,"[72] when a bullet fired from a Spanish rifle tore into his left shoulder.

Creelman's account of forcing the surrender of the Spanish troops at the blockhouse seems highly improbable. An editorial writer for the

Washington Post mocked Creelman's unlikely tale, writing: "When he really gets his blood up, what he wants to do is to surround and capture armies, to fly into the imminent deadly breach, to beat back regiments with his single sword, and to scale the dizziest heights in quest of glory. . . . But not everyone could have charged up the hill, . . . intimidated the Spaniards crouching there, and then modestly transferred the glory and the booty to the trembling forces of the United States. That's what Creelman did, however; he tells us so himself."[73]

There is little evidence the blockhouse at El Caney was captured as Creelman described. Official U.S. Army reports about the fighting there make no mention of Creelman's presence or his purported heroics. They say instead that the fortress was taken in a charge led by Captain Harry L. Haskell of the Twelfth Infantry Regiment. By the time of Haskell's assault, U.S. artillery had greatly reduced Spanish resistance inside the blockhouse.[74]

A far more plausible version of Creelman's actions at El Caney was offered by David Nasaw in *The Chief,* an admirably even-handed biography of Hearst published in 2000. Of the battle at El Caney, Nasaw said that Creelman, in the company of Hearst and his small party, mistakenly wandered onto the battlefield as the final American assault on the blockhouse was about to unfold. "Not fully understanding the lay of the land—and the position of the Spanish troops—Hearst's entourage, on arriving at El Caney, strolled up the hill toward the Spanish fort," Nasaw wrote. "Only when the American soldiers, lying prone on the ground to escape Spanish gunfire, shouted at the civilians to make themselves scarce, did those in the Hearst party realize that they were walking toward the Spanish fortifications. James Creelman drew fire from the Spanish soldiers and was wounded."[75]

Creelman, who recovered from his shoulder wound and cast himself in another starring role while covering the Philippine insurrection in 1899, was an adherent of the "journalism of action," a model or paradigm that Hearst developed in the late nineteenth century. The "journalism of action" anticipated that newspapers would go beyond editorializing about social ills and corruption and inject themselves, conspicuously, as active agents in righting the wrongs of public life. Newspapers would actively fill the void of government inaction and incompetence and render any public service they could.[76] For a time at the end of the nineteenth century, Hearst's vision of activist journalism attracted a fair amount of interest. No one embraced the "journalism of action" with more fervor than James Creelman.

He exulted in "the journalism of action," which critics disparaged as "yellow journalism." Creelman wrote in *On the Great Highway:* "How little they know of 'yellow journalism' who denounce it! How swift they are to condemn its shrieking headlines, its exaggerated pictures, its coarse buffoonery, its intrusions upon private life, and its occasional inaccuracies! But how slow they are to see the steadfast guardianship of public interests which it maintains! How blind to its unfearing warfare against rascality, its detection and prosecution of crime, its costly searchings for knowledge throughout the earth, its exposures of humbug, its endless funds for the quick relief of distress!"[77]

In offering the Remington-Hearst anecdote, which we now know is surely counterfeit, Creelman sought to illustrate the power and potential of the "journalism of action." He succeeded instead in constructing a media myth of remarkable tenacity. It lives on as Creelman's singular contribution to American journalism, an anecdote of timeless appeal that feeds popular mistrust of the news media and promotes the improbable notion that the media are powerful and dangerous forces, so powerful they can even bring on a war.

CHAPTER 2

Fright beyond Measure?

The Myth of *The War of the Worlds*

War of the Worlds is a science fiction with a social history.
—Lonna M. Malmsheimer, "Three Mile Island: Fact, Frame,
and Fiction," *American Quarterly* 38, no. 1 (Spring 1986): 47

No single program in American broadcasting inspired more fear, controversy, and unending fascination than the 1938 radio dramatization of the novel *The War of the Worlds*. So alarming was the show, so realistic were its accounts of invading Martians wielding deadly heat rays, that listeners by the tens of thousands—or maybe the hundreds of thousands—were convulsed in panic. They fled their homes, jammed highways, overwhelmed telephone circuits, flocked to houses of worship, set about preparing defenses, and even contemplated suicide in the belief that the end of the world was at hand. Fright beyond measure seized America that night, some eighty years ago. It was a night unlike any other; it was "the night the sky fell in," "the night that panicked America."[1]

Or so the media myth has it.

This chapter offers compelling evidence that the panic and mass hysteria so readily associated with the *War of the Worlds* program did not occur on anything approaching a nationwide scale. The program did frighten some Americans, and some others reacted in less than rational ways. But most listeners, overwhelmingly, were neither frightened nor unnerved. They recognized the program for what it was—an imaginative and entertaining show on the night before Halloween. Newspaper reports appearing the next day, however, advanced the notion that mass panic had swept the country. These reports were almost entirely anecdotal and largely based on sketchy wire service roundups that emphasized breadth over in-depth detail. As this chapter discusses, newspapers

RADIO FAKE SCARES NATION

Hysteria among radio listeners throughout the nation and actual panicky evacuations from sections of New York and New Jersey resulted from a too-realistic radio broadcast last night, describing a fictitious visitation of strange men from Mars.

FIGURE 4. Newspaper headlines across the country told of a scare that wasn't—how Americans in late October 1938 were pitched into mass panic and hysteria by the *War of the Worlds* radio dramatization. Here, the front page of the *Chicago Herald and Examiner*, October 31, 1938. [*Courtesy National Archives and Records Administration*]

simply had no reliable way of testing or ascertaining the validity of the sweeping claims they made about the radio show.

This chapter, which draws on a review of the *War of the Worlds* coverage in three dozen major daily newspapers from all regions of the United States, also offers evidence that muddled second- and thirdhand accounts—which spread rapidly as the broadcast unfolded—were significant and heretofore little-recognized sources of fright that October night. A false-alarm contagion took hold in many places of the country, briefly sowing fear and confusion among many people who had heard not a word of the program.

This chapter further describes how the broadcast offered American newspapers an exceptional and irresistible opportunity to rebuke radio—then an increasingly important rival source for news and advertising—as unreliable and untrustworthy. While newspapers seemed to delight in chiding an upstart competitor, their overwhelmingly negative commentary helped solidify the notion that the *War of the Worlds* dramatization had sown mass panic and hysteria among Americans.

In short, the notion that the *War of the Worlds* program sent untold thousands of people into the streets in panic[2] is a media-driven myth that offers a deceptive message about the power radio wielded over listeners in its early days and, more broadly, about the media's potential to sow fright, alarm, and hysteria. There is, however, no disputing that the *War of the Worlds* dramatization was great entertainment, worthy of distinction as "the most famous radio show of all time."[3] The broadcast was vivid, clever, fast-paced, and imaginative. Its dramatic quality was enhanced by what has been called *radio vérité*[4]—the highly effective use of overlapping dialogue, crowd noise, microphone feedback, and other effects. The program's references to well-recognized towns and cities, highways, and other landmarks further lent the broadcast a verisimilitude that heightened its appeal and entertainment value.

The *War of the Worlds* was an hour-long episode of *The Mercury Theatre on the Air* that aired live on October 30, 1938, over the CBS network.[5] The program's producer, director, and star actor was Orson Welles, a twenty-three-year-old prodigy who had already made the cover of *Time* magazine and who was destined for lasting fame as the director and star of the 1941 motion picture *Citizen Kane*.

The *War of the Worlds* program was an adaptation of the novel written by H. G. Wells and published in Britain in 1898. In H. G. Wells's treatment, the Martian invasion was set in England. In the 1938 adaptation, Orson Welles and his writers placed ground zero in rural central New Jersey, near the unprepossessing hamlet of Grovers Mill, not far from Princeton. From Grovers Mill, the Martians and their lethal heat rays and poison gas moved on to attack and devastate New York City. Their invasion was halted finally not by military force but by humble germs and bacteria, to which the Martians had no immunity. Telling such a story within an hour promised to be a significant challenge for *Mercury Theatre* writers and cast. The principal technique chosen to drive the performance and build suspense was a succession of simulated news bulletins, with which American radio listeners had become quite familiar during a recent war scare in Europe.

The first bulletin came within the first minutes of the broadcast, interrupting what seemed to be a snoozy program of orchestral music. As the performance unfolded, the interruptions became more frequent and more insistent, as fresh bulletins told of the mysterious bursts of gas on the Martian surface and the fall of a large meteorite on a farm near Grovers Mill. The bulletin series gave way to alarming-sounding on-the-scene reports. The fallen object was no meteorite but a cylindrical, extraterrestrial spaceship from which the leathery, hostile Martians soon emerged, taking aim with a heat ray that wiped out a crowd of human spectators. Just twenty minutes into the broadcast, it sounded as if Earth were under a full-scale alien attack.

Listeners who followed closely would have easily recognized that events moved far too quickly to be plausible.[6] In less than thirty minutes, the Martians had blasted off from their home planet, traveled millions of miles to Earth, set up lethal heat rays, wiped out units of American soldiers, disrupted local and national communications, and forced a declaration of martial law. In the next half-hour, they destroyed much of New York City and took control of swaths of the United States before falling victim to earthly germs.[7] But casual listeners (of whom there were many in 1938) as well as latecomers to the performance[8] were said to have been badly confused, mistaking the simulated news reports of an attack on America for the real thing. These listeners, apparently, failed to realize the broadcast was a dramatization and supposedly were most inclined to panic that night.[9]

The next day, newspaper headlines from coast to coast told of the fright, terror, and panic the program supposedly had caused. "Thousands Terrified by Radio War Drama," the *Boston Herald* said. "Radio Listeners in Panic, Taking War Drama as Fact," declared the *New York Times*. "Attack from Mars in Radio Play Puts Thousands in Fear," said the *New York Herald Tribune*. "Monsters of Mars on a Meteor Stampede Radiotic America," said the *Washington Post*. "Radio Listeners Become Panicky during Story of 'Mars Invasion,'" said the *Cincinnati Enquirer*. "Radio Fake Scares Nation," cried the *Chicago Herald and Examiner*. "Radio Skit Causes Wave of Hysteria over Nation," declared the Raleigh, North Carolina, *News and Observer*. "U.S. Terrorized by Radio's 'Men from Mars,'" said the *San Francisco Chronicle*.[10]

Welles seemed circumspect and even a bit chastened the day after the program, telling reporters at what he called a "mass press interview"[11] that he regretted "any misapprehension which our broadcast last night created among some listeners," but insisting it was unfathomable anyone could have mistaken the dramatization for an alien invasion.[12] Years later, though, Welles gleefully endorsed the notion that the broadcast had caused widespread panic, saying, "Houses were emptying, churches were filling up; from Nashville to Minneapolis, there was wailing in the street and the rending of garments."[13]

The belief that panic swept America that night was endorsed by the research of Hadley Cantril, a Princeton University psychologist who studied public reaction to the performance and published his results in 1940 in *The Invasion from Mars: A Study in the Psychology of Panic*.

FIGURE 5. The day after the *War of the Worlds* program, Orson Welles confronted reporters at what he called a "terrifying mass press interview." He said he was "bewildered" how the radio show could have been mistaken for news about an invasion from Mars. [*Bettman/Corbis*]

Based on assessments of public opinion surveys and on interviews with 135 people, most of them chosen "because they were known to have been upset by the broadcast,"[14] Cantril concluded, "Long before the broadcast had ended people all over the United States were praying, crying, fleeing frantically to escape death from Martians."[15]

Cantril's became the cornerstone study about the performance of *The War of the Worlds*—and something of a landmark in mass communication research. *Invasion from Mars* has been called the first study of panic and abnormal behavior linked to specific media content. And Cantril's research pointed the way to theories that mass media exerts variable influences that differ among recipients.[16] But his findings about *The War of the Worlds* have been challenged by sociologists and others, who point out that mass hysteria and panic are rare and, given their transient nature, difficult to study. Cantril, they say, failed to demonstrate that panicked reactions and flight were widespread among listeners to the show. Indeed, Cantril's own estimates were that at least 1.2 million listeners were "frightened," "disturbed," or "excited" by what they heard. That number represents a fraction of the audience, which Cantril estimated to have been at least 6 million people.[17] By Cantril's own calculations, then, most listeners were neither panic-stricken nor fear-struck. They presumably recognized and enjoyed the program for what it was—an entertaining and imaginative radio show.

Moreover, Cantril did not make clear the distinctions between "frightened," "disturbed," and "excited." Nor did he estimate how many listeners acted on their feelings. Indeed, one can watch a horror movie and feel "frightened," "disturbed," or "excited," but such responses are hardly synonymous with panic or hysteria.

Robert E. Bartholomew, an authority on mass hysteria and social delusions, has said there is "a growing consensus among sociologists that the extent of the panic, as described by Cantril, was greatly exaggerated." Only "scant anecdotal evidence," Bartholomew said, exists "to suggest that many listeners actually took some action—such as packing belongings, grabbing guns, or fleeing in cars after hearing the broadcast."[18] Similarly, Erich Goode has written that relatively few people "actually *did* anything in response to the broadcast, such as drove off in panic or hid in a cellar. . . . It becomes clear that whatever the public reaction to the *War of the Worlds* radio broadcast was, it did not qualify as an instance of mass hysteria."[19] And Jeffrey Sconce wrote in his book *Haunted Media*: "Direct evidence that thousands of Americans were in an actual panic over the broadcast is . . . limited at best. . . . And yet the legend of a paralyzing 'mass' panic lives on."[20]

Newspapers of the day offer the most detailed contemporaneous accounts of reactions to the broadcast, and a thorough review of the reports published in thirty-six major U.S. daily newspapers[21] after the program endorses the conclusions of the sociologists: the claims that the broadcast fomented mass panic and hysteria were dramatically overstated. It becomes clear in reading the accounts that newspapers based their characterizations of widespread panic and hysteria on small numbers of anecdotal cases of people who *were* frightened or upset. These anecdotes typically were not of broad scale. They described agitation and odd behavior among individuals, their families, or neighbors.

Although many small-bore accounts were published in newspapers in metropolitan New York and northern New Jersey, where reactions to the program were most pronounced, they collectively fall well short of documenting or substantiating claims that tens of thousands, or even hundreds of thousands, of listeners were terrorized or panic-stricken.[22] It is thus impossible to offer a persuasive case that the *War of the Worlds* broadcast set off nationwide panic and hysteria. That there was no mass panic and hysteria that night is further signaled by the paucity of follow-up reports: newspapers gave little sustained attention to the broadcast and the reactions it supposedly had stirred. Had there truly been mass panic and hysteria across the country that night, newspapers for days and even weeks afterward could have been expected to have published detailed reports about the dimensions and repercussions of such an extraordinary event.[23] But coverage of the broadcast faded quickly from the front pages, in most cases after just a day or two. The *New York Times* kept the story on its front page for two days after the program, as did the *Washington Post* and the *Los Angeles Times,* among other newspapers.

Moreover, none of the thirty-six newspapers examined reported deaths or serious injuries attributable to the supposed panicked reaction. Had mass panic and hysteria swept the country that night, the trauma and turmoil surely would have resulted in many deaths and injuries. But the newspaper reports were notably silent on casualties. The *New York Times* and *New York Herald Tribune* reported that at least fifteen people had been treated for shock at a hospital in Newark, New Jersey. A number of newspapers carried a photograph showing Caroline Cantlon, an otherwise obscure actress, with her arm in a sling. She reportedly became alarmed while listening to the broadcast at her home in New York, rushed into a street, and fell, breaking her arm and skinning her knees.[24] But otherwise, newspaper reports contained few references to injury or adverse health effects linked to the program. Their reports mentioned no suicides, either.

Not surprisingly, newspaper coverage was most extensive in New York City, the prime target of the invading Martians of *The War of the Worlds.* The New York newspapers offered detailed accounts of reactions to the broadcast. These accounts captured the individual-level fright that circulated that night but failed to demonstrate that panic was of extreme and far-reaching magnitude. The *New York Times,* for example, opened its report by stating that a "wave of mass hysteria seized thousands of radio listeners throughout the nation." The anecdote cited first to support that claim was strikingly modest. The *Times* described how "more than twenty families" from a single block in Newark had "rushed out of their houses with wet handkerchiefs and towels over their faces to flee from what they believed was to be a gas raid. Some began moving household furniture." The newspaper also reported that "Harlem was shaken by the 'news'" and as evidence described how thirty men and women had rushed to a police station in

Harlem, seeking advice. Twelve other people on a similar mission showed up at a police station a dozen blocks away.[25]

The *Times* report emphasized individual accounts of fear-stricken people, such as Louis Winkler of the Bronx, who was quoted as saying he "almost had a heart attack" while listening to the program. Despite his shock, Winkler said he "ran into the streets with scores of others and found people running in all directions." The newspaper reported that a caller to police in Jersey City, across the Hudson River from New York, asked whether the authorities could spare any gas masks. The *Times* told of another man, "white with terror," who rushed to a police station in Washington Heights at the northern end of Manhattan, "shouting that enemy planes were crossing the Hudson River and asking what he should do." Elsewhere in the neighborhood, curiosity seemed more commonplace than panic, as clusters of people gathered on street corners, "hoping for a sight of the 'battle' in the skies," the *Times* reported. Some callers to police stations in New York claimed to have seen smoke "from the bombs, drifting" toward the city.[26]

Newark's newspapers also spoke of widespread terror and panic. The *Star-Eagle* began its report about the broadcast by declaring, "War terror struck hundreds of thousands of persons throughout the nation, particularly in New Jersey." But for evidence of such a sweeping claim, the newspaper's lengthy report mentioned just a half-dozen specific cases that figured more than a few people. Among them was a report that told of twenty families, their "house hold possessions piled in their cars," arriving at police headquarters in Bergenfield, New Jersey, during the broadcast. The *Star-Eagle* also said that police in Union, New Jersey, reported seeing panicked people rushing into the streets. And the newspaper said nearly a half hour was needed to calm the thirty nurses on duty that night at Newark's hospital for infants.[27]

Beyond New York and Newark, newspaper accounts about the program and its reactions were briefer, with few detailed reports of people acting on their fears. Although some newspapers said thousands of people were panic-stricken, they offered scant detail to substantiate the claims. The *Philadelphia Inquirer,* for example, placed on its front page on October 31, 1938, a three-paragraph report that said that "thousands of Philadelphians were terrorized" by the program. But the newspaper offered little supporting detail beyond saying that "hundreds of persons in various parts of the city ran from their homes fearing an earthquake" and that it received "thousands of telephone calls of inquiry."[28]

In the capital, the *Washington Post* told of callers who, in "terrified, tearful voices, asked, 'What's it all about? Is it safe to stay here? Have they called the Army, the Navy, the Marines?' They wanted to know if anyone were yet alive in New Jersey, if New York was being evacuated, if Washington would be in danger before morning." The *Post* declared, "For an hour, hysterical pandemonium gripped the Nation's Capital and the Nation itself."[29] But the newspaper offered few specific accounts to support its characterization of "hysterical pandemonium." A few days later, a letter-writer chided the *Post* for having offered "a totally false impression" about reaction to the program. "Except for the scattered cases of ignorant or excitable people who telephoned police and newspapers in many cities, there was nothing approximating mass hysteria," the letter-writer wrote. "I walked along F street [in downtown Washington] at the hour of the broadcast. In many stores radios were going, yet I observed nothing whatsoever of the absurd supposed 'terror of the populace.' There was none."[30]

The *Post* fell victim to a prank-playing marine who told the newspaper that, during the broadcast, his fellow marines at their barracks in Quantico, Virginia, had been reduced to weeping and praying and protesting that "they didn't want to go to war in the winter."[31] Marine Corps officials soon issued a pointed denial and the *Post* backtracked, saying the source of the account was a marine playing "a joke on his buddies, but it was a joke that was not appreciated by the other enlisted men."[32]

RELYING ON THE WIRE SERVICES

The *War of the Worlds* broadcast aired late on Sunday evening in the Eastern Time Zone, a time when most newspaper newsrooms were thinly staffed. Covering the reactions to the program represented no small challenge, especially for morning newspapers having late-night deadlines. Given the constraints of time and staffing, relying on wire services such as the Associated Press became essential. This dependency, in turn, had the effect of promoting and deepening the notion that panic was widespread that night: on a late-breaking story of uncertain dimension and severity, many newspapers took their lead from wire service dispatches. They had little choice.

The Associated Press reports that night essentially were roundups of reactions culled from the agency's bureaus across the country. Characteristically, the roundups emphasized sweep—pithy anecdotal reports from many places—over depth and detail. Although the anecdotes tended to be sketchy, shallow, and small-bore, their scope contributed to the sense that panic was widespread that night. The reliance of newspapers on wire service roundups thus helps explain their consensus that the broadcast had created mass panic.

This dependency also gave rise to a striking similarity in newspaper coverage of the broadcast. Many anecdotes transmitted by the wire services found their way into newspapers across the country. One such story was about a woman in Pittsburgh who exclaimed, as her husband stopped her from poisoning herself, "I'd rather die like this" than fall victim to a Martian heat ray.[33] Another widely published anecdote told of fear-stricken students at Brevard College in North Carolina "fighting for telephones to tell their parents to come and get them."[34] Also widely reported was the story of a woman in Boston who told a local newspaper that she could "see the fire" caused by the Martian invasion and that she and her neighbors were getting ready to flee.[35]

The reports in several morning newspapers were even verbatim. These newspapers published the same Associated Press dispatch, the opening paragraphs of which read:

> New York, Oct. 30 (AP)—Hysteria among radio listeners throughout the nation and actual panicky evacuations from sections of the metropolitan area resulted from a too-realistic radio broadcast tonight describing a fictitious and devastating visitation of strange men from Mars.
>
> Excited and weeping persons all over the country swamped newspaper and police switchboards with the question:
>
> "Is it true?"[36]

As the dispatch suggests, the newspapers placed great emphasis on the unusually large volume of calls placed that night to their switchboards and to those of police and fire departments and local radio stations. The surge in call volume was routinely but mistakenly characterized by newspapers as evidence of widespread fright and hysteria. The *New York Times* said its telephone switchboard "was overwhelmed by the calls." The newspaper reported receiving 875 calls, including one from a man in Dayton, Ohio, who asked: "What time will be the end of the world?" The *Brooklyn Eagle* said it took more than 500 calls during and after the program. The *Washington Evening Star* reported receiving more than 400 telephone queries.[37] Many callers wanted to know whether the program was true or how they could reach friends and relatives.

The *Indianapolis Star* said its telephone switchboard and that of the city's police department "were flooded with queries. Several persons said they [had] packed their bags and wanted to know 'which was the best way to go.' . . . Several callers asked, 'People are running out into the streets—what's the matter?'" The *Los Angeles Times* said it received calls from "hundreds of persons. . . . within a brief period" during and immediately after the broadcast, and several people came to the newspaper's offices seeking firsthand information about the fictive invasion.[38]

Callers were readily deemed to be hysterical and terror-stricken. In a particularly colorful example of an overactive imagination, the *Hartford Courant* in Connecticut described how its telephone operator, "her board flooded with lights, got a mind picture of hundreds of people frozen with horror at real and impending doom, agony at the imagined fate of relatives and friends in the supposed stricken areas and quivering bewilderment at what to do." The *New York Times* likewise adduced panic in the voices of callers, saying that "large numbers" of them, "obviously in a state of terror, asked how they could . . . flee from the city." Cantril's study also directed attention to the unusually large number of telephone calls placed during and after the *War of the Worlds* broadcast. In northern New Jersey, the volume of telephone calls surged during the show by almost 40 percent, and in the hour afterward by 25 percent. Call volume on Long Island and in suburban Philadelphia also increased markedly during and immediately after the program, Cantril reported. Fifty of fifty-two radio stations surveyed reported receiving a far greater number of calls than usual for a Sunday night. "There seems little doubt then that a public reaction of unusual proportions occurred," Cantril wrote.[39]

But the volume of telephone calls that night is a crude and even misleading marker of fear and alarm. The call volume perhaps is best understood as signaling an altogether *rational* response of people who neither panicked nor became hysterical, but sought confirmation or clarification from external sources generally known to be reliable. And some newspapers congratulated themselves for being such a resource that night. "As is usually the case with wild radio rumors," the *Harrisburg Patriot* in Pennsylvania said the day after the broadcast, "the frightened listeners rushed to the telephone to ask the newspaper whether it was true."[40]

Moreover, the call volume surely included people who telephoned friends and relatives to talk about the unusual and clever program they had just heard.[41] Also, many callers to newspapers and police stations asked how and where they could volunteer their services. These callers likely were not fear-stricken. They included doctors and nurses who, the *New York Herald Tribune* reported, "called authorities in New Jersey . . . offering their services in the emergency they supposed to exist."[42] Some people placed calls to compliment CBS for airing such an entertaining program; others called to express anger and indignation about the stunt.[43] Welles reported receiving many telegrams from listeners who said they enjoyed the dramatization.[44] In Washington, D.C., radio station WJSV said the day after *The War of the Worlds* aired that it received as many as two hundred calls from people asking that the program be broadcast again.[45] There were, then, many reasons beyond fear and panic that account for the call volume that night.

Highways jammed with automobiles have been cited as another indicator of mass panic and hysteria: terrified people were said to have fled to the hills to escape the invading Martians.[46] The day after the program, New York and New Jersey newspapers contained references to such flight. The *Newark Evening News,* for example, said that streets "leading to the Orange Mountains became jammed with autos filled with fear-stricken persons."[47] But published reports of traffic jams are little more than a vague, imprecise measure of panic.[48] There is simply no way to distinguish between those people who were badly frightened and took to the highways to seek safety and the usual volume of highway traffic that night. The notion of highways crowded with terrified refugees also appears to have taken firm hold many months *after* the broadcast. For example, this colorful description of the automobile traffic fleeing Trenton, New Jersey, appeared in the *Saturday Evening Post* in 1940: "Hundreds of automobiles began to flash along at speeds which normally indicate gangsters leaving scenes of assassination. But there were family parties in most of the cars. . . . When a motorcycle [officer] tried to overhaul one speeding auto, he was passed by two or three others. The stampede was in all directions."[49]

News reports at the time described the roadways near Grovers Mill as "virtually impassible"—but they were jammed with curiosity-seekers attempting to get *to* the supposed Martian landing site as well as those who were trying to flee.[50] Such conditions hardly allowed for a "stampede in all directions." Among those who went to Grovers Mill that night were two of Cantril's faculty colleagues at Princeton, Arthur F. Buddington, the chairman of the university's geology department, and Harry H. Hess, a mineralogist. Neither had listened to the *War of the Worlds* program. But during the broadcast, they were told thirdhand about the landing of a meteorite near Grovers Mill and they went to search for it. "We got to Grovers Mill and spent an hour driving around looking for the meteor, but couldn't find any," Buddington told the

New York Post. "Finally somebody told us it was all a mistake, and naturally we felt quite foolish."[51]

Clearly, many people in America were confused, unnerved, and even frightened by the broadcast. But it was an untenable leap for newspapers to extrapolate mass panic and hysteria from a comparatively small number of anecdotal reports. The evidence the newspapers offered neither matched nor supported the claims in their headlines of mass panic and hysteria. Newspapers simply had no reliable way of ascertaining the validity of the sweeping claims they offered the day after the program.

SECONDHAND FEAR

U.S. newspapers reached indefensible conclusions that panic and mass hysteria prevailed in the aftermath of the *War of the Worlds* broadcast. But scrutiny of their contents reveals evidence that a false-alarm contagion took hold that night—a largely overlooked but scarcely insignificant source of fright. Mostly in New York and New Jersey, but occasionally in other places as well, well-intentioned people possessing little more than an incomplete understanding of the *War of the Worlds* broadcast set out to warn others of the sudden and terrible threat. These would-be Paul Reveres burst into churches, theaters, taverns, and other public places, shouting that the country was being invaded or bombed or that the end of the world was near.

It had to have been a cruel and unnerving way of receiving word of a supposedly calamitous event—to be abruptly disturbed in familiar settings by vague reports offered by people who themselves clearly were fear-stricken. The unsuspecting recipients of these jumbled, second- and thirdhand accounts had no immediate way of verifying the wrenching news they had just heard. Unlike listeners of the radio dramatization, they could not spin a dial to find out whether other networks were reporting an invasion. In more than a few cases, a contagion took hold: many *non-listeners* became quite frightened, thus compounding for a short time commotion and confusion stemming from the *War of the Worlds* program.

In New York, some apartment houses "were hurriedly emptied by frantic listeners to the program and by those who heard second- and thirdhand accounts multiplying the supposed peril," the *Newark Star-Eagle* reported, adding that "many of the panic-stricken did not hear the original broadcast but got their misinformation from others." The newspaper also described how a "panic-stricken" man stood in the middle of a busy intersection in Newark, "directing traffic to head for the Orange mountains."[52] The *New York Herald Tribune* said that "two or three motorists who had radios in their cars passed through Irvington, N.J., calling to every one to drive back into the country—that the state was being bombed." The newspaper also said, "Confused reports resulting from the broadcast led to various rumors, including one that a meteor had struck near Princeton and many persons had been killed."[53]

Some theater patrons in New York left abruptly upon hearing that an invasion from Mars, or a calamity of some kind, was unfolding. The manager of one theater told the *New York Times* that "the wives of two men in the audience, having heard the broadcast, called the theatre and insisted that their husbands be paged. This spread the 'news' to others in the audience."[54] In Rahway, New Jersey, a man tried without success to secure permission from police to drive a sound truck through town to warn of "the danger from the skies."[55] In Orange, New Jersey, Al Hochberg, the manager of the neighborhood Lido Theater, was credited with averting a panic by intercepting a man who rushed into the lobby exclaiming that a meteor had fallen nearby and that "little men [were] dashing around and growing into giants." The *Newark Evening News* quoted the intruder as shouting, "I've got to tell all the people to get out in the country, to get away from poison gases. They'll all be killed." Hochberg ordered the man to be kept in the lobby while he called police to find out what was going on. When Hochberg returned, the intruder had left, reportedly to rouse people elsewhere in town.[56] The newspaper also reported that a man rushed into a movie theater in Jamesburg, New Jersey, shouting, "The end of the world has come!" With that, the newspaper said, women screamed "and there was a rush for the exits."[57]

In Caldwell, New Jersey, a Baptist service was interrupted by a "wild young man" who, the *Evening News* reported, entered the sanctuary about 8:40 P.M., shouting, "Parson, a meteor has fallen in Central Jersey and wiped out several towns. Army troops are fighting poison gas." With that, the man rushed out. The minister, Rev. Thomas G. Thomas, told the congregation "that if disaster were on the way, church was a good place to be." His congregation of about one hundred people remained in the church.[58] A wedding reception at a restaurant on East 116th Street in Manhattan was disrupted when a latecomer arrived and took the microphone to announce that the city was under invasion from outer space. Guests reportedly grabbed their coats and began to leave, heedless of the bride's pleas not to ruin her wedding day. The groom took the microphone and began to sing hymns.[59]

In Indianapolis, a Methodist service was disrupted "when an hysterical woman member of the congregation entered shortly after worship had begun," the *Indianapolis Star* reported. The woman hurried to the pulpit, telling the pastor, "Something so terrible has happened that I must interfere." She announced that "New York has been destroyed" and added: "I believe the end of the world has come. I heard it over the radio." The pastor offered a short prayer and excused anyone who wanted to return home. Several members of the choir "doffed robes and went from the church, followed by a portion of the congregation," the *Star* reported. But the service continued, and the pastor delivered his sermon. Soon, several members of the congregation returned, explaining sheepishly that the alarm had been caused by nothing more than a misunderstood radio show.[60]

The *Baltimore Sun* reported a "near riot" at a grocery in suburban Baltimore after a girl came in and said that "a huge meteor" had fallen in New York City and "a lot of little men [had] jumped out and [begun] killing people."[61]

Although it is impossible to estimate the cumulative effects of the false-alarm contagion that night, second- and thirdhand accounts certainly provoked evanescent fear and apprehension among thousands of people who had *not* listened to the program. These second- and thirdhand accounts usually were not highlighted in newspaper reports of the broadcast, but they surely were potent, if only for a short while. Indeed, it is tempting to suggest that what radio-induced fear there was that night was mostly spread by credulous people who heard muddled and fragmentary accounts about the program and set about to alert others. This misguided Paul Revere effect also offers a plausible explanation for the many distorted, wildly inaccurate reports that circulated that night—reports of the smell of poison gas, fires seen on the New York City skyline, attack planes ready to drop bombs, and meteorites wiping out towns. The great variation in details suggests that many people who were fear-stricken that night had not heard the *Mercury Theatre* dramatization but were swept up in a wave of second- and thirdhand accounts. As those accounts proliferated, the storyline of *The War of the Worlds* became distorted, often beyond recognition.

DRESSING DOWN AN UPSTART MEDIUM

Editorial commentary in newspapers in the days following the airing of the program served to deepen and reinforce the notion that the *War of the Worlds* broadcast had created widespread panic and that culpability for such reactions rested squarely with radio. An editorial in William Randolph Hearst's *New York Journal and American* repeated unsubstantiated claims that the program caused hysteria that "was NATION-WIDE and literally MILLIONS OF PEOPLE understood the broadcast to be REAL."[62] It "goes without saying," the *Journal and American* declared, "that if the industry, or irresponsible units within the industry, cannot guard against incidents of this nature . . . it will not long be free from more drastic forms of censorship than it has yet known."[63] Similarly, the *Detroit Free Press* asserted, "Things are reaching such a pass that the radio simply must be cleansed of its evil sensationalism, and if there is no other way to perform the job, it must be through some sort of government action."[64]

Raising the prospect of censorship was one of several ways in which newspapers seized on the uproar of the *War of the Worlds* broadcast to chastise and admonish radio, an increasingly important rival in news gathering and advertising. The newspaper-radio rivalry certainly was not new in 1938. It had taken shape during the 1920s. But by 1938, radio's immediacy in bringing news to Americans had become all too apparent, and troubling, to newspapers. Radio was becoming the principal medium for reports of breaking news, a trend clearly demonstrated during the war scare in Europe in late summer and fall of 1938, when radio carried frequent reports about the territorial demands of Hitler's Nazi Germany and the acquiescence of Western European states, leading to the German annexation of Czechoslovakia's Sudetenland. American newspapers thus had competitive incentives to denounce radio and characterize it as irresponsible and unreliable. Many newspapers seized the chance to do so with enthusiasm. It was an opportunity they could not let pass.

The newspaper trade journal *Editor and Publisher* warned in an editorial about the *War of the Worlds* program that "the nation as a whole continues to face the danger of incomplete, misunderstood news over a medium which has yet to prove, even to itself, that it is competent to perform the news job."[65] In an editorial titled "Terror by Radio," the *New York Times* reproved the medium, stating: "Radio is new but it has adult responsibilities. It has not mastered itself or the material it uses. It does many things which the newspapers learned long ago not to do, such as mixing its news and advertising. . . . In the broadcast of 'The War of the Worlds' blood-curdling fiction was offered in exactly the manner that real news would have been given and interwoven with convincing actualities. . . . Radio officials should have thought twice before mingling this new technique with fiction so terrifying."[66] The *Richmond Times-Dispatch* insisted that "this innocent demonstration of radio frightfulness is no laughing matter" and declared, "The effect of this incident will probably be to impress upon radio stations the necessity of dealing more carefully with both truth and fiction."[67]

The *Mercury Theatre* troupe came in for a good deal of criticism as well. The *New York Sun* said it suspected that Welles and his colleagues "no doubt are sadder and wiser now, after their experiment with broadcasting dynamite. . . . It will require no lecture from the Federal Communications Commission to make them resolve never to do it again."[68] The *Chicago Tribune*, meanwhile, reserved a sneering attack for radio audiences, which it said were not "very bright," adding, "Perhaps it would be more tactful to say that some members of the radio audience are a trifle retarded mentally, and that many a program is prepared for their consumption." The *War of the Worlds* dramatization, said the *Tribune*, "was not a hoax; it was fiction, and any normally intelligent man, even if he tuned in late, could not have failed to recognize it for what it was within a minute or two."[69]

The broadcast exposed a fundamental flaw in radio, said the *Cincinnati Enquirer*. "At best," the newspaper said, "radio is a confusing medium of information. It lacks the means of check-back and confirmation so readily available on the printed page. Thus it is that radio listeners customarily telephoned newspapers for confirmation of important news bulletins broadcast by radio."[70] The *Harrisburg Patriot* in Pennsylvania likewise took up that theme, saying the *War of the Worlds* broadcast underscored the preeminent reliability of the print media: "Apart from questions of propriety in putting on the air broadcasts which, though not intended, brought panic to many minds, the significant feature of the Sunday night episode was the sense of dependence which the public continues to have on the newspaper. It continues to be a repository of reliable information and an essential part of the life of the people. . . . One hesitates to think what might have happened Sunday night had there been no newspapers to which horror-stricken persons could have turned for relief."[71]

Similarly, the *New York Herald Tribune* declared that "no hoax in print could be misunderstood and suddenly stir masses to panic as did this radio blunder."[72] The *Rocky Mountain News* in Denver, asserting that newspapers "through the years, have built up a high standard of responsibility," said that the *War of the Worlds* program "merely emphasizes the value of the familiar warning: Don't believe it until you read it."[73] The *Herald and Examiner* in Chicago said radio would do well to follow the lead of newspapers: "Radio news is frequently unreliable, and often sensational and alarming. Radio news ought to be presented with the same restraint that is exercised by newspapers."[74] The *Hartford Courant* said that the broadcast "ought to serve a double warning—to the radio industry to watch its step and to the listening public to be wary of believing wild rumors for which the only authority is 'I heard it over the radio.'"[75]

The newspapers soon finished their hectoring. But the notion of the panic broadcast, which newspapers had helped to implant, lives on as a delightfully good story, invariably recalled as that strange and exceptional moment when "millions of people . . . stampeded police stations and hospitals" and "terrified citizens [rushed] into the street and caused traffic jams along the East Coast."[76] The myth resides just at the margin of bizarre plausibility, which makes it all the more appealing and memorable.

The *War of the Worlds* broadcast also has become a frame of reference against which ostensibly exaggerated and irrational fears can be measured. For example, the *Wall Street Journal* once said: "The long-running scare over asbestos is turning out to be the 'War of the Worlds' of environmental panics. As with Orson Welles' famous scary radio broadcast, the asbestos panic has been whipped up by endless evening news reports about how the nation's schools were cancer traps" because of the chance of exposure to airborne asbestos.[77]

The War of the Worlds also offers a ready example of the malevolent effects of news media content. The famous broadcast suggests that, when circumstances are right, the media *can* create panic and other effects that are unpredictable, disruptive, and wide-ranging. The front-page headlines in American newspapers on October 31, 1938, stand as timeless evidence of such unwanted consequences. But reading closer, beyond the headlines, yields the rich and important insight of how overstated those headlines truly were. Inaccurate reporting gave rise to a misleading historical narrative and produced a savory and resilient media-driven myth.

CHAPTER 3

Murrow vs. McCarthy

Timing Makes the Myth

They'll have to rewrite the definition of journalism now.
—"They Listened to Murrow," *Broadcasting/Telecasting*
(15 March 1954): 132

Edward R. Murrow is without question the towering icon, the mythic figure, the "patron saint" of American broadcast journalism.[1]

The highest awards of the Radio-Television News Directors Association are named for Murrow. Documentaries have celebrated his exploits in journalism. Hagiographies have been written about his life and career. A corner of the Newseum, the $450 million museum of news in downtown Washington, D.C., extols Murrow's contributions to broadcast journalism. Elsewhere in Washington, a wedge of federal parkland on Pennsylvania Avenue, not far from the White House, is named for Murrow.[2] And in the lobby of CBS headquarters in New York, a plaque bears the image of Murrow, the network's most famous journalist. Murrow, the inscription says, "set standards of excellence that remain unsurpassed."[3]

Murrow became a household name as World War II swept across Europe. His radio reports about the Nazi aerial blitz of London in 1940 brought home to Americans the horrors and raw drama of war. His sign-on—"This . . . is London"—was readily identifiable. Murrow became so prominent and popular that, when he was on home leave in 1941, his boat was met by crowds as it docked in New York. CBS threw a banquet at the Waldorf-Astoria exclusively in his honor, and 1,100 people showed up. Millions more listened to the tributes on the radio.[4] "In the whole history of journalism," one of his admirers wrote, "perhaps no other reporter [had] become famous quite so fast."[5]

Forever sealing the image of Murrow as journalist-hero is the widely accepted view that he single-handedly confronted and took down the most feared and loathsome American political figure of the Cold War, Joseph R. McCarthy, the red-baiting Republican senator from Wisconsin. Murrow, it is often said, stood up to McCarthy when no one else would, or dared,[6] and in doing so produced one of American television's most treasured moments, its "finest half hour."[7]

The setting for the legendary confrontation with McCarthy was the episode of Murrow's *See It Now* program that aired on CBS at 10:30 P.M. on March 9, 1954. *See It Now* was a thirty-minute, documentary-style show sponsored by the aluminum manufacturer Alcoa. Through clever editing of film of McCarthy in action, Murrow and his team prepared a powerful indictment, one so compelling that it supposedly stopped the brutal senator in his tracks and set in motion events "that left the tyrant censured by his own Senate colleagues" later that year.[8] That Murrow's 1954 broadcast ended Joe McCarthy's reign of terror is a compelling story, one of the best known in American journalism. It also is a media-driven myth.

This chapter examines the emergence of the Murrow-McCarthy myth and offers several reasons for its tenacity, notably the unintended yet fortuitous timing of the *See It Now* program about McCarthy: the show aired amid a sudden convergence of developments that sent the senator into a tailspin from which he never recovered. In addition, the 2005 motion picture *Good Night, and Good Luck,* an imaginative cinematic treatment of the famous *See It Now* program, served to popularize and extend the Murrow-McCarthy myth to another generation of Americans.

Seeding the Murrow-McCarthy myth began soon after the *See It Now* program aired, with an editorial in *Broadcasting/Telecasting* magazine that declared: "They'll have to rewrite the definition of journalism now. No greater feat of journalistic enterprise has occurred in modern times than that performed by Ed Murrow last Tuesday on *See It Now.* He indicted Sen. McCarthy by word and deed, documenting it as it can be done by television only."[9] *Variety* soon afterward said Murrow was "practically . . . a national hero" for presenting such a devastating portrait of McCarthy.[10]

Admiring biographers helped solidify the myth. Among them was the broadcaster Bob Edwards, who wrote that "in 1954, Murrow demonstrated that TV news possessed a power beyond that of other forms of journalism. He and producer Fred Friendly focused the CBS eye on Senator Joseph McCarthy, exposing McCarthy as a despot and a bully."[11]

In her biography, *Murrow: His Life and Times,* Ann M. Sperber was even more expansive. She wrote that the report on McCarthy "served as a catalytic agent, mobilizing and coalescing opinion, hitherto fragmented, into a nationwide expression of popular sentiment," without fully explaining just how the thirty-minute program could have produced such an effect.[12]

Veteran journalists also have promoted the myth. Nat Hentoff, a First Amendment advocate who wrote a column for the *Village Voice,* once recalled that the program "ended Joe McCarthy's reign of fear."[13] Daniel Schorr, a veteran CBS newsman and onetime associate of Murrow, declared in 2005 that "Murrow launched the attack on McCarthy long before it was the popular thing to do, and Murrow set the standard for integrity in the media."[14]

Anniversaries inevitably have been occasions for recalling and celebrating Murrow's deed. At the twenty-fifth anniversary of the Murrow program, Joseph Wershba, a former reporter for *See It Now,* wrote in the *New York Times Sunday Magazine,* "It took more than one ax to topple Joe McCarthy, but [the *See It Now* program was] one of the first and most deadly blows."[15] On the fiftieth anniversary, in 2004, *Broadcasting and Cable* magazine recalled: "On March 9, 1954, television stood up and said, 'No more.' Edward R. Murrow used his See It Now program to present an unflattering, unvarnished portrait of Sen. Joseph McCarthy and his Communist witch hunt. . . . The world could see that the emperor had no clothes, and was nuts in the bargain."[16] On the sixtieth anniversary, in 2014, a CBS correspondent grandly described Murrow's program as "a turning point in the history of television and of CBS News."[17] At the hundredth anniversary of Murrow's birth, in 2008, Marvin Kalb, a former reporter for CBS and NBC, told an audience at the Newseum, "It was the . . . Murrow broadcast . . . that did in McCarthy."[18]

The never-ending accolades notwithstanding, the evidence is overwhelming that Murrow's famous program on McCarthy had no such decisive effect, that Murrow in fact was very late in confronting McCarthy, and that he did so only after other journalists had challenged the senator and his tactics for months or even years. Eric Sevareid, Murrow's friend and CBS colleague, chafed at the misleading interpretation attached to the *See It Now* program: "The youngsters read back and they think only one person in broadcasting and the press stood up to McCarthy and this has made a lot of people feel very upset, including me, because that program came awfully late."[19]

By the time Murrow's program on McCarthy aired in March 1954, the senator's favorability ratings had been sliding for three months, a sharp decline propelled in part by McCarthy's ill-considered clash with President Dwight D. Eisenhower over the direction of U.S. foreign policy. Gallup Poll data show that McCarthy's appeal crested in December 1953, when 53 percent of Americans said they had a favorable view of him. That rating had slipped to 40 percent by early January 1954, and to 39 percent in February 1954, when almost the same percentage of Americans viewed him unfavorably. By mid-March 1954, the proportion had shifted to 32 percent favorable and 47 percent unfavorable.[20]

Interestingly, this media myth took hold *despite* the protestations of its central figures. In the days and weeks after the *See It Now* program, Murrow said he recognized his accomplishments were modest and that, at best, he had reinforced what others had long said about McCarthy. Jay Nelson Tuck, the television critic for the *New York Post,* wrote that Murrow felt "almost a little shame faced at being saluted for his courage in the McCarthy matter. He said he had said nothing that . . . anyone might not have said without a raised eyebrow only a few years ago."[21] Murrow told *Newsweek,* "It's a sad state of affairs when people think I was courageous." He also dismissed the notion that the program about McCarthy represented television's coming of age, saying, "No single show can change a whole medium."[22] Murrow's collaborator and coproducer, Fred W. Friendly, also rejected claims that the program was pivotal or decisive, writing in his memoir, "To say that the Murrow broadcast of March 9, 1954, was the decisive blow against Senator McCarthy's power is as inaccurate as it is to say that Joseph R. McCarthy . . . single-handedly gave birth to McCarthyism."[23]

It wasn't as if Americans in early 1954 were hoping for someone to step up and expose McCarthy, or waiting for a white knight like Murrow to tell them what a toxic threat the senator posed. By then, McCarthy and his tactics were well known, and he had become a target of withering ridicule—a sign of diminished capacity to inspire dread. On the day the *See It Now* program aired, former president Harry Truman reacted to reports of an anonymous threat against McCarthy's life by saying, "We'd have no entertainment at all if they killed him."[24] Long before the *See It Now* program, several prominent journalists—including the Washington-based syndicated columnist Drew Pearson—had become persistent and searching critics of McCarthy, his record, and his tactics. McCarthy tried to destroy Pearson, whose little-remembered reporting on McCarthy is revisited in this chapter.

FIGURE 6. Edward R. Murrow, the chain-smoking "patron saint" of American broadcast journalism, took on Joseph R. McCarthy in a memorable television program on CBS in March 1954. By then, though, public opinion had begun shifting away from the demagogic senator. [*Bettman/Corbis*]

So why does deflating the Murrow-McCarthy myth matter now, long after the program was aired and long after McCarthy's death? The reasons are many, not the least of which is the inherent importance of placing in sharper context a famous early moment in American television. Another reason for examining the Murrow-McCarthy encounter is that it demonstrates how a media-driven myth can take hold despite the protests of its principal figures, a curious but not entirely uncommon outcome. Confronting the myth also matters because—as Murrow implicitly suggested in rebuffing acclaim for being courageous—the power and influence of television journalism is often assumed and frequently overstated.

SEE IT NOW, MARCH 9, 1954

Murrow had addressed McCarthy and McCarthyism on *See It Now* before March 9, 1954, but only indirectly or in passing.[25] On that night, however, *See It Now* was a full frontal attack on the man Murrow repeatedly, almost pejoratively, referred to as "the junior senator from Wisconsin." Murrow was cool, deliberate, and methodical as he went about puncturing a succession of McCarthy's half-truths and exaggerated claims.

The *See It Now* program was titled "A Report on Senator Joseph R. McCarthy," and it was powerful television. It also was a hearty dose of advocacy journalism. The program often is described as a skilled dissection in which Murrow allowed McCarthy's "own words [to] define and ultimately destroy him."[26] Murrow characterized the program as just that—a report told "mainly in his own words and pictures." But "A Report on Senator Joseph R. McCarthy" was far more clever than that: Murrow and his *See It Now* team assembled a series of film clips decidedly unflattering to McCarthy.[27] The result rightly has been called "a compendium of every burp, grunt, stutter, nose probe, brutish aside, and maniacal giggle the senator had ever allowed to be captured on film."[28]

Clips highlighting McCarthy's oddball appearance and mannerisms—his hulking, menacing presence, his nutty laugh, his five o'clock shadow, his careless grooming that allowed thin strands of greasy hair to creep down his forehead—were among the program's most revealing and most unforgettable moments. Philip Hamburger, the television critic for the *New Yorker*, wrote that the Murrow program allowed him his best look yet at McCarthy. "Most of the time," Hamburger wrote of McCarthy, "he has a petulant, droop-jaw expression, as though, at the very instant he was all set to challenge everybody in the place to step outside."[29]

At least one prominent critic in 1954 was troubled by Murrow's technique. He was Gilbert Seldes, a friend of Murrow's who was the radio-television columnist for the *Saturday Review of Literature*. Seldes pointedly criticized Murrow's selective use of footage of McCarthy. "It was not good politics, from my point of view, to present this menacing figure as an incompetent fool," Seldes wrote, adding, "Presented conspicuously as [the unflattering images of McCarthy] were, they became the equivalent of the partial truth and the innuendo." It is more important, Seldes wrote, "to use our communications systems properly than to destroy McCarthy."[30]

But the program's little-disguised advocacy and its confrontational style—elements rare these days in network news programs—help explain why it became so memorable and esteemed. "It was great television because it was a showdown between a journalist and a politician," Nicholas Lemann wrote in the *New Yorker* in 2006, "but the days when a major figure on network television can pick that kind of fight and openly state political opinions on prime time are long gone."[31]

The *See It Now* team had ample footage of the wild charges and bullying ways of McCarthy, who had burst into national prominence four years earlier. In a series of speeches in February 1950, McCarthy claimed that scores of communists, communist sympathizers, or persons of risk were embedded in the U.S. State Department. McCarthy at first placed that number at 57 in a speech at Wheeling, West Virginia. He soon raised the number to 205 and then 207. The shifting figures clearly suggested that McCarthy "was just 'winging it,' making it up as he went along,"[32] which he mostly was. Even so, his charges soon won national attention, turning an obscure first-term senator into something of a political celebrity. In the months and years that followed, McCarthy broadened and intensified his attacks, claiming that communists had penetrated the Democratic Party, the Voice of America, and the U.S. Army, among other institutions. He leveled withering and largely undocumented attacks against prominent Americans, accusing them of being willing accomplices in shielding communists or encouraging their anti-American designs. They included Adlai Stevenson, the Democratic presidential nominee in 1952 and 1956; General George C. Marshall, the author of the Marshall Plan for postwar relief in Europe; and Owen Lattimore, an authority on China and the Far East, whom McCarthy

FIGURE 7. McCarthy's bumbling response to Murrow was televised on CBS in early April 1954. The timing of McCarthy's unfocused rebuttal helped solidify a sense that Murrow was central to the senator's downfall. [*Bettman/Corbis*]

accused of being a spy for the Soviet Union. McCarthy even intimated that the loyalty of President Eisenhower should be regarded cautiously.

Few of McCarthy's wild and reckless accusations proved true. But his charges, usually hurled from the libel-proof protection of the Senate floor, deepened fears, darkened reputations, and inspired the enduring epithet "McCarthyism"—shorthand for the "stifling of free debate and the denial of constitutional rights by the imputation of communist sympathies."[33] McCarthyism of course predated Joe McCarthy. Truman had imposed loyalty oaths on federal employees in 1947, the year the House Un-American Activities Committee began investigating suspected Hollywood subversives.[34] The term *McCarthyism* first was used by the *Washington Post* political cartoonist Herbert Block in late March 1950, not long after McCarthy leveled his first charges about communists in the State Department.

Suspicions about communists in the government were neither far-fetched nor entirely baseless in the early 1950s. Shortly before McCarthy's speech in Wheeling, Alger Hiss, a former State Department official, had been sentenced to prison on charges linking him to a communist spy ring. Shortly after the speech, the physicist Klaus Fuchs was convicted on charges of delivering details about the U.S. atomic weapon program to the Soviets.

McCarthy gained power, if not prestige, as the Republicans won control of Congress in the fall elections of 1952. He was awarded the chairmanship of the Senate Permanent Subcommittee on Investigations and from that perch expanded his accusations about communists in government. By March 1954, Murrow and his *See It Now* team had collected 15,000 feet of film on McCarthy,[35] and they made devastatingly effective use of it.

Murrow seemed earnest, even grim, as he opened the show. "Because a report on Senator McCarthy is by nature controversial," Murrow intoned, staring at the camera in sidelong fashion, "we want to say exactly what we mean to say and I request your permission to read from the script whatever remarks Murrow and Friendly may make. If the Senator believes we have done violence to his words or pictures and desires to speak, to answer himself, an opportunity will be afforded him on this program."[36]

Murrow proceeded to demonstrate McCarthy's taste for half-truth and innuendo. McCarthy was shown laughing at his feigned mistake of confusing Stevenson, the 1952 Democratic presidential candidate, with Hiss, the convicted spy. The program showed the senator denouncing the

Democratic Party for "twenty years of treason." It showed him brow-beating obscure witnesses summoned to testify before his subcommittee about the communist threat in education. Murrow wrapped up by accusing McCarthy of repeatedly crossing the fine line between congressional investigation and persecution. "His primary achievement has been in confusing the public mind, as between internal and the external threats of communism," Murrow declared. "We must not confuse dissent with disloyalty. We must remember always that accusation is not proof and that conviction depends upon evidence and due process of law. We will not walk in fear, one of another. We will not be driven by fear into an age of unreason, if we dig deep in our history and our doctrine, and remember that we are not descended from fearful men—not from men who feared to write, to speak, to associate and to defend causes that were, for the moment, unpopular."

McCarthy's actions, Murrow said in closing, "have caused alarm and dismay amongst our allies abroad, and given considerable comfort to our enemies. And whose fault is that? Not really his. He didn't create this situation of fear; he merely exploited it—and rather successfully. Cassius was right. 'The fault, dear Brutus, is not in our stars, but in ourselves.'

"Good night," Murrow said, invoking his signature sign-off, "and good luck." The show was over, and Murrow slumped in his chair, his head down.[37]

The program drew mostly favorable reaction from television critics. Some of them were thrilled. Jack Gould, the television writer for the *New York Times,* wrote: "It was crusading journalism of high responsibility and genuine courage. For TV, so often plagued by timidity and hesitation, the program was a milestone."[38] Hamburger of the *New Yorker* said that Murrow had "brought off an extraordinary feat of journalism."[39] But other critics pointed out that *See It Now* had offered nothing new about McCarthy. "Murrow said nothing, and his cameras showed nothing, that this and some other newspapers have not been saying—and saying more strongly—for three or four years," the *New York Post*'s Jay Nelson Tuck said in his review. "The news was in the fact that television was saying it at all."[40]

Popular reaction to the program was said to have been something else—wildly enthusiastic and congratulatory. CBS headquarters in New York and its affiliated stations elsewhere in the country reportedly were inundated with telephone calls, letters, and telegrams, the sentiments of which were overwhelmingly in Murrow's favor. Friendly, Murrow's collaborator, estimated that CBS received as many as one hundred thousand letters about the program,[41] and messages came from the notable and the anonymous. Earl Warren, the chief justice of the U.S. Supreme Court, sent a note. So did Albert Einstein. And the reaction was "far from being an East Coast or liberal-elitist phenomenon," Sperber, Murrow's biographer, wrote. She said that "the show's success was based in large part on strong grass-roots support, . . . proving once again that Murrow knew his audience and the trap, to be avoided, of preaching to the converted."[42]

Everywhere he went, Ed Murrow seemed to be a man of the hour. The doorman shook Murrow's hand as he returned to his apartment after the program.[43] Patrons rose to applaud when Murrow and a colleague, Eric Sevareid, walked into a restaurant on the New Jersey Turnpike.[44] A similar scene unfolded at the Overseas Press Club awards dinner in late March 1954, at the Waldorf in New York. The fifteen hundred men and women attending "rose in a spontaneous standing ovation as Murrow entered the room," Sperber wrote. In Europe, the newspapers "went crazy, they were delighted; it was like America coming into her own again," according to Sperber's account.[45]

More recent research suggests that public reaction to the program on McCarthy was far more restrained than Sperber, Friendly, and other biographers suggested. In an exhaustive review of 2,107 editorials and 2,343 letters to the editor published in fourteen leading U.S. newspapers and four national magazines in the three weeks following the program, journalism historian Brian Thornton reported finding only three editorials and five letters that discussed the Murrow-McCarthy program. Had the program stirred "a powerful tidal wave of admiration . . . it is hard to explain why more enthusiasm did not show up in letters to the editor and editorial pages of the newspapers and magazines at that time," Thornton wrote.[46]

There is, he concluded, "little published evidence to support the notion, advanced in several Murrow biographies and in many journalism history books, claiming that the vast majority of the people publicly honored Murrow in March 1954, thanking him for exposing McCarthy." Thornton noted that intervening years "have added a golden glow to the reaction to Murrow's program about McCarthy that was not evident in much of the print press in March 1954."[47]

Even so, the See It Now program on McCarthy helped to seal Murrow's reputation as "the white knight of the airwaves."[48] But the legendary status that came to be associated with the program obscured and diminished the contributions of journalists who took on McCarthy years earlier, at a time when doing so was quite risky. And at least two of them paid a stiff price for challenging the senator.

A SEVENTEEN-PART EXPOSÉ

In September 1951—two and a half years before Murrow's *See It Now* program on McCarthy—the *New York Post* published an exuberantly bare-knuckled series about the senator. The series, which ran in seventeen installments, is seldom recalled in the historiography of the McCarthy period. It was raw, aggressive, unflattering, and insulting. And it represented "the first comprehensive newspaper account of [McCarthy's] curious public career."[49]

The *New York Post*'s series was accompanied by the logo "Smear Inc.," and the first installment carried the headline, "The One-Man Mob of Joe McCarthy." It made no bow to even-handedness. "This is the story of a hoax," the opening salvo read. "It may turn out to be the most fabulous hoax of the century. It is the story of Joseph Raymond McCarthy, the junior Senator from Wisconsin. The magnificence of the hoax would have intrigued Barnum."[50]

The article described the major topics to be addressed in installments to follow, including irregularities in McCarthy's income tax returns; his hypocrisy in impugning the patriotism "of thousands in government service" while having used political connections "to get out of the Marine Corps seven months before" the end of World War II, and his accepting $10,000 from a company that had received millions of dollars in government contracts. "McCarthy has raced to the fore with breakneck speed," the *Post* observed. "In the course of his careening, reckless, headlong drive down the road to political power and personal fame, he has smashed the reputations of countless men, destroyed Senate careers, splattered mud on the pages of 20 years of national history, confused and distracted the public mind, bulldozed press and radio."[51]

The first installment also pointed to the source of McCarthy's power: "By constant practice he has learned that all one needs to defeat or at least immobilize an opponent is to charge that he is linked with the Soviet enemy or just suggest that he has been in the past, might be now, or could conceivably be linked in the future."[52]

The series concluded on Sunday, September 23, 1951, with an article headlined: "Sen. McCarthy: Past Cloudy, Present Windy, Future Foggy." The closing installment likened McCarthy to "a drunk at a party who was funny half an hour ago but now won't go home. McCarthy is camped in America's front room trying to impress everybody by singing all the dirty songs and using all the four-letter words he knows. The jokes are pointless, the songs unfunny, the profanity a bore."[53] While acknowledging that "the McCarthy story isn't over; perhaps the biggest chapters are yet to come," the article zeroed in on the senator's political shortcomings and intellectual limitations: "McCarthy has neither a disciplined mind nor a master plan," the *Post* said. "He is strictly the operator eyeing the main chance. Communism is his gold mine and he is working it for all it has, but beyond that he has no strategy. His essential roguishness and irresponsibility—so grotesquely magnified and highlighted in this whole Communist fight—work to betray him."[54]

The *Post* closed the series on a hopeful note that proved premature: "In more places than ever before," it said, "the methods in McCarthy's madness are being questioned and men in high and low places are summoning up the nerve to ask questions about him. That could be the beginning of Joe McCarthy's end."[55] But in fact, the series turned out to be the source of no small amount of trouble for the *Post* and its editor, James A. Wechsler.

Wechsler was twice summoned before McCarthy's subcommittee in 1953, ostensibly to answer in closed hearings questions about books he had written during the three years he belonged to the Communist Youth League. But the sessions quickly became an inquiry into the *Post* and its editorial policies, as well as Wechsler's communist past. Wechsler styled himself a "responsive but not friendly witness,"[56] and the hearing transcript shows that on occasion he sparred deftly with McCarthy. At one point, Wechsler told the Senator his newspaper "is as bitterly opposed to Joe Stalin as it is to Joe McCarthy, and we believe that a free society can combat both."[57]

Wechsler characterized the hearing as little more than "a reprisal against a newspaper and its editor for their opposition to the methods of this committee's chairman. In short, I believe I have been called here by Senator McCarthy, not because of anything I wrote or did fifteen or eighteen years ago—none of which I ever concealed—but because of what my newspaper has said about the committee's chairman in very recent times."[58] Wechsler also characterized the experience as "something of a nightmare," given that he was placed in the position of "defending myself against the insinuation that I did not break with the Communists 15 years ago."[59] McCarthy was unimpressed by Wechsler's avowals and suggested that the *New York Post* was serving the communist cause. He likened the newspaper to the *Daily Worker,* the publication of the American Communist Party.[60]

Rival newspapers such as the *New York Times* and *Washington Post* condemned McCarthy's bullying of Wechsler. In an editorial following release of the hearing transcript, which ran to 189 pages,[61] the *Washington Post* declared: "It is outrageous that the vitally important power of the Senate to conduct investigations should be prostituted in this way to gratify the personal vindictiveness of an individual committee chairman."[62]

The closed-doors encounter with McCarthy ended unhappily for Wechsler. He ultimately complied with the senator's request and turned over names of people he had known to be communists during his days in the Communist Youth League. Wechsler said he agonized about whether to give the names to McCarthy. "I did not believe there was a clear-cut right or wrong, and I found myself weighing rival expediencies," he wrote in a memoir in 1953. "It was wrong to expose others to McCarthy's wickedness, but it was equally wrong, in my judgment, to embrace the principle that a former communist should tell nothing to anyone. Whatever I did was bound to be misconstrued."[63] Among the names Wechsler yielded was that of Murray Kempton, who had a long career as a columnist for the *New York Post* and, later, for *Newsday*, where he won a Pulitzer Prize for commentary.

MCCARTHY'S IMPLACABLE MEDIA FOE

During the years of his communists-in-government campaign, McCarthy had no more relentless, implacable, or scathing foe in the news media than Drew Pearson, the lead writer of the syndicated muckraking column Washington Merry-Go-Round. The column featured nuggets of gossip, leaked disclosures, and embarrassing scoops uncovered by Pearson and his legmen. Merry-Go-Round was hardly a model of elegant prose. Pearson, who stood six feet tall and wore a trademark mustache, wrote in a breathless, staccato fashion. *Time* magazine once likened the column to "jottings [written] on an envelope in a lurching taxicab."[64]

Pearson readily made enemies, and almost seemed to relish doing so. He received mail addressed to "SOB" after President Harry Truman invoked the epithet to describe him.[65] The biographer of James V. Forrestal, the first U.S. secretary of defense and one of the columnist's frequent targets, called Pearson "a muckraking journalist of demonic dimensions," and "the self-appointed Grand Inquisitor of Washington officialdom."[66]

Pearson was something of a throwback—an activist muckraker eager to inject himself as a participant in Washington's political scene. Jack

Anderson, a legman for Pearson who became a collaborator on Washington Merry-Go-Round, recalled: "Drew was forever meddling in affairs of state, needling congressmen to do his bidding, even writing speeches for them to deliver on the floor. He believed that to get the job done he must intrude during all phases of the battle. Not only would he expose the abuse, he would hound the tribunal until it investigated, instruct witnesses on their testimony, propagandize the galleries, help draft the remedial legislation, and write a popular history of the affair."[67]

Arthur Herman, the author of a revisionist study of McCarthy, noted that Pearson would be "hard to understand in terms of today's Washington media. A strong and fervent liberal, he was a political commentator, investigative journalist, gossip columnist, and political blackmailer rolled into one. No other single person, neither journalist nor politician, looms as large in the effort to derail McCarthy."[68]

By the time of McCarthy's rise in early 1950, Pearson had been writing Washington Merry-Go-Round for seventeen years and had branched out into radio and television. "Generally," Pearson said in an interview for a cover story in *Time* magazine in 1948, "I just operate with a sense of smell: if something smells wrong, I go to work."[69] For Pearson, the smell-detector alarm had to have been set to clanging upon learning of McCarthy's incendiary charges in early 1950 about communists in the State Department.

Pearson has been recognized as the first columnist to take on McCarthy and the first to identify the likely source of McCarthy's claims of communist infiltration of the State Department.[70] Pearson first wrote about McCarthy's wild allegations on February 18, 1950, just days after McCarthy had begun raising them. Pearson called McCarthy the "harumscarum" senator and said that, when he "finally was pinned down, he could produce . . . only four names of State Department officials whom he claimed were communists.

"A careful scrutiny of these names is important," Pearson wrote. "Of the four accused by McCarthy, one, Dr. Harlow Shapley, at no time worked for the State Department. Two, Gustavo Duran and Mrs. Mary Jane Keeney, resigned four years ago; the fourth, John Service, was reinstated after a prolonged and careful investigation and after virtual apologies to him for ever questioning his loyalty."[71] Pearson also called attention to similarities between McCarthy's charges and those that had been raised three years earlier by Bartel Jonkman, a Republican congressman from Michigan. And Jonkman's charges had been discredited, Pearson noted.[72]

McCarthy persisted in his allegations about communists in the State Department, and Pearson returned to the topic a week later, seeming almost to let the senator down softly while thoroughly dismantling his charges. "The Senator from Wisconsin has been a healthy watchdog of some government activities, but the alleged communists which he claims are sheltered in the State Department just aren't," Pearson wrote, dismissing them as "stale subversives." McCarthy, Pearson added, had based his allegations on an outdated and discredited list of subversives that had been examined by Congress three years earlier. Most of the suspects on McCarthy's list "were either ousted or, after thorough examination, found to be OK," Pearson wrote. Pearson also noted that he had covered the State Department for about twenty years, during which time he had been "the career boys' severest critic. However, knowing something about State Department personnel, it is my opinion that Senator McCarthy is way off base."[73]

Pearson soon after described the calculated and expedient way in which McCarthy landed on his communists-in-government campaign: it was a surefire issue on which to run for reelection in 1952. "Today," Pearson wrote in his column of March 14, 1950, " . . . Republican leaders are getting unhappier by the minute at the antics of the junior senator from Wisconsin." Pearson also reviewed McCarthy's tax troubles with Wisconsin authorities, who in 1943 claimed McCarthy had failed to disclose $42,000 in income: "Joe explained that he had made some money speculating in stocks while he was out of the United States and not a citizen of Wisconsin; therefore, he didn't have to pay a state income tax," Pearson wrote. "However, McCarthy still held office as a state judge at the same time he claimed he was not a citizen of Wisconsin, and in the end, tax authorities accepted a compromise payment."[74]

In 1944, McCarthy reported receiving $18,000 from his father, brother, and brother-in-law as campaign contributions in his unsuccessful Senate primary race. "But when the campaign smoke was over," Pearson wrote, "it was discovered that McCarthy's father didn't have enough income to file a tax return himself, while neither the brother [nor] brother-in-law filed an income of more than $2,000. Where they got the $18,000 nobody yet knows."[75]

Pearson renewed his probing of McCarthy's checkered past by revealing in his column of April 19, 1950, that the senator had been paid $10,000 for a seven-thousand-word article, the material for which McCarthy had "obtained in the course of his government-financed trip" in 1948. McCarthy was paid $1.33 a word, Pearson figured, a rate that "would make most authors green with jealousy." McCarthy's benefactor, Pearson said, was Carl Strandlund of Lustron Corporation, a manufacturer of prefabricated housing that had received millions of dollars in government support through the Reconstruction Finance Corporation.[76]

Driving the McCarthy-Lustron arrangement, Pearson wrote, was that the senator "was in need of financial aid" and the company "was in need of congressional aid" to fend off a prospective investigation into its management and production troubles. "Actually," Pearson wrote, "the $10,000 Strandlund paid to McCarthy was part of the [Reconstruction Finance Corporation] millions the government had advanced Strandlund."[77] Lustron filed for bankruptcy in 1950.

Pearson's inquiries embarrassed and angered McCarthy, who began entertaining thoughts of doing the journalist harm. Not long after Pearson reported Lustron's $10,000 payment to McCarthy, Joseph B. Keenan, an assistant U.S. attorney general, overheard McCarthy speaking with friends about killing Pearson or causing him serious injury. Pearson's diary entry for April 21, 1950, described Keenan as "very much worried" when he told Pearson what he had heard. "McCarthy pointed out to his friends that he would be a hero with many Senators if he could pull my teeth, break my insteps permanently, or break fifteen ribs," the diary read. "I don't know where he got the figure fifteen. Joe [Keenan] was so worried he wanted to talk to J. Edgar Hoover. He said that McCarthy was something of a madman." Pearson said he was undeterred, and two nights later he closed his radio program by likening McCarthy and his tactics to the late seventeenth-century witchcraft trials in Massachusetts.[78]

At first, Pearson did not believe that McCarthy seriously meant him harm. But he wasn't so sure after the senator delivered a threat in person in May 1950 at a Gridiron Club dinner in Washington, D.C. McCarthy placed a hand on Pearson's arm and muttered, "Someday I'm going to get a hold of you and really break your arm."[79] The threats turned out to be a prelude to a brief but violent encounter at the fashionable Sulgrave Club in Washington, D.C. The Sulgrave occupies a late Gilded Age, Beaux-Arts mansion at DuPont Circle. In the 1950s, it was a hush-hush meeting place for Washington socialites and powerbrokers. The club prided itself on insuring privacy and permitted no photographers to enter. "So when history is made, as it often is, it is pictorially unrecorded," the *Washington Post* once observed.[80]

In late 1950, a twenty-seven-year-old socialite named Louise Tinsley ("Tinnie") Steinman invited both Pearson and McCarthy to join her guests at dinner at the Sulgrave. Steinman seated the men at the same table, and they traded gibes and insults throughout the evening. Pearson and McCarthy "are the two biggest billygoats in the onion patch, and when they began butting, all present knew history was being made," *Time* magazine said about their encounter.[81] McCarthy repeatedly told Pearson of plans to attack the columnist in a speech in the Senate. Pearson in turn chided McCarthy on his tax troubles in Wisconsin.[82] As the evening ended, McCarthy confronted Pearson in the Sulgrave's coat check room. Accounts differ about what happened. Pearson said McCarthy pinned his arms to one side and kneed him twice in the groin. McCarthy said he slapped Pearson, hard, with his open hand. A third account, offered by a radio broadcaster friendly to McCarthy, said the senator slugged Pearson, a blow so powerful that it lifted Pearson three feet into the air.[83] Senator Richard Nixon, who also was a guest at Tinnie Steinman's party, intervened to break up the encounter.[84]

Pearson said he was keenly embarrassed by McCarthy's assault but insisted the senator had caused no harm. He also claimed to be unworried by McCarthy's threat to denounce him on the Senate floor, saying, "The Senator's speeches are as ineffective as his pugilistic powers."[85] But Pearson soon learned otherwise. McCarthy followed through on his threat and assailed the columnist in vicious speeches in the Senate. They were unalloyed McCarthyism. He denounced the columnist as the "diabolically" clever "voice of international communism," a "prostitute of journalism," a "sugar-coated voice of Russia," and a "Moscow-directed character assassin."[86] McCarthy aimed a threat at Adam Hat Stores Incorporated, principal sponsor of Pearson's Sunday night radio program, declaring that "anyone who buys from a store that stocks an Adams [sic] hat is unknowingly contributing at least something to the cause of international communism by keeping this communist spokesman on the air."[87] A week later, Adam Hat said it would not renew its sponsorship of Pearson's program, citing "a planned change in advertising media for 1951."[88]

Pearson's staff claimed that McCarthy reprinted his Senate speeches attacking the columnist and mailed them, at taxpayers' expense, to 1,900 newspapers. What's more, the staff wrote, "copies of these speeches have been put in the hands of rival newspaper syndicate salesmen for discreet use in efforts to sell rival columns."[89] Pearson brought a $5.1 million lawsuit against McCarthy and ten others in 1951, alleging assault, libel, and conspiracy.[90] In a deposition taken in the case, Pearson claimed that losing the Adam Hat sponsorship cut his gross radio income to $100,000 from $250,000.[91] "I suppose no one newspaperman suffered more economically than I did from Joe McCarthy," Pearson mused a few years later.[92]

In the wake of McCarthy's attack, Pearson discussed moving his radio program to CBS with the network's president, Frank Stanton, who seemed enthusiastic about the idea. Later, however, Stanton said that time could not be cleared on the CBS lineup to accommodate Pearson's program. Unofficially, Pearson was told that Murrow "was really the man who had emphatically turned thumbs down."[93] Precisely why is unclear. But Pearson never forgot the slight. A few weeks after the *See It Now* report on McCarthy, Pearson wrote in his diary: "I couldn't help but remember how Ed Murrow vetoed my going on CBS after McCarthy's first attack on me in December 1950."[94]

WHY WAS MURROW SO LATE?

So why *was* Murrow so late in confronting McCarthy? Why did Murrow wait until Pearson and Wechsler and other journalists had challenged McCarthy when the risks of doing so were acute and even painful? Why did Murrow make his move only after McCarthy's power had fallen into a terminal decline? Such questions have been posed many times over the years, and the answers have never been fully satisfactory. It's possible that Murrow before 1954 was in no mood for what would be an epic confrontation. He may have sensed that the early 1950s, when the United States was at war against communist North Korea, were not especially propitious for an all-out challenge to an anticommunist senator.[95] Or Murrow simply may have been resting on laurels won covering World War II while settling into the *Person to Person* interview show with celebrities on Friday nights.[96] Or he may have been figuring out ways of tapping the power of television, which in 1954 passed the threshold of acceptance into more than half the households in the United States.[97]

Another factor may have been the well-recognized tendency of television to follow the lead of print media. The *See It Now* program on McCarthy suggested this predilection in more than one respect. Journalists such as Pearson had long before prepared the way for Murrow's report on McCarthy. And Murrow borrowed sentiments expressed by his print colleagues. Murrow's closing commentary about McCarthy—which has been called "the most dramatic, eloquent, and influential oration ever delivered by a television journalist"[98]—echoed the words

FIGURE 8. Drew Pearson, the energetic muckraking columnist, took on McCarthy years before Murrow's program in 1954. McCarthy was so angered by Pearson's probing that he physically assaulted the columnist at an exclusive club in Washington in 1950. [*Courtesy Tyler Abell/American University Archives*]

and sentiments expressed just two days before in James Reston's column in the *New York Times*.

Reston wrote: "Senator McCarthy *did not create this situation; he merely exploited it,* increasing the fear in the process, but he has been permitted to exploit it so successfully that he has established a technique which is likely to go regardless of his presence."[99] Murrow said in his closing commentary: "The actions of the junior senator from Wisconsin have caused alarm and dismay amongst our allies abroad, and given considerable comfort to our enemies. And whose fault is that? Not really his. He *didn't create this situation of fear; he merely exploited it*—and rather successfully."

A far more interesting question, though, is: What explains the tenacity of the Murrow-McCarthy myth? Why did it take such firm hold, especially in the face of objections by the program's central actors, Murrow and Friendly? Several reasons present themselves.

Mythologizing the *See It Now* program of March 9, 1954, serves to affirm television's sometimes tenuous claim to seriousness of purpose. Enveloping the program in heroic terms is a way to identify and celebrate the potential of broadcast journalism, which often has been criticized for superficiality and a taste for the trivial. As it became an inescapable presence in American living rooms in the 1950s, television needed a hero and a heroic moment. Murrow and his "Report on Joseph R. McCarthy" represented a gold standard for an often-beleaguered and much-criticized medium.

The communications scholar Gary Edgerton has addressed this question notably well, writing: "In a deep and heartfelt sense, Murrow is the electronic media's hero for self-justification. Commemorating a 'patron saint of American broadcasting' is also an act of testimony to the tenets of fairness, commitment, conscience courage, and social responsibility which compose the Murrow tradition for broadcast journalism."[100]

The accidental factor of exquisite good timing further explains the myth's enduring quality. The *See It Now* program on McCarthy aired during a week when, coincidentally, the senator's fortunes made an unanticipated yet decisive turn for the worse. The *New York Times* identified the week as a turning point in a commentary published five days after the program: "With startling suddenness, there arose in the U.S. last week the question: Has the tide turned against McCarthy?"[101]

The pivotal moment of the decisive week was not Murrow's program but the disclosure that came two days later about the Army's allegations that McCarthy and his subcommittee's counsel, Roy Cohn, had exerted pressure in an attempt to gain favored treatment for G. David Schine, Cohn's friend and assistant, who had been drafted into military service. The Army's unwillingness to extend special treatment to Schine had inspired McCarthy's charges a few weeks earlier about suspected communists in the Army.

The Army's allegations were "the climax of a week of wide-ranging counter-attack against Mr. McCarthy," the *New York Times* said. "The counter-attack was not concerted. It seemed to spring up spontaneously on many fronts," and included the *See It Now* program. Other events that sent McCarthy reeling that week were a stinging attack leveled by Ralph W. Flanders, a fellow Republican senator, who accused McCarthy of trying to shatter the party. "It was a week of steady siege for Mr. McCarthy," the *Times* said, noting that "the general feeling was that he was on the defensive, and in the novel position of being forced to do battle on ground not of his own choosing."[102] Such auspicious timing certainly contributed to the *See It Now* program's being regarded as a moment of singular importance. It was, after all, far easier to recall Murrow's provocative television program than to keep straight the allegations the Army lodged against McCarthy, Cohn, and Schine. The senator's inept and clumsy televised response to Murrow in early April 1954 further highlighted Murrow's role, however belated, in McCarthy's unraveling.

The *Times* analysis was perceptive and on target: the week was decisive. The Army's charges posed an unparalleled threat to McCarthy and signaled his collapse. The charges were a centerpiece of thirty-six days of Senate hearings in the spring and summer of 1954, hearings that the then-fledgling ABC network televised live. The Army-McCarthy hearings left the senator badly weakened and enabled his censure by the Senate in December 1954. After that, McCarthy fell into political eclipse and died from alcohol-related illness in 1957.

Years later, Fred Friendly acknowledged the decisive importance of the televised Army-McCarthy hearings. "What made the real difference" in toppling McCarthy, Friendly said, "wasn't the Murrow program but the fact that ABC decided to run the Army-McCarthy hearings. People saw the evil right there on the tube. ABC helped put the mirror up to Joe McCarthy."[103] The Murrow-McCarthy myth was sealed for another generation with the release in 2005 of *Good Night, and Good Luck,* the dramatic cinematic retelling of the *See It Now* program on McCarthy. George Clooney directed the film and starred as a slightly pudgy, ever-earnest Fred Friendly. David Strathairn played a twitchy, mirthless, ever-smoking Murrow.

Good Night, and Good Luck was released in black and white, to lend a 1950s feel, and incorporated archival footage of McCarthy from the original *See It Now* program. Although the movie never explicitly said as much, it left an inescapable impression that Murrow courageously and single-handedly stopped McCarthy.[104] And many reviewers saw it that way. The *Baltimore Sun* called the movie a "factual account of how pioneer CBS broadcaster Edward R. Murrow . . . took down the rabid anti-communist witch-hunter Senator Joseph R. McCarthy at the height of the Cold War."[105] A critic for the *Christian Science Monitor* said that *Good Night, and Good Luck* paid "homage to CBS news legend Edward R. Murrow for going up against anticommunist crusader Sen. Joseph McCarthy, chairman of the House Un-American Activities Committee [sic], when few in the '50s-era media would dare."[106] The film, said the *New York Times,* offered a timeless reminder to journalists "that it may take a . . . willingness to risk career and more, to bring government to account."[107]

Roger Ebert of the *Chicago Sun-Times* said that *Good Night, and Good Luck* was about "a group of professional newsmen who with surgical precision remove a cancer from the body politic. They believe in the fundamental American freedoms, and in Sen. Joseph McCarthy they see a man who would destroy those freedoms in the name of defending them. . . . The instrument of his destruction is Edward R. Murrow, a television journalist above reproach."[108]

There is no small irony in journalism's veneration of Murrow, who died in 1965. He was hardly a "journalist above reproach." On his employment application at CBS, Murrow added five years to his age and claimed to have majored in college in international relations and political science.[109] In fact, he had been a speech major at Washington State University.[110] Murrow also passed himself off as holding a master's degree from Stanford University, a degree he never earned.[111] During the 1956 presidential election campaign, Murrow privately counseled Stevenson, the Democratic candidate for president, on "the finer points of speaking to the camera."[112] These days, such lapses would surely disqualify Murrow, or any journalist, from positions of prominence in America's mainstream news media.

CHAPTER 4

TV Viewers, Radio Listeners, and the Myth of the First Kennedy-Nixon Debate

Nothing in life is harder to unseat than a settled and comfortable assumption.

—Bret Stephens, "Iraq Tips Toward the Abyss,"
Wall Street Journal (22 October 2013): A15

The power of the image in U.S. presidential politics, it is often said, was never more vividly demonstrated than inside a Chicago television studio on the evening of September 26, 1960.

That was when John F. Kennedy, a Democratic senator from Massachusetts, handily won the first-ever televised debate between U.S. presidential candidates because, supposedly, he appeared so confident, cool, and telegenic compared to his uneasy, haggard-looking rival, Vice President Richard M. Nixon, who wore a shirt that was too large and perspired visibly in the hot lights of the studio. Most television viewers supposedly thought Kennedy won. But people who listened to the hour-long debate on radio, away from the unblinking eye of television, reached quite a different conclusion: they thought that Nixon, whose voice supposedly sounded more authoritative and sincere, won the encounter conclusively, that he "had cleaned his [rival's] clock."[1]

So goes the myth of viewer-listener disagreement—one of the most resilient, popular, and delectable memes about the media and American politics. Despite a feeble base of supporting documentation, it is a robust trope that emerged within months of the first of four Kennedy-Nixon debates and is often cited decades later as conclusive evidence of the power of television images and the triumph of image over substance.[2] It is described often and nonchalantly in books about American presidential politics,[3] in

FIGURE 9. This was scene at the start of an hour-long debate in September 1960 between Vice President Richard Nixon (right) and Senator John F. Kennedy. The first-ever joint televised encounter between major party presidential candidates gave rise to an enduring media myth about the clashing reactions of TV viewers and radio listeners. Howard K. Smith of CBS News (center) was the debate moderator. [*Associated Press photo*]

news articles recalling the 1960 debate,[4] and in commentaries ruminating about the legacies and lessons of the first Kennedy-Nixon encounter.[5] The websites of the Museum of Broadcast Communications[6] and the John F. Kennedy Presidential Library and Museum have invoked the notion of viewer-listener disagreement.[7] It is described on a display panel at the Internet, TV, and Radio Gallery of the Newseum, the museum of news in Washington, D.C.[8] References to viewer-listener disagreement have appeared in such diverse and unlikely contexts as an art exhibition review[9] and an illustrated booklet about U.S. presidents aimed at ten-year-old readers.[10]

While popular and resilient, the notion that television viewers and radio listeners reached starkly different conclusions about the first-ever presidential debate is a dubious bit of political lore: there is no persuasive evidence that millions of viewers and listeners diverged sharply and dramatically about the outcome of the first of the Kennedy-Nixon debates in 1960. Over the years, viewer-listener disagreement has become a defining feature of the debate and, in some extravagant retellings, was responsible for Kennedy's victory in the presidential election of November 1960.[11] "It's now common knowledge," *Time* magazine claimed in 2010, "that without the nation's first televised debate . . . Kennedy would never have been president."[12] Max Frankel, formerly executive editor of the *New York Times,* once observed, with tongue in cheek, that "Nixon lost a TV debate, and the Presidency, to John F. Kennedy in 1960 because of a sweaty upper lip."[13]

As with many media myths, the notion of viewer-listener disagreement rests more on assertion than on persuasive evidence. It is a plausible and compelling tale, one that is almost too good *not* to be true. That such an effect did occur—or must have occurred—is attractive for many reasons, not the least of which is that it makes understandable a long-ago encounter that is commonly regarded as a decisive moment in the rise of television in American politics.

The myth of viewer-listener disagreement has become so ingrained that it obscures more decisive elements of the debate—notably Kennedy's tactical and rhetorical superiority, especially in the opening portions of the encounter. The gray suit Nixon wore that night may have been a poor choice given the studio's drab setting, and his face may have betrayed the effects of a debilitating knee injury that had put him in the hospital not long before. But the perplexing me-too character of several of his statements and his seeming readiness to concur with his opponent's views were ill-advised, and his demeanor was no match for the potent, "get-America-moving-again" energy of Kennedy's debate narrative. Indeed, a compelling argument can be made that content rather than appearance swung the outcome of the first Kennedy-Nixon debate.

The enduring popularity of viewer-listener disagreement is also a reminder that thorough debunkings do not always take hold. The myth was utterly demolished in a scholarly journal article some thirty years ago,[14] but it has survived to circulate energetically and without serious challenge. The authors of the journal article, David L. Vancil and Sue D. Pendell, pointed out how the evidence typically offered to support the notion of viewer-listener disagreement was thin, flawed, and anecdotal. What they found even more telling was that no public opinion surveys conducted in the immediate aftermath of the debate were aimed at gauging reactions of radio audiences. Only one national survey, conducted by the Philadelphia marketing firm Sindlinger & Company, did identify radio listeners in its sample, but that pool was too small and unrepresentative to support broad conclusions.[15]

Sindlinger reported that respondents who heard the first debate on the radio thought Nixon won, by more than a two-to-one margin.[16] But as Vancil and Pendell pointed out, Sindlinger's subgroup of radio listeners included just 282 respondents, only 178 of whom offered an opinion about which candidate won the debate. Of the 178, 121 identified Nixon as the debate winner.[17]

Moreover, Vancil and Pendell pointed out that the Sindlinger sample of radio listeners did not identify where the radio listeners lived or what their political affiliations were—factors that could easily have distorted the results, and probably did. "A location bias in the radio sample," Vancil and Pendell wrote, "could have caused dramatic effects on the selection of a debate winner. A rural bias, [which was] quite possible because of the relatively limited access of rural areas to television in 1960, would have favored Nixon."[18] And it is not known, they wrote, how many of the 121 respondents who favored Nixon were registered Republicans or supported the vice president for reasons such as having misgivings about Kennedy's Catholicism.[19] Before 1960, Americans had never elected a Roman Catholic to the presidency.

The Sindlinger data were flawed and essentially useless in determining how radio listeners reacted to the debate. Yet the data are still cited in support of the belief that television viewers and radio listeners had starkly different impressions of the inaugural presidential debate.[20]

Vancil and Pendell's research also challenged the notion that Nixon's haggard look was decisive in shaping viewers' opinions about the debate. "Even if viewers disliked Nixon's physical appearance," they wrote, "the relative importance of this factor is a matter of conjecture."[21] It does stretch logic to argue that the opinions of millions of people turned simply on how a candidate looked on television—especially when television was still a novelty in American political life.[22]

As impressive as it was, Vancil and Pendell's debunking did not take hold for a number of reasons, not the least of which was that it was published in a scholarly journal. The outlet meant that it attracted little popular attention. Indeed, the article was even overlooked by scholars who later examined viewer-listener perceptions of the 1960 debate. Michael Schudson was one of them, and he conceded to having been unaware of Vancil and Pendell's research when he explored the notion of viewer-listener disagreement in his book *The Power of News.*[23] Another scholar, David Greenberg, offered a similar acknowledgment in a retrospective essay posted at *Slate* in 2010 about the 1960 debates.[24]

What's more, the notion of viewer-listener disagreement had become ingrained as something of an article of faith by the time Vancil and Pendell confronted the supposed phenomenon. They were taking on a

FIGURE 10. As the debate went on, Nixon perspired noticeably under the hot studio lights, contributing to a wan and haggard look that contrasted with the cool confidence projected by Kennedy. Nixon had lost weight before the debate, and the suit he wore that night fit poorly. [*Associated Press photo*]

dominant narrative about the debate, one that had been identified, with all apparent authority, by Theodore H. White, author of the most acclaimed popular work about the campaign, *The Making of the President, 1960*. White's book was a best seller and set a standard for nuanced, detail-rich reporting of presidential campaigns.

In what was surely one of the first references to viewer-listener disagreement, White wrote: "Those who heard the debates on radio, according to sample surveys, believed that the two candidates came off almost equal. Yet every survey of those who watched the debates on television indicated the Vice-President had come off poorly and, in the opinion of many, very poorly. It was the picture image that had done it—and in 1960, television had won the nation away from sound to images, and that was that."[25]

And that was that: White's characterization helped embed and solidify the notion of viewer-listener disagreement, even though he failed to cite the survey data to which he had referred. As Greenberg pointed out years later, White "provided no footnoting or other sourcing for others to track . . . down."[26] So from a remarkably thin evidentiary base, the powerful claim of viewer-listener disagreement took hold, becoming the most familiar and salient feature of the first Kennedy-Nixon debate.

But even now, another resource is available for examining the purported viewer-listener disagreement in 1960—a rich resource about the debate that has been almost entirely neglected by researchers: contemporaneous newspaper content—the articles, editorials, and commentaries published in leading U.S. newspapers in the immediate aftermath of the Kennedy-Nixon debate.

This chapter presents the results of the close reading of debate-relevant content that was published in three dozen U.S. metropolitan newspapers, a sample that includes large-city titles from across the country.[27] Their contents were scrutinized for references or suggestions in news reports and commentaries that television viewers and radio listeners were at odds in their interpretations of the debate's winner. Had such dramatic and widespread differences been prevalent, as the myth of viewer-listener disagreement suggests it was, journalists would have been well positioned to detect and report about such clashing perceptions—especially in the days immediately after the Kennedy-Nixon encounter, when curiosity about the debate, its novelty, and its consequences were especially keen.

But the review of newspaper content turned up nothing more than passing, oblique hints that at best were remotely suggestive of viewer-listener disagreement. None of the scores of newspaper articles, editorials, and commentaries examined made specific reference to the phenomenon. Leading American newspapers in late September 1960 spoke of nothing that suggested or intimated pervasive differences in how television viewers and radio listeners reacted to the landmark debate.

News organizations at the time were keenly interested in finding out how Americans had responded to the Kennedy-Nixon encounter, and they sometimes turned to fairly enterprising techniques in seeking reactions. For example, several metropolitan newspapers collaborated to locate a dozen men across the country with the commonplace name "Joe Smith" and ask them for their thoughts about the debate.[28] Reporters for the Associated Press news service interviewed ten people selected at random from telephone directories in ten cities.[29] The *New York Times* and *Boston Globe* sent reporters to barrooms to identify reactions to the debate.[30] The *Los Angeles Times, Washington Post,* and several other newspapers solicited the opinions of small numbers of people by telephone or in person.[31] None of that reporting, as earnest and searching as some of it was, turned up evidence that viewer-listener disagreement was afoot in the debate's immediate aftermath.

Even the oblique hints of viewer-listener disagreement were vague and few. The most proximate reference to the purported phenomenon appeared two days after the debate in a column by Ralph McGill, publisher of the *Atlanta Constitution.* McGill wrote that he had arranged for "a number of persons [to] listen to the great debate on radio. It is interesting to report they unanimously thought Mr. Nixon had the better of it. They could not see him. They listened without the diversion of looks and the consequent straying of the mind to that subject."[32]

McGill's experiment, while intriguing in its prescience, was more speculative than revealing. His column did not report how many people he had recruited to listen to the debate on radio, nor did it describe their party affiliations or where they lived. It was not a representative sampling; obviously, it was not meant to be.[33] Rather, it was McGill's opportunity to ruminate about the novelty of television as an instrument of political campaigns. The debate, he wrote, "was a triumph for television" and a benefit to newspapers, too, "as readers turned to the printed page to see what people 'thought about it.'"[34]

To be sure, many newspaper analyses recognized the debate as an exceptional moment. "American presidential campaigning will never be the same again," the *Milwaukee Journal* declared the day afterward.[35] The *Philadelphia Inquirer* hailed the debate as "a brilliant innovation."[36] The *San Francisco Chronicle* said Kennedy and Nixon had "launched a noble tradition."[37] The *Newark Evening News* said the encounter was "a campaign experiment that demonstrated politics may be waged intelligently, even urbanely."[38]

But the contemporaneous assessments of columnists and critics were hardly unanimous as to which candidate won the debate. The commonplace belief these days—that Kennedy looked so good on television that he won hands down—was not at all a dominant theme in news reports and commentaries after the debate. Leading U.S. metropolitan newspapers in the days after the debate teemed with diverse opinions about the encounter. Newspaper analysis was by no means fixated on Nixon's appearance. The barren studio setting, the absence of a live audience,[39] the challenge of addressing complex national issues in less than an hour,[40] the rigid question-answer format, and the debate's ground rules restricting time for replies were topics much discussed in the newspapers—and cited as factors that inhibited spirited exchanges between the candidates. For some analysts, the debate was a letdown.

"There were no flashes of wit, no memorable phrases, no give-and-take with a personal flavor," the *Chicago Tribune* observed.[41] The candidates, said the *Hartford Courant*, "seemed too much on their good behavior, almost like boys hoping for promotion to the next grade in Sunday school."[42] Richard Starnes, a columnist for the *New York World-Telegram*, wrote that Kennedy and Nixon were reduced to acting like "two terribly cautious ping pong players" fearful of blundering. He lamented that the debate lacked "any display of anger or righteous passion. There was no suggestion of emotion: no more was there humor, stinging sarcasm or—heaven forbid—bitter invective."[43] John Crosby, a syndicated radio-television columnist for the *New York Herald-Tribune,* wrote in a review of the debate, "I think Kennedy outpointed Nixon. I think it was a close fight. I think it was a slow fight and perhaps a disappointing one. The first of the great television debates seemed to lack fire." The acerbic former president Harry S. Truman "would have slaughtered both of them" in such an encounter, Crosby added.[44]

More significantly, and contrary to some contemporary interpretations,[45] there was no unanimity among newspaper columnists and editorial writers about Nixon's appearance. Not all analysts in late September 1960 thought Nixon's performance was so dreadful—or that Kennedy was necessarily all that appealing and rested. "Of the two performances," the *Washington Post* said in a post-debate editorial, "Mr. Nixon's was probably the smoother. He is an accomplished debater with a professional polish, and he managed to convey a slightly patronizing air of a master instructing a pupil. Mr. Kennedy was crisp and to the point, but his comments suffered somewhat from machine-gun delivery."[46]

Saul Pett, a prominent feature writer for the Associated Press who won a Pulitzer Prize several years later, gave Nixon high marks for cordiality. "On general folksiness both before and during the debate," Pett wrote, "my scorecard showed Nixon ahead at least 8 to 1. . . . He smiled more often and more broadly, especially at the start and close of a remark. Kennedy only allowed himself the luxury of a quarter-smile now and then."[47] The debate moderator, Howard K. Smith, later said he thought "Nixon was marginally better."[48] Russell Baker, who covered the debate for the *New York Times,* said he had a similar impression—that Nixon "had a slight edge in what little argument there had been."[49]

Other analysts found flaws in how both men looked on television. "The two antagonists contributed generously to the tension of the occasion as the probing close-up shots easily revealed," wrote the radio-television writer for the *Cleveland Press,* citing "Nixon's sweat glistening on his chin . . . Kennedy's Adam's apple nervously jiggling to and fro . . . Nixon's awkward attempt at a nervous smile . . . Kennedy's pursed lips which simply could not bring themselves to smile."[50] Syndicated columnist Harriett Van Horne wrote that both men were "visibly anxious, watching as a tiger while his opponent was speaking. . . . Mr. Nixon looked made up. Obviously somebody had de-fluffed his shaggy brows. Sen. Kennedy's hair no longer falls in his eyes . . . but he looked as if he'd not slept well recently."[51] The *Chicago Daily News* said in an editorial that Kennedy projected "more than a trace of arrogance" during the debate by implying "that he could conduct an administration that would please everybody."[52]

Commentators did not, of course, ignore how Nixon looked on television, but they did not necessarily assign great significance to his appearance. Walter Lippmann, who was perhaps the leading newspaper columnist of the time, turned to the topic of Nixon's appearance deep in his column the day after the debate, observing that the television cameras "were very hard on Mr. Nixon. . . . They made him look sick, which he is not, and they made him look older and more worn than he is." The effect, Lippmann wrote, "was a misrepresentation and we must make sure for the future that the cameras are in fact impartial."[53]

Gould Lincoln, a columnist for the Washington *Evening Star,* ruminated briefly about television's deceptive power, saying in a passing reference that Nixon "looked like a sick man on the screen which he does not in real life."[54] Decidedly more cutting was Thomas O'Neill, a political columnist for the *Baltimore Sun,* and no friend of Nixon. O'Neill, whose name appeared on Nixon's "enemies list," which was released in

FIGURE 11. Not everyone thought Nixon, shown here listening to a panelist's question, looked dreadful during the debate. Saul Pett, a prominent feature writer for the Associated Press, gave the vice president high marks for "general folksiness." [*Associated Press photo*]

1973 during the Watergate scandal,[55] likened the vice president's appearance on television to a mug shot on a wanted poster:

> The television camera was singularly unkind to Vice President Nixon. The electronic eye tends to present Vice President Nixon on the screen like a picture on a post office bulletin board. Attempts by the cosmeticians to produce a more loveable image were lamentably unsuccessful. Their ministrations, intended to obscure the 5 o'clock shadow the Vice President shows at any hour of the day, succeeded only in giving him the appearance of an invalid. . . . Special lighting arranged to accent Mr. Nixon's maturity (he is four years older than his opponent) had the effect when reflected on the television screen of showing him as gaunt and hollow eyed.[56]

Such detailed discussions about Nixon's appearance were not commonplace in the debate's immediate aftermath, however. And as O'Neill's observations suggested, partisan leaning also colored some post-debate assessments. The conservative *San Diego Union,* which vigorously opposed Kennedy, said in an editorial that the debate sharpened the differences between the candidates and "emphasized the painful superficiality and intellectual cynicism of Sen. Kennedy."[57]

A dominant and widespread theme in post-debate reporting and analysis was that the encounter had been a standoff—a "slow fight to a draw," as the Los Angeles Times observed in an editorial.[58] A reporter for the Philadelphia Evening Bulletin wrote that "it could hardly be said that either man had won."[59] The United Press International dispatch about the debate stated: "Political experts . . . viewed the historic first TV debate between Vice President Richard Nixon and Sen. John F. Kennedy as a draw. Early reaction from politicians suggested that both presidential nominees got in some licks but neither was hurt badly in the first round of their four-round nationwide TV bout."[60] The Boston Globe said in its report about the debate: "Who won? You can toss a coin."[61] The Boston Herald said the candidates "argued genteelly to what appeared to be a standoff."[62]

Syndicated columnist Roscoe Drummond wrote, "Neither candidate won. . . . Clearly neither side scored anything approaching a knock-out."[63] James Reston, a nationally prominent columnist who was then Washington bureau chief for the New York Times, wrote soon after the debate, "Who took the first round is a matter of individual opinion. My own view is that Kennedy gained more than Nixon, but it was a fielder's choice, settling nothing."[64]

The Associated Press reported that results of a post-debate survey of one hundred Americans in ten major U.S. cities found that just two respondents said the debate prompted them to shift their support, both switching to Kennedy from Nixon. Otherwise, the news agency reported, the respondents said their loyalties were unchanged, or deepened, by the debate.[65]

Probably more damaging to Nixon than his wan appearance and ill-chosen suit were his tactics, particularly at the outset of the debate. He committed the elementary mistake of arguing on his opponent's terms—of seeming to concur rather than seeking the initiative. Nixon projected a "me-too" sentiment from the start in answering Kennedy, who had spoken first. Kennedy asserted in his opening remarks that it was "time America started moving again"[66] and also said:

> I should make it very clear that I do not think we're doing enough, that I am not satisfied as an American with the progress that we're making. This is a great country, but I think it could be a greater country; and this is a powerful country but I think it could be a more powerful country. I'm not satisfied to have fifty percent of our steel-mill capacity unused. I'm not satisfied when

the United States had last year the lowest rate of economic growth of any major industrialized society in the world. Because economic growth means strength and vitality; it means we're able to sustain our defenses; it means we're able to meet our commitments abroad.[67]

In his opening statement, Nixon rather surprisingly said he agreed with much of what his opponent had said. Whether Nixon was trying to be gracious, seeking to appeal to wavering Democrats, or attempting to stifle his famously combative instincts, his remarks came across as diffident, uninspired, and oddly deferential. Worse, they effectively validated Kennedy's views and stature.[68] Here's what Nixon said in beginning his statement:

> The things that Senator Kennedy has said many of us can agree with. . . . There is no question but that this nation cannot stand still; because we are in a deadly competition, a competition not only with the men in the Kremlin, but the men in Peking. We're ahead in this competition, as Senator Kennedy, I think, has implied. But when you're in a race, the only way to stay ahead is to move ahead. And I subscribe completely to the spirit that Senator Kennedy has expressed tonight, the spirit that the United States should move ahead. Where, then, do we disagree? I think we disagree on the implication of his remarks tonight and on the statements that he has made on many occasions during his campaign to the effect that the United States has been standing still.[69]

"Republicans cringed," wrote syndicated political columnist Doris Fleeson, "at the frequency with which Nixon said 'I agree with Sen. Kennedy,' though he went on to explain that he had better ways of reaching the same goals."[70] Columnist Joseph Alsop wrote, sarcastically, that "Vice President Nixon insisted so strongly that he shared all Senator Kennedy's worthy goals that one expected a Nixonian endorsement of the Democratic platform at any moment."[71] In his book about the 1960 campaign, David Pietrusza described Nixon's opening statement as "grotesquely weak, defensive, and artlessly constructed and wretchedly delivered."[72] Herbert G. Klein, Nixon's press secretary during the 1960 campaign, claimed that the vice president's defensive, me-too approach "not only disappointed his own followers but lost vast numbers of undecided voters who had expected to see a strong, statesmanlike, tough leader."[73]

At another point early in the debate, Kennedy stated why he believed that voters should elect him in spite of his comparatively thin experience in national leadership:

> I come out of the Democratic party, which in this century has produced Woodrow Wilson and Franklin Roosevelt and Harry Truman, and which

supported and sustained these programs which I've discussed tonight. Mr. Nixon comes out of the Republican party. He was nominated by it. And it is a fact that through most of these last twenty-five years the Republican leadership has opposed federal aid for education, medical care for the aged, development of the Tennessee Valley, development of our natural resources. I think Mr. Nixon is an effective leader of his party. I hope he would grant me the same.[74]

Asked if he had a response to Kennedy's statement, Nixon said, unaccountably, "I have no comment."[75]

Going gracious and declining comment were not successful tactics for Nixon. Even so, it's not far-fetched to imagine that Nixon could have turned the tables and swung momentum to his favor by bluntly taking Kennedy to task in the following fashion:

Ladies and gentlemen, I cannot believe what you and I have just heard: A sitting U.S. senator, the Democratic party's candidate for president, has just spent his opening statement tearing down this country—and doing so at a time when the Soviet threat to international security and stability couldn't be greater. 'Get the country moving again': I can't believe it—the junior senator from Massachusetts is poor-mouthing the United States and the progress we have made, and he embellished quite a bit in doing so. I'll address his unfortunate errors and exaggerations in a minute. But first, let me tell you of my plan for keeping our country safe, strong, productive, and on the move in the next four years.[76]

Such a rejoinder—polite in a steely way, with a hint of anger and disdain—would have placed Nixon on the offensive and may have reinforced the impression that Kennedy was too raw and inexperienced for the presidency. An assertive opening statement along those lines surely would have been more attention grabbing than Nixon's ashen appearance. But by seeming to concur with Kennedy, Nixon irritated Republicans and squandered an opportunity to appeal to Democrats who were unsure about Kennedy's qualifications.

Over the decades, the memory of Nixon's ill-advised debate tactics has faded behind the enduring fascination with presumptive viewer-listener disagreement. And understandably so. After all, it is much easier, and more entertaining, to summon the myth than it is to recall the particulars of Nixon's clumsy debate performance.

Not only does viewer-listener disagreement remain a topic of public fascination, it is also the occasional spur for imaginative research. In 2003, James N. Druckman, then of the University of Minnesota, reported the results of a study in which 171 summer students at Minnesota either viewed a video of the first Kennedy-Nixon debate or listened to an audio recording of the encounter.[77] None of the participants had detailed prior knowledge about the Kennedy-Nixon debate, according to Druckman. He reported finding that television viewers in his experiment "were significantly more likely to think Kennedy won the debate than audio listeners." This, he declared, represented "the first clear empirical evidence consistent with the widespread assertion of viewer-listener disagreement in the first Kennedy-Nixon debate."[78] But in a footnote, Druckman reported that 81 percent of the viewers in his experiment thought Kennedy won, but so did 60 percent of listeners.[79] The finding that large majorities of both viewers and listeners were in agreement about a Kennedy debate victory is inconsistent with the central component of viewer-listener disagreement: that Kennedy won among television viewers, while Nixon prevailed among radio listeners.

What's more, participants in Druckman's experiment skewed Democratic. The "sample did underrepresent Republicans," he wrote in another footnote.[80] As such, participants may have been more readily sympathetic to Kennedy than to Nixon. Druckman also acknowledged that "younger people" in the early twenty-first century may process "televised information differently" than viewers did in 1960.[81]

CONCLUSION

Seven state and national surveys were conducted about the first debate in 1960, and each reported that a clear plurality of respondents thought Kennedy had prevailed, or had likely gained votes, or had done better than Nixon.[82] Among these surveys was the Gallup Organization's national poll, conducted during the week after the debate and released October 11, 1960. Gallup reported that 43 percent of voters thought Kennedy "did the better job" in the debate, 23 percent thought Nixon was better, and 29 percent said both candidates were about the same; 5 percent offered no opinion.

The same survey, however, detected no marked post-debate shift of support to Kennedy. Gallup reported Kennedy to be narrowly ahead, supported by 49 percent of voters to Nixon's 46 percent, with 5 percent undecided. Before the debate, Gallup found that Nixon was slightly ahead, with 47 percent of the vote to Kennedy's 46 percent.[83] But the head of the polling organization, George Gallup, warned against regarding the results as definitive. "The prudent reader can see," he wrote in an essay for the *Washington Post,* "that polling accuracy has not reached the degree of accuracy required to say with certainty which candidate is ahead in a close race such as the present one."[84]

The slight post-debate bump for Kennedy dissipated during the campaign's closing six weeks; Nixon's washed-out appearance in Chicago on September 26, 1960, surely did not cost him the election on November 8, 1960.[85] The race remained close to the end, although as the election approached, some newspaper analyses described scenarios in which Kennedy would win in a landslide.[86] The final pre-election Gallup poll showed Kennedy narrowly leading Nixon by 49 percent to 48 percent, with 3 percent undecided.[87] On Election Day, Kennedy carried 49.72 percent of the popular vote to Nixon's 49.55 percent, a margin of 112,000 votes.

What turned the election of 1960? If not the late September debate, what then was decisive in Kennedy's victory? Many factors contributed, of course.[88] Nixon's injured knee landed him in a hospital for eleven days early in the campaign. The vice president's ill-considered pledge to visit all fifty states—a promise he kept—took him to Wyoming and Alaska in the final days of the campaign, time that would have been better spent stumping for votes in closely contested states such as Illinois and Texas, where the election pivoted. Had he carried those two states, Nixon would have won the presidency in 1960. Lyndon B. Johnson's presence on the Democratic national ticket as Kennedy's running mate surely helped keep his native Texas, and perhaps several other Southern states, from straying to Nixon.[89]

Surely another factor was Kennedy's call to get the country moving again after eight years of the presidency of Dwight D. Eisenhower, a war hero who turned seventy in October 1960. Eisenhower, the last American president born in the nineteenth century, never campaigned enthusiastically for Nixon.

An amorphous sense that important change was afoot may have been a decisive factor, too. Theodore White touched on that vague awareness in his book about the campaign: "It was the atmospherics of 1960, more than anything else, that made it possible for John F. Kennedy's political exertions to triumph over the many divided pasts of the American people. . . . It was a year in which Americans sensed the world about them changing . . . and they knew their own world to be changing, too."[90]

But in the end, Pietrusza argued, it was "amazing . . . Nixon came so close" to victory, given that so much "had gone against him" during the campaign, including the knee injury that sent him to the hospital and his clumsy performance at the first debate. "He had started from behind," Pietrusza wrote. "He should have fallen even further behind. Jack Kennedy should have strolled to victory."[91] But there was something about Kennedy that many voters in 1960 found troubling, if vaguely so, Pietrusza added. Was it, he asked, that "cold glint in the Kennedy eye, the passionless passion in his voice that supporters portrayed as sureness of purpose but that may have merely portrayed ruthless lust for power?" Was Kennedy really a lot like Nixon, only "with a tan and a shave"?[92]

CHAPTER 5

The Bay of Pigs–*New York Times* Suppression Myth

Aside from the stories they are paid to tell, professional
journalists also invent myths about themselves.
—John J. Pauly, "Rupert Murdoch and the Demonology
of Professional Journalism," in *Media, Myths, and
Narratives: Television and the Press*, ed. James W. Carey
(Newbury Park, CA: Sage, 1988), 246

In the vernacular of American journalism, *spiked* is an especially loathsome term, evoking as it does the shame and humiliation of self-censorship. *Spiked* typically means that a perfectly good, usually provocative news story is suppressed for reasons other than accuracy or good taste. Pressures from outside sources—be they politicians, advertisers, or representatives of other powerful interests—usually are to blame when a news story is spiked.

In early April 1961, the *New York Times* bowed to pressure from the White House of President John F. Kennedy and spiked, or "killed," its detailed report about the pending Bay of Pigs invasion of Cuba.[1] The *Times*'s purported self-censorship took place just ten days before the invasion, which failed utterly in its objective of toppling the Cuban revolutionary leader, Fidel Castro. The invasion force of CIA-trained Cuban exiles gave up in less than three days, and the Kennedy presidency, as well as U.S. standing in the Caribbean and the world, suffered a humiliating setback. Had the *Times* not censored itself, had the *Times* gone ahead and reported all that it knew, the ill-fated invasion might well have been scuttled and a national embarrassment avoided.

Or so the story goes.

The story of the *Times*'s purported spiking has been called the "symbolic journalistic event of the 1960s."[2] It has been recounted in scores of books, journals, newspapers, and other periodicals over the years. It offers supposedly timeless lessons about the perils of self-censorship, the risks of yielding to pressure to withhold sensitive information on national security grounds, and the hazards of journalists surrendering to the government's agenda. It often is cited as an object lesson—"an instructive case study"[3]—about what can happen when independent news media give in to power-wielding authorities.

Versions vary as to what supposedly transpired between the *Times* and the Kennedy administration. The *Times* is often described as having yielded without much of a fight. Howard Kurtz, formerly the *Washington Post* media writer, wrote, for example, that "Kennedy pressed the Times successfully to withhold most details of the impending Bay of Pigs invasion."[4] The *Tampa Tribune* has called it a "classic example of the clash between the public's right to know and government secrecy . . . when The New York Times learned of a plan to invade Cuba. President Kennedy pressured Times executives to kill the story, which he insisted would be damaging. The Times agreed."[5]

It also has been said that the *Times*'s act of self-censorship cost untold lives: "Newspapers, including the mighty New York Times, have withheld stories after the government warned that national security and American lives could be jeopardized," a columnist for the *St. Petersburg Times* in Florida once wrote. "The Bay of Pigs fiasco is the best example. President Kennedy persuaded the New York Times, which had gotten wind of plans for the ill-fated invasion, to sit on the story. Had the Times gone with the story, the invasion might have been scratched and many lives saved."[6] Similarly, David K. Shipler declared in his 2015 book, *Freedom of Speech: Mightier Than the Sword*: "The most famous and catastrophic case of journalists' abandoning their role in getting the facts out was the *Times*'s decision to water down advance information on the Bay of Pigs invasion of Cuba." Shipler claimed that "a full-throated disclosure might have helped derail the plan, saving lives and preventing a humiliating defeat."[7]

Another durable version has it that Kennedy soon regretted arm-twisting the *Times*. The *Washington Post* once noted that Kennedy "went so far as to indicate his regret that he had successfully persuaded the New York Times to delay a story that would have revealed in advance the preparations for the Bay of Pigs."[8] And a columnist for the *Chicago Sun-Times* once wrote that "the New York Times' publisher agreed not to run reports of the upcoming Bay of Pigs invasion, an act of self-censorship that even President John F. Kennedy later regretted."[9]

In other retellings, the editors of the *Times* were the ones left with agonizing regret. The *Christian Science Monitor* once described how Kennedy "successfully appealed to the patriotism of the New York Times not to publish a story about the then-forthcoming Bay of Pigs invasion of Cuba. Times editors later publicly regretted acceding to the presidential plea."[10] The *New York Times* itself has found lessons in its purported spiking. "There have been times in this paper's history when editors have decided not to print something they knew," the *Times* once declared in an editorial. "In some cases, like the Kennedy administration's plans for the disastrous Bay of Pigs invasion, it seems in hindsight that the editors were over-cautious."[11] Bill Keller, then the executive editor of the *Times,* wrote shortly before the invasion's fiftieth anniversary: "I'm the first to admit that news organizations, including this one, sometimes get things wrong. . . . We may err on the side of keeping secrets (President Kennedy reportedly wished, after the fact, that The Times had published what it knew about the planned Bay of Pigs invasion, which possibly would have helped avert a bloody debacle) or on the side of exposing them. We make the best judgments we can."[12]

The anecdote about the *Times*'s self-censorship is potent, compelling, instructive, and timeless. It also is apocryphal, a media-driven myth. As this chapter shows, the *Times* did not spike reports about the pending invasion of Cuba. In fact, the *Times*'s reports about preparations for the invasion were fairly detailed and prominently displayed on the newspaper's front page in the days before the assault. Moreover, the notion that Kennedy asked or persuaded the *Times* to suppress, hold back, or dilute any of its reports about the impending Bay of Pigs invasion is utter fancy. There is no evidence that Kennedy or his administration knew in advance about the *Times* report of April 7, 1961, the front-page article that lies at the heart of this media myth.[13] There is no evidence that Kennedy or anyone in his administration lobbied or persuaded the *Times* to hold back or spike that story, as so many accounts have said.

Notably, the recollections of none of the principal figures in the Bay of Pigs–*New York Times* suppression myth say that Kennedy pressured the newspaper's editors. These include the memoirs of Turner Catledge, then the managing editor of the *Times;* James (Scotty) Reston, then the chief of the *Times*'s Washington bureau; Pierre Salinger, Kennedy's press secretary; and Arthur M. Schlesinger Jr., an award-winning Harvard historian who was a White House adviser to Kennedy. In addition, a compelling insider's account written by Harrison E. Salisbury, a former *Times* foreign correspondent and senior editor, says flatly that the Kennedy White

House neither knew about nor meddled in the newspaper's deliberations about its preinvasion coverage.[14] The evidence is persuasive that Kennedy was unaware of the *Times* article of April 7, 1961, before its publication. Kennedy did consider contacting the newspaper's executives after the fact—to call attention to a passage in the article that overstated the size of the Cuban exile force.

This chapter also presents evidence that the Bay of Pigs–*New York Times* suppression myth stems from confusion with a separate episode during the Cuban Missile Crisis in October 1962, when Kennedy *did* ask the *Times* to postpone publication of a report about the Soviets having deployed nuclear-tipped weapons in Cuba. On that occasion, when the prospect of a nuclear exchange seemed to be in the balance, the *Times* complied.

Addressing and dismantling the Bay of Pigs–*New York Times* suppression myth is essential for reasons that go beyond the importance of setting straight the historical record. Exposing the myth demonstrates how the Kennedy administration sought to deflect blame for the Bay of Pigs and make a scapegoat of the *Times*. On separate occasions in 1961 and 1962, Kennedy told the senior executives of the *Times* that, had the newspaper published more about the impending assault on Cuba, the invasion might have been scuttled. Such an interpretation, of course, shifts responsibility away from the authorities who possessed the power to order an invasion of a sovereign state. Puncturing the suppression myth, then, allows blame for the Bay of Pigs fiasco to be more properly and accurately apportioned.

THE HEART OF A MYTH

The suppression myth revolves around a report filed by Tad Szulc, a veteran Polish-born correspondent for the *Times*. Szulc was described by Salisbury as striking the quintessential look of a secret agent, with "classical tan trench coat and all."[15] Szulc also was notably "news prone," in that important developments seemed to break out wherever he went.[16] The *Times* would send him places, recalled his son, Anthony, and upon his arrival the bullets would suddenly be flying.[17]

Szulc's "news proneness" was with him in late March 1961 as he returned to the United States after a six-year assignment in Latin America. He was to take up a position in the *Times*'s Washington bureau. En route, Szulc stopped in Miami to visit acquaintances. "As I landed in Miami," he wrote later, "nothing could have been further from my mind than Cuba or the exiles' plans to launch an invasion to topple Premier Fidel Castro's regime. Having covered many phases of the Cuban story after Castro's capture of power, I was naturally aware of the exiles' activities in general. . . . But for all practical purposes, Cuba no longer was my story and I had no reason to concern myself with any of it. Yet," he added, "even before I finished that first martini [after arriving], I was suddenly and deeply enmeshed in the invasion story." Within two days, Szulc had pieced together the outline of CIA-backed plans to attempt to topple Castro with an invasion force of Cuban exiles who had been trained in Guatemala.[18]

The CIA's planning was enveloped in little or no secrecy, Szulc found. "It was," he said later, "the most open operation which you can imagine."[19] It had all the makings of an explosive story. Szulc soon went to New York to confer with senior editors at the *Times*. "I felt that it would not be advisable to discuss the story over an open telephone line with my superiors," Szulc wrote. "The details [about the preinvasion plans] were too startling and too unbelievable."[20] In New York, it was agreed that Szulc would return to Miami to continue gathering details about the invasion plans. He was on the story full-time.

On his way back to Miami, he stopped in Washington to confer with Reston, the *Times* bureau chief, and with officials in the Kennedy administration. According to his son, Szulc also met with the CIA director, Allen Dulles, at a private dinner in Georgetown, arranged by Szulc's uncle, John C. Wiley, a retired U.S. ambassador.

After dinner, "they got down to business," Anthony Szulc said. Dulles told Ted Szulc that he was familiar with the story Szulc was working on, and said "for the good of the country, it would be better if this [story] did not go out." Szulc thought for a moment and replied, "I appreciate everything you're saying, but I consider it my duty and obligation to report the news, . . . and I don't see any way I can withhold it."

OK, Dulles simply said, "I understand."[21]

Anthony Szulc recalled that his father related the story in 1997. "I told him," Anthony Szulc said, " 'That's quite a story.' And he said, 'Yeah, yeah.' He made it sound as if it was all in a day's work."[22]

Back in Miami, Szulc teamed up with Stuart Novins, a CBS reporter, with whom he exchanged information and impressions.[23] By noon on April 6, 1961, Szulc had collected enough details to begin composing a dispatch that said five thousand to six thousand Cuban exiles had been trained in a plan to overthrow Castro.[24] Szulc also wrote that invasion plans were in their final stages and that the operation had been organized and directed by the CIA.[25] He filed his dispatch by telephone to New York in the afternoon of April 6. The report ran to more than a thousand words and set off a flurry of intense consultations among senior editors. Their deliberations revolved around three elements: Szulc's characterization of the invasion as imminent, the reference to the operation as CIA-led and directed, and the prominence the report should receive on the *Times*'s front page.

Catledge, the managing editor, ordered the reference to the invasion's imminence removed. There were solid reasons for doing so. Reston, consulted at the Washington bureau, concurred. "I had no trouble with printing the facts of the situation," Reston recalled in his memoirs, "but *imminent* was a prediction and not a fact."[26] ("The tendency to predict," Catledge later wrote, "is one of the strongest and most dangerous urges of newspaper reporters.")[27] Moreover, a reference in Szulc's story to the assault's imminence would not have been accurate. The article appeared ten days before the invasion, which scarcely could be considered imminent. As Catledge noted, "Szulc himself had reservations about predicting the specific time of the invasion."[28] So references to imminence were deleted.

Catledge also removed reference to the CIA's sponsorship, instead inserting the more nebulous terms *U.S. officials* and *U.S. experts*. His reasoning was that the government had more than a few intelligence agencies, "more than most people realize, and I was hesitant to specify the CIA when we might not be able to document the charge."[29] To anyone familiar with the sometimes rough, give-and-take atmosphere of a newsroom, a place of sharp elbows and often-bruised egos, Catledge's characterizations carry the ring of authenticity. Catledge may have been cautious in his editing, but the alterations he ordered were modest, defensible, and well within the prerogatives of a senior editor on an important and sensitive article. Neither alteration significantly harmed the story.

A more controversial decision centered around the prominence to be given Szulc's report. The editors charged with designing the *Times*'s front page had planned to display Szulc's article beneath a four-column headline. They also were under the mistaken impression that the invasion of Cuba was a day away.[30] Four-column display was unusual, though not unheard of, at the *Times* in the early 1960s. Given the newspaper's gray, mostly vertical presentation of front-page news, a four-column headline would have signaled "a story of exceptional importance," as Salisbury noted.[31] But without a reference to the invasion's imminence, a four-column headline was difficult to justify.[32] In the end, Szulc's report remained on the front page, in a prominent position above the fold, displayed beneath a single-column headline that read: "Anti-Castro Units Trained to Fight at Florida Bases."[33]

Altering the story's prominence sparked near-insubordination by the two editors in charge of laying out the paper, assistant managing editor Theodore Bernstein and news editor Lewis Jordan. They were angered by the decision to change the headline size and went to Catledge in protest, saying that it appeared the change was being made for political reasons. They also demanded an audience with Orvil E. Dryfoos, the *Times*'s president and publisher-to-be.[34] According to Catledge, Dryfoos felt "the story must be played down for reasons of national security."[35] Bernstein and Jordan were hardly mollified, and years later they "still burned" with indignation because their judgment had been overridden. "To them the news evaluation ritual was sacred and they were its high priests," Salisbury wrote. "This process had been contaminated by infidels and they never really got over this."[36]

Although the headline size was modified, Szulc's report hardly can be said to have been played down. It certainly had not been spiked, diluted, or emasculated.[37] Szulc's report, Catledge wrote, made "perfectly clear to any intelligent reader that the U.S. government was training an army of Cuban exiles who intended to invade Cuba."[38] It began on the front page, above the fold[39]—a daily newspaper's most coveted real estate—and was continued onto another page in the front section.[40] It spelled out in detail the preparations for the invasion. Appended to the article was a brief report that quoted Novins of CBS as saying that preparations for the invasion of Cuba were nearing their "final stages."[41] So in the end, the disputed characterization of the invasion's imminence found its way into the *Times* after all.[42]

Szulc, though, later said he was "overcome with indescribable frustration" the next day when he saw his story in the *Times*. "But events were moving fast and I had no time to dwell on frustrations. For one thing, I was not aware of the drama that had taken place the night before in the newsroom of *The New York Times*."[43] And yet, two months later, Szulc spoke with a hint of pride about his report of April 7. In testimony before a closed hearing of a Senate Foreign Relations subcommittee, Szulc described how the article had gone "into very considerable detail on the training of Cuban forces in camps in Guatemala, movements then afoot in Florida, and I think we mentioned for the first time there was a camp in Louisiana outside of New Orleans."[44] Szulc had ample opportunity during the closed hearing to criticize or second-guess the editing of his dispatch. But he did not.

His report of April 7 was not without flaws, however. Notably, the article overstated the strength of what Szulc described as "the external fighting arm of the anti-Castro" exile organization, an umbrella group called the Revolutionary Council. He said the Cuban exile force was 5,000 to 6,000 strong. In reality, its strength was about 1,200 men.

SCANT TIME FOR PREPUBLICATION CONSULTATIONS

The second important component of the suppression myth is that Kennedy was in touch with *Times* executives, urging them to spike or downplay Szulc's article. To whom at the *Times* Kennedy had spoken varies with different versions of the story. David Halberstam claimed that the president called James Reston "and tried to get him to kill" the Szulc report. Kennedy "argued strongly and passionately about what the Szulc story would do to his policy," Halberstam wrote, adding that the president warned that the *Times* would risk having blood on its hands were the article published and the invasion a failure.[45] Another version was offered by Peter Wyden, who wrote that Dryfoos "was in touch with" Kennedy, who "was upset" by plans to publish the report. Wyden wrote that Kennedy "told Dryfoos that he had not even given orders to release the necessary fuel for the operation" and that Dryfoos "was gravely troubled."[46]

There is, however, no evidence that Kennedy spoke with anyone at the *Times* the day Szulc's dispatch was written, edited, and prepared for publication. The Kennedy Library in Boston says that the White House telephone logs reveal no calls that were placed to Reston, Catledge, or Dryfoos on April 6, 1961.[47] Moreover, Kennedy would have had almost no chance to speak with those executives during the interval from when Szulc's story arrived at the *Times* building in midtown Manhattan and when it was set in type. According to Salisbury's account in his book, *Without Fear or Favor,* the Szulc dispatch reached the *Times* during the afternoon of April 6. It was edited and readied for publication by early evening.

Kennedy was otherwise occupied during that time. He spent the last half of the afternoon of April 6, 1961, playing host to Harold Macmillan, the British prime minister, on a lengthy cruise down the Potomac River to Mount Vernon. They traveled aboard the *Honey Fitz,* a ninety-two-foot presidential yacht. The round trip from Washington on that chilled and windy afternoon lasted two hours and forty minutes. It was 6:25 P.M. when the yacht returned to an Army Engineers dock in Washington at the end of the outing. Kennedy and Macmillan rode together to the White House, arriving at 6:28 P.M.[48] From there, the prime minister went to a dinner at the British embassy. Salisbury's account indicates that Szulc's report had been edited and prepared for publication by 7 P.M., leaving only a very tight window for Kennedy to have been in touch with *Times* executives before the first edition of the newspaper hit the streets.

Salisbury's description in *Without Fear or Favor* offers the most detailed account of the *Times*'s deliberations on the Szulc article, and it is unequivocal: "The government in April 1961 did not . . . know that *The Times* was going to publish the Szulc story although it was aware that *The Times* and other newsmen were probing in Miami. Nor did President Kennedy telephone Dryfoos, Scotty Reston or Turner Catledge about the story. . . . The action which *The Times* took [in editing Szulc's report] was on its own responsibility," the result of internal discussions and deliberations. "Most important," Salisbury added, "*The Times* had not killed Szulc's story. . . . *The Times* believed it was more important to publish than to withhold. Publish it did."[49]

Kennedy's reaction to the Szulc article further indicates that he neither had advance knowledge about it nor had spoken with *Times* executives about its content. On the morning the article appeared, Kennedy met in the Oval Office for forty-five minutes with Chalmers M. Roberts, the chief diplomatic correspondent for the *Washington Post*. According to Roberts's account, Kennedy was seated in a rocking chair, appearing relaxed and smoking thin cigars. The conversation was off the record, Roberts said, and the Szulc report soon was brought up. Kennedy noted that Szulc's article estimated the strength of the exile force to be five thousand to six thousand men. That figure, the president told Roberts, was far too high. Kennedy telephoned Richard Bissell, the CIA operative heading the invasion planning, to confirm that impression. In Roberts's presence, Kennedy spoke with Bissell about whether he should dispatch Schlesinger or McGeorge Bundy, another presidential assistant, to speak with Reston "or someone else at the *Times*" about the article's flaws. Kennedy decided against doing so because the U.S. government did not want to give the impression of being involved in planning the invasion, Roberts later wrote.[50]

Szulc's overstated estimate of the size of the exile force appeared in the article's second paragraph—a prominent detail that surely would not have been overlooked had there been prepublication consultations between the president and *Times* executives. That Kennedy considered

FIGURE 12. The afternoon Tad Szulc filed his dispatch to the *New York Times* about preparations to invade Cuba, President John F. Kennedy was playing host to the British prime minister, Harold Macmillan, left, on a cruise on the Potomac River. [*John F. Kennedy Presidential Library*]

sending White House officials to speak with the *Times* after publication signals that he was unaware of the contents of Szulc's article before it appeared in print.

NOT A ONE-DAY STORY

The suppression myth fails to recognize or acknowledge that the *Times* coverage was not confined to Szulc's article ten days before the invasion. It ignores that several follow-up stories and commentaries appeared in the newspaper during the run-up to the invasion. The *Times* did not abandon the Cuba-invasion story after April 7, 1961. Far from it. Subsequent reporting in the *Times,* by Szulc and others, kept expanding the realm of what was publicly known about a coming assault against Castro.[51]

On April 8, 1961, the *Times* published a front-page article about the Cuban exiles and their eagerness to topple Castro. The article, which appeared beneath the headline "Castro Foe Says Uprising Is Near," quoted the president of the U.S.-based umbrella group of exiles, the Cuban Revolutionary Council, as saying that a revolt against the Castro regime was "imminent"[52]—the characterization in Szulc's report that had caused so much soul-searching among *Times* editors two days earlier. On April 9, 1961, the *Times* published two articles about Cuba on its front page, one of them the lead story. That report carried the headline "Castro Foes Call Cubans to Arms; Predict Uprising" and discussed the vow of the exiled Cuban Revolutionary Council to topple Castro's regime. "Duty calls us to the war against the executioners of our Cuban brethren," the Revolutionary Council said in its call to arms. "Cubans! To victory! For democracy! For the Constitution! For social justice! For liberty!"[53]

The *Times* front page on April 9 carried another report by Szulc, describing how the exile leaders were attempting to paper over deep rivalries and divisions in advance of what Szulc termed the coming "thrust against Premier Fidel Castro." The "first assumption" of the leaders' plans, Szulc wrote, "is that an invasion by a 'liberation army,' now in the final stages of training in Central America and Louisiana, will succeed with the aid of an internal uprising in Cuba. It is also assumed that a provisional 'government in arms' will be established promptly on the island."[54] With those sentences, Szulc effectively summarized the strategic objectives for what soon became the Bay of Pigs invasion.

Although none of the *Times*'s preinvasion reports included information about a prospective date for the invasion, they unmistakably signaled that an attempt to topple Castro was forthcoming. Two days later, on April 11, James Reston, the Washington bureau chief, reported on the *Times*'s front page that Kennedy administration officials were divided "about how far to go in helping the Cuban refugees to overthrow the Castro Government." Reston described in detail how Kennedy had been receiving conflicting counsel from advisers in the White House, the CIA, the State and Defense departments. Reston also identified the time pressures facing Kennedy, writing, "It is feared that unless something is done fairly soon nothing short of direct military intervention by United States forces will be enough to shake the Castro Government's hold over the Cuban people."[55]

Reston followed that report the next day with a commentary that addressed the moral dimensions of an armed attempt to topple Castro. His column noted that, "while the papers have been full of reports of U.S. aid to overthrow Castro, the moral and legal aspects of the question have scarcely been mentioned." Reston lamented the paucity of public debate about whether supporting efforts to topple Castro would contravene U.S. treaty obligations. He wrote, "President Kennedy and his advisers are discussing the question on an urgent basis, but the Congress is not talking about it, the press is ignoring the moral aspects of the question, nobody knows where the funds are coming from or where they are going."[56]

The *Times* continued to cover and comment on invasion preparations until the Cuban exiles hit the beaches at the Bay of Pigs. Not all its preinvasion reports were accurate. Besides overstating the size of the anti-Castro force, Szulc said a week before the assault that the exiles had "agreed to concentrate on multiple guerrilla landings in Cuba instead of attempting a large-scale invasion."[57] In so reporting, Szulc may have fallen victim to misinformation spread by the Revolutionary Council leadership. In any event, his report was in error; the invasion at the Bay of Pigs was to be the main show. Still, the newspaper's preinvasion reporting was fairly extensive. Not only does the suppression myth ignore this, it also fails to recognize that coverage of invasion preparations appeared in newspapers other than the *New York Times*.

Indeed, the coverage reached a point where Kennedy, a week before the invasion, told his press secretary, Pierre Salinger: "I can't believe what I'm reading! Castro doesn't need agents over here. All he has to do is read our papers. It's all laid out for him."[58] Salinger later noted, "To declare in mid-April of 1961 that I knew nothing of the impending military action against Cuba except what I read in the newspapers or heard on the air was to claim an enormous amount of knowledge."[59]

BEYOND THE *TIMES*

Dimensions of the pending invasion were widely reported, if in piecemeal and sometimes tentative fashion, by U.S. news organizations other than the *Times*. They included CBS News, the *Miami Herald*, the *New York Herald Tribune*, *Time* magazine, and *The Nation*. The preinvasion story "was covered heavily if not always well," according to a critique published in May 1961 in *The Reporter*, a journalists' trade publication. *The Reporter* noted, "Remarkably detailed reports were published and broadcast describing the stepped-up preparations" for the invasion.[60] Nine days before the invasion, the *New York Herald Tribune* reported that "anti-Castro troops are to begin converging on the island in ever-increasing numbers from various secret bases in the Caribbean area."[61]

A week before the invasion, the *Miami Herald* published an intriguing report that described how Cuban exile pilots had left Miami for staging areas in Central America. "This was the latest development here as exiles stepped up preparations for [a] promised attempt to overthrow the Cuban government," the *Herald* reported.[62] The *Herald*, though, was embarrassed by a misguided prediction about the invasion's timing. Beneath the headline, "Here's Cuban Invaders' Timetable," the *Herald* said the assault against Castro would be launched in fourteen to thirty-five days.[63] The invasion came the next day.

Although many of them were sketchy, incomplete, and even mistaken in some details, these and other news reports collectively signaled that moves were afoot in the Caribbean in the winter and spring of 1961 to strike at the Castro regime. Indeed, the coverage helped strip away the fiction circulated by the Kennedy administration that the invasion was strictly a Cuban affair. The first inklings of the U.S. role in training and arming the Cuban exiles appeared in late November 1960. *The Nation* that month published a report titled "Are We Training Cuban Guerrillas?" The journal offered details of a visit to Guatemala by Ronald Hinson, the director of the Institute of Hispanic-American Studies at Stanford University, who said the CIA had acquired a large tract in Guatemala that was "stoutly fenced and heavily guarded." Hinson was quoted as saying that it was "'common knowledge' in

Guatemala that the tract is being used as a training ground for Cuban counter-revolutionaries who are preparing for an eventual landing in Cuba. It was also said that U.S. personnel and equipment are being used at the base," which *The Nation* said was near the town of Retahuleu, not far from the Pacific coast.[64]

The Nation closed its strikingly accurate article by calling on U.S. news media with correspondents in Guatemala to follow up on Hinson's reports. Some news organizations did so. In early January 1961, *Time* magazine reported on a mystery airstrip "that Guatemalans have been whispering about for months." Could it be, *Time* speculated, "the base for a cooperative U.S.-Guatemalan-Cuban-exile airborne military operation against Fidel Castro?" *Time* did not fully answer its question, but it did note that opposition leaders in Guatemala claimed "that hundreds of Cubans were being given commando training by U.S. instructors at the air-base and at several coffee plantations in the area."[65] Soon after, the *New York Times* published a front-page article about the Guatemala base and airstrip. The report appeared beneath the headline "U.S. Helps Train an Anti-Castro Force at Secret Guatemalan Air-Ground Base."[66] In a separate article published a few days earlier, the *Times* had quoted a Cuban exile leader as saying his group was "almost ready" to invade Cuba and that he expected to be on the island in February.[67]

The *Times* article about the training base in Guatemala prodded the *Miami Herald* to break its self-imposed embargo of a report describing a "mysterious Miami-Guatemala air highway" by which Cuban exiles were secretly flown to Guatemala for training from a former Navy air-field at Opa-locka, north of Miami.[68] The *Herald* published the report on January 11, 1961. It appended a short note to the article saying that it had been "withheld for more than two months" and that its publication "was decided upon only after U.S. aid to anti-Castro fighters in Guatemala was first revealed elsewhere."[69] The *Herald's* editor, William C. Baggs, conceded that he agonized about delaying the report's publication. "Once you make a decision to withhold the news," he was quoted as saying, "it raises the question of how far you go and when you stop."[70]

The flurry of news reports in January 1961 effectively meant that "the scope and detail of the operation had been about as widely disseminated as possible, short of an official announcement by the CIA," Salisbury later wrote, adding, "One had to be blind and deaf not to know what was going on."[71] But for several weeks thereafter, the invasion-preparation story was oddly quiescent, not reemerging in the American press until early April 1961. By then, as Szulc recalled, preparations for the invasion had become an open secret in south Florida—so open that Castro agents in Miami "had simply to go to the usual restaurants and cafes where Cubans went to find out that a military operation was afoot, because people were departing daily, with tearful goodbyes to their families." By then, U.S. authorities knew of at least one hundred Cuban intelligence agents operating in the Miami area, Szulc said, and that meant "the whole operation was mounted in the full view not only of the American press but . . . of Fidel Castro."[72]

ACCOUNTING FOR THE SUPPRESSION MYTH

So what explains the emergence and tenacity of the Bay of Pigs–*New York Times* suppression myth? Why did Szulc's report of April 7, 1961, gain such singular focus, especially since several other articles were published in the *Times* and elsewhere that discussed invasion preparations? The best explanation is that Szulc's article of April 7 was singled out for discussion by a senior *Times* editor, Clifton Daniel, in a widely noted speech five years later.[73] Daniel addressed a meeting of the World Press Institute in St. Paul, Minnesota, in June 1966, and prefaced his remarks by saying, "This morning, I am going to tell you a story—one that has never been told before—the inside story of The New York Times and the Bay of Pigs, something of a mystery story."[74] Daniel recounted how *Times* editors had discussed Szulc's dispatch and had deleted references to the invasion's imminence and to the CIA's sponsorship. Daniel noted that editors Bernstein and Jordan vigorously opposed the decision to publish the report beneath a headline smaller than they had intended.

Daniel also disclosed comments Kennedy had made afterward, in separate conversations with Catledge and Dryfoos. At a meeting with Catledge and other newspaper editors at the White House in 1961, Kennedy "said in an aside to Mr. Catledge, 'If you had printed more about the operation you would have saved us from a colossal mistake.'" In a conversation at the White House in 1962, Kennedy told Dryfoos, "I wish you had run everything on Cuba. . . . I am just sorry you didn't tell it at the time."[75] In neither instance, though, did Kennedy refer specifically to the Szulc article of April 7. The president's comments, in any case, were quite self-serving. They represented an attempt to deflect blame for the debacle.[76] Reston aptly characterized Kennedy's remarks as "a cop-out,"[77] arguing, "It is ridiculous to think that publishing the fact that the invasion was imminent would have avoided this disaster. I am sure the operation would have gone forward" nonetheless.[78]

Daniel closed his speech in St. Paul by describing how the *Times* had cooperated with Kennedy's request on another occasion—during the Cuban missile crisis of October 1962. At that time, Reston was prepared to report that the Soviets had deployed nuclear-tipped weapons on the island. Kennedy telephoned Dryfoos asking that the newspaper refrain from publishing that report for twenty-four hours, to permit Kennedy to craft an announcement. Dryfoos complied, a decision that Kennedy later said "made far more effective our later actions [to defuse the crisis] and thereby contributed greatly to our national safety."[79]

What likely has happened over the years is that distinctions between the separate incidents became blurred—that Daniel's account of the *Times* postponing the publication of Reston's story during the 1962 Missile Crisis was confounded with the *Times*'s handling of Szulc's story in the run-up to the 1961 Bay of the Pigs invasion. That is, it was mistakenly thought that Kennedy had called the *Times* executives about the newspaper's coverage before the Bay of Pigs invasion when, in fact, he called about an entirely different matter in 1962.

Another, indirect factor contributing to the suppression myth was that some news organizations *did* comply with requests by the White House or State Department to withhold sensitive reports about the exiles and the plans to invade Cuba. According to Schlesinger's memoir, the *New Republic* magazine solicited prepublication review of an article it intended to publish beneath the headline "Our Men in Miami." Schlesinger said the *New Republic*'s report was "a careful, accurate and devastating account of CIA activities among the [Cuban] refugees, written, I learned later, by Karl Meyer," who collaborated with Szulc on a book titled *The Cuban Invasion: The Chronicle of a Disaster*. Schlesinger said he showed the *New Republic* article to Kennedy, "who instantly read it and expressed the hope that it could be stopped." The magazine "accepted the suggestion" not to publish the article—"a patriotic act that left me oddly uncomfortable," Schlesinger wrote.[80]

In addition, Szulc privately discussed how he had complied with a request eight months before the invasion to hold off reporting that camps had been established in Guatemala to train Cuban exiles. In testimony at the closed Senate hearing in 1961, Szulc said he had learned about the camps by August 1960 and was asked by the State Department "to consider this as a matter of national interest, not to write about it. We obliged and did not write about it."[81] Also, as noted, the *Miami Herald* delayed for two months publication of a report about the secret airlift taking Cuban exiles to training in Guatemala.

The cumulative effect of these separate cases of self-imposed restraint is to provide plausible context for the suppression myth of April 1961. The run-up to the Bay of Pigs invasion was hardly a finest hour for the *Times* or for American journalism. American journalists then were likelier to accede to requests of power-wielding authorities than they are today.[82] They were more inclined to withhold publication, if requested, so as not to undermine or compromise plans to challenge communist regimes. Such acquiescence was certainly misplaced in the Bay of Pigs episode: Castro claimed to have known a good deal about the invasion plans,[83] and by the end of March 1961 the Cuban exile community in Miami was abuzz about the coming assault.

In the final analysis, however, the *Times* did not spike the Szulc article that lies at the heart of the suppression myth. The article received editing that was judicious and comparatively minor and had the effect of improving its accuracy. Szulc later said, "I have no real quarrel with the handling of my stories" in the run-up to the invasion.[84]

The president did not know in advance about the Szulc report. He did not attempt to persuade *Times* executives to spike or dilute the report. That the story was not suppressed is readily apparent in reading the *Times* of April 7, 1961, and the thousand or so words Szulc filed about the pending invasion.

CHAPTER 6

Debunking the "Cronkite Moment"

If I've lost Cronkite, I've lost Middle America.

—Cited in "Walter Cronkite: The Most
Trusted Man," *Columbia Journalism Review,*
November–December 2001: 64

At the close of a thirty-minute special report televised in late February 1968, the avuncular CBS News anchorman Walter Cronkite declared that the U.S. war effort in Vietnam was "mired in stalemate." Drawing on his visit to Vietnam in the aftermath of the communists' surprise Tet Offensive that winter,[1] Cronkite said military victory seemed out of reach for U.S. forces. "We have been too often disappointed by the optimism of the American leaders, both in Vietnam and Washington, to have faith any longer in the silver linings they find in the darkest clouds," Cronkite said, suggesting that the moment was approaching when the United States should seek a negotiated settlement, "not as victors, but as an honorable people who lived up to their pledge to defend democracy, and did the best they could."[2]

The report by the popular and respected anchorman, it is said, produced immediate and stunning effects. At the White House, President Lyndon Johnson supposedly watched the program and, upon hearing Cronkite's concluding remarks, snapped off the television set and exclaimed, "If I've lost Cronkite, I've lost Middle America,"[3] or words to that effect. A month later, Johnson announced that he would not seek reelection—a decision said to have been tied to, and made inevitable by, Cronkite's piercing insight.[4] The Cronkite program supposedly had an even more powerful effect—that of shifting American public opinion from favoring the war to opposing it.[5] "Not since . . . Edward R. Murrow lifted Senator Joe McCarthy by the skunk tail for public inspection [in 1954] had one TV broadcast reflected such a fateful climate change in public opinion," *Vanity Fair* declared at the thirty-fifth anniversary of Cronkite's report.[6]

The program and Johnson's despairing response have become the stuff of legend—certainly among the most unforgettable moments in American journalism.[7] It was an occasion when the power of television news was unequivocally confirmed, a rare, pivotal nexus when a single broadcast "shook the nation,"[8] exposed "the hopelessness" of a faraway war,[9] and spurred a dramatic swing in foreign policy.[10] According to some interpretations, it was a turning point,[11] the moment when Johnson "lost heart" for the war in Vietnam.[12] It was an occasion that demonstrated "what an emotionally explosive combination television and war could be."[13] The program supposedly was so singularly potent that it has come to be remembered as the "Cronkite moment."

The journalist David Halberstam was among the first to recount the Cronkite-Johnson anecdote, doing so in his 1979 book, *The Powers That Be*. Interestingly, Halberstam did not place Johnson's purported remark about having "lost Cronkite" inside quotation marks. He paraphrased Johnson, saying the president made the comment to his press secretary, George Christian. Johnson was in Washington when the show was broadcast, according to Halberstam, who characterized Cronkite's program as "the first time in American history a war had been declared over by an anchorman."[14] A former CBS executive, Howard Stringer, offered a similar analysis, stating: "When Walter said the Vietnam War was over, it was over."[15] But there was more than a little hyperbole in the characterizations by Halberstam and Stringer: it was more than five years after the "Cronkite moment" when the last U.S. combat forces left Vietnam.

Even more serious flaws are associated with the presumptive "Cronkite moment." Scrutiny of the evidence associated with the program reveals that Johnson did not have—and indeed could not have had—the abrupt yet resigned reaction so often attributed to him. That's because Johnson did not see the program when it was aired. Moreover, Johnson's supposedly downbeat, self-pitying reaction to Cronkite's assessment clashes sharply with the president's aggressive characterization of the war. Hours before the Cronkite program, Johnson delivered a little-recalled but rousing speech on Vietnam, a speech cast in Churchillian terms. It seems inconceivable that Johnson's views would have pivoted so swiftly and dramatically upon hearing the opinion of a television news anchor, even one as respected as Cronkite. Even if he later heard—or heard about—Cronkite's one-off assessment, it certainly would have

FIGURE 13. CBS News anchor Walter Cronkite went to Vietnam in February 1968, shortly after the North Vietnamese communists launched their surprise Tet military offensive. Cronkite returned home to report that U.S. forces were "mired in stalemate." [*Bettman/Corbis*]

been no epiphany for Johnson. In the weeks after the program, the president gave several speeches in which he delivered robust defenses of his war policy and even urged a "total national effort" to win in Vietnam.[16]

Moreover, there is scant evidence that the Cronkite program had much influence at all on American popular opinion about the war. Polling data clearly show that American sentiment had begun shifting months before the program aired. And other U.S. news organizations had offered gloomy assessments about Vietnam in the days, weeks, and months before Cronkite described the war as "mired in stalemate." Nearly seven months before the program, the *New York Times* declared the war in Vietnam had reached that point.[17]

The "Cronkite moment," moreover, has been afflicted with acute version variability. That is, there is no single consensus version of what Johnson supposedly said in response to Cronkite's assessment. Johnson's remarks most often have been characterized as: "If I've lost Cronkite, I've lost Middle America." Sometimes, however, they have been quoted as: "If I've lost Cronkite, I've lost the country." Occasionally, they have been presented as: "If I've lost Cronkite, I've lost the American people" or even, "If I've lost Cronkite, I've lost the war." Version variability of that magnitude signals implausibility. It is a marker of a media-driven myth.

Interestingly, Cronkite's views of the program's effect shifted markedly over the years. In promoting his 1997 memoir, Cronkite likened the effect on Johnson to "a very small straw on a very heavy load he was already carrying."[18] But in the latter years of his life, Cronkite came to embrace the more flamboyant interpretation that his program had a powerful "effect on history."[19]

NOT AT THE WHITE HOUSE

Each of the points mentioned above will be discussed in detail in this chapter, which draws on a variety of primary and secondary sources in challenging the Cronkite-Johnson anecdote as a media-driven myth. The chapter expands on the largely overlooked research of David Culbert, who explored the Cronkite-Johnson anecdote within the broader context of the president's relations with the news media.[20]

The CBS special program was titled "Report from Vietnam by Walter Cronkite"[21] and aired at 9:30 P.M. Central Standard Time (10:30 P.M. Eastern Standard Time) on February 27, 1968. As the program began, Johnson was en route to Gregory Gymnasium on the campus of the Uni-

FIGURE 14. President Lyndon Johnson did not watch the Cronkite program when it was aired on February 27, 1968. At the time, Johnson was at a birthday party in Texas for Governor John Connally. "Today you are 51, John," the president said. "That is the magic number that every man of politics prays for—a simple majority." [*Lyndon B. Johnson Library*]

versity of Texas at Austin to attend a birthday party for Governor John B. Connally. He arrived there at 9:50 P.M. and shortly afterward offered remarks honoring Connally.[22] As Culbert pointed out, "Johnson could not have seen the broadcast as originally aired"[23]—which means the president could not have had the immediate, visceral reaction to Cronkite's assessment that has been so often claimed.

About the time Cronkite was offering his closing "mired in stalemate" commentary, Johnson was engaging in teasing, lighthearted banter about Connally's age: "Today you are 51, John. That is the magic number that every man of politics prays for—a simple majority. Throughout the years we have worked long and hard—and I might say late—trying to maintain it, too."[24]

Johnson left the campus soon after completing the cheery remarks. As his limousine drove away, about one hundred antiwar protesters booed and jeered him.[25] He boarded Air Force One to return to Washington, arriving at the White House at 2:11 A.M. on February 28. He slept a little more than five hours, rising at 7:45 A.M., and met the outgoing defense secretary, Robert S. McNamara, shortly after 8 A.M.[26] Johnson that morning missed NBC's *Today* show, which he often watched.[27]

Culbert held open the possibility that Johnson later viewed the Cronkite program on videotape. Audiovisual records at the Johnson Presidential Library show that the program had been taped, he noted. But Johnson's memoir about his presidency, *The Vantage Point*, is notably silent about the Cronkite program, offering no clue about whether he ever saw it or, if he did, what he thought of it. The power of the "Cronkite moment" resides in the sudden, unexpected, and decisive effect it supposedly had on the president:[28] such an effect would have been absent, or greatly diminished, had Johnson seen the program on videotape at some later date.[29]

Culbert attempted to resolve the uncertainties about the Cronkite-Johnson anecdote in a telephone interview with Christian, Johnson's former press secretary, in September 1979. He asked Christian about the president's reaction to the Cronkite program, and Christian gave this rambling and contradictory reply:

> Johnson did talk about Cronkite going to Vietnam and in effect turning against the war and it did worry him immensely that Cronkite had in effect become dovish, because he saw the impact was going to be tremendous on the country. Now whether or not Johnson saw that program at X time and that sort of thing, I don't know. He saw newscasts of other things, I'm sure that Johnson is bound to have seen the program. I remember being

with Johnson when he saw a commentary from Cronkite. Now whether it was on the morning news ... I think it probably was on the CBS Morning News, where it might have been an excerpt out of the program or something. I saw the programs ... I either saw them at home and I saw the videotapes. I don't remember ... I don't know whether he saw them. I'm pretty sure he saw all the [recorded] programs in some manner although I don't remember precisely. I know we talked about the Cronkite program and he was very concerned about Cronkite coming home from Vietnam and portraying the 'cause is lost' in effect, the impact it was going to have. Now when it was and where it was, I don't really have a clear recollection.[30]

John Wilson, an archivist at the Johnson Presidential Library, has said,"It is quite likely that Johnson did not see the show when it first aired, but saw either a tape of it or excerpts on another show at a later point. I can not identify just what or when he saw it."[31]

A BRAVADO SPEECH ON VIETNAM

What is quite clear is that at the time the Cronkite program aired, Johnson was forceful and adamant in his public statements about the war effort in Vietnam. He was not despairing in the aftermath of the shock of the Tet Offensive, which was launched in late January 1968 by North Vietnamese forces and their Viet Cong allies. They had attacked more than one hundred cities and towns across South Vietnam and even pressed their assault to the grounds of the U.S. embassy compound in Saigon. The offensive eventually was beaten back, and the communist objectives of inciting popular uprisings against the South Vietnamese government utterly failed. But more than 1,700 American troops were killed in action in the Tet Offensive, and South Vietnamese losses were about twice that number. As many as 40,000 communist forces were killed, most of them Viet Cong.[32]

The aftermath of the Tet Offensive, Johnson asserted in a speech in Dallas on the day the Cronkite program aired, was no time for retreat, no time for loss of resolve. Rather, he said, it was the hour for Americans to demonstrate unity and determination. "Persevere in Vietnam we will," Johnson declared, "and we must."[33]

Johnson's visit that day to Dallas was his first since President John F. Kennedy was assainated there in November 1963. He made the trip from his ranch in Johnson City, Texas, in low-key fashion. In Dallas, Johnson traveled in an unmarked car that rode ahead of a small motorcade of reporters and secret service agents. Motorists and pedestrians were unaware the president was in town.[34] "There were no crowds on the streets . . . and Mr. Johnson appeared to take no notice as he passed within sight of the place where President Kennedy was shot," the *New York Times* reported.[35]

At midday, Johnson spoke to several thousand convention-goers of the National Rural Electric Cooperative Association. Although his pledge to continue supporting rural electrification drew the warmest applause, Johnson devoted much of his speech to the war effort in Vietnam. He invoked Churchillian language, saying at one point: "There will be blood, sweat and tears shed." The president also declared, "I do not believe that America will ever buckle" in pursuit of its objectives in Vietnam. "I believe that every American will answer now for his future and for his children's future. I believe he will say, 'I did not buckle when the going got tough.'"[36]He further said:

> Thousands of our courageous sons and millions of brave South Vietnamese have answered aggression's onslaught and they have answered it with one strong and one united voice. "No retreat," they have said. Free men will never bow to force and abandon their future to tyranny. That must be our answer, too, here at home. Our answer here at home, in every home, must be: No retreat from the responsibilities of the hour of the day. We are living in a dangerous world and we must understand it. We must be prepared to stand up when we need to. There must be no failing our fighting sons.[37]

Johnson's speech—although rarely recalled in the context of the "Cronkite moment"—was reported the next day on the front pages of major newspapers, including the *Chicago Tribune, New York Times,* and *Washington Post.* The *Los Angeles Times* also reported Johnson's speech on its front page, beneath a bold headline that read: "NO VIET RETREAT." Johnson's speech, the newspaper said, was "perhaps his strongest public call yet for unity in pushing the Vietnam war."[38]

The bravado speech in Dallas was hardly consistent with the crestfallen and resigned tenor of Johnson's supposed reaction to the Cronkite program later that day. It is difficult indeed to imagine how the president's mood could swing so abruptly, from vigorously defending the war effort to throwing up his hands in self-pity and despair. But if the anecdote of the "Cronkite moment" is to be believed, such a dramatic change in attitude is exactly what happened, within hours of the hawkish speech in Dallas.

The vigor of the speech was consistent with the assertiveness Johnson expressed about Vietnam immediately after the Tet Offensive.

Washington-based syndicated columnists Rowland Evans and Robert Novak, writing at the end of February 1968, described Johnson as being "in an aggressively martial mood, privately vowing his mailed-fist determination to gain his objectives [in Vietnam] no matter what force of arms is required." Evans and Novak reported that the president had "never before . . . been so insistent about the absolute rightness of his policies. In long Johnsonesque monologues these days, he is praising the soldiers and denouncing the war correspondents, emphasizing the shooting war and deemphasizing pacification" of villages of South Vietnam.[39]

Even if he had seen Cronkite's program soon afterward on videotape, Johnson gave no indication of having taken the anchorman's message to heart. Just three days after the program aired, Johnson vowed in remarks at a testimonial dinner in Texas that the United States would "not cut and run" from Vietnam. "We're not going to be Quislings," the president said, invoking the surname of a Norwegian politician who helped the Nazis take over his country, "and we're not going to be appeasers."[40] Johnson spoke with similar force in mid-March 1968, telling business leaders meeting in Washington: "We must meet our commitments in the world and in Vietnam. We shall and we are going to win. . . . I don't want a man in here to go back home thinking otherwise—we are going to win."[41]

Two days later, he traveled to Minneapolis to deliver a rousing speech to the National Farmers Union convention, during which he urged "a total national effort to win the war" in Vietnam. Punctuating his remarks in Minneapolis by pounding the lectern and jabbing his finger in the air, Johnson declared, "We love nothing more than peace, but we hate nothing worse than surrender and cowardice." He disparaged critics of the war as inclined to "tuck our tail and violate our commitments."[42] And a day after that speech, Johnson insisted in a talk at the State Department: "We have set our course [in Vietnam], and we will prevail."[43] Thus, in the days and weeks after the Cronkite program, Johnson was adamant, robust, and unwavering in defending his Vietnam policy. On multiple occasions during that time, when Cronkite's view was most likely to have been circulating, the president remained openly and tenaciously hawkish on the war.

By the close of March 1968, however, such vigor had been drained from Johnson's views. He yielded reluctantly to pressures within his administration to make a peace overture to the North Vietnamese.[44] In a nationally televised speech on March 31, Johnson announced that he had decided to seek "peace through negotiations." He ordered a limited halt to U.S. aerial bombing of North Vietnam as an inducement to the Hanoi government to enter peace talks. Johnson closed the speech with the stunning announcement that he would not seek reelection to the presidency.[45]

Johnson's change of heart on Vietnam came about through a complex process, in which Cronkite's views counted for little. Among the far more prominent forces and factors that shaped Johnson's thinking in the days before March 31, 1968, was the counsel of an influential and informal coterie of outside advisers known as the "Wise Men." The Wise Men included such foreign policy notables as Dean Acheson, a former secretary of state; McGeorge Bundy, a former national security adviser to Kennedy and Johnson; George Ball, a former under secretary of state; Douglas Dillon, a former treasury secretary; General Omar Bradley, a former chairman of the joint chiefs of staff; and Abe Fortas, a U.S. Supreme Court justice and friend of Johnson's. The Wise Men had met in November 1967 and expressed near-unanimous support for Johnson's Vietnam policy. They met again, at the request of the White House, in late March 1968.[46]

The Wise Men, wrote George C. Herring in his study *LBJ and Vietnam,* persuaded Johnson "that something dramatic must be done" to seek peace in Vietnam.[47] They largely, though not unanimously, expressed opposition to America's escalating the war in Vietnam.[48] "The theme that ran around the table was, 'You've got to lower your sights,'" George Ball later recalled. "I think the thing that shook the President most was Acheson, who had been pretty much of a hawk up to that point."[49] Acheson said the Tet Offensive had made it clear that U.S. objectives in Vietnam were out of reach and that disengagement had to be considered.[50] Johnson "was shaken by this kind of advice from people in whose judgment he necessarily had some confidence, because they'd had a lot of experience," Ball noted a few years later.[51]

The counsel of the Wise Men probably represented the tipping point for Johnson on Vietnam. But the inklings of a policy change can be traced at least to February 28, 1968, at a breakfast meeting convened at the White House just hours after Johnson's late-night flight from Texas. The president's closest advisers and senior cabinet officers were there, and the topic was the war, specifically the request of General William C. Westmoreland to increase U.S. troop strength in Vietnam by 206,000 men.[52] To meet the general's request, the U.S. military faced calling up its reserves, extending enlistments for six months, and expanding the military draft—all unappealing options in an election year,[53] especially given that U.S. forces in Vietnam already numbered more than 520,000. The breakfast meeting on February 28 set in motion a thorough review of the administration's options and objectives in Vietnam,[54] culminating a month later in Johnson's speech proposing negotiations and offering a partial halt in bombing.

Had Johnson watched the Cronkite program on videotape during that period—that is, after the breakfast meeting on February 28 and before his speech on March 31—it may have contributed marginally to reservations about the war. But the videotaped program surely would not have represented a distinctive, remarkable, or decisive element in his thinking. Viewing the Cronkite program on videotape would have given Johnson no exceptional insights. His advisers already had begun to embrace the misgivings that Cronkite and others had noted, and those reservations were confirmed by the Wise Men.

Dismaying political developments also weighed on Johnson in late winter 1968. War supporters in Congress were becoming disenchanted with Vietnam.[55] More ominous was the growing popularity of Senator Eugene McCarthy and his insurgent run for the presidency. The unexpected potency of McCarthy's antiwar campaign was revealed in the Democratic primary election in New Hampshire on March 12, 1968, in which McCarthy won 42.4 percent of the vote, a far greater portion than expected.[56] Johnson won 49.5 percent, although his name was not on the ballot. Shortly after the primary, columnists Evans and Novak reported that many of the president's supporters had become "convinced he must soften his war policy—at the least, dropping his long-planned tactic of campaigning as patriot President, at most shifting somewhat his war policy—to keep down McCarthy and stave off [the impending candidacy of Robert] Kennedy."[57] Kennedy entered the race for the Democratic presidential nomination in mid-March 1968 and promptly assailed Johnson's Vietnam policy as "bankrupt."[58]

Other factors in Johnson's decisions to seek negotiations with North Vietnam and quit the presidential race were public opinion polls that signaled a softening of popular support for the war. That support was ebbing had been clear for some months.

SHIFTING PUBLIC OPINION

Periodically since late summer 1965, the Gallup Organization had included this question in its surveys: "In view of the developments since we entered the fighting in Vietnam, do you think the U.S. made a mistake sending troops to fight in Vietnam?" The question was a marker for gauging popular support for the war. In August–September 1965, only 24 percent of the respondents said "yes," it had been a mistake; 60 percent said "no," it had not. The percentage of respondents saying that U.S. military presence in Vietnam was a mistake steadily increased, and it reached a plurality—47 percent "yes" to 44 percent "no"—in the Gallup survey conducted October 6–11, 1967.[59]

That pivotal moment was three and a half months before the Tet offensive, four and a half months before the Cronkite program, and five and a half months before Johnson's peace overture at the end of March 1968. The proportion shifted slightly in December 1967—when 45 percent said "yes," it had been a mistake, and 46 percent said "no," it had not—but in the poll conducted in early February, three weeks before the Cronkite program, the proportion had swung back to 46 percent "yes" and 42 percent "no." Gallup asked the question again in a poll completed the day the Cronkite program aired. Forty-nine percent of the respondents said "yes," U.S. military intervention in Vietnam had been a mistake; 42 percent said "no."

Journalists also had detected a softening in support of the war. In December 1967, for example, Don Oberdorfer, then a national correspondent for the Knight newspapers, noted that the "summer and fall of 1967 [had] been a time of switching, when millions of American voters—along with many religious leaders, editorial writers and elected officials—appeared to be changing their views about the war."[60] And as the historian Daniel C. Hallin later observed, "Lyndon Johnson had essentially lost Mr. Average Citizen months before Cronkite's broadcast."[61] Additionally, Greg Mitchell of the trade journal *Editor and Publisher* declared, "Those who claim that [the Cronkite program] created a seismic shift on the war overlook the fact that there was much opposition to the conflict already."[62]

By late February 1968, then, Cronkite's "mired in stalemate" assessment was neither notable nor extraordinary. Mark Kurlansky wrote in his study of the year 1968 that Cronkite's view was "hardly a radical position" for the time.[63] The *Wall Street Journal* had said in an editorial published four days before the Cronkite program aired that the U.S. war effort in Vietnam "may be doomed" and that "everyone had better be prepared for the bitter taste of defeat beyond America's power to prevent."[64] And nearly seven months before the program, the *New York Times* correspondent R. W. Apple Jr. had cited "disinterested observers" in reporting that the war in Vietnam "is not going well." Victory, Apple wrote, "is not close at hand. It may be beyond reach." Apple's analysis was published on the *Times*'s front page, beneath the headline "Vietnam: The Signs of Stalemate."[65] Several months before Apple's downbeat assessment, the columnists Evans and Novak had ruminated about "the frustrations of . . . a seemingly endless war that will not yield to the political mastery of Lyndon Johnson. Never before in his career as a political leader . . . has Mr. Johnson been so immobilized."[66]

Leading American journalists and news organizations had thus weighed in with pessimistic assessments about the war long before Cronkite's special report on Vietnam. As Jack Gould, the *New York Times*'s television critic, noted in his column, Cronkite's closing assessment about America's predicament in Vietnam "did not contain striking revelations" but served instead "to underscore afresh the limitless difficulties lying ahead and the mounting problems attending United States involvement."[67]

Moreover, a close reading of the transcript of Cronkite's closing remarks reveals how hedged and cautious they really were. Cronkite did not urge immediate talks aimed at ending the conflict, as many accounts have stated.[68] He held open the possibility that the U.S. military might still force the North Vietnamese to the bargaining table and suggested the U.S. forces be given a few months more to press the fight in Vietnam. "On the off chance that military and political analysts are right, in the next few months we must test the enemy's intentions, in case this [the Tet Offensive] is indeed his last big gasp before negotiations," Cronkite said. "But it is increasingly clear to this reporter that the only rational way out *then* will be to negotiate, not as victors, but as an honorable people who lived up to their pledge to defend democracy, and did the best they could."[69]

Cronkite's closing comments were somewhat muddled and certainly far less emphatic than those offered less than two weeks later by Frank McGee of the rival NBC network. "The war," McGee declared on an NBC News program that aired March 10, 1968, "is being lost by the administration's definition."[70]

VERSION VARIABILITY

A marker of a media-driven myth can be version variability—the imprecision that alters or distorts an anecdote in its retelling. Often in such cases, the anecdote's original source is not mentioned or it is misidentified. Typically, the anecdote's content varies markedly, much like a tall tale in which the details change with frequent recounting. To some extent, version variability characterizes the often-told Remington-Hearst anecdote.[71] But it afflicts the Cronkite-Johnson anecdote in greater measure. Sometimes, Johnson is said to have made the "If I've lost Cronkite" comment to Christian, his press secretary; other versions have him speaking to Bill Moyers[72]—who had left the White House in January 1967 to become publisher of *Newsday*.[73] Still other versions have the president addressing unspecified "aides"[74] or "associates."[75]

According to the most common version of the anecdote, Johnson's purported remark was: "If I've lost Cronkite, I've lost Middle America."[76] Cronkite himself recounted this version in his memoir, *A Reporter's Life*.[77] But other accounts present Johnson as reacting more vigorously and dramatically. "If I've lost Cronkite, I've lost the war," one alternative version has it.[78] A variation on that goes: "I've lost Cronkite. I've lost the war!"[79] Another despairing version is: "If I've lost Cronkite, I've lost the American people."[80] Other versions are similarly sweeping: "If I've lost Cronkite, I've lost the country,"[81] and "If I've lost Cronkite, I've lost the nation."[82] A variation on that has Johnson saying: "If I've lost Cronkite, I've lost America."[83] In some versions, Johnson's reaction is blithely offhanded: "Well, that's the end of the war."[84] Another account, offered by Tom Hayden, a prominent antiwar activist of the Vietnam era, says the president "went berserk" upon hearing Cronkite's assessment.[85] And once in a while, a nonsensical version pops up, such as: "If I've lost Cronkite, I've lost the mid west."[86] Typographical lapses may have distorted the following version, in which Johnson was quoted as saying: "If I've lost Cronkite, the country."[87]

This degree of version variability suggests more than sloppiness in journalistic research or a reluctance to take time to trace the derivation of the popular anecdote. The varying accounts of Johnson's purported reactions represent another, compelling reason for regarding the "Cronkite moment" with doubt and skepticism.

Cronkite at first rejected the suggestion that his report on Vietnam had much of an effect on Johnson. But over the years, as the anecdote took on legendary dimensions, Cronkite embraced its purported power. His interpretation of the impact and consequences of the 1968 program became more emphatic in the years before his death, in 2009.[88] As noted, Cronkite characterized the program in distinctly modest terms, saying in his 1997 memoir that the "mired in stalemate" assessment represented for Johnson "just one more straw in the increasing burden of Vietnam."[89] It was an analogy he repeated in interviews promoting the book. He told the CNBC cable network that he doubted whether the program "had a huge significance. I think it was a very small straw on a very heavy load [Johnson] was already carrying."[90] Cronkite once again invoked the straw metaphor in 1999, in an interview with CNN: "I think our broadcast simply was another straw on the back of a crippled camel."[91]

But by 2001, Cronkite had begun to claim somewhat greater significance for the program, telling an interviewer for NBC's *Today* show that "apparently it had some influence" on Johnson.[92] In an interview a few years later, he said, "It never occurred to me it was going to have the effect it had." He added on that occasion, "President Johnson's comment after watching from the Oval Office gave it an importance that I don't think anybody really thought it had."[93] In 2006, Cronkite referred to his special report from Vietnam as having left the president with "another bullet in his rear end."[94] He later told *Esquire* magazine, "To be honest, I was rather amazed that my reporting from Vietnam had such an effect on history."[95] Cronkite further embraced the power of the anecdote in 2007, telling the *Gazette* of Martha's Vineyard in Massachusetts: "There are a lot of journalists out there today who if they chose to take that strong stand and course [in opposing the Iraq War] would probably enjoy a similar result."[96]

INVOKING THE "CRONKITE MOMENT"

For many American journalists, the "Cronkite moment" has become an ideal, a standard that suggests both courage and influence in war-time reporting. It is an objective that contemporary practitioners at times seem desperate to recapture or recreate. Other, would-be "Cronkite moments" have been identified or anticipated from time to time. The long, U.S.-led war in Iraq produced at least two such occasions. The decision by NBC News in 2006 to call the conflict a civil war, despite the objections of the administration of President George W. Bush, was likened to a "Cronkite moment."[97] So was the *New York Times* editorial in 2007 that said the time had come "for the United States to leave Iraq, without any more delay than the Pentagon needs to organize an orderly exit."[98] But neither civil war terminology nor the pullout editorial proved to be particularly influential. Neither presumptive "Cronkite moment" was remembered for very long. That they aspired to such status signals the enduring allure and importance of the "Cronkite moment" and suggests why debunking it still matters, some fifty years later.

The evidence presented here demonstrates that the "Cronkite moment" is a media-driven myth. It did not have the effects that Halberstam and many others have attributed to it: it was neither an occasion when "a war had been declared over by an anchorman"[99] nor a moment when a single newscast changed the course of history.[100] Not unlike the Murrow-McCarthy myth, the "Cronkite moment" parlayed coincidental but propitious timing into enduring recognition. The Johnson administration's policy review of Vietnam began soon after the Cronkite program, suggesting a linkage that is more deceptive than real. The administration's policy review was triggered not by Cronkite's assessment but by the surprise Tet Offensive and the proposed deployment of thousands of additional U.S. troops in Vietnam. Cronkite's program had nothing to do with initiating the review.

Critical to Johnson's decision in late March 1968 to deescalate the war and seek negotiations with the North Vietnamese was the advice and counsel of the Wise Men and the implications of Eugene McCarthy's insurgent bid for the Democratic nomination for president. In the end, Cronkite's first impressions about the program's effect were surely the most accurate: in its influence, the televised report of February 27, 1968, was at best like that of "a very small straw."

Under scrutiny, the "Cronkite moment" dissolves as illusory—a chimera, a media-driven myth. That it does is not so surprising. Seldom, if ever, do the news media exert truly decisive influence on decisions to go to war or to seek negotiated peace. Such decisions typically are driven by forces and factors well beyond the news media's ability to shape, alter, or significantly influence. So it was in Vietnam, where the war ground on for years after the "Cronkite moment."

CHAPTER 7

The Nuanced Myth

Bra Burning at Atlantic City

I wonder whether the historians whose job it will be to sift
through all the refuse we reporters deposit on the pile of
history might not notice some articles of value we did not
notice at the time.

—Remarks by Charles Kuralt, cited in "Charles Kuralt
Receives Allen H. Neuharth Award for Excellence in
Journalism," Business Wire (28 April 1995)

Myth-busting can be an uncertain pursuit. On occasion, a myth may
carry a bit more truth than debunkers are inclined to believe. So it is
with the nuanced myth of bra burnings, which took hold in the days
following the Miss America pageant in Atlantic City, New Jersey, on
September 7, 1968.

Early that afternoon, about one hundred women from New York
City, New Jersey, Boston, and elsewhere arrived by bus at the Atlantic
City boardwalk. They were, according to the *New York Times,* "mostly
middle-aged careerists and housewives,"[1] and they set up a picket line
at Kennedy Plaza, across from the convention center. They had come to
Atlantic City, as one participant declared, "to protest the degrading
image of women perpetuated by the Miss America pageant," which
took place that night inside the convention center. Their goal was: "No
more Miss America!"[2]

The demonstrators denounced the pageant as a "degrading Mindless-
Boob-Girlie symbol" that placed "women on a pedestal/auction block
to compete for male approval" and promoted a "Madonna Whore
image of womanhood."[3] They carried placards declaring: "Up against
the Wall, Miss America," "Miss America Sells It," "Miss America Is a

Big Falsie,"[4] and "Miss America Goes Down."[5] And they became visibly more animated when television cameras showed up.[6]

In time, the protest on the boardwalk came to be recognized as a decisive moment in the emergence of the women's liberation movement.[7] "Before September 7," Mark Kurlansky wrote in his study of the landmark events of 1968, "the common image of feminism was that it was a movement of long-skirted women in bonnets who fought from 1848 until 1920 to get women the right to vote."[8] The protest at Atlantic City also gave rise to the myth of bra burning, a media-driven myth that became a way to denigrate women's liberation and feminist advocacy as trivial and even a bit primitive.

Invoking bra burning was a convenient means of brushing aside the issues and challenges raised by women's liberation and discrediting the fledgling movement as shallow and without serious grievance. The columnist Harriet Van Horne was perhaps the first to do so. "My feeling about the liberation ladies," Van Horne wrote soon after the protest in Atlantic City, "is that they've been scarred by consorting with the wrong men. Men who do not understand the way to a woman's heart, i.e., to make her feel utterly feminine, desirable and almost too delicate for this hard world. . . . No wonder she goes to Atlantic City and burns her bra."[9]

Feminists have long despaired of the "bra burning" epithet and insisted that no bras or other objects were burned at the Atlantic City protest. This chapter, however, offers evidence that bras *were* set afire, briefly, during the protest that day. It further argues that the notion of flamboyant bra burnings is fanciful and highly exaggerated—a media myth whose diffusion can be traced to a humor columnist's riff.

The protest on the Atlantic City boardwalk was organized by a small group called New York Radical Women. Many of its members had participated in civil rights demonstrations and New Left protests. But Atlantic City was the group's first attempt at staging a public protest of its own. "It was our foray into the adult world," Robin Morgan, the principal organizer, was quoted as saying years later, "and we were all excited bunnies."[10] Morgan at the time of the protest was twenty-seven years old. The demonstrators were under instructions not to speak with male reporters. "Why should we talk with them? It's impossible for men to understand," said Marion Davidson, a protester from New York.[11] When Clara de Miha, a sixty-eight-year-old grandmother who belonged to the pacifist Jeannette Rankin Brigade, tried to remind a male reporter that there were "more important things to pay attention to than beauty," a younger protester pointedly told her, "We won't talk to men reporters."[12]

For all the stern rhetoric and blunt tactics, the daylong protest on the boardwalk wasn't disruptive, or even very raucous. "Intoxicated with our own leadership and freedom," Morgan recalled years later, "we picketed, leafleted, chanted, and sang all day outside the convention hall."[13] Mindful of the violence that had characterized protests at the Democratic National Convention in Chicago just a few weeks earlier, the organizers sought to avoid what Morgan called "heavy disruptive tactics"[14] and tried to inject a measure of frivolity into their demonstration at Atlantic City. There were, for example, moments of absurd street theater, such as when a sheep festooned in yellow and blue ribbons was crowned "Miss America." As they paraded the frightened animal, the protesters sang, "There she is, Miss America."[15]

THE FREEDOM TRASH CAN

The centerpiece of the protest was the so-called Freedom Trash Can, into which the protesters consigned "instruments of torture," such as brassieres, girdles, high-heeled shoes, false eyelashes, and magazines such as *Playboy* and *Cosmopolitan*.[16] The *New York Times* reported that one demonstrator tossed a bottle of pink liquid detergent into the trash can and declared her opposition to "such atrocities as having to do the dishes." Another woman held a girdle over the trash can and chanted, "No more girdles, no more pain. No more trying to hold the fat in vain."[17]

It was around the Freedom Trash Can that the myth of feminist bra burning emerged. In the days before the protest, the organizers had let it be known—or at least had hinted openly[18]—that brassieres and other items would be set afire in the Freedom Trash Can. At least a few news reports in advance of the protest referred to plans for a "bra burning" at the Atlantic City boardwalk. The day before the demonstration, for example, the *Wall Street Journal* said organizers had promised "picket lines, leaflets, bra-burning and 'lobbying visits to the contestants urging our sisters to reject the pageant farce and join us.'"[19] The *Star-Ledger* newspaper in Newark also made reference to "news reports about a New York women's group" that had announced plans to "burn women's undergarments in protest" of the Miss America pageant.[20]

But once in Atlantic City, protesters' plans to set bras afire supposedly were abandoned in favor of what Morgan termed a "symbolic

FIGURE 15. The nuanced myth of "bra burning" emerged from around the so-called Freedom Trash Can, shown here. It was a centerpiece of a women's liberation demonstration in Atlantic City on September 7, 1968, during the Miss America beauty pageant. The protest's principal organizer, Robin Morgan, is in the striped outfit at center. [*Courtesy* Press *of Atlantic City*]

bra-burning."[21] The Atlantic City mayor, she said, had expressed fears about burning anything[22] given that, a week before the protest, fire had destroyed or damaged fourteen stores in a half-block section of the boardwalk.[23] In the years since, Morgan and other participants have insisted that bras were not set afire at Atlantic City that day.

But almost immediately, the notion took hold that bra burning had been a centerpiece of the protest at Atlantic City. In her column in the *New York Post* two days later, Van Horne derided the demonstrators as having wanted "to be liberated from their femininity, such as it is." Van Horne, who was not at the Atlantic City protest, also wrote that the highlight "was a bonfire in a Freedom Trash Can. With screams of delight they consigned to the flames such shackling, demeaning items as girdles, bras, high-heeled slippers, hair curlers and false eyelashes."[24] It was a highly imaginative characterization, one that was taken up a few days later by Art Buchwald in his nationally syndicated column.

Buchwald was the country's preeminent humor columnist, and his wry send-ups appeared in no fewer than three hundred newspapers. Frequent readers knew that Buchwald's columns usually contained at least a small element of truth, but it was not always easy to judge just how far the columnist had planted tongue in cheek.[25] And so it was with the column published September 12, 1968, beneath headlines that read, "The Bra Burners"[26] or "Uptight Dissenters Go Too Far in Burning Their Brassieres."[27] Buchwald wrote that he "was flabbergasted to read that about 100 women had picketed the Miss America pageant in Atlantic City against 'ludicrous beauty standards that had enslaved the American woman.'" He added, "The final and most tragic part of the protest took place when several of the women publicly burned their brassieres."[28]

Buchwald concluded, "If the women in Atlantic City wanted to picket the Miss America beauty pageant because it is lily-white, that is one thing, and if they wanted to picket because it is a bore, that is also a legitimate excuse. But when they start asking young American women to burn their brassieres and throw away their false eyelashes, then we say dissent in this country has gone too far."[29]

Buchwald's characterization of the protest introduced the notion of flamboyant bra burning to a national audience, conjuring as it did a powerful mental image of angry women setting fire to bras and twirling them, defiantly, for all on the boardwalk to see. Buchwald's humor column thus helped solidify the evocative, though entirely misleading, representation of the angry bra burners.[30]

Other national publications fortified that impression. At the end of September 1968, the *New York Times* published a brief wire service article that referred to "bra-burnings and other demonstrations" at Atlantic City.[31] The following August, the *Wall Street Journal* reported in a front-page article about the increasingly popular "no-bra" look that the "fad got a push . . . when a group called the Women's Liberation Movement [had] staged a mass bra-burning at Atlantic City" the year before.[32] The syndicated political columnist James J. Kilpatrick also linked the no-bra fashion to the protest on the Atlantic City boardwalk, writing in September 1969, "The first organized demonstration against the bra apparently occurred in Atlantic City in September of 1968, when a group of women burned their bras outside the Miss America pageant."[33]

The *Washington Post* indulged in a striking flight of fancy about bra burning in a series of articles in 1970 that explored the emergent women's liberation movement: "When the Women's Liberation members first surfaced at the 1968 Miss America contest, their protest took the form of bra burning. A rash of bra burnings followed. No matter how opposed you were to sit-ins, lie-ins, marches and other demonstrations, none of them seemed to represent quite as bad a case of the sillies as bra burning. And though they had a point to make, the stigma of silliness has stuck to Women's Liberation ever since."[34]

The notion of numerous and demonstrative bra burnings eventually became ingrained in American popular culture. And the term "bra burning" remains convenient shorthand for describing the upheaval of the 1960s and early 1970s. It is casually invoked as a defining phrase, or cliché, of those troubled times—as in "the era of bra-burning,"[35] "the hysteria of bra-burning,"[36] the time of "raucous bra burning,"[37] when there were "bra burnings across the land,"[38] "the bra-burning days of the turbulent 1960s,"[39] and "the 1970s, when bra burning became the most popular fashion statement."[40] A lawyer named Wendy Kaminer wrote in the *New York Times* in 1988, "No one has burned a bra in 20 years, but the image of those little bonfires remains."[41]

More significantly, the phrase became an offhand way of ridiculing feminists and mocking their sometimes militant efforts to confront gender-based discrimination in the home and the workplace. Characterizations such as "bra-burning feminists,"[42] "the bra-burning women's movement,"[43] "loud-mouthed, bra-burning, men-hating feminists,"[44] and "a 1960s bra-burning feminist"[45] have had currency for years. Betty Friedan, a women's rights advocate who helped establish the National

FIGURE 16. The humor columnist Art Buchwald propelled the notion that flamboyant "bra burning" had marked a feminist protest at Atlantic City. The puckish Buchwald wrote in his nationally syndicated column published September 12, 1968: "The final and most tragic part of the protest took place when several of the women publicly burned their brassieres." [*Bettman/Corbis*]

Organization for Women but rejected radical feminism, reportedly advised college students to avoid "the bra-burning, anti-man, politics-of-orgasm school."[46]

Women's rights advocates were keenly sensitive to, and even mortified by, such epithets and the images they conjured. Bra burning, they claimed, was a "media misrepresentation" that deflected attention from the gender inequality that had encouraged the rise of feminism.[47] Bra burning quite clearly suggested that women's liberation advocates really had "little of substance to complain about,"[48] and it signaled how the news media could promote contempt for an emergent and uncertain social movement that nonetheless "disturbed many people."[49] As the feminist authors Judith Hole and Ellen Levine wrote, "The phrase 'bra-burning' was sufficiently provocative to make headlines and with steady usage by the media . . . it even assumed an historical reality. In all cases, its usage, ostensibly as a statement of 'fact' or description, served to ridicule."[50]

Feminists long have insisted that no bras were burned at Atlantic City in 1968—or at any feminist protest, for that matter. Among the first to make such a claim was Joanna Foley Martin, who wrote in the *Chicago Journalism Review* in 1971: "No one in the women's liberation movement has ever burned or otherwise mutilated a bra. At least not in public. If you find this hard to believe, that's not surprising. The myth has been repeated constantly by the media over the past three years, building on itself in the classic pattern of the Big Lie. Every time women's liberation is mentioned, bras are, too, and vice versa." She also asserted that the news media had never "documented a specific case in which a women's liberation group was involved in a bra destruction, despite their constant repetition of the myth."[51]

Prominent writers on women's issues have offered similar assertions over the years. Ellen Goodman, a nationally syndicated columnist, wrote in 1981 that "no piece of lingerie was ever kindled in anger" by women's rights advocates.[52] "In fact," Susan Faludi wrote in her book, *Backlash: The Undeclared War against American Women*, "there's no evidence that any undergarment was ever so much as singed at any women's rights demonstration" in the late 1960s and 1970s.[53] Suzanne Braun Levine, a former editor of *Ms.* magazine and of *Columbia Journalism Review*, scoffed at what she called "the apocryphal bra burning," saying, "nothing was actually burned" during the Miss America protest in 1968.[54] Flora Davis, in her study of the modern women's movement, said of the purported bra-burning demonstration at Atlantic City, "America's most famous bonfire was strictly a media invention."[55]

And Robin Morgan, the protest's principal organizer, has asserted, "There were no bras burned [at Atlantic City]. That's a media myth."[56]

The insistent claims that it was all a media myth were, however, overwhelmed by the alliterative and faintly lascivious appeal of the term "bra burning." The term seemed to fit the times as well: "bra burning" resonated as an extension of "draft card burning," which by 1968 had emerged as a way to protest the Vietnam War. "Bra burning" took hold and gained tenacity because it seemed to define a highly charged moment in a confused and angry time given readily to drama and dissent.

"Bra burning" offered something of a faint historical connection as well, alluding to the "watch fire" protests of the women's suffrage movement of the early twentieth century. In pressing demands for the right to vote, members of the suffragist National Woman's Party tended to "watch fires" just beyond the White House fence. The watch fires were set in urns and fed with wood and, imaginatively, with pages from speeches in which President Woodrow Wilson made references to promoting "freedom" in the world.[57]

Even the watch fires, mild and nonconfrontational though they were, could stir hostile reactions. On New Year's Day, 1919, soldiers, sailors, and civilians attacked a National Woman's Party demonstration in Lafayette Park, across from the White House, knocking down the protesters and destroying the urn in which their watch fire burned. The assault came soon after the protesting women had unfurled a banner declaring Wilson a "false prophet of democracy." The suffragists regrouped and started another watch fire in a large urn in the park. Soon, five of them were arrested for violating park regulations, the *New York Times* reported the next day.[58]

BRA BURNING AND THE LOCAL PRESS

Long overlooked in the claims and counterclaims surrounding the 1968 protest at Atlantic City is intriguing, contemporaneous evidence that gives dimension to the bra-burning legend and complicates its debunking. The evidence is offered by two eyewitness accounts—one of them published the day after the protest—that said bras and other items *were* burned, however briefly, in the Freedom Trash Can at Atlantic City. The published account appeared in the local Atlantic City daily newspaper, the *Press*, on September 8, 1968. The newspaper that day published two articles about the Miss America protest, both appearing on page four. The more prominent of the two articles was displayed at the upper left corner of page four, beneath the headline "Bra-Burners Blitz Board-walk."[59]

The article described what it called "the first such protest in the history of the Miss America pageant," and its ninth paragraph included this passage: "As the bras, girdles, falsies, curlers, and copies of popular women's magazines burned in the 'Freedom Trash Can,' the demonstration reached the pinnacle of ridicule when the participants paraded a small lamb wearing a gold banner worded 'Miss America.'"[60]

The article did not elaborate about the fire and the articles that were burned in the Freedom Trash Can, nor did it suggest that the fire was all that important. Rather, the article conveyed a sense of astonishment that an event such as the women's liberation protest could take place near the venue of the pageant. Nonetheless, the passage stands as a contemporaneous account that there *was* fire in the Freedom Trash Can that day—a firsthand report that was ignored and left unexamined for many years. In the many strenuous efforts to characterize bra burning as a myth, the reporting of the local newspaper had gone overlooked.

The "Bra-Burners Blitz Boardwalk" article was written by John L. Boucher, a newspaper reporter for nearly forty years who died in 1973. Boucher was locally prominent and had built a reputation as a conscientious and highly ethical reporter who took pains not to embroider or exaggerate. He won nine awards for writing and reporting, according to an article published in the *Atlantic City Press* on June 6, 1964, the day the governor declared John L. Boucher Day in New Jersey.[61]

Boucher's son, Jack, a photographer for the National Park Service, recalled his father as a "meticulous reporter" who "didn't embellish stories to make them hot news. He was known for that" kind of ethical regard. Although Jack Boucher was not familiar with the "Bra-Burners Blitz Boardwalk" article, he said that his father would have had no reason to contrive a reference to fire in the Freedom Trash Can. "I would take that article as gospel truth," Jack Boucher said.[62]

John Boucher was gruff and tough, but he also acted as an informal adviser to young reporters at the *Press*. Among them was Jon Katz, who in 1968 was at the outset of a career that took him to the *Philadelphia Inquirer* and *Boston Globe,* and to the *CBS Morning News* as executive producer. After leaving daily journalism, Katz became a media critic and commentator on digital media, as well as a prolific writer of mysteries and nonfiction.

Katz's first reporting job was at the *Atlantic City Press*, where John Boucher was his informal mentor. "He was very, very careful," Katz said of Boucher. "He was quite scrupulous about accuracy. . . . I remember him lecturing me all the time about accuracy." Boucher would often remind Katz that "'reputation is all you have.' He'd say that a lot," Katz said, adding, "I would give enormous credence to what he wrote."[63]

Katz recalled that Boucher felt an affinity for the police he covered and was inclined to look the other way were they to rough up a suspect. But it would have been exceedingly out of character for Boucher to have fabricated the reference to fire in the Freedom Trash Can, Katz said. "He was not creative enough" to have made up such a story.[64] Katz was the other reporter the *Press* sent to cover the women's liberation protest on the boardwalk, an event, he said, that was "formative in terms of my reporting" career. Significantly, Katz said he recalls that bras and other items *were* set afire during the demonstration and burned briefly. "I quite clearly remember the 'Freedom Trash Can,' and also remember some protestors putting their bras into it along with other articles of clothing, and some Pageant brochures, and setting the can on fire. I am quite certain of this," Katz stated.[65]

"I recall and remember noting at the time that the fire was small, and quickly was extinguished, and didn't pose a credible threat to the Boardwalk. I noted this as a reporter in case a fire did erupt. . . . It is my recollection that this burning was planned, and that a number of demonstrators brought bras and other articles of clothing to burn, including, I believe some underwear."[66] When the fire flickered out, Katz said, the police dragged the trash bin to the sand. Otherwise, Katz said, "Nobody made a big deal of it." He said he remembers Mario Floriani, Atlantic City's public safety commissioner, telling demonstrators, "You can protest but you just can't set fire to things."[67]

Katz wrote a sidebar article that the *Press* displayed beneath Boucher's "Bra-Burners Blitz Boardwalk" report. Katz's sidebar described the puzzled and mostly unfriendly reactions to the demonstration, quoting one confused passerby as saying, "I don't care if they march, but I wish to God I knew what they were marching about." Although Katz's article included references to demonstrators "throwing away their bras" and "waving their bras," it made no reference to fire in the Freedom Trash Can.[68] Asked about that, Katz said his article focused on boardwalk strollers and their reactions to the protest, not the demonstration itself. "I actually have no doubt about the fire," he said.[69]

Informed about Boucher's contemporaneous article and Katz's more recent recollections, Robin Morgan said through a spokeswoman, Carol Newton, "There were NO bras EVER burned at the 1968 protest."

Newton also said that "Morgan was present on the boardwalk the entire time" of the demonstration. "Steno pads, diapers, stiletto heels, corsets, bras, etc., were DUMPED into the [Freedom Trash] can but not burned."[70]

Other published news reports about the women's liberation protest included no mention of bras or other items having been set afire. The *New York Times* report, written by Charlotte Curtis, the women's editor, referred to "a symbolic bra-burning."[71] Katz turned to that phrase three years later in writing a retrospective account about the protest for the *Philadelphia Daily News.* "The program called for the now-famous 'burn-in,' featuring bras, girdles, and other 'repressive' female garments," Katz wrote in 1971, recalling how Floriani, the public safety commissioner, was "resplendent in full uniform" as he "marched onto the Boardwalk and informed the demonstrators that the burning of bras, or anything else, was forbidden by city ordinance. The demonstrators thought it over, and the burning became symbolic, with symbolic bras and a symbolic fire."[72]

Asked about that account, Katz said that the retrospective article does not contradict his recollections about fire in the Freedom Trash Can. The phrase "the burning became symbolic" refers to a sequence of events in which the small fire was extinguished and became "a symbolic fire," he said. "They stopped the burning and made it a symbolic burning."[73]

Katz's recollections about the 1968 protest are detailed and certainly support the passage in Boucher's article about bras and other items having been "burned in the 'Freedom Trash Can.'" Boucher's article carries a ring of authenticity. Had he intended to ridicule or belittle the protesters, Boucher surely would have given greater prominence in his article to burning bras. The passing reference to burning bras also suggests that Boucher assigned little significance to that aspect of the demonstration on the boardwalk. It was only *after* the protest—in columns by Van Horne and, more important, by Buchwald—that "bra burning" took on significance and became a term of derision. Similarly, Katz would seem to have little incentive to contrive an account of bra burning at the Miss America protest. The demonstrators at Atlantic City, he said, "were very exotic to me." It was at that protest, he said, that he first heard the epithet "sexist pig."[74]

And what is the broader significance of Boucher's article and Katz's recollections? At the very least, their reports offer fresh dimension to the bra-burning legend. They represent two eyewitness accounts that bras and other items were burned, or at least smoldered, in the Freedom

Trash Can. These descriptions offer compelling evidence that bras and other items *were* set afire, if briefly, at the 1968 Miss America protest in Atlantic City. This evidence cannot be taken lightly, dismissed, or ignored.

But it must be said as well that the eyewitness accounts of Boucher and Katz lend no support to the far more popular and vivid imagery that many bras went up in flames in flamboyant protest that September day. Their accounts offer no evidence to corroborate a widely held image of angry feminists demonstratively setting fire to their bras and tossing the flaming undergarments into a spectacular bonfire. Boucher's long-over-looked article and Katz's recollections offer no endorsement for that central and alluring feature of the media-driven myth. Demonstrative bra burning at Atlantic City would have been reckless and hazardous, coming so soon after the fire that destroyed a portion of the boardwalk,[75] and surely would have commanded prominence in Boucher's article. As such, Boucher's article and Katz's recollections effectively *bolster* the view that bra burning is a media-driven myth exaggerated by Van Horne, Buchwald, and many others. There was no "mass bra-burning."[76] Fire was, at most, a modest and fleeting aspect of the protest that day.

But the accounts by Boucher and Katz do suggest that the myth of mass or demonstrative bra burning needs to be modified. Their accounts offer compelling evidence that bras were set afire that day, though not with the flamboyance as the stereotype has it. Shorn of the adjectives *mass* or *flamboyant,* the term "bra burning" becomes nuanced, an epithet not entirely misapplied to the women's liberation protest at Atlantic City.

It is interesting to note, moreover, how the implication of *bra burning* has slowly morphed over the decades to take on a meaning that is somewhat less pejorative and less demeaning. In recent years, the term sometimes has been associated with female empowerment—a metaphor for assertiveness, audacity, and dedication to women's rights. It is not unusual for female college students to express such views. For some of them, "bra burning" has few negative associations. They find little reason to cringe at the epithet. Rather, they view bra burning as bold symbolism that connotes a refusal to conform to standards and expectations set by others—sentiments that certainly echo the views of the women who tossed undergarments into the Freedom Trash Can.

An early representation of bra burning's revised significance appeared in *Ms.* magazine in 1991, in a retrospective article by Lindsy Van Gelder, who in 1968 was a reporter for the women's pages of the *New York Post*. Writing twenty-three years after the Miss America protest, Van

Gelder argued that, however misleading the epithet may have been, "bra burner" carried moral weight in 1968. At the height of the war in Vietnam, "thousands of young men had set fire to their draft cards in public demonstrations. It was an act associated with dignity, bravery, and impeccable politics," Van Gelder wrote. "To talk about bras being burned was at one and the same time to speak in a language that the guys on the city desk could understand (i.e., tits) and to speak in code to the radicals of our generation."[77]

Another example of bra burning's evolving meaning came during a protest near the Ohio State University campus in 1999, when members of the Feminist Majority group attempted to burn a brassiere on the rickety porch of the residence of Bob Hewitt, a cartoonist for the student daily newspaper, the *Lantern*. The attempted bra burning was to protest Hewitt's unflattering caricature of students in Ohio State's women's studies program and, by extension, to demonstrate the group's assertiveness. The bra failed to catch fire,[78] however, and after a few awkward moments the demonstrators left the porch and their impromptu protest sputtered out.[79] The failed bra burning gained a measure of unsought attention for the Feminist Majority. It won top billing that year in the Campus Outrage Awards, given by the conservative Intercollegiate Studies Institute to call attention to acts of "extreme political correctness."[80]

A further example of bra burning's changing significance took place in February 2008 on *The Tyra Banks Show,* an afternoon television program that ended a five-year run in 2010 Banks took members of her studio audience into the chill of a winter's afternoon in New York for a made-for-television stunt about what women could do with ill-fitting brassieres. Banks wore an unzipped gray sweatshirt that revealed a powder-blue sports bra. Most of the women were clad only in brassieres above the waist. They clutched other bras as they stood before a burn barrel from which flames leapt hungrily. On Banks's word, they tossed the bras they were holding into the fire.

So finally, there it was: unmistakably, a bonfire of burning bras. Forty years after the myth of mass bra burnings emerged and was propelled by the riff of a humor columnist, the image had become a reality—in a gratuitous and puzzling gesture on afternoon television.

CHAPTER 8

Picture Power?

Confronting the Myths of the
Napalm Girl *Photograph*

Some things we think we know with certainty are simply
wrong. But we've heard them repeated so many times that
fact-checking no longer seems necessary.

—Daphne Bramham, "Truth Is Often a Casualty of Peace,"
Vancouver Sun (17 September 2015): B7

Few photographs of the Vietnam War era are as immediately recognizable or possess such raw emotional power as *The Terror of War,* a
black-and-white image showing a cluster of horror-stricken Vietnamese
children fleeing napalm bombs mistakenly dropped on their village by a
South Vietnamese attack plane.

At the center of the image is a naked girl, her arms outstretched, her
face contorted in agony. She was nine years old. The photograph was
taken June 8, 1972, near Trang Bang, in what was South Vietnam, by
Huynh Cong ("Nick") Ut of the Associated Press, who learned the craft
of photography as a teenager while working in a darkroom for the news
agency's bureau in Saigon.[1] Ut was twenty-one years old when he took
Terror of War, and was already a seasoned combat photographer.[2] His
photograph won a Pulitzer Prize in 1973. The naked girl in the photograph, Phan Thi Kim Phuc, suffered severe burns to her back, shoulder,
left arm, hairline, and part of her chest.[3] Thanks in part to Ut's efforts in
securing her hospitalization,[4] she recovered, although she still receives
treatment for her wounds.[5] In 1992, while traveling from Russia to Cuba,
where she was studying, Kim Phuc and her husband, Bui Huy Toan, left
the plane on a refueling stop in Newfoundland and sought and were
granted asylum in Canada.[6] She and her family live near Toronto.

FIGURE 17. One of the most powerful photographs of the Vietnam War was *The Terror of War*, taken by Nick Ut. It shows the effects of a misdirected napalm attack in June 1972 near the village of Trang Bang in South Vietnam. The naked girl at center is Phan Thi Kim Phuc, then nine years old. She suffered burns so severe that she nearly died from her wounds. [*Associated Press photo/Nick Ut*]

Terror of War is better known by its colloquial title, *Napalm Girl*. In its visceral power and presumptive impact, *Napalm Girl* rivals other iconic images of the war period—such as the 1963 photograph of the self-immolation of a Buddhist monk in Saigon and the 1968 photograph of the summary execution in that city of a suspected Viet Cong guerrilla. *Napalm Girl* has received many accolades. It was deemed one of ten photographs "that changed the world" in a ranking by Britain's *Daily Telegraph*.[7] It was said to have helped define "a golden era for photojournalism."[8] In the words of Horst Faas—the Associated Press photographer and editor who helped make sure *Napalm Girl* cleared the news agency's wires despite its depiction of frontal nudity[9]—it is "an icon of photography for all times,"[10] "a picture that doesn't rest."[11]

Faas, who supervised Ut in Saigon, was quite right. In the decades since it was taken, *Napalm Girl* has indeed become a photograph that "does not rest," a rare image that remains an insistent statement about the horrors of war and its terrorizing effects on civilians.[12] And *Napalm Girl* has become much more than that. Over the years, the superlatives associated with the image have edged into hyperbole and exaggeration. *Napalm Girl* has become invested with mythic qualities and a power that no photograph, however distinctive and exceptional, can project.

Napalm Girl has become embroidered with media myths—false, dubious, or improbable tales about and/or propagated by the news media that masquerade as factual. The myths of *Napalm Girl* are fourfold and include these often-invoked claims: the photograph depicted the consequences of an aerial bombing by American-piloted or American-directed warplanes; it hastened an end to the Vietnam War; it galvanized American public opinion against the conflict; and it appeared on the front pages of newspapers across the United States. None of these claims is accurate; none can be sustained by dispassionate assessment of relevant evidence.

The purpose here is by no means to excuse or rationalize the errant aerial attack at Trang Bang. Rather, this chapter calls attention to and seeks to correct distortions in the historical record. It recognizes the importance of not confounding the aesthetic and emotional impact of *Napalm Girl* with its political effects.[13]

Debunking the myths of *Napalm Girl* is vital for a number of reasons, not the least of which is to insist on a more complete understanding of a prominent visual artifact of a bitter and prolonged war. Confronting the myths serves to puncture the post hoc causality commonly associated with the image and deflate the notion that a single still photograph was decisive to the outcome of the Vietnam conflict. To assert that it was decisive is to indulge in media-centrism; it is to stretch logic.

This chapter draws on a variety of sources, notably a detailed review of forty leading U.S. daily newspapers published in June 1972. The newspapers were examined to determine how—or if at all—they displayed *Napalm Girl* in the immediate aftermath of the photograph's distribution by the Associated Press. Other sources for this chapter include transcripts of oral history interviews conducted with Ut, Faas, and other principal figures behind the *Napalm Girl* story, as well as news reports and commentaries published in U.S. and international media that, over the years, have referred to the presumed effects of *Napalm Girl*. Such references tend to be more than casual or offhand: they are tireless and are sometimes invoked in assessing other powerful and more recent news images—such as the widely published photograph in 2015 of the body, face down in the sand, of a little Syrian Kurdish boy who drowned near a resort in Turkey. He and his family had fled violence in Syria and were headed for Greece when their overcrowded boat capsized.

The photograph of the boy's lifeless body on the beach inspired many references to *Napalm Girl*,[14] including this observation by Daphne Bramham, a columnist for the *Vancouver Sun:* "The poignant image of the little boy is reminiscent . . . of a Vietnamese girl running, crying, her clothes burned off by a napalm bomb dropped by Americans."[15] In stating that the aerial attack was carried out "by Americans," Bramham fell victim to the most tenacious and perhaps most perplexing of the four media myths associated with *Napalm Girl*.

ATTACK WAS CARRIED OUT BY U.S. WARPLANES

Bramham is one of many journalists who have asserted that Americans dropped the napalm that wounded Kim Phuc. Similar claims—usually presented without attribution—have been made over the years, and sometimes in curious contexts. For example, the *New Yorker* magazine in 2012 published a brief retrospective review that likened the napalm attack at Trang Bang to a scene in Alfred Hitchcock's film *The Birds,* in which "screaming schoolkids fleeing down a lonely road disturbingly presage[d] the iconic news image of Vietnamese children escaping from American napalm attacks."[16]

Even the Associated Press, Ut's employer and owner of the rights to *Napalm Girl,* has erroneously described the circumstances of the bombing at Trang Bang. The news agency said in a dispatch in 2000 that a "U.S. napalm attack . . . seared" Kim Phuc's body.[17] A few years earlier, the Associated Press said in a report about Kim Phuc's taking Canadian citizenship that her village in Vietnam had been "hit by a U.S. napalm bomb."[18]

Lawrence O'Donnell, host of the MSNBC program *The Last Word,* invoked the myth on his show in 2013 during an angry commentary about the effects of napalm. He referred to Kim Phuc as "the most famous napalm victim in history," noting that she was nine years old "when we [Americans] dropped napalm on her village in Vietnam" and that she spent months "recovering in an American hospital in Saigon." O'Donnell said, "We dropped napalm on her, and then we saved her life."[19]

References to the myth have surfaced in international news outlets as well. London's *Independent* newspaper said in 1993 in an overview of powerful wartime photography that *Napalm Girl* depicted "terrified children after an American attack."[20] In 1989, the *Sunday Mail* in Queensland erred twice in a single sentence in stating that "US bombers dumped a planeload of napalm onto the pagoda where [Kim Phuc and] her family [were] hiding." Not only were U.S. bombers absent at Trang Bang, but the village pagoda was not targeted.[21]

The notion that Americans dropped the napalm that wounded Kim Phuc and other civilians at Trang Bang took hold, slowly, in the months following the attack. Senator George S. McGovern, the Democratic nominee for president, referred to the photograph in a nationally televised speech October 10, 1972, in which he invoked the image of "the little South Vietnamese girl, Kim, fleeing in terror" and "running naked into the lens of that camera. That picture ought to break the heart of every American," McGovern said. "How can we rest with the grim knowledge that the burning napalm that splashed over little Kim and countless thousands of other children was dropped in the name of America?"[22]

How he determined that Kim Phuc was representative of "countless thousands of other children" sprayed by napalm, McGovern did not say.[23] But the candidate's metaphoric claim that the napalm had been "dropped in the name of America" plainly overstated what happened at Trang Bang on June 8, 1972. The attack was an errant attempt by South Vietnamese forces to roust North Vietnamese troops from bunkers dug at the outskirts of the village, which is quite clear from contemporaneous news reports about the fighting that day. Those reports were unequivocal in stating that the misdirected napalm bombing had been carried out by a South Vietnamese Air Force pilot flying a propeller-driven, American-made A-1 Skyraider.

Fox Butterfield of the *New York Times,* for example, reported that "a South Vietnamese plane mistakenly dropped flaming napalm right on his troops and a cluster of civilians. In an instant five women and children and a dozen South Vietnamese soldiers were badly burned, their skin peeling off in huge pink and black chunks."[24] Donald Kirk of the *Chicago Tribune* wrote of "napalm dropped by a Vietnamese air force Skyraider diving onto the wrong target."[25]

Christopher Wain, a correspondent for Britain's ITN network, wrote a detailed witness account of the bombing for the United Press International news agency that described how four napalm canisters came to be dropped on civilians and soldiers:

> South Vietnamese army troops were getting the worst of the firefight . . . with about 100 North Vietnamese infantry, who were dug into bunkers . . .

on the outskirts of Trang Bang. At about 11:30 a.m. the heavy monsoon rains lifted enough for the South Vietnamese to call in an airstrike, but we—a group of watching newsmen—were surprised when the A1 Skyraiders turned up. The cloud base was very low at about 600 feet, and the A1s kept disappearing into the clouds. A forward air control plane flew in and, ignoring bursts of gunfire, sent in two white marker rockets to indicate the North Vietnamese positions. The ARVN [South Vietnamese troops] showed their own lines in the traditional way with a purple smoke grenade. But the white smoke dissipated in the rain. It was then when things started going wrong. An A1 came in and, as we saw the four high explosive bombs fall from his wings, we realized they had been released over the wrong side of the road at least 300 yards from the North Vietnamese bunkers. The bombs exploded and then we could see the ARVN troops racing across the road. Their own positions had become death traps. Among the olive-green ARVN uniforms, I could see white shirts of the villagers who had been caught in the crossfire and also were trying to get to safety, and I could also see what they couldn't— another A1 coming in, straight at them.[26]

Wain surmised that the Skyraider pilot could see the figures running on the ground but mistook them for fleeing North Vietnamese troops. "You cannot identify people when you are 100 feet up and flying at 300 miles per hour," he wrote, "so he flew in and dropped four canisters of napalm on top of them. They exploded right on target."[27] While he did not mention her by name, Wain described the wounds Kim Phuc suffered:

Out of the dense black smoke caused by the flaming [napalm] bombs, a group of figures eventually emerged. . . . A little girl, about 9, stumbled forward, barefoot, naked, whimpering. . . . The girl's back was in shreds with the skin hanging off, as if she had suffered a sudden instant case of third-degree sunburn. As she reached me, she stopped. An ARVN soldier asked me if I had any water. I emptied my water-bottle on her back. There's not much you can do for napalm burns, but water does reduce the surface temperature. The little girl stopped whimpering.[28]

Wain concluded his dispatch by writing: "These were South Vietnamese planes dropping napalm on South Vietnamese peasants and troops. I believe the usual Vietnamese phrase is 'Xin Loi'—or 'Sorry about that.'"[29] The fight at Trang Bang was an all-Vietnamese encounter.

While exaggerated, McGovern's claim that the napalm had been dropped "in the name of America" corresponded to the antiwar thrust of his campaign. The protracted conflict in Vietnam was one of the strongest issues in McGovern's struggling and ill-fated run for the presidency in 1972. His remark, "in the name of America," implied American culpability and surely strengthened the mistaken view then taking

FIGURE 18. Newsmen and South Vietnamese troops clustered around Kim Phuc after she was badly burned in an errant napalm attack in June 1972. One of the journalists poured water on her back, seeking to calm the pain of her wounds. She was taken to a hospital soon afterward. [*Associated Press photo/Nick Ut*]

hold that the attack had been carried out by U.S. forces. As Nick Thimmesch, a syndicated political columnist, wrote after McGovern's speech in late October 1972, "Many casual readers and viewers think that a U.S. plane was bombing civilians."[30]

McGovern's claim was perhaps the first to blur the circumstances of the attack and suggest that responsibility extended to Americans—who weren't at Trang Bang, but who manufactured the warplane and the napalm it dropped. The American writer and filmmaker Susan Sontag likewise did so in her acclaimed work *On Photography,* which came out in 1973. Sontag referred in the book to Kim Phuc as "a naked South Vietnamese child . . . sprayed by American napalm, running down a highway toward the camera."[31] Sontag's reference to "American napalm" insinuated direct U.S. involvement in, or at least responsibility for, the bombing. It was a reference that Sontag repeated in *Regarding the Pain of Others,* which was published in 2002. In it, Sontag wrote of "children from a village that has just been doused with American napalm."[32]

Other writers have invoked similar allusions to American culpability for the aerial attack. Nancy K. Miller, for example, wrote of "the horror-struck girl running from American napalm,"[33] and Sylvia Shin Hue Chong claimed in her book *The Oriental Obscene* that "many viewers experience Ut's photograph as a call to culpability, even if the facts of the bombing allow for an alibi of [American] blamelessness."[34]

The *New York Times* also has insinuated American responsibility for the civilians wounded at Trang Bang. In its obituary in 2012 about Horst Faas, the newspaper said the photograph depicted "the aftermath of one of the thousands of bombings in the countryside by American planes: a group of terror-stricken children fleeing the scene, a girl in the middle of the group screaming and naked, her clothes incinerated by burning napalm."[35]

It was pointed out to the *New York Times* that the attack was carried out by South Vietnamese pilots, as contemporaneous news reports had made clear. Peter Keepnews, an assistant obituary editor at the newspaper, said in reply: "You are correct that the bombing in question was conducted by the South Vietnamese Air Force. However, the obituary referred only to 'American planes,' and there does not seem to be any doubt that this plane was American—a Douglas A-1 Skyraider, to be precise."[36] As if the warplane's manufacturer was central or relevant to who carried out the attack.

This was pointed out to Keepnews, and yet the newspaper resisted for weeks before publishing a grudging semi-correction that embraced

Keepnews's labored reasoning: "While the planes that carried out that attack were 'American planes' in the sense that they were made in the United States, they were flown by the South Vietnamese Air Force, not by American forces."[37]

Daphne Bramham, the *Vancouver Sun* columnist, was not so reluctant to correct her mistaken reference to *Napalm Girl*. Shortly after her column was published, Bramham's attention was directed to the erroneous passage that the napalm had been "dropped by Americans." A few days later, she wrote another column acknowledging the error and stating: "It is often said that in war, truth is the first casualty. But . . . it is also a battle to keep truth from being a casualty after the peace."[38]

The mistaken notion that Americans were central to the attack at Trang Bang hardened in 1996, when John Plummer, a troubled former U.S. Army captain, came forward to say he had ordered the bombing.[39] He also implied that he had piloted the Skyraider that dropped the napalm. Plummer's claim was widely publicized after he met Kim Phuc in Washington, D.C., following a ceremony at the Vietnam Veterans Memorial on Veterans Day in 1996. Kim Phuc was a speaker at the program, during which Plummer passed a note addressed to her saying, "I am that man"[40]—that is, the person responsible for the napalm attack years before at Trang Bang.

In June 1997, Plummer went on the ABC News program *Nightline* to describe what he said was his torment about the attack. "Had I not ordered that air strike," he said, Kim Phuc "wouldn't have gotten burned like that."[41] Plummer referred to *Napalm Girl* as "one of the most expressive photographs I've ever seen and, I mean, you could almost look at that photograph and hear that little girl and the little boy on the left side of the frame screaming. And then to realize that it was a result of something that I had done just really devastated me."[42]

Plummer's claims were startling, suggesting an unequivocal and previously unknown American dimension to the napalm attack. But in December 1997, Plummer's account was exposed as fanciful in a report by Tom Bowman, then of the *Baltimore Sun*. Bowman quoted Plummer as acknowledging that he was neither the pilot who dropped the napalm at Trang Bang nor the person who ordered the attack. Bowman's article also quoted James F. Hollingsworth, the lieutenant general who in 1972 was leader of the U.S. Third Regional Assistance Command, which advised South Vietnamese forces in a district that included Trang Bang. Hollingsworth said that he himself "couldn't order Vietnamese planes into the air," let alone a low-level staff officer who, the general said, essentially filled the role of a "handyman" to the operations chief. Hollingsworth made clear that Plummer "would have [had] no authority to order anyone to do anything."[43]

In an interview in 2015, Bowman said he did not know why Plummer had made up the account about having had a direct role in the bombing. He may have been "wrapping himself in the pain of the Vietnam veteran," Bowman said. "Who knows?" He added, "Everybody thinks they were American planes" that dropped the napalm at Trang Bang.[44]

The attack at Trang Bang was carried out by aircraft of the 518th Fighter Squadron of the South Vietnamese Air Force. The pilot of the warplane that dropped the napalm was identified in a poem titled "The Skyraider," which was included in a book of poetry published in 2000. The poem and accompanying textual material said the pilot was Duc Tu Nguyen,[45] who fled South Vietnam just before Saigon fell to the communists in 1975. He settled in the United States.

"The Skyraider" was written by Linh Duy Vo, a Vietnamese poet who endowed aircraft with voice to tell of the bombing run at Trang Bang. Vo's poem reads in part:

> Trang Bang is under attack, there come the North Vietnamese
> Children, men, and women keep running
> The Communists are so close, Duc, let me in.
> Just you, Duc, and me now,
> Stop the enemy from charging South Vietnamese units,
> Get the napalm in, go ahead, release it from my body
> They are firing upon me; oh, I am hit, not bad.
> . . .
> Oh, no, who took the photo of my fight?
> That's awful, I burned the little girl, Duc, I did it.
> You fought the Viet Cong, stopping their atrocities
> Don't cry now, Duc, our country needs you, keep fighting
> Another sortie request just came in, hurry, get on my wing.[46]

The poem closes with the line, "Duc, say it, say: 'I am that man.'"[47] The passage refers to the note Plummer passed to Kim Phuc on Veterans Day in 1996. Vo said he helped arrange that meeting.[48] Vo said in an interview that he learned of the pilot's identity from another member of the 518th Fighter Squadron, Chuyen Van Nguyen. "Everyone in the squadron knew," Vo said.[49]

In a separate interview, Chuyen Van Nguyen confirmed the pilot's identity as Duc Tu Nguyen and said that knowledge had come from "talk among ourselves" in the squadron.[50] Nguyen said he had completed training in the United States and joined the 518th Fighter Squadron a few weeks after the attack at Trang Bang and subsequently flew many missions with Duc Tu Nguyen. They once were very close, Nguyen said, adding that he and Duc Tu Nguyen were aboard a C-119 military transport aircraft that made a perilous escape from South Vietnam's Tan Son Nhut Air Base in late April 1975. "It was a very close call," Nguyen said. "We were under attack" by North Vietnamese forces as the aircraft took off. "It was very, very scary."[51] Nguyen said Duc Tu Nguyen lives in Northern California and has not spoken publicly about the attack at Trang Bang since coming to the United States.[52] Duc Tu Nguyen did not reply to the author's email requests for an interview.

NAPALM GIRL HASTENED THE WAR'S END

In June 2012, at the fortieth anniversary of *Napalm Girl,* the Associated Press distributed a retrospective story about the photograph, an article that appeared widely in U.S. news media. "In the picture," the article stated, "the girl will always be 9-years-old and wailing 'Too hot! Too hot!' as she runs down the road away from her burning Vietnamese village." It said the photograph "communicated the horrors of the Vietnam War in a way words could never describe, helping to end one of the most divisive wars in American history."[53] The article, however, presented no evidence about how *Napalm Girl* had accomplished this.

Claims that the photograph hastened an end to the war have circulated for years. For example, Nancy Miller wrote that *Napalm Girl* "crystallized anti-war sentiment and may even 'have stopped the war,' as many anti-war veterans claimed."[54] In an article in 1995 about Kim Phuc, Scotland's *Daily Mail* described the photograph as having "packed enough explosive power to help end a war."[55] The *New York Daily News* asserted in 2012 that *Napalm Girl* arguably "sped up America's retreat" from Southeast Asia.[56] In a review of an exhibition of images of war at the Louvre in Paris in 2014, the *Guardian* newspaper of London declared that the photograph had "expedited the end of the Vietnam war."[57]

Additionally, a report in April 2015 by KABC television in Los Angeles said the photograph "is credited with shortening a conflict that was already being called unwinnable."[58] An exhibits review published that year in a magazine supplement of Hong Kong's *South China Morning Post* newspaper said the image was "so horrific that it helped prompt the American withdrawal from Vietnam."[59] In her column discussing

FIGURE 19. Forty years after the taking the *Napalm Girl* photograph, Nick Ut of the Associated Press received a Leica Hall of Fame award. Kim Phuc, the girl in the photograph, joined in congratulating Ut. She lives in Canada, he in California. They have been friends for years. [*Associated Press photo*/Damian Dovarganes]

the images of the Syrian boy on the beach and of Kim Phuc, Bramham of the *Vancouver Sun* wrote that *Napalm Girl* had "helped end a war."[60]

Moreover, Ut has given interviews that encouraged the notion that his photograph had ended the war. For example, he was quoted in an article in *LA Weekly* in 2014 as saying: "When I pressed the [camera's shutter] button, I knew. This picture will stop the war."[61] In another interview in 2014, Ut said: "That picture stopped the war in Vietnam. . . . People, when they see the picture, say, 'I don't want any more war.'"[62] In an oral history interview with the Newseum, the museum of news in Washington, D.C., Ut said American war veterans have told him that the reason "we all [went] home was your picture."[63] In 1999, Kim Phuc was quoted by the *Toronto Star* as saying: "I accept that the pictured changed the world. If it stopped the war, then I am happy. Because of that, there are children who didn't die."[64]

Invariably, claims that the photograph hastened the war's end are accompanied by little or no supporting evidence and by little or no explanation about how a still photograph could have exerted such influence. Sometimes, temporal proximity is invoked as ostensible evidence. Seven months after *Napalm Girl* was taken, the United States and the North Vietnamese reached a peace agreement after prolonged negotiations in Paris.[65] But that agreement did not end the war. Not until late April 1975, when North Vietnamese forces routed South Vietnamese troops and entered Saigon (now Ho Chi Minh City), did the protracted conflict reach its end. The North Vietnamese takeover came nearly three years after *Napalm Girl* was published.

Claims that the photograph was a factor in ending the war are untenable in other respects as well. *Napalm Girl* had no discernable effect or influence on the U.S. policy of "Vietnamization"—the shifting of the burden of the ground war to the South Vietnamese while dramatically reducing the U.S. combat presence in the country. Vietnamization was announced early in the presidency of Richard M. Nixon, and as the policy was put in place, U.S. troop strength in Vietnam fell steadily from a peak of 543,000 men in April 1969.[66] By early June 1972, about 60,000 U.S. troops remained in Vietnam,[67] a drawdown neither accelerated nor otherwise influenced by the publication of *Napalm Girl*. In fact, a broad North Vietnamese offensive launched in South Vietnam at the end of March 1972 had the temporary effect of slowing the pace of U.S. troop withdrawals.[68]

Vietnamization sharply reduced the death toll of U.S. forces; for all of 1972, 759 U.S. military personnel were killed in Vietnam, the lowest number of fatalities since 1964, the year before the escalation of U.S. forces in the country.[69] For American ground forces, then, the war was winding down long before the aerial attack at Trang Bang. By June 1972, nearly all U.S. combat troops had been removed from Vietnam.[70]

This is not to say that Nixon was oblivious to *Napalm Girl*. The president briefly discussed the photograph with his top aide, H. R. Haldeman, on June 12, 1972, in a conversation captured by Nixon's secret White House tape-recording system. The tapes show that Haldeman brought up what he called the "napalm thing" and Nixon replied by saying, "I wonder if that was a fix"—that is, had it been staged? "Could have been," Haldeman said, "because they got that picture of the little girl without any clothes. It made a hell of a bounce out of that one, but, it was North Viet—South Vietnamese bombing South Vietnamese, by accident. They thought they were hitting the enemy but they got their own refugees, apparently. Napalm bothers people. You get a picture of a little girl with her clothes burnt off." Nixon replied, "I wondered about that."[71]

William Westmoreland, the former U.S. commander in Vietnam, also questioned the authenticity of *Napalm Girl*. In a speech in Florida several years after the war, Westmoreland said he had been told that Kim Phuc was injured not in an aerial attack but "burned by a hibachi," or an open grill. The general's remarks were disputed by Ut[72] and roundly dismissed.

In any case, *Napalm Girl* had no known effect on Nixon's thinking about the war. His attention was soon diverted: on June 17, 1972, burglars linked to his reelection campaign were arrested inside the headquarters of the Democratic National Committee in what was the seminal crime of the Watergate scandal. Six days later, Nixon approved Haldeman's suggested plan to divert the FBI's investigation into Watergate, a decision that was disclosed in 1974 and ended his presidency.[73]

While the U.S. troop presence in Vietnam was winding down, Nixon in April 1972 ordered American warplanes to conduct extensive bombing raids over Hanoi and Haiphong, the largest cities in North Vietnam. The attacks were a retaliatory response to the massive Easter Offensive that North Vietnamese forces had launched in the northern provinces of South Vietnam in late March 1972. The aerial attacks on Hanoi and Haiphong and other targets in North Vietnam continued until October 1972—uninterrupted or undeterred by the publication of *Napalm Girl*.[74] Nixon ordered the bombing resumed shortly before Christmas in 1972, a gambit to force the North Vietnamese to reopen peace talks that had broken down in Paris. The so-called Christmas Bombing of North Vietnam continued until December 29, and the talks were resumed the following month.

A search of a database of leading U.S. newspapers found no articles, editorials, or commentaries published from December 1, 1972, to January 15, 1973, (or before, during, and immediately after the Christmas Bombing) that specifically mentioned or referred to *Napalm Girl*. The nearest proximate reference to the photograph came in a comment by Father Richard T. McSorley, a Jesuit priest and Georgetown University professor, who joined a small anti–Vietnam War protest outside the White House on Christmas Day 1972: "As long as a child can be torn apart with napalm and B-52 bombs, . . . we are not going to celebrate Christmas in the usual way."[75] But in no way did *Napalm Girl* alter or otherwise influence the broad trajectory of U.S. troop withdrawal from Vietnam.

NAPALM GIRL GALVANIZED PUBLIC OPINION
AGAINST THE WAR

Not only did Susan Sontag refer to "American napalm" in *On Photography,* but she also claimed that Ut's photograph "probably did more to increase the public revulsion against the war than a hundred hours of televised barbarities."[76] Sontag offered no evidence to substantiate that claim, and neither did George Esper when he visited Trang Bang in 1993. Esper, a veteran Associated Press correspondent, recalled the aerial attack there and said that it had "tilted American public opinion against the war."[77] Similar assertions have resonated over the years and in many contexts. The "single, searing image played no small part in deepening opposition in the United States to the war," Samuel G. Freedman, a veteran reporter and journalism professor, wrote in his book, *Letters to a Young Journalist.*[78] *Napalm Girl* said a reporter for ABC's affiliate station in Los Angeles in 2012 had stirred in the United States "a firestorm of outrage over Vietnam."[79] In 2014, *LA Weekly* said the photograph "is credited with swaying public opinion against the war."[80] Similarly, London's *Guardian* said in 2015 that the photograph "was widely credited with turning the tide of public opinion against the war."[81] A commentary in London's *Independent* newspaper in 2015 said, "That single picture turned American public opinion against that terrible war."[82] The tabloid *Sun* of London said in 2015 the photograph of Kim Phuc "screaming with agony of napalm burns as she fled her village swung American public opinion against the war in Vietnam."[83]

None of these assertions was accompanied by compelling documentation or supporting evidence. That's because, by June 1972, American public opinion had long since turned against the Vietnam War. Sixty-one percent of respondents to a Gallup poll conducted in May 1971—more than a year before the napalm bombing at Trang Bang—said it had been a mistake to send U.S. troops to fight in Vietnam, while only 31 percent said it had not been a mistake. When Gallup next asked the question, in a survey in January 1973, about the time the United States and the North Vietnamese reached a peace agreement, the results were essentially unchanged: 61 percent of respondents said sending U.S. forces to Vietnam had been a mistake, and 29 percent said it had not.[84]

American public opinion had begun to turn against the war by October 1967, when 47 percent of respondents to the Gallup poll, a plurality, said it was a mistake to have sent troops to Vietnam; 44 percent said it had not been a mistake. When Gallup first asked the question in late summer 1965, 24 percent of respondents said it had been a mistake to send troops to Vietnam; 60 percent said it had not.[85]

Americans' changing views about the war have been defined in four discrete phases: the first was an "innocence" phase, lasting from 1964 to mid-1965, or just before the deployment of sizable numbers of U.S. combat troops in Vietnam; a "rally-round-the-flag" period, from mid-1965 to mid-1966; an "escalation" phase, from mid-1966 to early 1968; and a lengthy "withdrawal" phase that stretched from 1968 to the end of U.S. military presence in Vietnam in 1973.[86] These phases further signal that American sentiment for leaving Vietnam had begun building long before *Napalm Girl*. As such, it is untenable to assert that the photograph turned Americans against the war.

Ut has offered an intriguing dimension to the notion that his photograph had powerful effects on public opinion. He said in an interview in 2012 that *Napalm Girl* prompted antiwar protests in major international cities: "The next day, there were anti-war protests all over the world. Japan, London, Paris. . . . Every day after that, people were protesting in Washington, D.C., outside the White House. 'Napalm Girl' was everywhere."[87] The claim is extravagant. A review of the front pages of leading U.S. newspapers reveals no reports of antiwar protests of the sort that Ut described in the interview. Disturbing though it was, *Napalm Girl* did not prompt Americans to take to the streets in rallies or demonstrations against the war.[88]

It is no doubt asking too much of a still photograph to stir far-reaching protest. Philip Kennicott, a Pulitzer Prize–winning critic for the *Washington Post,* considered this matter in an essay about the modest outrage stirred by images of children killed and wounded in Syria's brutal civil war that began in 2011: "We choose to look, we bear as much as we can, yet we often turn away in anger or annoyance when an image seems to demand too much of us. Images of suffering children, in particular, are subject to a kind of emotional deflation, losing power if used too often or without regard to how we can channel the feelings they invoke."[89]

NAPALM GIRL WAS ON FRONT PAGES EVERYWHERE

It often is said that *Napalm Girl* was so arresting and so extraordinarily newsworthy that it was published on the front pages of newspapers across the United States and around the world. In her book about Kim Phuc, Denise Chong wrote that the photograph "was picked up by editors of newspapers around the world and printed on their front pages."[90] In their journal article about the image, Robert Hariman and John Louis Lucaites said *Napalm Girl* was "published all over the world" the day after it was taken.[91] An Associated Press newsletter published in June 1972 said of *Napalm Girl:* "No single photo in recent weeks has won so many big [newspaper] displays."[92]

Such observations suggest that *Napalm Girl* received universally prominent treatment in newspapers—an interpretation disputed by a review of the contents of forty leading U.S. daily newspapers published at the time. These newspapers, all subscribers to Associated Press services, were far from unanimous in publishing *Napalm Girl* on their front pages.

The forty newspapers, all of which were published in major American cities, were reviewed from June 8 to June 12, 1972, inclusive.[93] That period includes the date *Napalm Girl* was taken and the days immediately afterward—when interest in the photograph would have been keen, and when articles, editorials, and other commentaries about it were most likely to have been published in American newspapers.

Of the forty titles examined, twenty-one—slightly more than half—published *Napalm Girl* on the front page, most of them doing so on June 9, 1972. (The photograph was transmitted in time for some U.S. evening newspapers to publish the image in editions of June 8, 1972.) Of these twenty-one newspapers, fourteen displayed the photograph at or above the front-page fold, a newspaper's most prominent and coveted placement. Six of the forty newspapers published *Napalm Girl* on inside pages.

But thirteen newspapers examined—nearly one third of the sample—did not publish the photograph at all. Those newspapers were: *Arizona Republic, Dallas Morning News, Denver Post, Des Moines Register, Detroit Free Press, Hartford Courant, Honolulu Star-Bulletin, Houston Post, Indianapolis News, Los Angeles Herald Examiner, Newark Star-Ledger, Omaha World Herald,* and *Pittsburgh Post-Gazette.* Competitive factors may explain why a few of those titles did not publish the photograph. The *Indianapolis Star,* for example, displayed *Napalm Girl* at the top of its front page, accompanied by Christopher Wain's first-person report; such prominent treatment may have discouraged the rival *Indianapolis News* from publishing the image.

Reservations about the frontal nudity shown in *Napalm Girl* no doubt led some U.S. newspapers to decline to publish the photograph prominently, if at all. The depth of such reluctance remains largely speculative, however. Publications that might have discussed editors' objections to publishing frontal nudity—the *Editor & Publisher* trade journal, for example, and the *Columbia Journalism Review*—did not address the matter. Horst Faas said in an oral history interview in 2007 that he believed the *New York Times* and "other papers" debated whether to publish the photograph because they "didn't see a burning girl, they saw a naked girl. They didn't see a child, they saw a girl and they looked between her legs and they saw something dark and it wasn't pubic hair, it was dirt. We even printed the photo in a way that pubic hair does not come out strongly in the wire transmission, so we didn't doctor it, but we printed it softly, softly," said Faas, a German national who spoke English as a second language. "There was a gray overtone, which helped in getting the picture across" the Associated Press wire, he said.[94] Faas credited Hal Buell, the news agency's executive news photo editor at the time, for his decisive intervention in approving the picture for transmission.[95] In an interview, Buell recalled having no hesitation about sending the photograph to Associated Press clients. "How could you not move it?" he said, adding that *Napalm Girl* did not come across as prurient. Rather, it was an "extremely dramatic horror-of-war picture."[96]

The *New York Times* was one of the few newspapers to publish *Napalm Girl* twice during the period examined. The newspaper placed the photograph at the lower left corner of its front page on June 9, 1972, and published a cropped version two days later to accompany a Week in Review essay about napalm.[97] The *Philadelphia Inquirer* published the photograph twice in as many days—above the front-page fold on June 9, 1972,[98] and inside the main section on the following day as a tightly cropped version to accompany a follow-up story about the Trang Bang attack.[99] The *Atlanta Constitution* gave the photograph similar treatment, publishing it below the fold of its front page on June 9, 1972,[100] and as a tightly cropped version the next day on its second page.

The *Washington Post* displayed *Napalm Girl* in a rather odd and jarring fashion, placing it at the lower right-hand corner of its front page on June 9, 1972, adjacent to two articles that offered upbeat assessments about war-related developments.[101] The articles were side-by-side, beneath a shared headline that read: "Vietnam: Scents of Success." Next to that headline was the photograph. The bombing at Trang Bang was mentioned in the *Post* that day in an Associated Press dispatch on page A20.[102]

While many of the forty newspapers published articles about the Trang Bang napalm attack, only three of them printed editorials specifically about the photograph and its significance. The three news-papers were the *Boston Globe, New York Post,* and *New York Times,* all of which described the misdirected bombing as emblematic of the terrible blunder the Vietnam War had become. "When," asked the *New York Post,* "will this bloodiest and most bestial of wars also be recog-nized as the monstrous mistake that it is? The picture of the children [fleeing the napalm attack] will never leave anyone who saw it."[103]

Just three newspapers examined—the *Boston Globe, Los Angeles Times,* and *Philadelphia Inquirer*—published editorial cartoons that clearly were inspired by the photograph or the Trang Bang attack. Of the three, the *Inquirer's* sketch, by staff cartoonist Tony Auth, was the most stark and powerful. Auth drew the likeness of Kim Phuc and the other children in their flight. "Suffer the little children . . . " the caption read.

CONCLUSION

Timothy Snyder, a history professor at Yale University, has noted that "all good history revises and corrects the errors of collective memory, which follows its own muses."[104] Snyder's observation has relevance to this discussion about *Napalm Girl.* Excising the myths of *Napalm Girl* allows the image to be regarded and assessed more fairly and on its own terms. Debunking the myths of *Napalm Girl* does nothing to diminish the photograph's exceptionality. But removing the barnacles of myth effectively frees the photograph from association with feats and effects that are quite implausible.

It is remarkable that a still photograph has been linked to such a variety of outcomes, and the question that inevitably follows is, why? Why is so much presumptive power and influence invested in a single image, more than forty years after it was taken? One explanation can be found in the photograph's graphic rawness and in what Horst Faas identified as its disturbing restlessness. Because the image is so visceral, and because it captures the pain and terror of innocents, it surely *must* have had significant effects at the time it was published. Assigning such presumed effects to *Napalm Girl* allows contemporary audiences to understand, and to ratify, the photograph's exceptionality.

Napalm Girl also demonstrates the allure of the post hoc fallacy of causation: *post hoc ergo propter hoc,* or "after this, therefore because of this." U.S. troop withdrawal from Vietnam was completed and the peace treaty was reached in 1973, both after *Napalm Girl* was taken.

As such, *Napalm Girl* must have been an important causal influence. But of course no single photograph, and no single event, hastened the war's end or turned American public opinion against the conflict. The war's duration, its uncertain policy objectives, its contested morality, and its toll in dead and wounded were far more decisive factors in how the conflict ended for Americans.

This leaves some powerful, lingering questions: Why is *Napalm Girl* invoked so readily as an example of, or metaphor for, the consequences of America's failed military intervention in Vietnam? Why is the photograph so often mischaracterized as showing the effects of "U.S. napalm" or a "U.S. air strike"? Perhaps it is a matter of what Shelby Steele has termed "poetic truth"—the bending of "the actual truth in order to assert a larger *essential* truth that supports one's ideological position. It makes the actual truth seem secondary or irrelevant."[105] Since the days of George McGovern's doomed campaign for the presidency, the photograph has been associated with a narrative that the U.S. role in Vietnam was amoral and foolhardy and that Kim Phuc's wounds were, in the words of the critic Philip Kennicott, "the collateral damage of a war we made."[106] In that telling, *Napalm Girl* has been appropriated to illustrate the consequences of America's intervention. But to make that argument is to misrepresent the photograph, distort its meaning, and garble the circumstances of its making.

CHAPTER 9

It's All about the Media

Watergate's Heroic-Journalist Myth

It was not the press which exposed Watergate; it was agencies
of government itself.

—Edward J. Epstein, *Between Fact and Fiction: The Problem
of Journalism* (New York: Vintage Books, 1975), 32

Watergate was easily America's greatest political scandal of the twentieth century. Twenty-one men associated with the presidency of Richard
M. Nixon or his reelection campaign in 1972 were convicted of Watergate-related crimes, nineteen of whom went to prison.[1] Nixon himself
resigned in August 1974, less than halfway through his second term, to
avoid certain impeachment and conviction. By then, it had become clear
that Nixon had conspired with senior aides to cover up the scandal's
signal crime, the burglary in June 1972 at the national headquarters of
the rival Democratic Party at the Watergate office-apartment complex
in Washington, D.C.

To roll up a scandal of such dimension required the collective, if not
always coordinated, efforts of special prosecutors, federal judges, both
houses of Congress, and the Supreme Court, as well as the Justice
Department and the FBI. Even then, Nixon likely would have served
out his term if not for the audiotape recordings he secretly made of most
conversations in the Oval Office of the White House. Only when compelled by the Supreme Court did Nixon surrender those recordings,
which captured him agreeing to the cover-up and authorizing payments
of thousands of dollars in hush money.[2]

The complexity of Watergate—the lies, deceit, and criminality that
characterized the Nixon White House, the multiple lines of investigation
that slowly unwound the scandal, and the drama of what was an excep-

tional and long-running constitutional crisis—is not routinely recalled these days. The epic scandal has grown so distant that not many Americans can accurately describe what took place.[3] A survey taken for ABC and the *Washington Post* in June 2002, at the thirtieth anniversary of the Watergate burglary, found as much: nearly two-thirds of American adults said they were not conversant with the scandal's fundamental elements.[4]

What does stand out amid the scandal's many tangles is the heroic-journalist version of Watergate—the endlessly appealing notion that the dogged reporting of two young, hungry, and tireless *Washington Post* journalists, Bob Woodward and Carl Bernstein, brought down Nixon and his corrupt presidency. It has become the most familiar story line of Watergate, serving as ready shorthand for understanding Watergate and its denouement, a proxy for grasping the scandal's essence while avoiding its forbidding complexity. How the *Post* and its reporters uncovered Watergate is deeply ingrained in American journalism as one of the field's most important and self-reverential stories.

Inevitably, the tale of the heroic journalist has been cast as a story of "two Davids"—Woodward and Bernstein—who "slew Goliath."[5] By taking down "a mendacious American president," political journalist Matt Bai wrote in 2014, Woodward and Bernstein came "to symbolize the hope and heroism of a new generation."[6] That Woodward and Bernstein exposed Nixon's corruption is a favored theme in textbooks of journalism and mass communication, as in Melvin Mencher's *News Reporting and Writing*,[7] Shirley Biagi's *Media/Impact: An Introduction to Mass Media*,[8] and Tim Harrower's *Inside Reporting*.[9] It has been cited in works as disparate as Robert M. O'Neil's *The First Amendment and Civil Liability*[10] and Edward Kosner's *It's News to Me: The Making and Unmaking of an Editor*.[11]

Even the *New York Times*—the *Washington Post*'s foremost rival—has embraced the heroic-journalist interpretation, noting how "two young Washington Post reporters cracked the Watergate scandal and brought down President Richard M. Nixon."[12] There's even a sinister and conspiratorial variation to the heroic-journalist theme. "The Watergate witch-hunt . . . was run by liberals in the media," Paul Johnson wrote darkly in *Modern Times: The World from the Twenties to the Nineties*. Johnson claimed that Nixon's sweeping reelection victory in 1972 "was overturned by what might be described as a media *putsch*. The 'imperial presidency' was replaced by the 'imperial press.'"[13]

But to explain Watergate through the lens of the heroic journalist is to abridge and misunderstand the scandal and to indulge in a particularly beguiling media-driven myth. The heroic-journalist interpretation mini-mizes the far more decisive forces that unraveled the scandal and forced Nixon from office. This interpretation of Watergate is especially power-ful, the sociologist Michael Schudson has written, because it "offers journalism a charter, an inspiration, a reason for being large enough to justify the constitutional protections that journalism enjoys."[14] Simi-larly, Jay Rosen, a media scholar, has called the heroic-journalist con-struct "*the* redemptive tale believers learn to tell about the press and what it can do for the American people. It is a story of national salva-tion: truth their only weapons, journalists save the day."[15]

THE DOMINANT POPULAR NARRATIVE

The heroic-journalist myth has become the dominant popular narrative of the Watergate scandal for several reasons. They include: the timing of Woodward and Bernstein's book about how they reported the unfolding scandal; the popular cinematic version of their book; and the endless parlor game about the identity of the helpful but anonymous high-level source with whom Woodward surreptitiously met while investigating Watergate. These factors combined to place Woodward and Bernstein at the center of Watergate in popular consciousness and project the notion that the scandal's outcome pivoted on disclosures reported by the news media.[16]

The myth began to take hold in June 1974, with publication of *All the President's Men,* Woodward and Bernstein's Watergate memoir. "All America knows about Watergate," the book's dust jacket declared. "Here, for the first time, is the story of how we know. In what must be the most devastating political detective story of the century, the two young *Washington Post* reporters whose brilliant investigative journal-ism smashed the Watergate scandal wide open tell the whole behind-the-scenes drama the way it really happened."[17] *All the President's Men* was a runaway success. *Playboy* carried two prepublication excerpts. The book's first print run of seventy-five thousand quickly sold, and in late June 1974, *All the President's Men* reached the top of the *New York Times*'s nonfiction best-seller list. It remained there for fifteen weeks,[18] through Nixon's resignation and the decisive days of Watergate, and beyond.[19] When the book came out, Woodward was thirty-one; Bern-stein was thirty.

The book's impeccable timing—it appeared as the scandal neared its climax—helped promote the impression that Woodward and Bernstein

FIGURE 20. *Washington Post* reporters Bob Woodward (left) and Carl Bernstein (right) were the *Washington Post* reporters often credited with bringing down Richard Nixon's corrupt presidency. The notion endures even though Woodward has dismissed it, as have other authorities at the *Post*. [*Bettman/Corbis*]

were central to Watergate's ultimate outcome. As Stanley I. Kutler, Watergate's leading historian, wrote: "However self-serving or exaggerated the work, [the timely publication of *All the President's Men*] undeniably gave an added impetus to the growing understanding and awareness of Watergate. . . . In an important sense, the book offered a journalistic brief to the nation as it prepared to understand and judge for itself" the deepening evidence of Nixon's guilt.[20] Not only was *All the President's Men* well timed, but it was useful in making sense of the scandal's sprawl. If nothing else, wrote a reviewer for the *Wall Street Journal*, the book "is a great guide for people like me who still have trouble figuring out where Ehrlichman begins and Haldeman ends."[21] John Ehrlichman and H. R. Haldeman were top aides to Nixon who were convicted of crimes and imprisoned in the Watergate scandal.

All the President's Men introduced to journalism and American culture the intriguing character known as "Deep Throat." He has been called the "dark star of *All the President's Men*"[22] and the "most important . . . whistle-blower in modern American political history."[23] "Deep Throat" was a stealthy, high-level government source who sometimes conferred with Woodward in the small hours of the morning at an underground parking garage in northern Virginia, across the Potomac River from the Watergate complex.[24] The code name "Deep Throat" stemmed from the source's cloak-and-dagger ways and from his willingness to speak with Woodward only on "deep background." That meant "Deep Throat" would confirm information obtained elsewhere but would not be quoted, even anonymously, in articles in the *Post*.[25]

"Deep Throat" lent a measure of mystery and intrigue to the narrative of *All the President's Men*, and the source's identity became the topic of not infrequent speculation in the three decades that followed the book's publication. Woodward and Bernstein kept to their pledge to protect "Deep Throat's" identity until his death, or until he decided to make known that he was the famous source. In 2005, W. Mark Felt, formerly the second-ranking official at the FBI, revealed that he had been the "Deep Throat" source. By then, Felt was in his early nineties and suffering from dementia. He died in 2008.

All the President's Men was an even greater and more lasting success in its adaptation to the screen. The book in fact had been written with the cinema in mind. Robert Redford had taken a keen interest in the Woodward-Bernstein collaboration in reporting the scandal and had encouraged the reporters to structure the book around their experiences.[26] "From the very beginning," Woodward once said, Redford "saw and talked about our story in terms of movie scenes."[27] Redford paid $450,000 for the movie rights to *All the President's Men* after seeing only an incomplete draft of the manuscript.[28] The cinematic version, which starred Redford as Woodward and Dustin Hoffman as Bernstein, was released by Warner Brothers in April 1976, as the wounds of Watergate had only begun to close. The film was a commercial and critical success.[29] It rang up more than $68 million in gross receipts and was the most popular movie of the year after Sylvester Stallone's pugilist melodrama *Rocky*. *All the President's Men* was nominated for eight Academy Awards, winning four, including best supporting actor for Jason Robards's portrayal of Ben Bradlee, the *Post*'s executive editor during the Watergate period.

Warner Brothers promoted the film extravagantly, lionizing Woodward and Bernstein as "the two young reporters who cracked the Watergate conspiracy ... [and] solved the greatest detective story in American history. At times, it looked as if it might cost them their jobs, their reputations, perhaps even their lives."[30] The movie suggested that their reporting was more hazardous than it was—that by digging into Watergate, Woodward and Bernstein exposed themselves to not insignificant risk and peril. To an extent far greater than the book, the cinematic version of *All the President's Men* placed Woodward and Bernstein at the center of Watergate's unraveling while minimizing, and even denigrating, the efforts of investigative agencies such as the FBI. The effect was to solidify and elevate the heroic-journalist myth, giving it dramatic power and sustaining it in the collective memory.[31]

The film closes with the Woodward and Bernstein characters at their respective desks in the *Post*'s brilliantly lighted newsroom, pounding at their typewriters. The newsroom is otherwise empty at first. Woodward and Bernstein remain oblivious to their colleagues as they slowly drift in. It's inauguration day 1973, and the *Post* editors and reporters are shown gathering at television sets in the newsroom to watch as Nixon is sworn in to a second term. Woodward and Bernstein, however, remain hard at work. They do not budge from their desks or look up from their typing. The television sets show Nixon smiling as he completes the oath of office. The first volleys of a twenty-one gun salute begin to boom. Woodward and Bernstein continue their frantic typing, and the cannonade resounds ever louder. The newsroom scene dissolves to a close-up of an overactive teletype machine noisily battering out summaries of the indictments, trials, and convictions of Nixon's men. The clattering machine spells out "Nixon resigns" and stops abruptly a moment later. With that, the film ends.

It is a deft conclusion that pulls together the many strands of Watergate. But more than that, it offers an unmistakable assertion of the power and centrality of the press in Nixon's fall. *All the President's Men* allows no other interpretation: it was the work of Woodward and Bernstein that set in motion far-reaching processes that brought about the first-ever resignation of a U.S. president.[32] And it is a message that has endured. More than forty years later, what remains most vivid, memorable, and accessible about Watergate is the cinematic version of *All the President's Men*. Woodward said he expected as much, that the story of the exploits of Woodward and Bernstein would be the one "people know and remember" about Watergate.[33]

Frank Rich of the *New York Times* is among the commentators to have noted the effectiveness of *All the President's Men* in that regard. "Such is the power of movies," Rich has noted, "that the first image 'Watergate' brings to mind . . . decades later is not Richard Nixon so much as the golden duo of Redford and Hoffman riding to the nation's rescue in 'All the President's Men.'"[34] Similarly, David Brooks, another *New York Times* columnist, has observed that "Watergate in today's culture ... isn't about Nixon and the cover-up anymore. It's about Woodward and Bernstein. Watergate has become a modern Horatio Alger story, a real-life fairy tale, an inspiring ode for mediacentric college types—about the two young men who found exciting and challenging jobs, who slew the dragon, who became rich and famous by doing good and who were played by Redford and Hoffman in the movie version."[35]

The cinematic adaptation of *All the President's Men* possessed what might be called "stickiness," the elusive quality that makes some films, books, and ideas particularly memorable and enduring.[36] *All the President's Men* has had long-term influence. The film "holds up extraordinarily well—as both history and entertainment," Jonathan Kirshner, a government scholar at Cornell University, wrote in a review at the film's thirtieth anniversary in 2006. That it has retained such appeal "is remarkable," Kirshner wrote, "considering how easily it might have become a faded period piece."[37] An explanation for its enduring appeal was suggested by Matthew Ehrlich in his study *Journalism in the Movies:* "If American mythology holds that any boy can grow up to be president, the movie suggests that any boy can grow up to topple a corrupt president, especially if he is 'hungry' and has an equally hungry partner."[38]

NEAT, TIDY, AND SIMPLIFIED

The cinema was more than an agent in projecting and promoting the heroic-journalist myth of Watergate; it helped ensure the myth would live on by offering a neat, tidy, and vastly simplified account about Watergate, one that allowed viewers to sidestep the scandal's complexity while following an entertaining story line. No other Watergate-related movie has retained an appeal that transcended decades or has been seen by as many people.[39] In addition to the moviegoers who bought nearly thirty-four million tickets to *All the President's Men* in 1976, millions have seen the film on television, "another generation would see it on video cassettes, [and] still others would view it in high schools and colleges as part of history or journalism classes," as Adrian Havill noted in *Deep Truth,* a critical, unauthorized biography of Woodward and Bernstein.[40]

What really happened in unraveling the Watergate scandal was, of course, vastly more complex than what was shown on the screen. The arrests of the Watergate burglars in the early hours of June 17, 1972, began the dismantling of illegal intelligence-gathering operations conducted by Nixon's White House and officials of his Committee to Re-elect the President. Their objective was to collect embarrassing information about the rival Democrats that could be used to good effect in the presidential election campaign in the fall of 1972. Six days after the burglars were arrested at the Watergate complex, Nixon and his top White House aide, Haldeman, conspired to cover up the break-in. Their plan was to call on the CIA to block the FBI's nascent investigation, ostensibly for reasons of national security. Nixon and his aides also approved the payment of hush money to the burglars and others caught in the web of Watergate.

Decisive to sorting out this complex web of criminality were John Sirica, a federal judge whose threat of stiff prison sentences for the Watergate burglars forced one of them, James McCord, to crack and implicate others in the break-in and cover-up;[41] the Senate Select Committee on Watergate, which in 1973 uncovered the existence of the White House audiotapes, a discovery that proved crucial to the scandal's outcome; the two federal special prosecutors on Watergate, one of whom Nixon ordered fired and the other of whom won the release of the White House tapes that incriminated the president; and the Supreme Court, which ruled unanimously in July 1974 that the president could not hide behind executive privilege and had to turn over the audiotapes subpoenaed by the special prosecutor. "The fact is," Kutler wrote, "an incredible array of powerful actors all converged on Nixon at once—the FBI, prosecutors, congressional investigators, the judicial system."[42]

Amid this tableau of prosecutors, courts, federal investigations, and bipartisan congressional panels, the contributions of Woodward and Bernstein were at best modest, and certainly not decisive. Principals at the *Post* have acknowledged as much. Katharine Graham, the newspaper's doughty publisher, often insisted that the *Post* did not topple Nixon. "Sometimes people accuse us of bringing down a president, which of course we didn't do," Graham said in 1997, at a program marking the scandal's twenty-fifth anniversary. "The processes that caused [Nixon's] resignation were constitutional," she insisted.[43] In earthier terms, Woodward concurred: "To say that the press brought down Nixon, that's horseshit."[44] In 2005, Michael Getler, then the *Post*'s ombudsman, wrote: "Ultimately, it was not The Post, but the FBI, a Congress acting in bipartisan fashion and the courts that brought down the Nixon administration. They saw Watergate and the attempt to cover it up as a vast abuse of power and attempted corruption of U.S. institutions."[45]

This is not to say that the *Post*'s reporting on Watergate was without distinction. As the scandal slowly unfolded in the summer and fall of 1972, Woodward and Bernstein progressively linked White House officials to a secret fund used to finance the burglary. The *Post* was the first news organization to demonstrate that campaign funds to reelect Nixon were used to fund the break-in, the first to implicate the former attorney general John Mitchell in the scandal, and the first to link Haldeman to Watergate.[46]

"OUT OF GAS" ON WATERGATE

Those reports were published in the four months following the Watergate break-in.[47] But by late October 1972, the *Post*'s investigation into Watergate "ran out of gas," as Barry Sussman, then the newspaper's city editor, later acknowledged. "After the Haldeman story [in late October 1972] we didn't have anything else to print" about Watergate for weeks.[48] Woodward conceded that he and Bernstein "really weren't concentrating" in the aftermath of the November election: "We had taken some time off, and were working on our book and traveling around making speeches."[49] Meanwhile, Nixon was reelected, defeating George McGovern, the hapless Democratic candidate, in a forty-nine-state landslide.

The *Post*'s Watergate reporting won the 1973 Pulitzer Prize for Public Service—the most prestigious award in American print journalism. But as earnest and revealing as their reporting was, Woodward and Bernstein did not uncover defining and decisive elements of the Watergate scandal— the cover-up and the payment of hush money to the Watergate burglars. Those aspects of the scandal, Woodward was quoted as saying in 1973, were "held too close. Too few people knew. We couldn't get that high."[50] They also had a lead about, but failed to report on, the White House audiotaping system that proved critical to determining Nixon's fate. According to *All the President's Men*, Woodward was tipped about the taping system a day or two before it was disclosed by Alexander Butterfield, a former presidential aide, in July 1973. Bradlee, in what perhaps was a lapse of judgment, suggested that Woodward not expend much energy pursuing the tip. And Woodward did not.[51]

Principals at the *Post* say the newspaper's key contribution was to keep the Watergate story alive during the summer and fall of 1972, when few other news organizations seemed interested in pursuing the break-in and its aftermath.[52] "For months we were out there alone on this story," the *Post*'s managing editor, Howard Simons, once said.

"What scared me was that the normal herd instincts of Washington journalism didn't seem to be operating. . . . It was months of loneliness."[53] Sussman similarly characterized the *Post* as "out on a limb by itself" covering the Watergate story.[54] Although potent and memorable, such characterizations are not entirely accurate. The *Post* may well have led other newspapers on the Watergate story—principally because Watergate at first was a local story, based in Washington, D.C. But rival news organizations such as the *Los Angeles Times* and the *New York Times* did not ignore Watergate as the scandal slowly took dimension during the summer and fall of 1972.[55]

The *Los Angeles Times,* for example, published an exclusive first-person account in early October 1972 by Alfred C. Baldwin III, a former FBI agent who had acted as the lookout man in the Watergate burglary.[56] Baldwin described how he had delivered to Nixon's Committee to Re-elect the President sealed eavesdropping logs from wiretaps that had been placed at Democratic national headquarters shortly before the burglars were arrested in June 1972. Baldwin's account "was powerful stuff," David Halberstam observed in *The Powers That Be.* "It brought Watergate right to the heart of the Nixon reelection campaign, in a more dramatic way than any other story" to that point.[57]

In late summer 1972, the *New York Times* called for an independent prosecutor "of unquestioned political independence and judicial integrity" to investigate what it called the "sinister affair" of Watergate.[58] "What is involved in these tawdry proceedings is not an obscure political caper but the integrity of the election process and of government itself," the *Times* said in an angry and prescient editorial about Watergate.[59] More significantly, the *Times* was the first news organization to report the payment of hush money to the Watergate burglars,[60] a pivotal disclosure that made clear that efforts were under way to conceal the roles of others in the scandal. Unlike most other Watergate-related news reports in 1972 and early 1973, the *Times* story about hush money "hit home!" John Dean, Nixon's former counsel, recalled years later. "It had everyone concerned and folks in the White House and at the reelection committee were on the wall."[61]

Additionally, Edward Jay Epstein noted in his classic essay disputing the heroic-journalist myth of Watergate that the *Post* and other newspapers were joined during the summer of 1972 by the General Accounting Office, the investigative arm of Congress,[62] and Common Cause, a foundation that seeks accountability in government office, in calling attention to the scandal. Within a few days of the Watergate break-in, moreover, the Democratic National Committee filed a civil lawsuit against the Committee to Re-elect the President, which ultimately compelled statements under oath. And Nixon's Democratic challenger for the presidency, George McGovern, repeatedly invoked Watergate in his campaign appearances in the summer and fall of 1972. At one point, McGovern charged that Nixon was "at least indirectly responsible" for the Watergate burglary. McGovern also termed the break-in "the kind of thing you expect under a person like Hitler."[63] In its reporting on the emergent scandal in the summer and fall of 1972, the *Post* in fact was one of several institutions seeking to delineate the reach and contours of Watergate.[64] The *Post,* in other words, was very much *not* alone.

Epstein's essay also noted that Woodward and Bernstein had been "diverted" in their investigation to focus on what was a minor sideshow of Watergate—a "dirty tricks" campaign directed by a Republican lawyer named Donald Segretti. "The quest for Segretti," Epstein pointed out, "dominates the largest section" of Woodward and Bernstein's book.[65] But nearly all of Segretti's "dirty tricks" took place during the Democratic primary election, before the Watergate break-in, Epstein noted. In October 1972, Woodward and Bernstein reported that Segretti was one of "at least fifty undercover Nixon operatives" who "traveled throughout the country trying to disrupt and spy on" challengers for the Democratic nomination for president. Woodward and Bernstein characterized "numerous acts of political sabotage and spying" as perhaps "the most significant finding of the whole Watergate investigation."[66]

But none of the many Watergate-related investigations uncovered evidence endorsing such a claim. An internal FBI memorandum disputed as "absolutely false" Woodward and Bernstein's claim about fifty undercover Nixon operatives.[67] In short, Epstein wrote, "neither the prosecutors, the grand jury, nor the [Senate] Watergate Committee . . . found any evidence to support the Bernstein/Woodward thesis that Watergate was part of the Segretti operation." The Segretti–dirty tricks element represented "a detour, if not a false trail," in the *Post*'s Watergate coverage, Epstein concluded.[68] Over time, though, such distinctions have become blurred. So has recognition of the contributions by agencies and organizations besides the *Washington Post*.

"DEEP THROAT" GUESSING GAME

Significantly, the thirty-year guessing game about the identity of the "Deep Throat" source provided periodic and powerful reminders about the *Post* and its Watergate coverage, serving to keep Woodward and Bernstein in the public eye far longer than they otherwise would have been. They and the mysterious "Deep Throat" became central figures in what one newspaper termed "the parlor game that would not die. . . . With each passing year, as 'Deep Throat's' cloak of anonymity remained securely in place, his perceived role in Watergate gained gravitas."[69] And so, in a sense, did the roles of Woodward and Bernstein. In public appearances, they often were asked about the identity of "Deep Throat."[70] The guessing game became "a convenient means of journalistic self-congratulation," Kutler wrote, a ready way for the news media to assert that they had figured decisively in exposing the scandal.[71]

Speculation about "Deep Throat's" identity began in June 1974, soon after publication of *All the President's Men,* with a front-page article in the *Wall Street Journal* that appeared beneath the whimsical headline "If You Drink Scotch, Smoke and Read, Maybe You're 'Deep Throat.'"[72] In the years that followed, countless articles and columns and at least a couple of books were written about the mysterious source and who he may have been. The list of candidates seemed endless and included, at one time or another, George H. W. Bush, the former CIA director who was elected president in 1988; Henry Kissinger, Nixon's secretary of state; Alexander Haig, Nixon's former chief of staff; L. Patrick Gray, the former acting FBI director; Ron Ziegler, the White House press secretary; Diane Sawyer, a network television newswoman who worked for a short time at the Nixon White House; Bobby Ray Inman, a former deputy CIA chief; and John Dean, former White House counsel to Nixon.

Identifying "Deep Throat" was the inspiration for a multiyear assignment in an investigative journalism class at the University of Illinois. Under the guidance of William Gaines, a professor and former reporter, the students sifted clues that appeared in *All the President's Men* and reviewed thousands of pages of FBI documents, congressional testimony, and Watergate memoirs. In 2002, Gaines's students placed Patrick Buchanan, a former speechwriter and special assistant to Nixon, atop their short list of "Deep Throat" suspects. "One of the things that swayed the students on Buchanan," Gaines told an interviewer, "was the trucker's bar" near Washington where Woodward and "Deep Throat" once met. Of all the candidates the students reviewed, Buchanan was a native of Washington, D.C., "and knew his way around" the capital and its environs. Buchanan presumably would have been familiar with the trucker's bar.[73]

Still, the archconservative Buchanan, who ran for president three times after the Watergate era, was a highly improbable candidate. The student-sleuths went back to their work, sifting clues. About a year later, they announced that Fred Fielding, a lawyer and former assistant to John Dean, most likely was "Deep Throat."[74] Meanwhile, a former White House aide named Leonard Garment brought out a book, *In Search of Deep Throat*, that told of his years-long sleuthing to pierce the mystery. Garment's conclusion: John Sears, a Republican strategist, was "Deep Throat."[75]

Suspicions also abounded that "Deep Throat" was a literary device, a composite character developed to embody a number of government sources and inject a sense of suspense into the narrative. Epstein embraced that view.[76] So did Robert L. Jackson and Ronald Ostrow, reporters who covered the unfolding Watergate scandal for the *Los Angeles Times*. "We were trying to compete with them and when we got some of the same stories, we know they did not all come from the same person," Ostrow once said.[77] Adrian Havill hypothesized in his critical biography of Woodward and Bernstein that "Deep Throat" was "a hybrid of three or four main sources."[78]

Even so, Mark Felt was fingered early and often as a leading "Deep Throat" candidate. The *Wall Street Journal* article that initiated years of speculation about the source's identity described Felt as the top suspect.[79] Epstein wrote in his Watergate essay in 1975 that "prosecutors at the Department of Justice now believe that the mysterious source was probably" Felt.[80] The *Atlantic Monthly* also identified Felt in a detailed account published in 1992.[81] Felt, though, repeatedly denied he was "Deep Throat." "I'm just not that kind of person," he told the *Wall Street Journal* in 1974, adding that he, too, thought "Deep Throat" was a composite character.[82] In a memoir published in 1979, Felt insisted, "I never leaked information to Woodward and Bernstein or to anyone else!"[83] Twenty years later, Felt told a Connecticut newspaper that had he been "Deep Throat," he "would have done it better."[84]

Woodward engaged in occasional misdirection over the years that served to deflect attention from Felt. For example, Woodward said in an interview with *Playboy* in 1989 that "Deep Throat" was not part of the "intelligence" community, a statement that seemed to rule out anyone at the FBI. Felt finally acknowledged that he was "Deep Throat," in an article published in 2005 in *Vanity Fair*. He did so partly because his family urged him to do so while he was still alive, possibly to pursue ways of capitalizing on his status.[85]

Felt was hardly a noble character or a self-sacrificing whistleblower. By passing information to Woodward, Felt sought to undercut the acting

FBI director, L. Patrick Gray III, and thereby enhance his chances of being named to the bureau's top position. Max Holland argued this point persuasively in his 2012 book, *Leak: Why Mark Felt Became Deep Throat*. The book makes clear that Felt was motivated by ambition in the internal struggle at the FBI to replace J. Edgar Hoover, the long-serving director who died in May 1972.[86] Felt's ambition, however, went unfulfilled. Clarence M. Kelley became Hoover's successor in July 1973.

At roughly the time he was meeting privately with Woodward about Watergate, Felt authorized warrantless break-ins as part of the FBI's investigations into associates of the radical Weather Underground. Felt was indicted on felony charges related to the burglaries and convicted in 1980. He was ordered to pay a $5,000 fine, but the following year, Felt was granted an unconditional pardon by President Ronald Reagan.[87]

WATERGATE'S SUBSIDIARY MYTH

The disclosure that Felt was "Deep Throat" gave fresh life to the heroic-journalist myth and to a stubborn subsidiary myth of Watergate—namely, that the exploits of Woodward and Bernstein were a profound stimulus to enrollments in collegiate journalism programs. *All the President's Men* supposedly made journalism sexy and caused enrollments in journalism schools to surge. The *Post*'s media writer, Howard Kurtz, invoked the subsidiary myth in recalling the evanescent "golden glow" that Woodward and Bernstein were said to have cast on the news business in the mid-1970s. "Newspapermen became cinematic heroes," Kurtz wrote of those days. They were "determined diggers who advanced the cause of truth by meeting shadowy sources in parking garages, and journalism schools were flooded with aspiring sleuths and crusaders."[88]

Many other newspapers invoked the subsidiary myth as well. The *Philadelphia Inquirer* referred to "the muckraking duo who launched a million journalism majors."[89] Jay Bookman, a columnist for the *Atlanta Journal-Constitution* wrote that journalism schools in the 1970s became "overcrowded with students aspiring to be the next Woodward and Bernstein."[90] And the journalism scholar Philip Meyer, writing in *USA Today*, declared that *All the President's Men* and its film version "persuaded thousands of young people who might otherwise have been English or accounting majors to choose journalism."[91] In a posthumous tribute to Felt, the *Washington Post* declared that "he inspired thousands and thousands of campus misfits to get journalism degrees, each one of them in pursuit of bad haircuts, smoking habits and the next Deep Throat, the next huge story."[92]

But there is no evidence to support the notion that enrollments in journalism programs surged because of Woodward, Bernstein, "Deep Throat," and *All the President's Men.* The subsidiary myth lives on despite its thorough repudiation in scholarly research. In one such study, financed by the Freedom Forum media foundation, the researchers Lee B. Becker and Joseph D. Graf reported that "growth in journalism education result[ed] not from specific events [such] as Watergate . . . but rather to a larger extent from the appeal of the field to women, who ha[d] been attending universities in record numbers. The growth also in part reflect[ed] the applied nature of the field and its link to specific job skills."[93] They added: "There is no evidence . . . that Watergate had any effect on enrollments."[94]

Becker and Graf's study was published in 1995. It was not the first to challenge Watergate's subsidiary myth. Seven years earlier, Maxwell E. McCombs reported in the *Gannett Center Journal* that "the boom in journalism education was underway at least five years before" the Watergate break-in in 1972. McCombs, a veteran mass communication scholar, wrote: "It is frequently, and wrongly, asserted that the investigative reporting of Woodward and Bernstein provided popular role models for students, and led to a boom in journalism school enrollments. The data . . . reveal, however, that enrollments already had doubled between 1967 and 1972."[95]

The subsidiary myth appears to derive from an *Atlantic Monthly* cover story in March 1977, nearly a year after the release of the cinematic version of *All the President's Men.* The article was titled "Woodstein U" and included an image from *All the President's Men,* the movie. The image showed Hoffman telling Redford: "Would you believe it! More than 60,000 kids studying journalism!" Redford replies: "Yeah. And they're all after our jobs."[96]

The tenacity of the subsidiary myth is easily understood: it endures because it seems irresistibly logical and straightforward—too obvious, almost, *not* to be true. But as the journalism educator Reese Cleghorn once noted, the "popular mythology" of American journalism "knows no bounds."[97] And media-driven myth can build on media-driven myth, a phenomenon that will be apparent again in this study.

CHAPTER 10

The "Fantasy Panic"

*The News Media and the
"Crack-Baby" Myth*

The Worst Threat Is Mom Herself.

—Douglas J. Besharov, "Crack
Babies: The Worst Threat Is
Mom Herself," *Washington Post*
(6 August 1989): B1

The drug wars of the 1980s and 1990s produced few images more wrenching or despairing than those of "crack babies," helpless infants born to women who, while pregnant, took cocaine or its potent, smokable derivative, crack. Prenatal exposure supposedly left these infants neurologically damaged, addicted at birth, and prone to all kinds of suffering—convulsions, withdrawal, chronic irritability, and an unwillingness to be touched or held. They were given to emitting ear-piercing, unearthly shrieks and cries.[1] And worse. Much worse. Prominent journalists declared crack babies the harbingers of a social disaster from which there would be unending consequences.

"The inner-city crack epidemic," Charles Krauthammer, a conservative syndicated columnist for the *Washington Post,* wrote in 1989, "is now giving birth to the newest horror: a bio-underclass, a generation of physically damaged cocaine babies whose biological inferiority is stamped at birth." Krauthammer added: "In the poorest, most desperate pockets of society, it has now become a menace to the future. For the bio-underclass, the biologically determined underclass of the underclass, tomorrow's misery will exceed yesterday's. That has already been decreed." The crack-induced bio-underclass, Krauthammer said, promised to become "a horror worthy of Aldous Huxley" and his *Brave New World.*[2]

Writing from the other end of the political spectrum, Courtland Milloy, another *Washington Post* columnist, also invoked the specter of a "bio-underclass." He declared in 1989 that cocaine-damaged children were "turning up in first- and second-grade classrooms around the country, wreaking havoc on themselves and others. Severe emotional damage and even physical deformities not so readily apparent today may mushroom in the near future. The children's irritability and anger—along with their need for love and understanding—will surely grow."[3]

Jane E. Brody, an award-winning medical writer for the *New York Times,* likewise described a gathering "epidemic of damaged infants, some of whom may be impaired for life because their mothers used cocaine even briefly during pregnancy." New research, Brody wrote in 1988, "has found a wide spectrum of ill effects that can result from fetal exposure to cocaine. These include retarded growth in the womb and subtle neurological abnormalities, which may afflict a majority of exposed newborns. In more extreme cases, cocaine can cause loss of the small intestine and brain-damaging strokes. . . . The litany of threats to newborns is long and growing." So powerful was the drug, Brody wrote, that "research suggests that a single cocaine 'hit' during pregnancy can cause lasting fetal damage."[4]

Newsweek declared in 1990 in a report about "crack children" that "the country now must confront a whole new facet of the crack epidemic: an entire generation that may never be free of the scourge."[5] Dr. Elaine M. Johnson, the director of the Federal Office of Substance Abuse Prevention, warned that the crack babies represented "a new generation of innocent addicts."[6] In an editorial in 1989, the *New York Times* likened crack to a disaster of historic dimension: "Crack may be to the 80's and 90's what the Great Depression was to the 30's or the Vietnam War was to the 60's and 70's."[7]

The anticipated consequences were jaw-dropping, and the scare was full-blown, bolstered by what seemed to be inescapable logic: taking crack or other forms of cocaine during pregnancy seemed a surefire way to devastate the human fetus. And because crack was a fairly new, still-mysterious drug of the inner city, it became a ready and inviting target, a "popular demon in the war on drugs" of the second half of the 1980s.[8] So intense was the crack-baby scare that, in some jurisdictions, pregnant women who used crack risked prosecution and imprisonment for child abuse.[9] At some hospitals, pregnant women were secretly tested for cocaine exposure.[10] By the late 1980s and early 1990s, wrote Mariah Blake in the *Columbia Journalism Review,* the crack-baby scare had become "an emblem of the havoc drugs wreak and a pretext for draconian drugs laws."[11]

But the much-predicted social catastrophe—the dreaded "bio-underclass"—never materialized. The crack-baby scare turned out to be an "epidemic that wasn't."[12] Fears that American society would be over-whelmed by a lost generation of crack-damaged misfits proved wildly exaggerated, "a grotesque media stereotype," in the words of Deborah A. Frank, a leading authority on prenatal drug exposure.[13] The crack-baby scare, Frank has said, was "an unscientific panic based on minimal data. . . . This fantasy panic around crack had to do with the social aspect of the drug, with the inner city, with violence."[14] It was, in short, a compelling story that fit a media-conjured template about the out-of-control, inner-city nature of the crack epidemic. It was a media-driven myth based more on anecdote than solid, sustained research, a myth that had the effect of stigmatizing underprivileged children presumed to have been born damaged and despised as "crack babies."[15]

To be sure, smoking crack during pregnancy is hardly risk-free, and certainly neither prudent nor sensible. But the effects of prenatal cocaine exposure proved more subtle than sweeping: newborns exposed to crack during pregnancy tend to be smaller in birth weight, in length, and in head circumference.[16] Some research suggested that mild cognitive deficiencies, such as difficulties in concentrating on tasks at hand, might be attributable to prenatal cocaine exposure,[17] especially as cognitive demands on children intensify as they grow older.[18] But biomedical research has found nothing akin to a "bio-underclass," a "new generation of innocent addicts," or even a "crack-baby syndrome." There is no recognizable set of neonatal defects attributable to cocaine, nothing akin to fetal alcohol syndrome, which can be characterized by low birth weight, diminished cranium size, distorted facial features, and cognitive disorders.

The adverse effects that journalists so often attributed in the late 1980s and early 1990s to prenatal exposure to crack turned out to be associated with a variety of factors—such as use during pregnancy of tobacco, alcohol, or marijuana—as well as the quality of the newborn's environment and the quality of the mother's prenatal care.[19] Women who consumed cocaine during pregnancy also tended to smoke cigarettes, drink alcohol, take other illegal drugs, and receive inadequate prenatal care. "It's astonishing that so much fuss has been raised about cocaine when kids born with fetal alcohol syndrome are so much worse off," Claire D. Coles, a clinical psychologist at Emory University, has said about the crack-baby scare.[20]

Revisiting the myth of the crack baby allows insights into a tendency among journalists to neglect or disregard the tentativeness that characterizes serious scientific and biomedical research and to reach for certainty and definitiveness that are not often found in preliminary findings. The tendency of journalists to push hard on tentative data has been apparent in coverage of subsequent drug scares, notably that of methamphetamine in 2004 and 2005. Parallels in exaggerated coverage of "crack babies" and "meth babies" were striking. "Meth addicts are pouring into prisons and recovery centers at an ever-increasing rate, and a new generation of 'meth babies' is choking the foster-care system in many states," *Newsweek* magazine reported in 2005. The methamphetamine scourge seemed to know no bounds. "Anytown, U.S.A., can be turned into a meth den almost overnight," *Newsweek* declared.[21] Such reporting prompted the media critic Jack Shafer to declare, "Proving that the press corps has no memory, they're at it again, proclaiming without any scientific evidence that a generation of damaged 'meth babies' is on the way."[22]

This chapter points to the risks of anecdote-driven reporting, which characterized news coverage of the crack-baby phenomenon. Disturbing images and heart-wrenching descriptions of helpless newborns supposedly damaged by their mothers' toxic indulgence were frequent and irresistible elements of the coverage. Anecdotes were fuel for a powerful but misleading story line. This chapter also calls attention to the reluctance or unwillingness of journalists to revisit and correct erroneous interpretations of scientific phenomena. In the case of crack babies, the news media presented a powerful, perhaps indelible misimpression that crack-exposed children faced empty, hopeless futures. It was irresistibly "hot copy to write about screaming little monsters birthed from the wombs of dope fiends," *City Paper,* an alternative weekly newspaper in Washington, D.C., said in 1991 in a lengthy report critical of crack-baby coverage.[23] It was far less appealing to report that the crack-baby story was really not so hot after all. As the crack-baby scare suggests, the news media often are not inclined to revisit and explain their mistakes in a meaningful or sustained fashion.

THE MYTH EMERGES

The derivation of the crack-baby myth can be traced to 1985 and an article titled "Cocaine Use in Pregnancy" that was published in the *New England Journal of Medicine.*[24] The article reported on a study of twenty-three cocaine-using women who were found to have increased rates of spontaneous abortions and developmental disorders. The results were tentative, as the study took care to point out: "These preliminary observations suggest that cocaine influences the outcome of pregnancy as well as the neurologic behavior of the newborn, but a full assessment will require a larger number of pregnancies and longer follow-up."[25] On the eve of the study's release, the CBS Evening News program devoted a brief segment to the topic and quoted the study's lead author, Ira J. Chasnoff, as likening cocaine's effects on pregnant women to those of heroin. A wire service article published the next day in the New York Times quoted Chasnoff as saying, "This is a tremendous problem." The article stated, "Cocaine use may be dangerous for pregnant women and their babies, causing spontaneous abortions, developmental disorders and life-threatening complications during birth, doctors reported today."[26]

The news media's fascination with the phenomenon intensified during the second half of the 1980s, with flurries of anecdotal reports in print and on broadcast outlets describing the dire and lasting effects of cocaine use during pregnancy. Reporters, correspondents, and columnists for several of the country's leading news organizations—including the New York Times, the Washington Post, USA Today, and CBS News—embraced powerful anecdotal evidence and then failed to follow up promptly when the evidence proved not so strong or compelling. For example, USA Today declared in 1989 that "crack babies enter the world with a long list of medical and behavioral problems destined to grow as they do." The newspaper quoted a woman who said that she had smoked crack "'from the time I got up until I went to sleep. . . . One hit trembled the [fetus] so much it was like it was looking for some place to hide.' But there is no hiding." The USA Today account said 375,000 babies were born in the United States "after exposure to cocaine and other drugs during pregnancy."[27]

In a commentary headlined "Crack Babies: The Worst Threat Is Mom Herself," the Washington Post in 1989 claimed that the incidence of crack babies was on the rise everywhere, "in cities, suburbs and even rural areas." Crack, the commentary said, "is uniquely dangerous. Other drugs have plagued our society since the 1960s, but cocaine, and especially its derivative, crack, poses a threat to many more young children—because mothers use it." The article described, without attribution or anecdotal examples, how crack had left some new mothers so depraved that they "abandon their sick babies in the hospital—not returning, even if the infant dies, to help bury it."[28] A columnist for the Post struck a similarly despairing tone, writing: "We are faced here with an unprecedented phenomenon in this city and nation. And it affects the relationship of that deepest and most sacred of bonds: that between a

Crack Babies: The Worst Threat Is Mom Herself

By Douglas J. Besharov

LAST WEEK in this city, Greater Southeast Community Hospital released a 7-week-old baby to her homeless, drug-addicted mother even though the child was at severe risk of pulmonary arrest. The hospital's explanation: "Because [the mother] demanded that the baby be released."

The hospital provided the mother with an apnea monitor to warn her if the baby stopped breathing while asleep, and trained her in CPR. But on the very first night, the mother went out drinking and left the child at a friend's house—without the monitor. Within seven hours, the baby was dead. Like Dooney Waters, the 6-year-old living in his mother's drug den, whose shocking story was reported in The Washington Post last week, this child was all but abandoned by the authorities.

FIGURE 21. This commentary in the *Washington Post* said that crack was "uniquely dangerous" and told of crack-using mothers who had abandoned "their sick babies in the hospital—not returning, even if the infant dies, to help bury it." [Washington Post]

mother and a child. In the case of crack cocaine, the most extraordinary and dreadful quality of its use is that it totally erodes all natural maternal tendencies. This is a development that is taking place from coast to coast and is a breakdown of profound proportions."[29]

Hints that the scourge was overstated and probably something less than "uniquely dangerous" began appearing in the early 1990s. The *Post* published a lengthy article in April 1990, reporting that, in many states, alcohol outstripped crack as the leading problem drug. By then, state and federal governments had devoted billions of dollars to combating cocaine and other illegal drugs. The *Post* said that "a growing number of public health officials fear that this effort has overshadowed the far more damaging and pervasive problems caused by alcohol abuse. This is especially true in many Midwestern and Rocky Mountain states where officials say the toll from alcohol—measured by highway fatalities, teenage drinking and thousands of babies with fetal alcohol syndrome—dwarfs the problems created by cocaine and other illegal drugs."[30]

The article raised an early, tentative challenge to the crack-baby scare, stating: "Even the mounting national concern over crack-addicted babies may be out of proportion, some health officials say. In Iowa, local hospitals report that they continue to see far more babies suffering from fetal alcohol syndrome. . . . Some doctors and researchers now believe that at least some of the adverse symptoms detected in 'crack babies' may actually be the consequence of alcohol use by the mother."[31]

A more pointed challenge to the crack-baby phenomenon was published late in 1991 by *City Paper,* the alternative newspaper in Washington. The article, written by Kathy Fackelmann, declared the phenomenon a myth, stating: "The tragedy of the 'crack-baby' myth is that it taught at-risk mothers the wrong lesson, instilling in them the belief that there is no hope for their developing child, that nothing they do will ameliorate the impact of their addiction. Nothing could be further from the truth."[32]

Ellen Goodman, a columnist for the *Boston Globe,* wrote in early 1992 that the crack baby was a myth and misnomer. The terms "crack babies" and "crack kids," she wrote, had become "shorthand for monster-children who are born addicted. These are the kids destined to grow up without the ability to pay attention or to learn or to love. But just when the name has stuck, it turns out that 'crack baby' may be a creature of the imagination as much as medicine, a syndrome seen in the media more often than [in] medicine." She wrote that researchers were beginning to raise doubts about the singular destructiveness of crack and noted: "Cocaine is rarely taken by itself. It's part of a stew of substances taken in a variety of doses and circumstances. No direct line has been drawn from the mother's use of cocaine to fetal damage. Alcohol and tobacco may do as much harm to the fetus as cocaine."[33]

About the time Goodman's column appeared, the prestigious *Journal of the American Medical Association* published a withering commentary, deploring "a rush to judgment" about the effects of prenatal cocaine exposure. The commentary criticized the news media's frequent characterization of cocaine-exposed infants "as severely or even irrevocably brain damaged—to the point that they may never function normally in society. On this account, a very large group of children is in danger of being 'written off.'" The commentary pointedly noted, "Predictions of an adverse developmental outcome for these children are being made despite a lack of supportive scientific evidence." It was a stinging rebuke by the medical profession's most authoritative publication of what it called "the lay media." The commentary closed with a call for "a suspension of judgment about the developmental outcome of cocaine-exposed babies until solid scientific data are available."[34]

AN UNEVEN ROLLBACK

The news media's retreat or rollback on crack babies was neither as extensive nor as prominent as the dramatic and ominous reports about the scourge in the late 1980s and early 1990s. There was little sustained effort to revisit and dismantle the media-driven myth, even as a consensus took hold among scientists and biomedical researchers that exposure to crack during pregnancy was not as destructive as preliminary research had suggested. As the alternative magazine *Mother Jones* noted in 1995, "The publicity blitz that spread the crack-baby myth has not been matched by an attempt to unmake the myth—and many, many people still believe in it."[35]

Revisionist accounts appeared sporadically in the mainstream media, with a notable spurt in the mid-1990s. Beneath the headline "'Crack Baby' Fears May Have Been Overstated," the *Washington Post* said in 1997 that much of the reporting eight to ten years earlier had been based "more on anecdotal reports than scientific studies." The *Post* quoted a neonatologist as saying, "If there is a cocaine effect, it's not a tomahawk between the eyes." Interestingly, though, the article was assigned an obscure place in the newspaper, on page Z10 in the Tuesday health section.[36] About the same time, *Newsweek* reported, "Most likely, the effects of cocaine are real but small," and quoted Barry Kosofsky of the Harvard Medical School as saying, "Cocaine is not a sledgehammer to the fetal brain."[37]

The rollbacks on crack babies continued sporadically into the first years of the twenty-first century. E. R. Shipp, a columnist for the *Daily News* in New York, conceded in 2004, "We probably overreacted with forecasts of harm to so-called 'crack babies.' . . . I'm no apologist for drug abusers," she wrote, but "what we're finding out is that crack may not have been as permanently 'whack' as we rather hysterically thought it would be. The response, in hindsight, was as off-kilter as that now-comical 1930s movie meant to warn young people against marijuana. Remember 'Reefer Madness'? If not, please do check it out."[38] In March 2005, the *Denver Post* published a 2,000-word account that acknowledged that "cocaine did not appear to be the demon originally feared."[39] In January 2009, the *New York Times* devoted 1,440 words to "the epidemic that wasn't," quoting researchers as saying, "the long-term effects of [prenatal cocaine] exposure on children's brain development and behavior appear relatively small."[40]

So how could the news media have been so spectacularly wrong about crack babies, so badly in error about the prospect of a social catastrophe rippling outward from the inner city? What may be called the "something for everyone"[41] syndrome helps account for the tenacity of the media-driven myth. As suggested in the columns of Krauthammer and Milloy, the crack-baby phenomenon inspired fearful commentary across political and ideological boundaries. The crack baby was a rare social issue that had appeal across the political spectrum—appeal that made the phenomenon especially powerful, compelling, notable, and tenacious. For conservatives, the specter of crack babies underscored the importance of imposing stiff penalties in the country's war on drugs. And penalties were stiffened for crack possession during the second half of the 1980s. For liberals, meanwhile, crack babies represented an opportunity to press for costly assistance programs aimed at helping crack users and their children.[42] The absence of skeptical or dissenting opinion at either end of journalism's ideological spectrum helped sustain the crack-baby myth. When challenges to the dominant narrative about crack babies did begin to emerge, they often appeared in alternative weekly newspapers before turning up in mainstream news media.

The crack-baby myth also was sustained by the perverse appeal of the would-be apocalyptic—an impulse or mindset not uncommon in journalism. It is a truism that bad news is news. The emphasis local television news places on coverage of crime and disaster long ago spawned the cliché "if it bleeds, it leads." A richer and more sophisticated variant of the would-be apocalyptic impulse can be seen in the periodic Malthusian indulgence in the terrifying specters of acute resource depletion, unstoppable disease, and nation-state deterioration—what Robert Kaplan called "the coming anarchy" in a memorable article years ago in the *Atlantic*.[43]

Journalists do at times seem unthinkingly eager to report on trends and developments that seem so exceptional or frightening as to be without precedent. This is not to characterize them as morbid or macabre in their news gathering. But they respond with undeniable excitement and energy when trends of exceptional and hazardous proportion seem to be taking hold. The "uniquely dangerous" is seductive and perversely appealing among journalists. And the crack baby promised to become just such a scourge, a curse derived from unfathomably selfish and amoral behavior of women who, in effect, were sentencing their newborns to a life of deviancy and an unavoidably bleak future. Such a story line was irresistible in an apocalyptic and oddly fascinating sort of way. "Of all the drug horror stories ever told," it has been pointed out, "perhaps none has provoked as much public concern as that of the crack baby."[44]

The rush to report shocking findings before research-based consensus emerges is not uncommon in American journalism. Nor is the related tendency to extrapolate broadly from tentative data. Journalists covering the crack-baby phenomenon were caught in such a predicament: their deadlines were vastly shorter than those of medical researchers, the best of whom work incrementally and deliberately. In reporting the crack-baby scare, journalists not infrequently overlooked or ignored methodological shortcomings in scientific research and presented preliminary findings as if they were well-established fact.[45] Their descriptions of a social catastrophe in the making often were extrapolated from anecdotal evidence that proved misleading and unreliable, and from preliminary, and in some cases even flawed, scientific studies.

The crack-baby scare was hardly the first time that alarming news media predictions about medical and scientific phenomena proved erroneous or exaggerated. In the 1970s, for example, *Newsweek* and other print media warned about the gathering threat of global *cooling*. "There are ominous signs that the earth's weather patterns have begun to change dramatically and that these changes may portend a drastic decline in food production—with serious political implications for just about every nation on earth," *Newsweek* declared in 1975, demonstrating that the perverse appeal of the would-be apocalyptic is hardly a recent phenomenon. "The evidence in support of these predictions has now begun to accumulate so massively that meteorologists are hard-pressed to keep up with it," *Newsweek* reported.[46]

Inevitably, the pace and pressures of daily journalism conflict with the rhythm of scientific and biomedical research. Scientists typically operate without the urgency that characterizes the professional life of journalists. At their best, scientists insist on time to test hypotheses and conduct experiments, repeatedly, before reaching sure conclusions. "Research findings are tentative, undigested, preliminary—and therefore not newsworthy [in the view of scientists]—until they are certified by peers to fit into the existing framework of knowledge," the British medical journal *Lancet* has said of the inherent tension between science and journalism. "For journalists, by contrast, established ideas may be 'old news,' and of far less interest than fresh or dramatic, though possibly tentative, research."[47]

Even so, scientists are not always beyond reproach. Some of them seek media coverage of tentative findings in hopes of gaining recognition and financial support for their research.[48] Researchers were not blameless in the crack-baby scare. Some of them pushed hard at tentative findings. In addition, methodological flaws plagued a good deal of the early research about prenatal cocaine exposure, the *Journal of the American Medical Association* noted in 1992. These shortcomings included the difficulties in disentangling cocaine-specific effects from the additive or synergistic effects from exposure to other drugs. Crack-using pregnant women often drank alcohol, smoked tobacco, and received little prenatal care. Teasing out discrete effects was problematic in the early studies. Other methodological shortcomings included the reliance on self-reporting, which tended to under-identify cocaine users, and the difficulty in identifying and accounting for differences in the timing and duration of prenatal exposure to cocaine.[49]

Beyond methodological complications was an apparent bias, at least in some quarters, against studies that reported few or no adverse effects from prenatal cocaine exposure. A team of researchers led by Gideon Koren, a pediatrician at the University of Toronto, reported in 1989 that research indicating adverse effects was significantly more likely to be accepted for presentation at the Society of Pediatric Research than were studies showing few or no effects. "This bias . . . may lead to distorted estimation" of the potential of cocaine to cause birth defects "and thus cause women to terminate their pregnancy unjustifiably," Koren reported in *Lancet* in 1989. The rejected research showing few or no adverse effects tended to be better grounded methodologically, Koren wrote, adding: "This strengthens the suggestion that most negative studies were not rejected because of scientific flaws, but rather because of bias against their non-adverse message. The subconscious message may be that if a study did not detect an adverse effect of cocaine when the common knowledge is this is a 'bad drug,' then the study must be flawed."[50]

Moreover, scientists who argued in the 1980s that insufficient research had been conducted about prenatal exposure to cocaine to allow definitive conclusions sometimes became targets of withering criticism. Claire Coles of Emory University, who raised pointed challenges to the crack-baby scare, recalled several years later that because she had warned that "the information on prenatal exposure to cocaine was not yet complete and that it was too soon to draw conclusions or to take actions on such conclusions," she was "attacked as advocating drug use," called "an inept researcher," and dismissed as "personally corrupt." Her outspoken challenges, Coles said, led to her "being excluded from committees, losing foundation funding, and being criticized by both a state legislator and a medical school official."[51]

While fears of a "bio-underclass" of crack-damaged children dissipated without much attention from the news media, references to crack babies are neither rare nor difficult to find in the mainstream media. The references were common enough for thirty prominent doctors and scientists to sign a collective appeal several years ago, urging the news media to abandon use of "crack baby" and "crack-addicted baby," as the terms lacked scientific validity.[52] "Through almost 20 years of research," the doctors and scientists asserted in the statement, "none of us has identified a recognizable condition, syndrome or disorder that should be termed 'crack baby.' . . . The term 'crack addicted baby' is no less defensible. We are deeply disappointed that American media continues to use a term that not only lacks any scientific basis but endangers . . . the children to whom it is applied." Leading authorities on fetal exposure to cocaine were among those who added their names to the appeal. They included Claire Coles, Deborah Frank, and Ira Chasnoff, whose preliminary study in 1985 had been the basis for the news reports that helped ignite the crack-baby scare. Chasnoff had long since become skeptical of the crack-baby scare. "I personally have never seen a 'crack kid,'" he wrote in 1993, "and I doubt I ever will."[53]

"CRACK BABIES" IN THE TWENTY-FIRST CENTURY

The appeal of the thirty doctors and scientists did little to stem the appearance of the term "crack baby" in the media. It remained in circulation, invoked casually and idiomatically, as something of a cliché. For example, the entertainer Bill Cosby spoke of crack babies during an appearance in 2007 on the Sunday television talk show *Meet the Press*. The program was devoted to Cosby's campaign to call attention to social pathologies in African-American communities. "If I give it to a woman," Cosby said of illegal drugs, "that knocks her out of doing anything other than being a user. She also can become pregnant, and this goes to her child, better known as 'crack babies.'"[54]

Colbert I. King, a columnist for the *Washington Post,* casually referred to the term in writing about directionless inner-city youths: "Kids by the dozens, if not hundreds, who barely attend school or don't attend at all. They are, in some cases, crack babies of the '90s grown up and with emotional and mental disorders they don't even know about."[55] Another writer for the *Post,* DeNeen Brown, reported in 2007 that while "the skinny 'crack babies' have grown," crack itself "has hung on, never really left." Deep into the article of 1,900 words, Brown offered this contradictory passage: "The one light spot in the crack epidemic—if you can call it light—is that recent studies have shown there are really no crack babies."[56]

In some ways, the dread associated with term "crack baby" has dissipated, and the idiom has been morphed into a slightly eccentric emblem of self-congratulation and self-promotion, a badge of sorts for peculiar accomplishment. That became apparent several years ago, when sixteen-year-old Denise Jackson declared during an audition for a spot on television's *American Idol* talent show that she had been born a crack baby. Buoyed perhaps by the sympathy that her admission may have generated, Jackson advanced to the next round of auditions before being cut.[57]

Other self-congratulatory testimonials have appeared in the news media from time to time, about how crack babies have grown up to beat the odds and triumphed over low expectations and how they have entered adulthood with few emotional or psychological disorders and no record of crime and drug abuse. One such triumphant testimonial appeared in the *Atlanta Journal-Constitution.* "I was supposed to be an emotional 'crack baby,' a problem child, a troublemaker, a statistic," the writer declared. "I was born in 1983, conceived by two parents who both used drugs at the time. When I was born in Atlanta's Grady Hospital, my mother was asked to participate in a scientific study that would monitor my cognitive reception, intelligence, personality, habits and overall attitude for the next 24 years. . . . Last summer, I participated in one of the final portions of the study. I impressed the testers in every test I took."[58]

More bizarrely, the term has been associated with the nocturnal adventures of Prince Harry, fifth in line to the British throne. Several years ago, Harry developed a taste for a cocktail called the Crack Baby, a potent tipple intended to be downed in a single gulp or sucked through a straw. The Crack Baby is a signature cocktail at Boujis, a private celebrity nightclub the prince has frequented in the South Kensington section of London.[59]

In March 2007, after a night spent downing what a London newspaper called a "vat of Crack Baby cocktails,"[60] the prince emerged unsteadily from the nightclub's rear door. It was about three in the morning, and paparazzi were waiting, cameras at hand. Seeing the photographers, the prince shouted an obscenity and took an awkward swing at one of them.[61] As he was guided to his chauffeur-driven Range Rover, the prince lost his balance and toppled into the gutter. Harry's pink socks and boxer shorts were exposed as bodyguards helped him to his feet.[62] "Harry the crack baby," sneered London's *Mail on Sunday* newspaper after the incident.[63]

And what is the heady cocktail that the prince so favored? A Crack Baby is a blend of vodka, champagne, passion fruit, and raspberry liqueur—or what the *Daily Telegraph* called "a combustive mix . . . that sounds more like vomit-in-waiting than a drink."[64] The prince's taste for the concoction and his embarrassing tumble into the gutter are far removed, of course, from the biomedical scare stoked years earlier by the American news media. Even so, Harry's conduct offered a measure of how media-driven myths, once loosed, can turn viral and take on altered new meaning—morphing, in this case, from a term of dread to a catalyst for low farce.

CHAPTER 11

"She Was Fighting to the Death"

Mythmaking in Iraq

Jessica Lynch was G.I. Jane come to life.

—Steve Ritea, "Jessica Lynch's Story:
A Little Too Perfect?" *American
Journalism Review,* August/September
2003: 10

Scholars call the phenomenon "intermedia agenda-setting." It typically occurs when large news organizations with the wherewithal to cover news across the globe set an agenda for outlets that are smaller and have fewer resources. Intermedia agenda-setting is not at work all the time. But it certainly was in evidence in propagating the hero-warrior myth of Jessica Lynch, a blonde, waiflike, nineteen-year-old Army private from West Virginia who, through no exceptional effort of her own, became the single best-known American military figure of the war in Iraq.

Her trajectory from obscurity to celebrity status began on March 23, 2003, the fourth day of the U.S.-led invasion of Iraq. Lynch was a supply clerk, in charge of paper, pencils, toilet paper, and the like,[1] for the 507th Maintenance Company, which had been deployed to Kuwait in the run-up to the war. The unit entered Iraq on March 21, in a lumbering convoy of heavy trucks and Humvees, at the end of a column of six hundred U.S. military vehicles that stretched for miles across the desert. The men and women of the 507th had been trained to shoot firearms, but they were not combat soldiers. They were cooks, clerks, and computer technicians. Their first mission in Iraq was to reach an Army base near Najaf and help deploy Patriot antimissile batteries there.[2]

On Sunday morning, March 23, elements of the 507th convoy made a wrong turn that took them across the Euphrates River and headlong into

Nasiriyah, a southern city controlled by Iraqi forces. Soon realizing their mistake, the American soldiers turned their vehicles and began to double back through the city. As they did, gunfire erupted all around them: Iraqi irregulars had caught them in an ambush. Some vehicles of the 507th escaped the attack; others did not. When it was over, eleven American soldiers were dead or dying, and six others were taken prisoner. Among those captured was Jessica Lynch, who suffered grievous injuries and had been knocked unconscious in the crash of a fleeing Humvee. The Iraqis took Lynch to a military hospital and then to a civilian facility, the Saddam Hussein General Hospital in Nasiriyah. She was bedridden, and at times in the days afterward seemed near death from the shattering injuries she had suffered to her arms, back, legs, and spine.[3]

Early on April 1, nine days after the deadly ambush, a U.S. Special Operations unit swooped down on the hospital and rescued Lynch in a swift and well-coordinated helicopter-borne raid. Lynch, who was taken from the hospital on a stretcher, became the first captured American soldier retrieved from behind enemy lines since World War II. She was quickly transported to a U.S. military hospital in Germany for treatment, quite unaware that she was about to become the subject of an international media frenzy.

A SENSATIONAL WORLD EXCLUSIVE

Two days after her rescue, the *Washington Post* published a sensational world exclusive on its front page, reporting that Lynch had "fought fiercely" in Nasiriyah and "shot several enemy soldiers after Iraqi forces ambushed" her unit, "firing her weapon until she ran out of ammunition." Citing "U.S. officials" who otherwise were unidentified, the *Post* said that Lynch had "continued firing at the Iraqis even after she sustained multiple gunshot wounds and watched several other soldiers in her unit die around her in fighting March 23." One official was quoted anonymously as saying: "She was fighting to the death. She did not want to be taken alive."[4]

It was an electrifying account of heroism, unlike any to emerge from the war. It was not entirely far-fetched to imagine the frail, blonde teenager pouring fire into the ranks of her attackers, fighting desperately even as she was shot and stabbed. It was all rather evocative of the actress Meg Ryan firing away at Iraqis in the 1996 film *Courage under Fire*.[5]

The *Post*'s story about Lynch quickly became a classic illustration of intermedia agenda-setting. News organizations around the world

FIGURE 22. Pfc. Jessica Lynch was honorably discharged from the Army following her return to the United States for treatment of the shattering injuries she suffered in Iraq. In July 2003, Lynch received the Purple Heart, the Prisoner of War Medal, and the Bronze Star. [*Department of Defense/Brett McMillan*]

followed the *Post*'s lead by prominently reporting the supposed heroics of young Jessica Lynch and contemplating their significance. The *Pittsburgh Post-Gazette* said that Lynch "appears headed for life as an American icon, regardless of whether she likes it."[6] Even more expansively, a columnist for the *Hartford Courant* in Connecticut suggested that Lynch was destined to join the likes of Audie Murphy and Alvin York in the gallery of improbable American war heroes. Lynch, the columnist noted, "does share qualities with her illustrious predecessors.

Like them, she is from rural America, daughter of a truck driver, raised in a West Virginia tinroofed house surrounded by fields and woods." The *Courant*'s columnist quoted the historian Douglas Brinkley as likening Lynch to an "Annie Oakley of the high-tech world."[7]

A reporter for the *Plain Dealer* in Cleveland went to Lynch's hometown, Palestine, West Virginia, and filed a front-page story that read: "For many Americans, and certainly in this part of the country, the face of [the Iraq War] will forever be the smiling young woman under the camo-colored Army cap against the background of an American flag. It belongs to rescued POW Jessica Lynch. It's the face of a hero, America's hero, folks around here say. The stuff she's got inspires songs and action figures and sit-downs with Oprah [Winfrey] and Barbara [Walters]."[8]

In *USA Today*, Robin Gerber, a scholar at University of Maryland, declared Lynch "the latest in a long line of women who prove their sex's capacity for steely heroism." Lynch's battlefield derring-do, Gerber wrote, "shows that the time is right to blast through the armored ceiling that keeps women second-class citizens in the military."[9] The *New York Times* published a commentary by Melani McAlister, an American Studies scholar, who likened Lynch to Hannah Dunston and other long-ago American heroines. In 1697, Dunston was taken hostage by Indians in Massachusetts but escaped after killing and scalping ten of her captors. The Lynch story, McAlister wrote, "resonates because it is the latest iteration of a classic American war fantasy: the captivity narrative." Like Dunston, McAlister wrote, Lynch "was 'fighting to the death.'"[10]

In London, the tabloid *Daily Mirror* repeated the essentials of the *Post*'s report, saying it "was only when lightly-armed Jessica, 19, ran out of ammunition that she finally gave up." The *Mirror* also said Lynch had "fought like a lion."[11] The *Times* of London wondered "where she found the strength to shoot back while her comrades lay dead and dying around her and she bled, apparently, from multiple bullet wounds." But "one thing is certain," the *Times* declared. "Private Lynch has won a place in history as a gritty, all-American hero, to rival the likes of Bonnie and Clyde."[12] The flashy *Daily Telegraph* of Sydney, Australia, reported Lynch's heroics on its front page, saying that she had "staged a one-woman fight to the death" and was "certain to become a national icon."[13]

Broadcast media in the United States couldn't get enough of the Lynch exploits. On ABC's *Good Morning America* program, Robin Roberts reported: "This morning, we are learning dramatic new details of her rescue and her capture a week ago by Iraqi forces. According to 'The Washington Post,' Lynch fought fiercely after her unit was ambushed near Nasiriyah, shooting several Iraqis during the attack. Emptying her weapon before being stabbed and finally taken prisoner."[14]

On NBC's *Today Show*, anchor Katie Couric asked Lynch's mother, Deadra, about the *Post*'s report, saying: "Apparently, she fought fiercely and shot several enemy soldiers after Iraqi forces ambushed her company. She fired her weapon until it ran out of ammunition. She sustained multiple gunshot wounds. She watched several soldiers in her unit die around her. She was fighting so hard, [she] did not want to be taken alive. . . . Are you surprised at the tenacity she showed when—when she was faced with this?" No, Deadra Lynch replied, "I'm not surprised. She's a fighter. That's—that's our Jessi. She's a fighter, and I think that that's exactly what I would [have] expected . . . out of her."[15] Vernon Loeb, one of the authors of the *Post*'s "fighting to the death" story, went on NBC's Sunday evening *Dateline* program to say that Lynch "had literally fired her weapon until it ran out of ammunition."[16]

It was all quite remarkable, fascinating, and irresistible:[17] the shy, petite clerk who, in the *Post*'s telling, had fought her attackers with Rambo-like ferocity. But little of it proved true. Lynch, it turned out, had been neither shot nor stabbed. She had not fired her assault rifle during the ambush. "I didn't kill nobody," Lynch would tell her biographer, who wrote that she "seemed ashamed" in making the acknowledgment.[18] Her weapon had jammed, and as the ambush raged around her, Lynch had cowered in the back seat of a speeding Humvee, her head between her knees, praying, "Oh God help us. Oh God, get us out of here."[19] Moments later, a rocket-propelled grenade slammed into the Humvee, sending it crashing into a disabled tractor-trailer just ahead. The driver and four others in the Humvee were fatally injured. The impact tossed Lynch around like a rag doll, crushing her arms and legs and knocking her unconscious for several hours.

This chapter explores the many and enduring consequences of the inaccurate newspaper report that propelled the media-driven myth of Jessica Lynch. The *Post*'s account that Lynch was "fighting to the death" became a foundation myth, enabling and encouraging the emergence of subsidiary media myths, including the enduring notion that Lynch's dramatic rescue was "completely manufactured,"[20] a propaganda stunt manipulated by the U.S. military[21] to boost morale at home. This chapter also notes that the *Post* never fully acknowledged or explained its extraordinary error about Jessica Lynch and that the newspaper's retreat from its false report was belated, incomplete, misleading, and even disingenuous.

The *Post*'s hero-warrior tale thrust Lynch into an international spotlight that has never fully receded.[22] Years after the erroneous account of her exploits in Iraq, the fame and riches associated with hero status still attach to Lynch, despite her protestations that in her case, "hero" is a characterization both inaccurate and undeserved. The media myth of Jessica Lynch had the additional effect of diverting attention from the real Ramboesque hero of the ambush at Nasiriyah, an Army cook from Oregon who laid down covering fire as elements of the 507th fled the ambush and fought the Iraqis until running out of ammunition.

THE HERO-WARRIOR STORY UNRAVELS

The *Post*'s "fighting to the death" story about Lynch was reported by respected veteran journalists: Loeb and Susan Schmidt shared the byline, with contributions by Dana Priest and others. The careers of these journalists suffered little, if at all, from the debacle of the Lynch report. Loeb moved from the *Post* to become an investigations editor at the *Los Angeles Times,* then a deputy managing editor at the *Philadelphia Inquirer,* and, more recently, managing editor at the *Houston Chronicle.* Schmidt won a Pulitzer Prize in 2006 for investigative reporting, and Priest won a Pulitzer and other awards as lead reporter in the *Post*'s disclosures in 2007 about scandalous conditions for some wounded soldiers at the Walter Reed Army Medical Center in Washington.

Their stunning story about Lynch began unraveling within hours after its publication, when Lynch's father told reporters that doctors treating Lynch at the U.S. military hospital in Landstuhl, Germany, said she had suffered neither gunshot nor knife wounds.[23] The implications of that report, and others that followed, were clear enough: the "fighting to the death" story was seriously flawed. The *Post,* though, was hardly eager to follow up on those implications. "The story had an odor to it almost from the beginning," wrote Michael Getler, then the *Post*'s ombudsman, or in-house critic, "and other news organizations blew holes in it well before The Post did." Why, Getler asked in his column in the *Post,* "did the information in that first story, which was wrong in its most compelling aspects, remain unchallenged for so long?"[24]

The *Post* waited ten weeks before revisiting the Lynch story,[25] doing so in a 5,500-word report that began on the front page and continued on two inside pages.[26] The article's first paragraphs were worded to suggest it was an update about Lynch and her slow recovery from serious injuries. But the article's continuation on page 16 presented the embarrassing news—or what one critic called "the journalistic equivalent of Napoleon's retreat from Moscow."[27] The *Post* acknowledged what by then was becoming widely known: Lynch "was neither shot nor stabbed." Her broken bones and other injuries were suffered in the crash of the Humvee as it tried to flee the ambush at Nasiriyah.[28]

But the article included a nervy attempt to deflect blame from the *Post*'s central role in spreading the hero-warrior myth of Jessica Lynch. The *Post* faulted the U.S. military and the administration of President George W. Bush for failing to correct an error for which the *Post* was responsible. "Neither the Pentagon nor the White House publicly dispelled the more romanticized initial version of her capture," the *Post* said, "helping to foster the myth surrounding Lynch and fuel accusations that the Bush administration stage-managed parts of Lynch's story."[29] It was an astounding assertion, because the *Post* alone was responsible for propagating the "romanticized initial version" that created the hero-warrior myth. To claim that the Pentagon and the White House should have done more to dispel that report was as brazen as it was misguided.[30]

The article contained another sleight of hand: it referred to "initial reports, including those in The Washington Post," that depicted Lynch as "emptying her M-16 into Iraqi soldiers." It was a disinguous reference that implied that the *Post* had company in breaking the hero-warrior story. And that was untrue, as Getler pointed out. "The Post . . . put this tale into the public domain," Getler wrote in a column on the editorial page, and the "rest of the world's media picked it up." The report about Lynch's heroics was, he added, "the single most memorable story of the war, and it had huge propaganda value. It was false, but it didn't get knocked down [by the *Post*] until it didn't matter quite so much."[31]

Given that the hero-warrior narrative proved untrue, it was scarcely surprising that other suspicions arose about the Lynch saga, namely that Pentagon officials had planted the "fighting to the death" report; that the rescue of Lynch was "something of a scam,"[32] a stunt concocted for propaganda purposes; and that the rescue was contrived to boost flagging morale at home. Each of these subsidiary myths will be examined, and dismantled, in turn.

PENTAGON NOT THE SOURCE

Loeb, Schmidt, and Priest have never spoken publicly about the specific identity of the sources for their "fighting to the death" account. They said in the article that their information about Lynch and her heroics was from "U.S. officials" with access to what the reporters called "battlefield intelligence" compiled from "monitored communications and from Iraqi sources in Nasiriyah whose reliability has yet to be assessed." The article said that "Pentagon officials . . . had heard 'rumors' of Lynch's heroics but had no confirmation" to offer.[33] Pentagon officials were said to have been mortified by the "fighting to the death" story and treated the *Post's* account "as if it were radioactive."[34]

Even so, it was soon widely suspected that the "U.S. officials" cited in the *Post's* report were Pentagon sources—or, as a columnist in Lynch's native West Virginia put it, "the armed forces' PR machine."[35] A columnist for the *Post* speculated that Loeb, Schmidt, and Priest "may have been misled or misinformed by their sources in the military" and suggested, "Maybe the Pentagon hyped the Lynch story."[36] It was hardly far-fetched to suspect that the military had had a hand in the *Post's* report. None of the *Post* reporters was with Lynch's unit when it was attacked. No reporters were. Loeb, Schmidt, and Priest put together the "fighting to the death" report in Washington, D.C. Loeb at the time was the *Post's* defense writer. The Pentagon was his beat. Given those elements, the Pentagon seemed a logical source for a story about battlefield derring-do. But Loeb, belatedly perhaps, insisted that was not so.

In a little-noted interview on National Public Radio's *Fresh Air* program in late 2003, Loeb made it clear the *Post's* sources were not Pentagon officials. "And, in fact," Loeb said, "I could never get anybody from the Pentagon to talk about those reports at all. I got indications that they had, in fact, received those intelligence reports, but the Pentagon was completely unwilling to comment on those reports at all. They wouldn't say anything about Jessica Lynch." Loeb scoffed at the interviewer's suggestion that the "fighting to the death" report was the result of clever manipulation by the Pentagon. "I just didn't see the Pentagon trying to create a hero where there was none," Loeb said. "I mean . . . they never showed any interest in doing that, to me."[37]

On another occasion, Loeb was quoted in the *New York Times* as saying, "Far from promoting stories about Lynch, the military didn't like the story."[38] Victoria Clarke, then the Defense Department spokeswoman, was quoted by the Associated Press as saying, "We were downplaying [the Lynch hero-warrior story]. We weren't hyping it."[39]

Although Loeb did not identify the newspaper's sources for its "fighting to the death" report, he characterized them on *Fresh Air* as "U.S. officials" who were "really good intelligence sources" in Washington.

He said that they were privy to the battlefield reports from Iraq and had shared those reports with what Loeb called "senior members of the U.S. government."[40] In a separate interview broadcast on CNBC, Loeb said that "Iraqi informants on the ground who either witnessed the battle or heard stories of the battle" were "the ones who basically told American intelligence that Jessica Lynch fought until she ran out of ammunition and that they—it was the Iraqis themselves who were basically stunned at her fierce resistance on the battlefield."[41]

It is clear that the top spokesman at the U.S. Central Command in Qatar, Navy Captain Frank Thorp, passed along aspects of the *Post's* flawed story. Thorp was quoted as saying in a *Military Times* report, posted online on April 3, 2003, that Lynch had "waged quite a battle prior to her capture." He also said the military had "very strong indications that Jessica Lynch was not captured easily. Reports are that she fired her (M-16 rifle) until she had no more ammunition."[42] Thorp, who later became a rear admiral and the Navy's chief of information, told congressional staff members in 2007 that his interview with *Military Times* was brief and that the news media then "desperately wanted me to confirm the story [about Lynch's heroics] that was running in the States." He added: "I may have said I am familiar with 'the reports' meaning the press reports, but as you can see I did not confirm them. . . . We did have reports of a battle and that a firefight had occurred. . . . That is what I stated."[43]

Had the Pentagon planted or concocted the story about Lynch's fighting to the death, it failed miserably in keeping the ruse from unraveling. The day after the *Post's* sensational report was published, Colonel David Rubenstein, commander of the Army's hospital at Landstuhl, Germany, told journalists that Lynch had been neither shot nor stabbed,[44] undercutting crucial elements of the hero-warrior narrative. If the military had been complicit in fabricating the Lynch saga, it defies logic to believe it would permit one of its own, an Army colonel, to impugn that narrative just as it began to circulate around the world.

Mark Bowden, the author of *Black Hawk Down*, a critically acclaimed book about the failed U.S. military mission in Somalia in 1993, dismissed as implausible the notion that the Pentagon concocted and planted the *Post's* "fighting to the death" report. "For one thing," Bowden wrote in the *New York Times*, "it would hardly have taken a secret plot to get the American press to make a hero out of Lynch, any more than it would take a plot to make a thirsty horse drink. . . . What happened often happens on big breaking stories, especially from a war zone. The bits and pieces of information that emerge from the fog are fit into a familiar frame. . . . There is no doubt that the American media took these bits and pieces from the fog of war and assembled them into a heroic tale. . . . This is how the media works today, for better or worse." And this happens, Bowden wrote, "without any prompting from the Pentagon."[45]

A STAGE-MANAGED STUNT?

The Lynch case produced an international variation of intermedia agenda-setting: the notion that her rescue was contrived drama emanated from news media in Britain. The day after the *Post* published its "fighting to the death" report, the *Evening Standard* newspaper in London cast a wary eye on the story, saying it smacked of "a dirty little piece of propaganda in a morally suspect war."[46] Such suspicions reached full expression in May 2003, in a documentary broadcast on the BBC, one of the world's most respected news organizations. Relying almost entirely on the accounts of Iraqi medical personnel at the hospital, the BBC concluded that the rescue of Lynch was "one of the most stunning pieces of news management ever conceived," a shameless bit of stagecraft done for propaganda purposes.

The program, which the BBC called "War Spin," quoted an Iraqi doctor at the hospital as saying the rescue "was like a Hollywood film." The extrication team, he said, "cried 'go, go, go,' with guns and blanks without bullets . . . and the sound of explosions. They made a show for the American attack on the hospital—action movies like Sylvester Stallone or Jackie Chan." The BBC's report also said that the Pentagon, in organizing the Lynch rescue, "had been influenced by Hollywood producers of reality TV and action movies," notably by Jerry Bruckheimer, who made the war film *Black Hawk Down*.[47]

The Pentagon dismissed the BBC's claims as "void of all facts and absolutely ridiculous." Other experts scoffed at the notion that Special Operations units would enter a hostile environment with blanks in their weapons. A Pentagon spokesman insisted that the military had employed tactics and procedures that were consistent with the prospect of facing hostile forces[48]—and an investigation by the Defense Department's inspector general supported that version. The inspector general's inquiry had been requested in the wake of the BBC's allegations by Rahm Emanuel, Louise Slaughter, and Pete Stark, all of whom were then members of the U.S. House of Representatives.

In testimony to Congress in 2007, Thomas F. Gimble, the Defense Department's acting inspector general, said the BBC's allegations had not been substantiated and that no evidence had been uncovered to support the notion that the rescue "was a staged media event." Rather, Gimble said, the rescue operation was "a valid mission" to rescue a prisoner of war "under combat conditions." That the Lynch rescue was videotaped was not unusual, Gimble said, noting that combat cameramen routinely filmed high-priority operations. In the Lynch case, he said, there was "no indication that any service member was acting for the camera during the rescue mission."[49] More than thirty witnesses were interviewed in the inspector general's inquiry, including members of the Special Operations rescue team, Gimble said in his written testimony. Few if any of those witnesses had been interviewed by news organizations, he said. In undertaking the Lynch rescue, Gimble said, the extrication team "fully expected to meet stiff resistance" and had come under enemy fire from the hospital building and areas nearby.[50]

Gimble's report was an unequivocal rebuke to the BBC's account. Even so, by the time Gimble testified, four years had passed and the BBC's version had become an unshakable, widely accepted element of the Lynch saga.[51] Gimble's contrary report did not fit what had become the dominant narrative about the rescue. It made little news. After all, the notion of a theatrical but counterfeit rescue operation fit well with the curdled popular view of the war in Iraq. U.S. forces had toppled Saddam Hussein's brutal regime, but they became bogged down in a lethal insurgency that took years to dampen. The weapons of mass destruction that Saddam supposedly developed and stockpiled were never found. Not surprising, it wasn't long before the American news media turned harshly skeptical about the war effort and the Lynch saga.

Her rescue, said the *Philadelphia Inquirer,* seemed at first to be "a balm to American hearts. Except that much of it now appears to be untrue. The British Broadcasting Corp. cast cold water on the tale," and only belatedly "the American media have begun examining the story they had swallowed" so readily.[52] The Associated Press wire service gave the BBC's version a significant endorsement, reporting in late May 2003 that its interviews of doctors, nurses, and medical staff at the hospital from which Lynch was rescued supported a conclusion that "the dramatics that surrounded Lynch's rescue were unnecessary."[53]

But such skeptics invariably ignored the critical variable of uncertainty, which shaped and defined the rescue operation. Lynch's rescuers could not have known whether, or to what extent, they would encounter resistance at the hospital.[54] The dangers and uncertainties in Nasiriyah obliged the rescuers to arrive in force.[55] Being uncertain about what they would encounter, they had no option but to prepare for the worst.[56] Above all, military planners wanted to avoid a botched rescue mission like the aborted attempt in 1980 to extricate U.S. diplomatic personnel held hostage in Tehran.[57] That operation ended in disaster, when a would-be rescue helicopter collided with a military transport aircraft at a rendezvous zone in the Iranian desert during the mission's early stages.

The hospital in Nasiriyah had been a command post for Iraqi irregulars, the Fedayeen, until the day before the rescue. Lynch's biographer called the place "a safe haven" for Iraqi militia, who knew that U.S. forces "would not—intentionally—bomb a hospital. The Americans would certainly not bomb a hospital with a female U.S. soldier lying helpless in her bed." Lynch, he wrote, was in effect "a human shield." In the basement of the hospital, the Iraqis kept a cache of rifles, mortars, and ammunition.[58] Not long after Lynch's rescue, the hospital's wards came under attack by men "in long gowns and head scarves, carrying grenades and machine guns," the London *Daily Telegraph* reported. "Hospital workers said the men rampaged through the wards stealing drugs and generators as terrified patients on all floors fled."[59] Even weeks later, Iraqis were still shooting at Marines in the vicinity of the hospital.

LITTLE NEED FOR MORALE BOOST

Portions of the videotape of Lynch's rescue were released almost immediately. Critics slammed the military, claiming the rescue had been orchestrated and choreographed to deliver a needed boost to spirits back home at a difficult moment in the war.[60] "Her story broke during the stalled early days of conflict, with morale reaching low tide, and had a galvanizing effect," David Lipsky wrote in the *New York Times*.[61] "Just when the war in Iraq seemed to drag and was losing public support, there was America's heroine on the front page of the Washington Post," wrote Steve Ritea in the *American Journalism Review*. "It was the perfect story at the perfect time."[62]

It is an enticing notion. But it finds little support in public opinion surveys taken during the first days and weeks of the war. Those surveys show there was little need for morale boosting. It may be little recalled nowadays, but the U.S.-led invasion of Iraq was widely supported by the American public. Polling data from the opening days and weeks of the war in March and April 2003 show an overwhelming percentage of

Americans supported the conflict and believed the war effort, overall, was going well. A CNN/*USA Today*/Gallup poll, taken of 1,012 American adults on March 29 and 30, 2003—just days after the ambush in Nasiriyah and shortly before Lynch's rescue—found that 85.5 percent of respondents thought the war effort was going "very well" or "moderately well" for U.S. forces; 72 percent thought that U.S. military action was proceeding according to plan, and 69 percent of respondents said that they felt sure the United States would win the war. Only 0.98 percent felt certain the United States would lose.[63]

Washington Post–ABC News polls conducted in late March and early April 2003 also dispute the notion that the Lynch rescue came at a time of sagging spirits and declining support for the war. A *Washington Post*–ABC News poll on March 23, 2003, found that eight of ten Americans felt that the war effort was unfolding well and 71 percent approved of the Bush administration's handling of the Iraq situation.[64] Another *Washington Post*–ABC News poll, taken on April 3, 2003, the day the *Post* published its "fighting to the death" report about Lynch, found that nine of ten Americans thought the war was going well and 69 percent said they believed the war was justified even if weapons of mass destruction were not found.[65]

At the time of the Lynch rescue, U.S. forces were closing in on Baghdad. So it is illogical to argue that the American military would have singled out and hyped the Lynch rescue for morale-building purposes when its vastly more important and central wartime objective was within reach. Yet the improbable notion that the Lynch rescue was contrived as a morale booster caught on and endures, notably in the news media in Britain and Ireland. For example, the *Observer* newspaper in London returned to that theme on the fifth anniversary of the start of the Iraq War, saying the "rescue" had been "used to bolster public backing for the war" and that "the facts surrounding [Lynch's] capture had been manipulated by the United States military."[66] The *Irish Times* recalled the Lynch case in cheeky fashion, stating, "A non-victim called Jessica Lynch was non-saved by U.S. soldiers in a non-heroic non-event."[67]

The most lasting and ironic consequence of the *Post*'s "fighting to the death" report was to help turn an Army private who had never fired a shot in anger in Iraq into the war's most recognizable soldier. So powerful and unexpected was the *Post*'s account that it stamped the Lynch story into the collective memory of the American public. No other

American soldier or Marine in Iraq, hero or otherwise, received so much attention or was the beneficiary of so many rewards.

In the weeks and months that followed the *Post*'s article, Lynch's photograph appeared on the cover of *Time* and *Newsweek* magazines. She starred in a welcome home parade in her hometown in West Virginia upon her release from the Walter Reed Army hospital. She accepted a book deal estimated at $1 million, half of which reportedly went to her biographer, Rick Bragg, a former *New York Times* correspondent. She went on morning and evening television shows to promote the book, *I Am a Soldier, Too,* which Bragg completed in time for publication on November 11, 2003—Veterans Day. She inspired a television movie, *Saving Jessica Lynch,* the title of which evoked Steven Spielberg's war film *Saving Private Ryan.*[68] Lynch was offered tuition-free education at West Virginia University. She was named West Virginian of the Year in 2003.[69]

She also won an award from *Glamour* magazine, was a guest in the Gator Bowl parade, attended parties after the Golden Globe awards program, and visited the Bahamas after christening a cruise ship.[70] A year after her rescue, she told an interviewer: "I do want my life back to normal, because it's hard—it's so hard. But at the same time I'm like—wow, I get to go to New York, I get to go to Hollywood. I get to hang out with people like Britney [Spears] and Leonardo [DiCaprio]."[71] Those and other rewards and accolades all had as their primal source the *Post*'s "fighting to the death" story. Absent that report, Jessica Lynch the soldier never would have encountered such fame and fortune.

Lynch placed herself in the peculiar and paradoxical position of denying that she was a hero while accepting the riches and rewards associated with hero status.[72] She attempted to explain the incongruity by saying in an interview with *Time* magazine: "I don't feel that I'm a hero or that I've done anything spectacular. I'm not trying to take advantage of the situation. These things are coming my way. If they [her critics] were put in my shoes, they would be doing the same thing."[73]

A MISTAKE IN TRANSLATION?

More significantly, the hoopla associated with the Lynch myth had the effect of blurring recognition of the American soldier whose actions at Nasiriyah *were* heroic but initially were attributed to Lynch. He was Sergeant Donald Walters, a cook in the 507th Maintenance Company. Walters was the father of three daughters and a veteran of the 1990–1991

Gulf War. He told his parents of premonitions that he would not return alive from Iraq this time.[74] During the ambush in Nasiriyah, as the lumbering vehicles of the 507th came under Iraqi fire, Walters either stayed behind, or was left behind, to lay down covering fire as his fellow soldiers tried to make their escape. Walters fought his attackers in a fashion that the *Post* attributed to Lynch.[75] The most detailed account of Walters's bravery appears in Richard Lowry's book about the fighting at Nasiriyah, *Marines in the Garden of Eden*. Left alone on a dusty Iraqi highway, far behind enemy lines, "Walters fought his way south . . . killing several Iraqis before he was surrounded and captured" by Iraqi irregulars, the Fedayeen, Lowry wrote.[76]

Walters was taken to the headquarters of an Iraqi brigade in Nasiriyah. Soon, his body was "carried out of the building and placed in an ambulance," Lowry wrote. The driver was ordered to take the body to Saddam Hospital, where it was hastily buried.[77] "We will never really know the details of Walters' horrible ordeal," Lowry wrote. "We do know that he risked his life to save his comrades and was separated from the rest of the convoy, deep in enemy territory. We know that he fought until he could no longer resist."[78] The Army ultimately acknowledged that Walters's conduct "likely prevented his unit from suffering additional casualties and loss of life"[79] and posthumously awarded him the Silver Star, the U.S. military's third-highest decoration for valor.

But how was it that Lynch came to be confused with Walters, who was slim, ruddy, and thirty-three years old? The probable sources of confusion were Iraqi radio communications that the U.S. forces intercepted. These battlefield communications reportedly included references to a blond American soldier's fierce resistance in the fighting at Nasiriyah. In translating the intercepted reports to English, the pronoun "he" was mistaken for "she." As Lynch was the only blonde woman in the 507th, the battlefield heroics were attributed to her, not Walters.[80] A brigade commander, Colonel Heidi Brown, offered that explanation in an interview broadcast in 2004 on National Public Radio's *All Things Considered* program. "What I was told," Brown said, "was that it was just a faulty translation." She said that everyone made "a huge assumption that it was Jessica Lynch, when, in fact it probably . . . was Sergeant Walters." She added, "But you know, no one knows for sure."[81]

Walters's heroics, when they became known, attracted little more than passing interest from the American news media—certainly nothing akin to the intensity of the Lynch coverage after the *Post*'s "fighting to the death" story appeared. Nicholas D. Kristof, a columnist for the

FIGURE 23. The heroics that the *Washington Post* misattributed to Jessica Lynch most likely were the battlefield deeds of Sergeant Donald Walters, a cook who fought Iraqis until his ammunition ran out. Walters was captured and executed in Iraqi custody. [*Department of Defense/Courtesy Norman and Arlene Walters*]

New York Times, looked into the Walters case and wrote that it "seems that the heroism originally attributed to Private Lynch may actually have been Sergeant Walters's. Iraqi radio intercepts had described a blond U.S. soldier fighting tenaciously, and the Army . . . awarded him a posthumous Silver Star in implicit acknowledgment that he was probably that soldier."[82] The *Oregonian* newspaper in Portland also explored the case and concluded that it was "likely that Walters was one of the real heroes behind the story of Jessica Lynch."[83] But the *All Things Considered* program, Kristof's column, and the *Oregonian* article were the notable exceptions.[84] Interest in Walters's actions proved thin and the corrective account soon faded.

Walters's parents said they have no doubt that their son performed the heroics that were attributed to Lynch. "I'm 100 percent certain that it was our son," Norman Walters said by telephone from his home in Salem, Oregon.[85] He and his wife, Arlene, said that Lynch never called or spoke with them, and they conceded they felt frustrated by the news media's scant interest in the case of mistaken identity. Arlene Walters noted that Lynch's photograph had appeared on the cover of *Time* magazine, but when the editors "found out it wasn't her, there was never any story about Don. I called all these magazines. . . . They didn't really care."[86] What happened during the ambush at Nasiriyah deserves to be understood fully, she said. "Don has three kids and when they grow up, they would like to hear what their dad did, instead of giving the credit to someone else."[87] Jessica Lynch, said Norman Walters, "got the million-dollar book deal, and our son got a gravestone."[88]

The *Post*'s mistaken hero-warrior story about Lynch has had many effects and unintended consequences. It was, as we've seen, the foundation from which subsidiary myths sprang. It vaulted Lynch to celebrity status, paving the way for a lucrative book contract and a measure of wealth. It obscured the actions of an unheralded Army cook whose conduct at Nasiriyah probably saved the lives of some of his fellow soldiers but won little lasting recognition. And the *Post* never fully explained or accounted for its error about Jessica Lynch. Beyond Loeb's comment that he "could never get anybody from the Pentagon to talk about" the Lynch case, the sources he consulted in the *Post*'s hero-warrior story remain undisclosed. Loeb bristled when asked to discuss the Lynch case for this book, saying he was tired of talking about the matter.[89]

For its part, the *Post* has sought to deflect blame from its erroneous world exclusive about Lynch. That was apparent years later, when Lynch gave testimony to a congressional oversight committee inquiring into misreporting from the battlefield. On that occasion, the *Post* referred to Lynch as "a former soldier whose ordeal in Iraq in 2003 was inaccurately portrayed *in the media* as a heroic fight against insurgents [*sic*], when in fact Lynch never fired a shot."[90] The phrase "in the media" sidestepped the *Post*'s singular role in promoting the hero-warrior myth. The wording suggested that the "fighting to the death" report in April 2003 had not been the *Post*'s responsibility alone. But it was.

Lynch, who received an honorable discharge from the military in 2003, still struggles with the effects of the severe injuries she suffered at Nasiriyah. "I continue to deal with bladder, bowel and kidney problems as a result of my injuries," Lynch told the congressional hearing in 2007. "My left leg still has no feeling from the knee down and I am required to wear a brace so that I can stand and walk."[91] She has undergone more than twenty operations. She also has said she has nightmares of Iraqi men chasing her. CNN reported in 2015 that Lynch "constantly walks around her house locking and rechecking doors and windows to make sure they're secure." She has seen a psychiatrist, CNN also reported.[92]

Lynch accepts invitations from veterans' organizations and other groups to speak about her ordeal in Iraq and her struggles with injuries. A theme of these talks typically is "perseverance."[93] She also accepted an acting role in a Christian-themed movie titled *Virtuous*. And she has spoken in favor of assigning women to combat roles in wartime.[94]

Rick Bragg's book about Lynch, *I Am a Soldier, Too,* debuted atop the *New York Times*'s best-seller list in late November 2003[95] but sold far fewer copies than the publisher had expected.[96] A reviewer for the *Washington Post* called the book a "treacly embarrassment" and observed that "once the original myths surrounding her capture are stripped away, Lynch, as unworldly as she is sweet, simply doesn't have much of a story to tell."[97]

CHAPTER 12

Hurricane Katrina and the Myth of Superlative Reporting

Accurate reporting was among Katrina's many victims.
—*A Failure of Initiative: Final Report of the Select Bipartisan Committee to Investigate the Preparation for and Response to Hurricane Katrina* (Washington, DC: U.S. Government Printing Office, 2007), 360

The first decade of the twenty-first century brought harsh and painful times to America's mainstream news media. Metropolitan newspapers and television networks hemorrhaged audiences and lost advertising to online media. Newspapers shrunk their pages to curb expenses. Staffs were cut deeply, through layoffs and buyouts. Salaries were trimmed and unpaid leaves were imposed. Predictions appeared with increasing frequency that newspapers might not long survive.[1] Warned the now-defunct *American Journalism Review*: "Adapt or die."[2] Well-known metropolitan dailies such as the *Rocky Mountain News* in Denver and the *Post-Intelligencer* in Seattle ceased publication. Once-powerful media enterprises such as the Tribune Company in Chicago sought Chapter 11 bankruptcy protection.

Midway through the grim decade came a moment of ostensible triumph for the beleaguered news media: their reporting of Hurricane Katrina, one of America's worst-ever natural disasters. The storm packed winds of up to 145 miles an hour as it plowed into the Gulf Coast in late August 2005. Katrina brought vast flooding to New Orleans and devastated coastal Mississippi and Alabama. More than 970 people were killed in Louisiana, most of them in New Orleans.[3] Across the Gulf Coast, tens of thousands of people were displaced, including 20,000 who took shelter at the Louisiana Superdome and 30,000 who fled to the Ernest N. Morial Convention Center in New Orleans. Looting broke out in New Orleans soon after the hurricane passed, and more than two hundred New Orleans police officers deserted their posts or failed to report for duty in the storm's aftermath.[4] Some officers even joined in the looting spree.[5]

In the face of the deepening disaster, federal, state, and city emergency relief efforts proved sluggish, erratic, and stymied, especially in New Orleans. The plight and despair of evacuees gathered at the hot, fetid Superdome and the Convention Center represented compelling testimony about the failure to provide relief and necessities. Evidence of government incompetence at all levels was abundant and became a powerful element of the post-Katrina story. People were suffering in New Orleans, and journalists went after the story vigorously, posing lacerating questions of federal, state, and city authorities: Where was the aid? Why had it not arrived? What was to be done to help the evacuees?

Conditions turned so dreadful that the *Times-Picayune,* the daily newspaper in New Orleans, published an open letter to President George W. Bush, urging the dismissal of every official at the Federal Emergency Management Agency (FEMA). "We're angry, Mr. President, and we'll be angry long after our beloved city and surrounding parishes have been pumped dry," the newspaper said, adding, "Our people deserved rescuing. Many who could have been were not. That's to the government's shame."[6]

Television journalists, meanwhile, were notably unrestrained, unafraid to show their frustration or express their barely disguised contempt. A frequent target was the beleaguered FEMA director, a Bush political appointee named Michael D. Brown, who had almost no emergency management experience when named to the position. In the hurricane's confused aftermath, Brown conceded to being unaware that the Convention Center had been turned into a shelter for thousands of people in New Orleans. Journalists were incredulous. "How is it possible that we're getting better intel than you're getting?" Soledad O'Brien, an anchor for the CNN network, asked the hapless official. "We were showing live pictures of the people outside of the Convention Center. . . . And also, we've been reporting that officials have been telling people to go to the Convention Center if they want any hope of relief. I don't understand how FEMA cannot have this information."[7] Ted Koppel of ABC News upbraided Brown for being unaware of the plight of Convention Center evacuees. "Don't you guys watch television?" Koppel asked him. "Don't you guys listen to the radio?"[8]

FIGURE 24. Journalists covering Hurricane Katrina's aftermath were withering in their appraisals of Michael D. Brown, the director of the Federal Emergency Management Agency. Brown seemed to possess only a tenuous grasp of posthurricane conditions in New Orleans. [*Jocelyn Augustino/Federal Emergency Management Agency*]

"ESSENTIAL AGAIN"?

It was all powerful, very moving stuff. In the turmoil that followed the hurricane's landfall, traditional news media seemed vital, aggressive, and authoritative. "Essential Again," *American Journalism Review* proclaimed in a flattering cover story about the news media and their Katrina coverage. "Those first days were a time for intrepid TV cameramen to take us into the stench and the sweat, the anger and the not knowing, the fear of those who seemed abandoned by their own country," the magazine declared. "Those first days were a time for newspapers to put aside jitters about their declining importance and worries about layoffs and cutbacks. The old papers instead reasserted the comfort and utility of news you could hold in your hand."[9] It added: "In this era of blogs, pundits and shouted arguments, the coming of Katrina reunited the people and the reporters. In a time of travail, parts of the media landscape that had seemed faded, yea, even discarded, now felt true."[10]

The miseries for the news media seemed suddenly to have lifted, and journalists congratulated one another on their gritty, searching, no-holds-barred reporting. "People were starved for information. And journalists, brave, committed journalists, went out and got it for them, often under harrowing conditions," Rem Rieder, the editor of *American Journalism Review,* wrote in a preface to the "Essential Again" article.[11] "Journalism seems to have recovered its reason for being," declared Howard Kurtz, the *Washington Post*'s media writer, in a tribute to the Katrina coverage. "For once, reporters were acting like concerned citizens, not passive observers. And they were letting their emotions show."[12]

Dan Rather, a former evening news anchor for CBS News whose early career had been propelled by his coverage of hurricanes, was extravagant in his praise. Rather went on the CNN talk show *Larry King Live* to declare the Katrina coverage "one of the quintessential great moments in television news," ranking it "right there with the Nixon/Kennedy debates, the Kennedy assassination, Watergate coverage, you name it." The reporting, Rather declared, was nothing short of a "landmark."[13]

The praise was effusive, self-reverential—and more than a little misleading. Journalists did let their emotions show, and they did confront incompetent government officials who seemed to dither in the face of the disaster. Many of them took great risks in New Orleans to report demanding, multidimensional stories in a city that was 80 percent under water. Some journalists there went days without much of a break, sleeping little and toiling amid despairing conditions.

FIGURE 25. The *New Orleans Times-Picayune* reported on September 2, 2005, that chaos and lawlessness had seized the city in Katrina's aftermath. The newspaper subsequently revisited the accounts of mayhem and said that "most of the worst crimes reported . . . never happened." [*© 2005 The Times-Picayune Publishing Co. All rights reserved. Used with permission of the* Times-Picayune]

But Katrina's aftermath was no high, heroic moment in American journalism. The coverage was in important respects flawed and exaggerated. On crucial details, journalists erred badly and got it wrong. In the days following Katrina's landfall, news reports described apocalyptic horror that the hurricane supposedly had unleashed. They reported that snipers were aiming at medical personnel. They reported that shots were fired at helicopters, halting evacuations from the Convention Center. They told of bodies being stacked there like cordwood. They reported that roving gangs were preying on tourists and terrorizing the occupants of the Superdome, raping and killing. They said children were victims of sexual assault, that one seven-year-old was raped and her throat was slit. They reported that sharks were plying the flooded streets of New Orleans.

None of those reports was verified or substantiated: no shots fired at rescue helicopters,[14] no child rape victims, no bodies stacked like cordwood, no sharks.[15] No single news organization committed all of these errors. And not all of the lapses were committed at the same time. But the erroneous and exaggerated reporting had the cumulative effect of painting for America and the rest of the world a scene of surreal violence and terror, something straight out of *Mad Max* or *Lord of the Flies*.[16] "The picture that emerged," the *Times-Picayune* said in a detailed retrospective report about the flawed news coverage, "was one of the impoverished, overwhelmingly African-American masses of flood victims resorting to utter depravity, randomly attacking each other, as well as the police trying to protect them and the rescue workers trying to save them."[17] The reports had made it seem as though the city were a haven for lurking criminals waiting for the opportune moment to inflict violence on others.

CONSEQUENCES OF FLAWED COVERAGE

The exaggerated, over-the-top reporting was neither benign nor without consequences. It had the very real and serious effects of delaying the arrival of aid to New Orleans, of diverting and distorting the deployment of resources and capabilities, of heightening the anxiety of evacuees at the Superdome and Convention Center, and of broadly stigmatizing a city and its people.

"Americans depend on timely and accurate reporting, especially during times of crisis," a bipartisan select committee of the House of Representatives said in a six-hundred-page report about the hurricane's aftermath. "But it's clear [that] accurate reporting was among Katrina's many victims. If anyone rioted, it was the media," the report declared. "Many stories of rape, murder, and general lawlessness were at best unsubstantiated, at worst simply false. And that's too bad because this storm needed no exaggeration."[18] When accurate reporting was most urgent, the news media too often failed to deliver.

The central focus of the House select committee was not the performance of the news media. The panel's report identified and criticized "failures at all levels of government" in Katrina's aftermath, including the Bush administration.[19] But the report presented what in effect was a compendium of adverse consequences traceable to the news media's flawed and inaccurate reporting.

Principal among the effects was to impede or delay the relief effort in New Orleans. By reporting exaggerated or unsubstantiated rumors of mayhem and violence, journalists "unwittingly helped slow an already slow response and further wound an already wounded population," the House report said. Commercial truck drivers transporting badly needed supplies of water, food, ice, shelter, and medicine read or heard the reports of nightmarish violence and were too frightened to enter New Orleans. Convoys of National Guardsmen were organized to escort the truckers into the city, but doing so diverted the guardsmen from other relief assignments.[20]

Exaggerated reporting had another complicating effect, that of encouraging spontaneous self-deployments of law enforcement officials from other parts of the region. According to the House select committee, local and state police officers responded at their own initiative to the media accounts of lawlessness in New Orleans. The committee said it could not estimate the extent of these self-deployments, given their ad hoc nature. But it noted that the "'self-deployed' personnel were acting without proper authority, without liability protection, and without eligibility for expense reimbursement."[21]

The reports of mayhem in New Orleans also forced National Guardsmen to delay their deployment to the Convention Center until September 2—one hundred hours after the hurricane struck—to be sure of mustering a force of sufficient size to confront the lawlessness and security problems that had been reported there. Those problems turned out to be wildly overstated.[22] In addition, one thousand FEMA employees who were set to arrive in New Orleans two days after the hurricane struck turned back because security in the city seemed so tenuous, the House report said, quoting the chief of staff of then Louisiana governor Kathleen Blanco.[23]

The exaggerated news reports not only complicated and impeded the relief effort, the House report said, they also "affected decisions on where to direct resources."[24] A senior National Guard official, Lieutenant General H. Steven Blum, told the select committee that in the absence of reliable communication networks, National Guardsmen and relief officials turned to news reports to gauge conditions on the ground—for what the general called "situational awareness." The news media, he said, "failed in their responsibility to get it right," noting that the National Guard "sent forces and capabilities to places that didn't need to go there in numbers that were far in excess of what was required."[25] Similarly, in a retrospective article published in late September 2005, the *New York Times* reported that "terror from crimes seen and unseen, real and rumored" had the effect of altering troop deployments in New Orleans and slowing medical evacuations.[26]

Reports of mayhem in New Orleans forced authorities and rescue workers to adopt unnecessary and cumbersome precautions to complete what otherwise would have been routine tasks. The *Wall Street Journal* reported that "federal rescuers and doctors were required to secure armed escorts even for short trips across the street" in Katrina's immediate aftermath. Moreover, the *Journal* said, the reports of "unspeakable violence" in New Orleans raised the possibility, at least for a short time, that American soldiers might be called on to confront "or even kill American citizens" to restore order. Such a scenario, the newspaper said, would have "added political and tactical complications to the job of filling the city with troops and set back relief efforts by days."[27]

While the Superdome and Convention Center went days without electricity, many evacuees turned to battery-powered transistor radios to keep up with news reports.[28] This created a feedback loop, in which the exaggerated reports about rampant lawlessness at the Superdome and Convention Center reached the evacuees inside those places, raising their fears and pushing some of them almost "to the boiling point."[29] Major Ed Bush of the Louisiana National Guard, who was stationed at the Superdome during the most wretched days after the hurricane struck, offered a sense of how the feedback loop caused confusion, consternation, and fresh rumors. "People would hear something on the radio and come and say that people were getting raped in the bathroom or someone had been murdered," Bush told the *Washington Post*. "I would say, 'Ma'am, where?' I would tell them if there were bodies, my guys would find [them]. Everybody heard, nobody saw."[30]

IMPUGNING A CITY AND ITS PEOPLE

The exaggerated reporting had the broader effect of impugning the reputation of New Orleans and its residents, depicting them as having shed all restraints. They have been "kind of cheated," Bush said, "because now everybody thinks that they just turned to animals, and that there was complete lawlessness and utter abandon" in the days after Katrina's landfall. "And that wasn't the case."[31] The hurricane did unleash spasms of looting in New Orleans. But often, looters were seeking necessities such as food and water. The House select committee cited the National Guard and law enforcement authorities as saying that "the people in the Superdome were very unhappy and anxious, but they were never out of control."[32]

The exaggerated reporting was not occasional, a slip or a mistake here or there. It came to characterize coverage of Katrina's aftermath, and it was noticeable within seventy-two hours after the hurricane's landfall. Banner headlines in newspapers across the country on September 2, 2005, told of the city's supposed slide into chaos and anarchy. "Anger, Anarchy, Desperation," declared the *San Francisco Chronicle;* "Crisis to Chaos," proclaimed the *Scottsdale Tribune* in Arizona; "Toward Anarchy," stated the *Waterbury Republican* in Connecticut; "Descent into Chaos," said the *San Diego Union-Tribune.*[33]

On her CNN program on September 1, 2005, Paula Zahn referred to "very discouraging reports out of New Orleans tonight about bands of rapists going from block to block, people walking around in feces, dead bodies floating everywhere. And we know that sniper fire continues." Zahn also said: "We are getting reports that describe it as a nightmare of crime, human waste, rotten food, dead bodies everywhere. Other reports say sniper fire is hampering efforts to get people out."[34] That day, John Burnett of National Public Radio said on the *All Things Considered* program: "We understand that there was a 10-year-old girl who was raped in the convention center in the last two nights. People are absolutely desperate there. I've never seen anything like this."[35]

Meanwhile, the *Miami Herald* reported that a "major American city all but disintegrated . . . and the expected death toll from Hurricane Katrina mushroomed into the thousands. Bodies floated down streets. Defeated survivors waded waist-deep and ghost-like through floods. Packs of looters rampaged through the ruins and armed themselves with stolen weapons, and gunfire echoed through the city."[36] The *New York Daily News* offered similarly horrific accounts: "Corpses littered the sodden streets. Snipers fired on cops and rescue workers. Gangs of looters took anything that wasn't nailed down."[37]

The Associated Press reported that New Orleans had "descended into anarchy" as "corpses lay abandoned in street medians, fights and fires broke out, cops turned in their badges and the governor declared war on looters who have made the city a menacing landscape of disorder and fear."[38] The news agency also said that shots had been fired at a military helicopter near the Superdome, suspending efforts to remove evacuees from the place.[39] It turned out that the evacuation was never suspended[40] and that the gunshots were fired most likely in an attempt to attract attention, not deter the relief helicopters.[41]

In some instances, news organizations passed on unadulterated rumors—and even identified them as such. Gannett News Service, for example, reported on September 3 that, inside the Convention Center, evacuees "spoke of dead bodies stacked up," of "toilets overflowing with waste and looters demanding payment for food they'd plundered from stores. Feverish rumors shot through the crowd—authorities wouldn't let people onto buses out of the city unless they cleaned up the area first, chemicals were being sprayed on them, the Mississippi River was about to be unleashed."[42]

Estimates of Katrina's death toll in New Orleans were wildly exaggerated. U.S. Senator David Vitter, a Louisiana Republican, said on September 2 that fatalities in the state could reach ten thousand or more[43]—which would have made Katrina the country's worst natural disaster. Vitter characterized his estimate as "only a guess," but it was taken up and repeated by the New Orleans mayor, Ray Nagin, and reported widely.[44]

Nagin and the city's police commissioner, Eddie Compass, were sources for some of the most shocking and exaggerated reports about the disaster. During a joint appearance on Oprah Winfrey's popular television talk show on September 6, Nagin said "hundreds of armed gang members" were terrorizing evacuees inside the Superdome. He declared that conditions there had deteriorated to "an almost animalistic state" and evacuees had been "in that frickin' Superdome for five days, watching dead bodies, watching hooligans killing people, raping people."[45] Compass spoke of other horrors. "We had little babies in there, little babies getting raped," the police commissioner said on the show.[46] Compass also claimed police officers had been shot at inside the Superdome. They had not returned fire, he said, for fear of wounding evacuees. Compass also claimed that police had made thirty arrests inside the Superdome by tracking the flashes made as weapons were fired.[47] Winfrey even joined in, declaring that gangs had "banded together" in the Superdome "and had more ammunition, at times, than [did the] police."[48]

These accounts were widely reported—and proved to be almost totally without foundation. In all, six people died in the Superdome during the Katrina aftermath. None of those deaths was related to violent crime. At the Convention Center, where the *Times-Picayune* had reported that National Guardsmen found thirty to forty corpses stacked in a freezer, four bodies were recovered.[49] Reports that infants and young girls were raped were likewise unfounded.

FIGURE 26. Then New Orleans mayor Ray Nagin was a source of highly exaggerated reports about death and violence in the city following Katrina's strike. Nagin said on Oprah Winfrey's television show that "hundreds of armed gang members" had been terrorizing evacuees inside the Louisiana Superdome. [*Marvin Nauman/Federal Emergency Management Agency*]

Compass was asked months afterward why he had depicted New Orleans as swept by mayhem in Katrina's aftermath. He offered a baffling reply. "I didn't want people to think we were trying to cover anything up," he said. "So I repeated these things without being substantiated, and it caused a lot of problems."[50] Within a few weeks of his appearance on Oprah, Compass was forced to resign. Nagin, though, was reelected in 2006 to a four-year term as mayor. He left office in 2010. In 2014, Nagin was sentenced to ten years in federal prison for bribery and other crimes committed in a kickback scheme with contractors.[51]

International news organizations were keen in Katrina's aftermath to report the horror stories from New Orleans, as if the hurricane had exposed pathologies in American society that otherwise would remain obscure. The international media "played the unfounded reports for all they were worth," noted David Carr in the *New York Times,* "with hundreds of news outlets regurgitating tales of lawlessness."[52] The British press, including the upscale "quality" newspapers, were particularly eager to indulge in tales of mayhem. "Girls and boys were raped in the dark and had their throats cut and bodies stuffed in the kitchens while looters and madmen exchanged fire with weapons they had looted," the usually staid *Financial Times* said of conditions inside the Convention Center.[53] The *Guardian* of London called New Orleans "a city . . . subsumed beneath waves of violence, rape and death" and said it was "clear from talking to survivors that what happened in New Orleans . . . was far more extensive, bloody and terrifying than the authorities have admitted so far."[54]

A columnist for London's *Independent* newspaper offered this colorful and highly imaginative account: "Reports from New Orleans ring like prophecies of the apocalypse. Corpses float hopelessly in what used to be a thriving and distinctive downtown; coffins rise from the ground; alligators, sharks and snakes ply the poisonous waters."[55] The *Times* of London erroneously and excessively reported that ambulances "were hijacked or tipped on their sides, and one fully functioning hospital asked to be evacuated after a supply truck carrying medical supplies was held up at gunpoint. Staff at another hospital came under sniper fire as they tried to evacuate patients."[56] The *Times* offered a short corrective article in mid-September, conceding that "there was much we thought we knew that turns out to be wildly exaggerated or plain false." That included estimates of ten thousand deaths in New Orleans. The *Times* said that "it was clear that 10,000 people could have died only if more than 90 per cent of them had locked themselves into their homes, chained themselves to heavy furniture and chosen to drown instead of going upstairs as the waters rose."[57] But the *Times* rationalized the flawed reporting, saying it was inevitable: when "nature and the 24-hour news industry collide, hyperbole results."[58]

REVISITING THE REPORTS OF MAYHEM

The London *Times*'s acknowledgment of error anticipated a flurry of reports in U.S. newspapers that revisited the descriptions of anarchy and mayhem in New Orleans and attempted to set the record straight. Among the first and most detailed of these retrospective accounts appeared in the *Times-Picayune* in late September 2005. The article, written by Brian Thevenot and Gordon Russell, opened with the account of a doctor who was associated with FEMA. In preparing to take possession of the dead bodies at the Superdome, the doctor had ordered a refrigerated, eighteen-wheel tractor-trailer. "I've got a report of 200 bodies in the Dome," the doctor was quoted as saying. The actual total was six—four of whom died of natural causes, one from an overdose of drugs, and one from an apparent suicide.[59]

"Four weeks after the storm," Thevenot and Russell wrote, "few of the widely reported atrocities have been backed with evidence. The piles of murdered bodies never materialized, and soldiers, police officers and rescue personnel on the front lines assert that, while anarchy reigned at times and people suffered unimaginable indignities, most of the worst crimes reported at the time never happened."[60]

The report by Thevenot and Russell was followed by similar accounts in the *Los Angeles Times*,[61] *New York Times*,[62] *Philadelphia Inquirer*,[63] *Washington Post*,[64] and *Washington Times*,[65] as well as on network and cable television,[66] all revisiting and criticizing the media's coverage. "The media joined in playing whisper-down-the-lane," the *Philadelphia Inquirer* said in explaining the exaggerated reporting, "and stories that defied common sense were treated as news."[67] The *Inquirer* had identified an important point. Much of the reporting about the nightmarish violence in New Orleans seemed so shocking as to defy believability. To accept those reports required a willing suspension of disbelief.

Jim Dwyer of the *New York Times* addressed this element of the Katrina coverage, writing, "I just thought that some of the reports were so garish, so untraceable and always seemed to stop short of having actual witnesses to the atrocities . . . like a galloping mythical nightmare had taken control."[68] Dwyer said he went to Louisiana after the hurricane struck "specifically to ascertain the truth of early wild reports of crime," especially those unattributed reports recounting "nightmarish scenes that seemed to defy common sense."[69] Dwyer's skepticism was reflected in a 2,100-word, front-page article in the *Times* in late September 2005, which said that many "of the most alarming stories that coursed through the city [in Katrina's wake] appear to be little more than figments of frightened imaginations, the product of chaotic circumstances that included no reliable communications."[70]

The bimonthly *American Journalism Review* also revisited Katrina. In the issue immediately after its cheerleading "Essential Again" cover article, the magazine offered a far more critical and sober assessment of the media's performance. Gone were the admiring remarks about traditional media and how they demonstrated their value and relevance in New Orleans. Instead, the magazine acknowledged that "hundreds of myths got reported in the early days of Hurricane Katrina's aftermath."[71] The article, titled "Myth-Making in New Orleans," was written by Thevenot of the *Times-Picayune,* who did not exempt himself from the bath of media criticism.

He opened the "Myth-Making in New Orleans" article by describing how he had taken the word of an Arkansas National Guardsman named Mikel Brooks that a freezer at the Convention Center contained the bodies of thirty or forty victims. "I didn't push it," Thevenot conceded. "Now I wish I had, as gruesome as that may seem. The soldiers might have branded me a morbid fiend and run me the hell out of there, but my story in the September 6 edition of the *Times-Picayune* would have been right, or at least included a line saying I'd been denied the opportunity to lay eyes on the freezer. Instead, I quoted Brooks and another soldier, by name, about the freezer's allegedly grim inventory, including the statement that it contained a '7-year-old with her throat cut.' Neither the mass of bodies nor the allegedly expired child would ever be found."[72] Thevenot traced the tale to a rumor that had circulated on a food line at Harrah's Casino a block away. In the storm's aftermath, the casino was used as a law enforcement and military staging area.[73]

Thevenot noted that, "in the worst of the storm reporting, tales of violence, rapes, murders and other mayhem were simply stated as fact with no attribution at all. I am among those who committed this sin," having described the Convention Center as "a nightly scene of murders, rapes and regular stampedes."[74] The news media's contrition and introspection did not last for long, however. The self-critical articles tended to be one-off assessments that usually received little prominence. The

Los Angeles Times, Philadelphia Inquirer, and *Washington Post* all placed their retrospective articles on inside pages, for example. After the flurry of post-Katrina assessments in late September and early October 2005, the news media demonstrated little interest in sustaining or revisiting the self-critique. The report of the House select committee was scathing in its criticism of the news media, but that criticism was rarely noted in news reports about the panel's report.

Instead, the dominant narrative about news coverage of the hurricane was that it represented a welcome counterpoint to the supposedly hesitant and noncritical reporting in the run-up to America's war with Iraq in 2003. Unlike the Iraq story, journalists covering Katrina's aftermath had demonstrated courage and temerity in standing up to public officials and holding them accountable for their inept and muddled response. "In the week following Katrina's marauding of the Gulf Coast," wrote James Wolcott in *Vanity Fair* in November 2005, "American journalism magically awakened, arose from its glass coffin, and roused itself to impromptu glory."[75] The authors of a slim study, *When the Press Fails,* saw it that way, too. The Katrina coverage "was a heady moment," they wrote. "Everywhere one turned, there seemed to be an impassioned journalist expressing public outrage and seeking to hold officials accountable." Whether in print or on the air, journalists "were suddenly and surprisingly taking adversarial positions with officials, even informing those officials about the realities of the situation at hand."[76]

Jeffrey Dvorkin, the executive director of Committee of Concerned Journalists, identified Katrina coverage as a moment when American journalism took to the offense after what he said was a prolonged period of defensiveness in response to accusations of media bias and distortion. "I sense that the days of journalistic defensiveness are if not over, at least journalism appears less defensive than it used to be," Dvorkin told an audience in 2006. "Part of that is because of one event which allowed journalists in the U.S. to start reporting with a critical and skeptical eye. That event was Hurricane Katrina."[77]

The media's back-patting was notably apparent at the first few anniversaries of the Katrina disaster. In 2007, at the hurricane's second anniversary, news reports revisited nearly every element of the disaster, particularly the federal government's sluggish and uncertain response. "But there was one thing missing from the coverage of this natural, social, economic, and political disaster," noted Jonah Goldberg, a columnist for the conservative *National Review,* and that was "the fact that Katrina represented an unmitigated media disaster as well. . . . Katrina unleashed a virus of sanctimony and credulity for urban legends almost without precedent," an embarrassment that the news media were loath to revisit.[78] The media, Goldberg observed, "are often good watchdogs of government, but rarely of themselves."[79] They mostly avoided referring to their flawed coverage in retrospective reports published at the fifth and tenth anniversaries of Katrina's landfall.

In failing to sustain their self-critiques, the news media largely missed the opportunity to extract useful lessons from the inaccurate reporting. Opportunities to do so often presented themselves. The prestigious *Nieman Reports,* published quarterly by Harvard University's Nieman Foundation for Journalism, devoted its fall 2007 issue to twenty articles and photo essays about the news media and the coverage of Katrina. But not one addressed the news media's errors in the hurricane's aftermath or considered the enduring lessons to be learned from those lapses.

Those lessons are many and include the recognition that it is a near certainty that erroneous reports will circulate in a disaster's immediate aftermath. On that point, the House select committee's report quoted Kathleen J. Tierney of the Natural Hazards Center at the University of Colorado Boulder as saying that "misleading or completely false media reports should have been among the most foreseeable elements of Katrina."[80] Similarly, initial and worst-case estimates of disaster casualties almost always are exaggerated. This happened in the wake of the September 11 terrorist attacks on New York City, offering a ready point of reference for reporters covering Katrina's aftermath. The initial estimates of ten thousand deaths in New York were considerably overstated. Casualty predictions in other crises—"from the refugee emergency in eastern Zaire after the Rwandan genocide, through the Kosovo crisis, to the U.S. wars in Afghanistan and Iraq, to the 2004 South Asian tsunami"—likewise were overstated.[81] Recognition of this tendency might well have helped to temper or curb the exaggerated reports of lawlessness and violence in post-Katrina New Orleans.

To their credit, some reports about mayhem in New Orleans contained a measure of skepticism. The Knight Ridder news service reported Nagin's "grim estimate of Katrina's human toll" of ten thousand dead with the caveat that "he didn't cite the basis for that statement."[82] The phrase was meant to signal caution and uncertainty. But such qualifiers seldom are much of a roadblock: the shocking estimate—ten thousand dead—was still reported and still appeared in headlines, and the cautionary phrase did little to dilute the impact. In the end, the caveat dissolved to little more than an afterthought.

DISASTER COVERAGE OFTEN IN ERROR

The news media's susceptibility to reporting falsehoods and rumors in disaster coverage has long been recognized. A Canadian research team struck a prescient tone in an article in 1986 titled "Coping with the Media in Disasters." The authors observed that news organizations "can spread rumors, and so alter the reality of disaster, at least to those well away from it, that they can bias the nature of the response. They can and do create myths about disasters, myths which will persist even among those with contrary disaster experience."[83]

Reporters for American news media typically receive scant, if any, training in covering disasters. And when they find themselves amid the uncertainties of a postdisaster environment, their ability to filter rumors may be significantly reduced, leaving them susceptible to repeating and circulating what later prove to be outlandish reports. In such circumstances, they are well advised not to report more than what they can see for themselves. But even that inclination can be trumped by what can be called the "out-there" syndrome: if other news organizations are "out there" reporting what seems to be an important element of a disaster-related story, pressures intensify to match those reports.[84] As a result, thinly documented accounts can gain wide circulation.

Av Westin, a former vice president and executive producer for ABC News, invoked the out-there syndrome in Thevenot's "Myth-Making in New Orleans" critique. The out-there syndrome, Westin said, helps explain why flawed reporting circulated so widely in Katrina's aftermath. "With 24/7 news," he said, "the deadline is always now, you go with whatever you've got, you stick it on the air."[85] There certainly is truth to Westin's observations. The out-there syndrome does add pressure to publish or broadcast accounts that have been incompletely reported. But the excuse "the competition made me do it" is untenable when thinly documented accounts turn out to be false or exaggerated.

Another quite obvious factor cited by Thevenot was the breakdown in communication networks. Telephone service was out in New Orleans after Katrina swept through. Cell phones did not function. Electricity was scarce. Amid such conditions, Thevenot wrote, "Stone-age storytelling got amplified by space-age technology." Stories that at first may have had some factual underpinning became "exaggerated and distorted as they were passed orally—often the only mode of communication—through extraordinarily frustrated and stressed multitudes of people, including refugees, cops, soldiers, public officials and, ultimately, the press," he wrote.[86]

And yet another factor for getting it wrong was the reliance on officials such as Nagin and Compass, both of whom were presumed to possess authoritative information. Usually, the imprimatur of officialdom translates to adequate sourcing for journalists. But in Katrina's aftermath, Nagin and Compass became the very public sources of alarming but false and exaggerated reports about their city and its inhabitants. And they offered their erroneous reports seemingly in all confidence, without equivocation or qualification.

Although these explanations certainly help explain why myths took hold in the aftermath of Katrina, none of them exonerate the flawed news coverage or let journalists off the hook. None of those factors—neither competitive pressures, nor communications breakdowns, nor outlandish public officials—was peculiar to Katrina. In varying degrees, they are elements familiar in all disasters. And there is no reason why each of those factors could not have produced alternate outcomes in covering Katrina. It would not have been unreasonable for the collapse of communication networks to have given reporters pause, leaving them more cautious and more wary about what they heard and reported, and thus less likely to traffic in wild and dubious claims.

The extravagant descriptions offered by Nagin and Compass were remarkable not only for their luridness—"little babies getting raped"—but also for being utterly false. Journalists covering disasters must often rely on public officials for critical details about casualties and relief efforts. But in doing so, they are not expected to shed the skepticism they are encouraged to develop about the officials and personalities they cover. Journalism, after all, is not stenography. As Duncan Campbell pointed out in London's *Guardian* newspaper in a look back at the flawed Katrina coverage, "when reporters get their information from their own eyes rather than from a government spokesperson, we inevitably get a truer story."[87]

It is hard to quarrel with advice offered by Scott Libin of the Poynter Institute, a Florida-based journalism training and resource center. Libin referred to the Katrina coverage in suggesting: "Even when plausibly reliable sources such as [government] officials pass along information, journalists should press for key details—respectfully and courteously, but assertively. Mr. Mayor, tell us more about how you found out. Chief, can we talk to the officer or officers who actually responded to those rapes?" Libin's former colleague at Poynter, Bob Steele, recommended that journalists keep in mind the "What if?" question—as in: "What if that information isn't true?" or, "What if the source is wrong?"

Professional skepticism, he said, "is part of a vigorous checks and balances process that debunks rumors, reveals false assumptions and clarifies misconceptions. Ideally, professional skepticism produces high-quality, believable reports."[88] And as the House select committee pointed out, "Skepticism and fact-checking are easier when the sea is calm, but more vital when it is not."[89]

Two other related explanations offer themselves as to why journalists got it so badly wrong in covering Katrina's aftermath. The first is the perverse appeal of the would-be apocalyptic. Not only is daily journalism driven by what loosely can be termed "bad" news—events that are extraordinary and potentially harmful. There is a perverse appeal among journalists for exceptionally "bad" news, for "the latest big scare story."[90] In mild form, the perverse appeal is evident almost daily in local television news coverage of building fires. Not only do fires offer dramatic footage, they also carry the potential to spread wildly out of control. "It could have been worse" is a phrase not uncommon among local television reporters. Hurricane Katrina unleashed the perverse appeal of the would-be apocalyptic, the appeal of the truly big scare story. Here, after all, was a disaster of almost Biblical proportion: storms and floods, death and mayhem, criminal gangs run amok in a city collapsing in chaos. New Orleans seemed to promise a descent into the truly apocalyptic. And for a time, the reporting matched that premise: it was as if some of the most dreadful events imaginable were taking place in New Orleans.

Related to the perverse appeal of the would-be apocalyptic is a second explanation: a latent readiness to assume the worst about the "other"—in this case, the poor, mostly black urban dwellers, with whom affluent mainstream journalists usually have little sustained contact and few shared interests. In the immediate aftermath of the hurricane, reporters engaged in unintentional stereotyping of New Orleans and its poor people and minorities. Thevenot wrote in "Myth-Making in New Orleans" that he had "little doubt that, consciously or unconsciously, some white reporters, and probably a smaller number of black ones found it more plausible that babies had been raped and children had been knifed in a black crowd than they would in a theoretical white one."[91] Jim Amoss, the editor of the *Times-Picayune*, addressed the topic, too, saying that it would be "hard to imagine that if the Dome and the Convention Center had been filled with sweaty, hungry, desperate white people, middle-class white people—it's hard to believe that these kinds of myths would have sprung up quite as readily."[92] Responding to that observation, Donna Britt, a columnist for the *Washington Post,* declared, "No kidding." It is, Britt wrote, "always easier to recount—and believe—the alleged inhumanity of those who are poor, less educated or of different ethnicities than . . . those reporting their supposed actions." Rumor, Britt added, "becomes part of the official record more often than journalists, historians and other 'authoritative' chroniclers care to acknowledge."[93]

THE LOVE OF PRIZES

American journalism loves giving prizes—to its own. Among other effects, prizes and awards can help lift the spirits and puncture the gloom enveloping an industry in decline. Journalism's prize culture has become so entrenched, the media critic Alicia Shepard once wrote, that the field seems "locked in the iron grip of prize frenzy."[94] It has been that way for years. "Were there ever members of any profession so keen on giving each other prizes as journalists?" the author Alexander Cockburn asked in the *Wall Street Journal* in 1984. Cockburn speculated that American journalists were so keen to give each other awards out of a sense of shared insecurity. To alleviate such pangs, he wrote, "British journalists turn to drink and American ones to prizes."[95]

The year after Katrina struck, many of American journalism's most prominent awards were given to print and broadcast journalists and their news organizations for coverage of the hurricane and its aftermath. The New Orleans television station WWL won a Peabody Award and the Radio-Television News Directors Association's Edward R. Murrow Award for "best continuous coverage by a large-market station." WWL was the city's lone television station with a local news operation to remain on the air throughout the hurricane.[96]

The *Times-Picayune* and the *Sun-Herald* of Biloxi, Mississippi, shared the coveted Pulitzer Prize for Public Service for their Katrina coverage. The *Times-Picayune* won a separate Pulitzer for Breaking News Reporting. The award citation noted the newspaper staff's "courageous and aggressive coverage of Hurricane Katrina, overcoming desperate conditions facing the city and the newspaper." The *Times-Picayune* also won a Polk Award for Metropolitan Reporting.

Less prominent in the constellation of awards for Katrina reporting was the Mongerson Prize for Investigative Reporting on the News. The award was initiated in 2001 to recognize journalists who set the record straight on inaccurate, incomplete, or misleading news stories. The Mongerson Prize was administered by Northwestern University and had a five-year run. It never attracted much attention, certainly nothing approaching the prominence of the Murrow Awards or the Pulitzer Prizes.

The Mongerson Prize was given for the last time in 2006, and the winners that year were Thevenot and Russell of the *Times-Picayune*. They were honored for the report they prepared in late September 2005 about the highly exaggerated accounts of mayhem in post-Katrina New Orleans. In announcing the winners, Northwestern said that Thevenot and Russell had "exposed the dangers of pack journalism in a difficult reporting environment."[97] More accurately, they were recognized for challenging, or at least poking at, the myth of superlative reporting.

CHAPTER 13

Counterfeit Quotations

Swelling with a Digital Tide

Fake quotes are often better than the things famous people actually said.

—Megan McArdle, "Great Quote. A Little Too Great," *Bloomberg View* (18 May 2015)

Thomas Jefferson—founding father, wealthy planter, principal author of the Declaration of Independence, and third U.S. president—liked to relax by smoking hemp outside at his mountaintop estate, Monticello. That, at least, is the improbable claim of a quotation of murky origin that has gained circulation online. "Some of my finest hours," Jefferson is alleged to have said, "have been spent on my back veranda, smoking hemp and observing as far as my eye can see."[1]

No one has identified the source of this comment, although it's sometimes accompanied by the date 1781. But the utterance is found in none of Jefferson's writings. And there is no evidence Jefferson ever smoked hemp or any other substances, including tobacco.[2] Hemp was grown at Monticello for making rope and clothing for slaves.

Despite the considerable evidence arrayed against it, and even though it is obviously preposterous, the hemp-smoking quotation endures online. It is too alluring and amusing to drift away as so much historical rubbish.[3]

So it is with this quotation, attributed to another founding father, Benjamin Franklin: "Beer is proof that God loves us and wants us to be happy." It is a colorful and pithy line at home on social media—and on T-shirts adorned with Franklin's smiling likeness. It, too, is a phony quotation, a distortion of Franklin's observations in a letter written in French around in 1779, in which he ruminated about the natural world,

FIGURE 27. A phony quotation of murky origin has it that Thomas Jefferson, founding father and third U.S. president, liked to relax by smoking hemp on a "back veranda" at his Monticello estate. While patently absurd, the quotation has gained some velocity online. This bust of Jefferson is displayed at the Jefferson Building of the Library of Congress in Washington, D.C. [*Photo by author*]

the growing of grapes, and the making of wine. "We hear of the conversion of water into wine at the marriage in Cana, as of a miracle," Franklin wrote. "But this conversion is, through the goodness of God, made every day before our eyes. Behold the rain which descends from heaven upon our vineyards, and which incorporates itself with the grapes to be changed into wine; a constant proof that God loves us, and loves to see us happy."[4] Franklin's ruminations had nothing to do with beer.

Mark Twain is another prominent dead person to whom bogus quotations are often attributed. The famous humorist and writer of the late nineteenth and early twentieth centuries is credited with observations he never made, including this gem: "History doesn't repeat itself, but it does rhyme." It's a witty turn of phrase that sounds at least faintly like something Twain might have said. The quote can be irresistible,[5] and it, too, turns up regularly on social media, sometimes as commentary about the similarities of events over time.[6] But the quotation that has not been found anywhere in Twain's writings or public remarks. And it appears to have been first attributed to Twain in 1970—sixty years after his death.[7]

Bogus quotations, especially those attributed to prominent people, are hardly novel. They have circulated for decades and longer.[8] Jefferson was known to have griped about them. He didn't call them bogus or misattributed quotations, but they annoyed him nonetheless. "So many persons have of late found an interest or a passion gratified by imputing to me sayings and writings which I never said or wrote," Jefferson stated in 1797, " . . . that I have found it necessary for my quiet & my other pursuits to leave them in full possession of the field, and not to take the trouble of contradicting them even in private conversation."[9]

In contemporary contexts, counterfeit quotations tend to be succinct, often recited, and not infrequently droll. They spring from many sources. Some simply have been made up; others were legitimate quotations but have been mangled or twisted beyond their original meaning. Some, like the beer quotation attributed to Franklin, are lighthearted and flippant. Others—like this guidance supposedly offered by Einstein: "You have to learn the rules of the game; and then you have to play better than anyone else"—hint at profundity. And not all bogus quotations are so obviously phony.

They almost always are attached to towering figures of the past— such as Jefferson, Franklin, Twain, and Einstein, as well as Lincoln, Churchill, Martin Luther King Jr., and, sometimes, even contemporary pop culture celebrities like Kayne West. The quotations gain authority and prestige from association with their presumed authors. Such ties ensure that the quotations, even if improbable, will gain attention and be repeated. As quote-debunker Richard Keyes once observed, "Famous quotes need famous mouths."[10] Similarly, Louis Menand noted in the *New Yorker:* "Quotations are in a perpetual struggle for survival. They want people to keep saying them. They don't want to die any more than the rest of us. And so, whenever they can, they attach themselves to colorful or famous people."[11]

Bogus quotations may not be new, but they can gain impressive reach and velocity thanks to the accelerant properties of the Internet and its social media platforms, notably Twitter and Facebook. Social media allow these sayings to circulate at light speed while they insinuate their way into popular consciousness. Before Internet use became widespread in the first years of the twenty-first century, the range and circulation of bogus quotations was "self-limiting," Keyes has noted: "The seed of a misquote that was planted in some speech, or a piece of writing, or reporter's notes, could only grow fitfully in the arid soil of print on paper. Not so online."[12] Keyes offered that observation before the emergence of Twitter, which, with its limit of 140 characters per post, is particularly well suited for popularizing pithy but bogus sayings. Such quotations flourish in the digital hothouse that Twitter promotes. As Carl M. Cannon, a well-known journalist in Washington, D.C., has noted, Twitter "lends itself to one of the Internet's most noxious features—the dissemination of bogus and misattributed quotations."[13]

Indeed, to search Twitter for quotations known to be spurious is to confront something resembling a cascade of seldom-challenged error. Rare are tweets that question or confront a quotation's authenticity. Rarer still are tweets offering a quotation's context, derivation, and attribution. The deluge can be such that social media have been characterized, perhaps a bit unfairly, as "a vast twilight zone of historical misinformation."[14] To arrest this flood of bogus quotations online would be Sisyphean—"a hopeless task," as Richard M. Langworth, a scholar of Winston Churchill has observed. "You would need an army of secretaries to reply to all these tweets."[15] Online quotation-verification sites, such the inimitable *Quote Investigator* blog, are not designed to stand up to, let alone reverse, the flow of dubious quotations online. And this speaks to a larger and thornier issue of verifying content on the Internet; after all, the repercussions of posting phony content invariably are small at most, and represent no practical deterrent.

Bogus quotations disseminated online are more than nuisances, bemusing distractions, or digital flotsam. They pose special challenges for journalists. After all, quoting accurately is fundamental to newsgathering. Moreover, bogus quotations can become embryonic media myths—prospective media myths of the future. There is precedent, as we've seen, for bogus quotations to congeal into full-blown myths. The delicious, though dubious, warmongering quote attributed to William Randolph Hearst—"You furnish the pictures, and I'll furnish war"—is a telling example. So, too, is the remark attributed to President Lyndon B. Johnson after Walter Cronkite, the CBS News anchorman, concluded in early 1968 that the U.S. war effort in Vietnam had become stalemated. "If I've lost Cronkite," the president supposedly said, "I've lost Middle America"—or something to that effect. Such remarks seem to defy debunking, and social media platforms can prolong the life spans of these quotations while enhancing their familiarity with contemporary audiences.

Bogus quotations share many of the defining features of media-driven myths. They tend to be concise and simplistic, easy to remember, fun to retell, tenacious, and often thinly sourced. Like media myths, bogus quotations tread indecorously on the historical record, distorting an understanding of the past. And they are known to leach from social media to traditional mainstream news outlets. The hemp-smoking remark attributed to Jefferson is an example. A few years ago, a reporter for the *Detroit Free Press* wrote that Jefferson "is thought to have smoked some of his crop, used then to make rope, on the veranda of Monticello, according to websites on early American history."[16] The websites were not identified. Gary Johnson, a former governor of New Mexico, invoked the hemp-smoking quotation on a Fox Business Network program in 2012, during his first run for president on the Libertarian Party ticket. "Well," Johnson asked, "didn't Jefferson say that his best times were spent out on the veranda, smoking weed? Didn't he say that? Didn't he?" The show's host, John Stossel, was skeptical. "I don't think so," he replied.[17]

A columnist for a newspaper in New Brunswick cited the quotation in 2013 in discussing overtures in Canada to legalize marijuana. He closed his commentary by writing: "Here's [a quotation attributed to] Thomas Jefferson: 'Some of my finest hours have been spent on my back veranda, smoking hemp and observing as far as my eye can see.'"[18] Also that year, a small newspaper in British Columbia publicized the hemp-smoking remark as its quotation of the day and cited Jefferson.[19] And a newspaper in India, noting that medicinal marijuana is increasingly tolerated in the United States, said such moves "would have pleased Thomas Jefferson, who declared, 'Some of my finest hours have been spent on my back veranda, smoking hemp and observing as far as my eye can see.'"[20]

A fictional interview with the celebrity Kayne West offers another example of how bogus quotations can migrate from a digital source to a leading mainstream publication. The fake interview with West was posted in 2014 at the online site of the *Daily Currant,* a satirical newspaper. It was meant to be a sendup of the rapper's egocentrism, and it included a passage in which he compares his derrière to the ample posterior of his wife, Kim Kardashian.

In the *Daily Currant*'s account, West told an interviewer for WGYN, a fictitious Chicago radio station: "I don't understand why everyone is focusing on Kim's booty. . . . My booty is like Michelangelo level, you feel me? It's like a sculpture. It's like something that should be sitting in a museum for thousands of thousands of years." And his wife's derrière? Nice, West said, "but it's not at that [Michelangelo] level." Portions of the fake interview were taken as genuine and quoted in a column posted at the website of the *New York Times,* without attribution.

The stunning lapse was soon called out. The *Times* acknowledged its error, saying in a correction that "the interview was fictitious, and should not have been included in the column."[21] Daniel Barkley, the founder of *Daily Currant,* was quoted by the *Washington Post* as saying the spoof interview "was clearly satirical and should never have been cited as fact. Kanye West comparing his own behind to a Michelangelo sculpture should have been a clue."[22] But, as a fact-checking blog for the *Washington Post* has noted, it sometimes seems as if the "more bizarre the quote, the quicker it gets retweeted, reblogged or reposted."[23]

Credulous journalists have been duped not only by satire but also by the irresistible, pitch-perfect character of quotations they encounter online. A few years ago, a twenty-two-year-old undergraduate student in Ireland inserted made-up quotations in the Wikipedia biography of Maurice Jarre shortly after the French composer's death. The student, Shane Fitzgerald, said his intention was to demonstrate how some journalists imprudently rely on Wikipedia as a primary source. Fitzgerald inserted the following wholly fabricated quotes to Jarre's biography: "One could say my life itself has been one long soundtrack. Music was my life, music brought me to life, and music is how I will be remembered long after I leave this life. When I die there will be a final waltz playing in my head and that only I can hear."[24] The bogus comments fooled journalists at a couple of prominent newspapers in Britain—the *Guardian*[25] and the *Independent*[26]—as well as at the website of the *BBC Music Magazine.*

What's more, the faux quotations went unnoticed until Fitzgerald sent emails to the news outlets about a month later to let them know they had been fooled. "I am 100 percent convinced that if I hadn't come forward, that quote would have gone down in history as something Maurice Jarre said, instead of something I made up," Fitzgerald told one of the newspapers he had duped. "It would have become another example where, once anything is printed enough times in the media without challenge, it becomes fact."[27]

Such sentiment encouraged comedian John Oliver, host of the HBO satire program *Last Week Tonight,* to set up a website called Definitely-RealQuotes.com, which allows visitors to post to Twitter and Facebook a variety of faintly plausible but intentionally counterfeit quotations. The supposed authors include Confucius, Albert Einstein, Amelia Earhart, Theodore Roosevelt, Karl Marx, Marie Curie, and Thomas Jefferson. The site was Oliver's way of calling attention to, and lampooning, bogus quotations—especially those invoked by contemporary politicians. "Quotations make us sound smart," Oliver said on his show in 2015. "That's why politicians love throwing them around." The Internet, he added, "is only making this epidemic of misattributed quotes worse."

In faux high dudgeon, Oliver said: "It seems we have got a decision to make at this point. Either we care about the accuracy of quotes and make sure they're correctly sourced, or we don't care at all. Which is why we have created a website called DefinitelyRealQuotes.com, which will generate random misquotes from historical figures, such as Thomas Jefferson saying, 'Yeah, I pronounce it "pasketti." Why? Is there another way?' Because if quotes no longer have to be real, they should at least be fun."[28]

Oliver's satiric treatment is an extreme example of how bogus quotations are parodied and deprecated. He had a point about how readily they circulate online and how utterly absurd they can be. He also was on target in his remarks about politicians and their eagerness to embrace irresistible expressions. They often are responsible for injecting bogus quotations into popular discourse.

A hardy perennial, a favorite among Republicans, is this specious aphorism, attributed to Lincoln: "You can't build a little guy up by tearing the big guy down." Former president Ronald Reagan invoked a variation of the saying in 1992, telling the Republican National Convention in Houston: "[What Democrats] truly don't understand is the principle so eloquently stated by Abraham Lincoln: 'You cannot strengthen the weak by weakening the strong. You cannot help the poor by destroying the rich. You cannot help men permanently by doing for them what they could and should do for themselves.'"[29] Variations of the quotation have popped up over the years. In 2015, the governor of Ohio, John Kasich, offered a slightly altered version in an interview on a Sunday talk show. "You can't build a little guy up by tearing the big guy down," he declared. "Abraham Lincoln said it then, and he's right."[30] But Lincoln never said it. The quotation apparently is a mash-up, and it has been traced to a collection of maxims called "10 Cannots," written in 1916 by the Reverend William John Henry Boetcker. He was born in Germany in 1873, eight years after Lincoln's assassination, and immigrated to the United States, where he became a lecturer and pamphleteer. In 1942, his list of "cannots" was printed on one side of a leaflet issued by a conservative group called the Committee for Constitutional Government; on the reverse side was an authentic Lincoln quote. Before long, the "cannots" became attached to Lincoln, and Boetcker's authorship of the maxims was largely forgotten,[31] a not uncommon case of authorship flowing from the obscure to the prominent.

Democrats also have fallen for bogus Lincoln quotes, a bipartisan impulse that is not all that surprising. As the scholar John J. Pitney has observed, "By quoting the Great Emancipator's words, public figures try to capture some of his magic for themselves. The temptation to touch the hem of [Lincoln's] garment is so great that they sometimes get sloppy about fact-checking and grab for a knockout."[32] President Barack Obama turned to Lincoln in 2010 in speaking with congressional Democrats on the eve of their vote on national health care legislation. "I have the great pleasure of having a really nice library at the White House," he said. "And I was tooling through some of the writings of some previous presidents, and I came upon this quote by Abraham Lincoln: 'I am not bound to win, but I'm bound to be true. I'm not bound to succeed, but I'm bound to live up to what light I have.'"[33]

Obama didn't specify which writings he had been "tooling through," but they couldn't have been the collected works of Lincoln; no documentary evidence exists that he ever made the statement.[34] The passage is pithy—and popular on social media. With punctuation and attribution to "Abraham Lincoln," the saying comes to 139 characters, one short of Twitter's limit for posts.

Politicians also have been the targets of malicious bogus quotations. Michelle Bachmann, a conservative former congresswoman who sought the Republican nomination for president in 2012, was quoted on a Facebook page as having said, "If English was good enough for Jesus when he wrote the Bible, it should be good enough for Coke." Bachmann, who favored a constitutional amendment designating English as the official language of the United States, supposedly was upset by a Coca-Cola television advertisement that aired during the Super Bowl in 2014. The advertisement featured "America the Beautiful" sung in seven languages. The purported quotation was posted at a satirical Facebook group called "Christians for Michele Bachmann," which claimed she had made the "good enough for Jesus" remark on February 3, 2014, in an interview on Fox News. But it was utterly untrue: Bachmann never said it and had not appeared on Fox News that day. What's more, versions of the saying have circulated since at least 1881, according to the fact-checking site PolitiFact.[35]

Certainly one of the most popular made-up lines in American media and politics is "Follow the money," the urgent-sounding advice immortalized in the cinematic version of All the President's Men, a dramatization of Bob Woodward and Carl Bernstein's eponymous book about their Watergate reporting for the Washington Post. The line was delivered with raspy urgency by the actor Hal Holbrook, who portrayed a marvelously twitchy and conflicted "Deep Throat," the code name for Woodward's stealthy, high-level source. In 2005, when he was ninety-one years old, W. Mark Felt came forward to say he had been the "Deep Throat" source. Felt, who once was the FBI's second-ranking official, was not known to have advised Woodward to "follow the money."[36] The line does not appear in notes Woodward made at the time.[37] The quotation was not included in any Watergate-related article or editorial in the Washington Post before 1981. Nor is it to be found anywhere in the book All the President's Men. But it was written into the screenplay of All the President's Men[38] and has become perhaps the most famous turn of phrase associated with Watergate, a cinematic anagram that is invoked often and taken as genuine. It also is popular on social media, which undoubtedly will keep the phrase from dying away any time soon.

The unshakable appeal of "Follow the money" suggests how made-up quotes can become memorable supplements to entrenched media myths. In this case, the phrase enhances the mythical notion that Woodard and Bernstein exposed the high-level crimes of Watergate and, in doing so, brought down Richard Nixon's corrupt presidency.[39] Just as the movie inaccurately places Woodward and Bernstein at the center of Watergate's unraveling, "Follow the money" offers a deceptive sense about how the Nixon administration's coverup of the Watergate scandal was unraveled.

"Follow the money"—meaning, investigate the suspect contributions to Nixon's reelection campaign in 1972—would have given the reporters only a partial understanding of what was a labyrinthine scandal. Watergate was more than Nixon's improper use of campaign funds and following "the money" would not, alone, have brought about Nixon's resignation. His downfall was sealed by the content of Watergate-related tape recordings that he secretly made of private conversations in the Oval Office. The tapes clearly showed Nixon approving a plan intended to thwart the FBI investigation into the Watergate scandal as it was unfolding in June 1972.

Bogus quotations are problematic beyond their power to supplement and solidify media myths. They can be acutely embarrassing to unwitting users. Take, for example, this half-true quotation attributed to broadcasting legend Edward R. Murrow: "We must not confuse dissent with disloyalty. When the loyal opposition dies, I think the soul of America dies with it." Murrow spoke the first sentence in 1954 during his fabled *See It Now* program about Senator Joseph R. McCarthy. The rest of the quotation, however, was appended by persons unknown many years later. But the full quotation, a semiaccurate mash-up, has gained considerable popularity. For a time, it was displayed on the welcome page of the dean of the Edward R. Murrow College of Communication at Washington State University.

Asked about the provenance of the suspicious quotation, the dean, Lawrence E. Pintak, replied by email, saying, "My suspicion is that the site was built by the university marketing comm. people and they may well have just pulled it from the web, rather than original source. If it's not correct, we certainly need to get it pulled."[40] He asked Paul Mark Wadleigh to look into the matter. Wadleigh, an instructor on the school's faculty who is knowledgeable about Murrow, soon reported: "While it seems to reflect the Murrow spirit, the lack of evidence that he phrased it that way is indeed suspicious." He added, "I feel the evidence says no, Murrow did not say this."[41] By day's end, the suspect quote had been removed from Pintak's welcome page.[42]

As the half-true Murrow expression suggests, bogus quotations can have the deceptive effect of making the thoughts and wisdom of historical figures seem close at hand and strikingly relevant,[43] conveying a sense of proximity that is misleading and unwarranted. Megan McArdle, who sometimes discusses bogus quotations in her column for *Bloomberg View,* referred to the deceptive sense of proximity in writing: "We become invested in these quotes because they say something important about us—and they let us feel that those emotions were shared by great figures in history. We naturally search for reasons that they could have said it—that they could have felt like us—rather than looking for reasons to disbelieve."[44]

Reasons to doubt the hemp-smoking remark attributed to Jefferson are several and include its uncertain derivation. The quotation appears to have begun circulating early in the twenty-first century, long after Jefferson's death in 1826. It probably was born digital. The staff at the Jefferson Library at Monticello, the former president's estate near Charlottesville, Virginia, scoffs at the hemp-smoking statement, noting that it has been found in none of Jefferson's writings, and adding that it "appears to be of extremely recent vintage." The quotation does not appear in secondary print sources available online, according to the Jefferson Library.[45]

The quotation's wording also invites its debunking. The phrasing is casual, almost colloquial, and the tone is uncharacteristic of Jefferson. What's more, *veranda* is not a word Jefferson would have used, said Anna Berkes, a reference librarian at Monticello. More common in his time, she said, was *portico*.[46] Berkes, who has conceded to frustration in battling "what often seems like an overwhelming ocean of bogus quotations"[47] about Jefferson, also said there is no evidence that the third president was a smoker, although he did grow tobacco as well as hemp. "If he were smoking at all," Berkes said, "I think we would have some record of it." Jefferson's many visitors to Monticello recorded no reference to his smoking, and there are no records of his having ordered smoking implements such as pipes.[48] Peter Hatch, then the director of gardens and grounds at Monticello, once said in an interview on NPR's *Science Friday* program, "Jefferson certainly grew hemp for cloth, but I don't think Thomas Jefferson was smoking marijuana in Monticello, despite what we—a lot of people would like to believe."[49]

Not only that, but 1781, the date sometimes given in Twitter posts as when Jefferson made the hemp-smoking comment, was a tumultuous time for him. Invading British forces spilled across much of Virginia in June 1781, chasing Jefferson, then the state's governor, out of the capital at Richmond and forcing his narrow escape from Monticello. Jefferson spent five weeks hiding from the British at a plantation near Lynchburg, Virginia.[50] It was hardly a tranquil interlude conducive to smoking leisurely on a veranda. "I don't think he was sitting on his back porch very much" in 1781, Berkes said.[51]

The hemp-smoking line is one of some fifty "spurious quotations" that Berkes and her colleagues have identified, discussed, and discredited in a "Spurious Quotations" section (what Berkes calls "debunk pages") at Monticello's website.[52] Together, the bogus quotations represent an amusing and offbeat collection that surely isn't exhaustive. Among the "spurious quotations" in Monticello's online collection are the following (all of which are commonly found on social media sites):

- "Bad government results from too much government." (The quotation probably originated in a speech about Jefferson.)
- "Dissent is the highest form of patriotism." (There is no evidence Jefferson uttered or wrote the passage.)
- "Eternal vigilance is the price of liberty." (The statement's more likely author was the Irish orator John Philpot Curran.)
- "Peace is that brief glorious moment in history when everybody stands around reloading." (An inelegant quotation attributed to Jefferson only in recent years.)

The "glorious moment" quotation, like the hemp-smoking remark, is ludicrous and suspect on its face. Its wording is too casual, too clumsy, and clearly too contemporary sounding to have been of Jefferson's time. And therein lies a key for disputing suspect quotations: Do they *sound* like something the presumed author would have said? Or, rather, do they sound suspiciously up-to-date? The Monticello site notes, in an understatement, that the "glorious moment" quote is "somewhat uncharacteristic of Jefferson's style" of writing.[53]

Being wary of quotations that sound too current can be a useful way of keeping a distance from bogus sayings. Of course, quote-skepticism is not fail-safe. This statement attributed to Lincoln could, on first reading, seem contrived and, in places, a bit too contemporary to be authentic: "From whence shall we expect the approach of danger? Shall some trans-Atlantic military giant step the earth and crush us at a blow? Never. All the armies of Europe and Asia . . . could not by force take a drink from the Ohio River or make a track on the Blue Ridge in the trial of a thousand years."[54]

The passage appeared in the introductory material to an essay posted in late 2015 at the website of the *National Review*. A skeptic who turned to the *Collected Works of Abraham Lincoln* online would find that the quotation is more-or-less accurate that Lincoln made approximate remarks in a speech in 1838: "At what point shall we expect the approach of danger? By what means shall we fortify against it? Shall we expect some transatlantic military giant, to step the Ocean, and crush us at a blow? Never! All the armies of Europe, Asia and Africa combined, with all the treasure of the earth (our own excepted) in their military chest; with a [Bonaparte] for a commander, could not by force, take a drink from the Ohio, or make a track on the Blue Ridge, in a trial of a thousand years."[55]

Turning to online sources to verify quotations demonstrates how the Internet, for all its culpability as a platform for transmitting bogus quotations, can be a bulwark against phony sayings. Lincoln's collected works are searchable online. So, too, are the papers of Franklin and the works of John Stuart Mill. Online resources like Snopes.com, the *Quote Investigator*, and the debunk pages at Monticello.org are a few of the important online tools for authenticating quotations. Berkes said links to the Monticello.org debunk pages typically turn up first in Google searches of dubious quotations attributed to Jefferson. The online site of the Churchill Centre has similarly posted a page of quotes falsely attributed to the former British prime minister.[56]

But what of Twitter and its flow of bogus quotations? Unmasking them as counterfeit can be accomplished by looking for authoritative citations. Typically, dubious quotations posted on Twitter lack specific reference to when and where the remarks were made. The absence of documentation is an obvious and immediate signal that the quotation is of suspicious origin. Standing advice from quote detectives like Keyes is to treat sourceless and unattributed quotations found online as if they were radioactive.[57] The advice extends to online quotation-aggregation sites such as BrainyQuote.com. "Even though the Internet hosts thousands of websites devoted to quotations," Keyes has noted, "these sites rarely concern themselves with accuracy."[58]

The patent absurdity of many quotations attributed to famous people of the past can be another tipoff and reason for skepticism. After all, wasn't it Lincoln who said, "Don't believe everything you read on the Internet"?[59] The quotation obviously is as bogus as they come, but in amusing and cautionary fashion, it reminds us anew of the abundant misattribution that circulates online.

Conclusion

We have been cock-sure of many things that were not so.

—Oliver Wendell Holmes, "Natural Law," *Harvard Law Review* 32, no. 1 (November 1918): 40

The tales examined on the preceding pages often ascribe power, significance, and courage to the news media and their practitioners. Edward Murrow crushing the McCarthy menace, Walter Cronkite effectively ending a faraway and unpopular war, and Bob Woodward and Carl Bernstein toppling a corrupt president are prominent examples. These purported achievements are compelling and exert an enduring allure; to expose them as exaggerated or untrue is to take aim at the self-importance of American journalism. To identify these tales as media myths is to confront the reality that the news media are not the powerful agents they, and many others, assume them to be. It is exceedingly rare for any news report to trigger a powerful, immediate, and decisive reaction akin to President Lyndon Johnson's purported response to Cronkite's televised assessment about Vietnam: "If I've lost Cronkite. . . ." Researchers long ago dismissed the notion that the news media can create such profound and immediate effects, as if absorbing media messages were akin to receiving potent drugs via a hypodermic needle.[1]

Debunking media-driven myths enhances a case for limited news media influence. Media power tends to be modest, nuanced, diffused, and situational. But too often, the ubiquitous presence of the news media is mistaken for power and influence. Robert J. Samuelson, an economist and a columnist for the *Washington Post,* has described this fallacy notably well. "Because the media are everywhere—and inspire much resentment—their influence is routinely exaggerated," Samuelson wrote. "The mistake is in confusing visibility with power, and the media are often complicit in the confusion. We [in the news media] embrace the mythology, because it flatters our self-importance."[2]

The notion that the news media are powerful forces seems almost intuitive. As the media scholar Denis McQuail has noted, "the entire study of mass communication is based on the assumption that the media [exert] significant effects." Yet as McQuail has said, "there is little agreement on the nature and extent of these assumed effects." In an observation of particular relevance to this study, McQuail has noted that the news media "are rarely likely to be the only necessary or sufficient cause of an effect, and their relative contribution is extremely hard to assess."[3]

The influence of the news media typically is trumped by other forces. American journalists traditionally have considered themselves as messengers, principally, rather than the makers and shapers of news.[4] These days, the American media are far too splintered and diverse—print, broadcast, cable, satellite, online—to exert much in the way of collective and sustained influence on policymakers or media audiences. As Herbert Gans, a sociologist who has written widely about the news media, noted, "If news audiences had to respond to all the news to which they are exposed, they would not have time to live their own lives. In fact, people screen out many things, including news, that could interfere with their own lives."[5]

Large numbers of Americans are beyond news media influence in any case. They choose to go newsless—they mostly ignore the news altogether. They are nonaudiences for news. Nearly 20 percent of American adults go newsless on a typical day, according to studies by the Pew Research Center for the People and the Press. The newsless option is most pronounced among young adults, eighteen to twenty-four years old. Almost 30 percent of that cohort goes newsless, according to Pew Research.[6] And among those who do keep up with the news, what topic do they follow most avidly? Weather. Pew Research reports that more than half of all American adults say they follow news about the weather very closely. "No other type of news comes close" in popularity, the research center has reported.[7]

Debunking media-driven myths, then, can help to place questions of media influence in a more coherent, more precise context. But what might be done to keep media myths from taking hold in the first place? What can be done to guard against their rise and proliferation? An elemental step lies in the recognition that media myths spring from diverse yet fairly recognizable sources. Among the most common of these sources is the tumult of war. Nearly half of the myths examined in this work had their origins in armed conflict.

That war can be a breeding ground for myth is scarcely surprising. The stakes in war are quite high, and the shock of combat is alien and unfamiliar to most people. Given their limited firsthand experience with war, media audiences usually find themselves in no position to challenge reports from the battlefield. The confusion and intensity inherent in warfare can lead journalists to place fragmented information that emerges from conflict into recognizable if sometimes misleading frames. In the process, distortion can arise and media myths can flourish. Mark Bowden, the author of one of journalism's finest recent war stories, *Black Hawk Down,* noted this inclination in the case of Jessica Lynch. In wartime, Bowden wrote, the tendency is "to weave what little we know into a familiar shape," and this can resemble "the narrative arc of a film."[8] Hence the *Washington Post's* flawed account of Jessica Lynch as a female Rambo, pouring lead into attacking Iraqis—an image that seemed at least vaguely familiar and not entirely implausible.

Hurried and sloppy reporting, which certainly characterized the sensational story about Lynch's purported heroics, also contributes to the rise of media myths. The myth of "crack babies" was propelled by hurried reporting, overeager journalists, and premature medical findings. Reporters and columnists pushed too hard and eagerly on preliminary and inconclusive research. And the horrors they predicted, that crack babies would grow up to be a vast permanently dependent class—a "bio-underclass" of staggering dimension—proved decidedly wrong.

Serendipitous timing figures in media mythmaking, too, as the "Cronkite moment" suggests. Cronkite's assessment in February 1968 that the United States was "mired in stalemate" in Vietnam took on significance in part because it coincided with—but certainly did not set in motion— the Johnson administration's extensive review of war policy in Vietnam. The "Cronkite Moment" preceded by one month—but surely did not prompt—Johnson's surprise announcement that he would not be seeking reelection. Fortuitous timing also helps explain the lasting importance attached to Murrow's *See It Now* program on CBS television about Senator McCarthy. Murrow's report came after other journalists had challenged the senator's tactics and reckless claims for months, even years. But Murrow's assessment was aired during the week in March 1954 when, for reasons quite independent of *See It Now,* the senator's fortunes irrevocably hit the skids. The Army that week accused McCarthy of having sought special treatment for a staff member who had been drafted into military service, charges that were to culminate in McCarthy's censure, disgrace, and political eclipse.

High-quality cinematic treatments are powerful agents of media myth-making and can enhance a myth's durability. Untold millions of Americans born after 1954 were introduced to the Murrow-McCarthy confrontation through *Good Night, and Good Luck,* a critically acclaimed film released in 2005 that cleverly promoted the myth that Murrow stood up to McCarthy when no one else would or could. The 1976 cinematic version of *All the President's Men* solidified the notion that young, diligent reporters for the *Washington Post* brought down President Richard Nixon. That myth of Watergate may be stronger than ever, given that *All the President's Men* is the first and perhaps only extended exposure many people have to the complex scandal that was Watergate.[9] Thanks in part to Hollywood, the heroic-journalist myth of Watergate has become the most familiar and readily accessible explanation of why Nixon left office in disgrace.

The quest for scapegoats further accounts for the rise of media myths. It is, after all, not unheard of to blame the news media for policy failures—as John Kennedy did in the aftermath of the Bay of Pigs debacle, claiming that, if only the *New York Times* had told all it knew about the Bay of Pigs invasion, perhaps the invasion plans would have been scrapped. That notion is absurd, as we've seen. But what can be striking is that the news media do not always protest when they've been made scapegoats. Sometimes they are complicit in the act. Leading U.S. newspapers were eager to condemn their upstart rival, radio, for supposedly pitching thousands of Americans into mass panic and hysteria in late October 1938. The torrent of newspaper criticism helped solidify the myth that the radio adaptation of *The War of the Worlds* had panicked America.

Media myths also take hold because of the timeless lessons they supposedly offer. The clashing impressions of television viewers and radio listeners of the 1960 presidential debate between Kennedy and Nixon supposedly revealed how appearance trumps substance. Yielding to government pressure can bring news organizations all sorts of problems and embarrassment, as supposedly was dramatized by the *New York Times* and its decision to muzzle itself about the coming Bay of Pigs invasion. William Randolph Hearst's purported vow to "furnish the war" offers a purported lesson about the hazards of unchecked media power: unscrupulous media moguls can distort public policy and even lead us into wars we otherwise would not fight.

Though they spring from multiple sources, it is not as if media-driven myths are beyond being tamed. To thwart media myths, journalists can start by applying a measure of skepticism to pithy, telling quotations such as Hearst's vow to "furnish the war" and even to euphonic phrases such as "bra burning." Turns of phrase that sound too neat and tidy often are too perfect to be true. Journalists also would do well to cultivate greater recognition of their fallibility. Too often, they seem only faintly concerned with correcting records they tarnish. They tend not to like revisiting major flaws and errors. As media critic Jack Shafer has written, "The rotten truth is that media organizations are better at correcting trivial errors of fact—proper spellings of last names, for example—than they are at fixing a botched story."[10] Not surprisingly, then, there was little sustained effort to explore and explain the distorted and badly flawed reporting from New Orleans in Hurricane Katrina's aftermath. There was no extensive effort by the news media to set straight the record about the chimerical scourge of crack babies.

Enhancing the training journalists receive in covering disasters and in analyzing medical and scientific research could be a preventive measure against media-driven myths. By recognizing that implausible rumors and exaggerated casualty tolls almost always are among the first effects of major disasters, journalists could spare themselves considerable embarrassment and their audiences great confusion. Journalists might also learn to resist the temptation of reporting results of preliminary studies as if those findings were solid and unequivocal. News coverage, it has been noted, "can easily mislead when reporters don't make it sufficiently clear that premature science may well not offer the truth."[11] Initial findings almost always are open to revision and substantial reinterpretation.

There is scant evidence that American journalists reporting on issues of health and science have taken lessons from the misreported crack baby scare. A survey conducted several years ago of nearly four hundred newspaper and magazine journalists covering health-related beats found that only 18 percent had received specialized training in health reporting.[12] A separate study of five hundred news reports on medical-related topics published and broadcast by U.S. news media in 2006–2008 found that most of the reports "failed to adequately address costs, harms, benefits, the quality of evidence, and the existence of other options when covering health care products and procedures." Such sketchy reporting, the study said, "raises important questions about the quality of the information U.S. consumers receive from the news media on . . . health news topics."[13]

Suggesting that journalists seek enhanced training may ring hollow and improbable at a time of unrelenting retrenchment in the news business and deep uncertainty about the future of America's mainstream media. Even so, there are plenty of good reasons to encourage a culture of skepticism and a tolerance for viewpoint diversity in American newsrooms, places that sometimes seem to be bastions of groupthink. Michael Kelly, the former editor of the *National Journal,* once observed, with only a small measure of hyperbole: "Reporters like to picture themselves as independent thinkers. In truth, with the exception of 13-year-old girls, there is no social subspecies more slavish to fashion, more terrified of originality and more devoted to group-think."[14] Kelly had a point, and polling data tend to lend support to such claims. For example, few journalists for mainstream American media consider themselves politically conservative. A survey conducted in 2004 for the Washington-based Committee of Concerned Journalists, found that 7 percent of national correspondents for U.S. news media considered themselves "conservative." The overwhelming majority were "moderate" or "liberal."[15] Similar findings were reported in 2008.[16]

Viewpoint diversity is an issue not much discussed in American journalism. But it is hardly irrelevant. "The perception of liberal bias is a problem by itself for the news media. It's not okay to dismiss it," Tom Rosenstiel, formerly the director of the research organization Project for Excellence in Journalism, has said. "Conservatives who think the press is deliberately trying to help Democrats are wrong. But conservatives are right that journalism has too many liberals and not enough conservatives. It's inconceivable that that is irrelevant." Rosenstiel called for "more intellectual diversity among journalists," saying, "More conservatives in newsrooms will bring about better journalism."[17] Rosenstiel probably is correct. It is certainly not inconceivable that a robust newsroom culture that embraces viewpoint diversity, encourages skepticism, invites challenges to dominant narratives, and rewards contrarian thinking would have helped thwart publication of embarrassing tales such as the *Washington Post*'s "fighting to the death" story about Jessica Lynch.

Similarly, journalists would do well to deepen their appreciation of complexity and ambiguity. All too often, the news media seem complexity-averse and exceedingly eager to simplify and synthesize. This tendency is explained in part by the tyranny of deadlines and the limitations of on-air time and newsprint space. Even so, few important events can be explained without recognizing and acknowledging their context and their intricacies. More than a few media-driven myths addressed in the preceding chapters arose from an impulse to offer easy answers to complex issues and abridge and simplify topics that are thorny and intricate.

The digitization of newspapers and other media content offers another antidote to media-driven myths. Digitization has made it easier than ever to consult and scrutinize source material from the past. Never has American journalism's record been more readily accessible. Reading what was written makes it clear that the *War of the Worlds* radio broadcast created nothing approaching nationwide panic and hysteria. Reading what was written makes clear that Murrow's critique of McCarthy was belated and unexceptional. Reading what was written makes clear that the *New York Times* reported in detail about the run-up to the Bay of Pigs invasion and that its preinvasion coverage was not limited to the controversial dispatch filed by Tad Szulc many days before the ill-fated attempt to topple Fidel Castro. Reading what was written makes clear that South Vietnamese warplanes dropped the napalm that burned Kim Phuc in Vietnam in 1972.

Reading what was written can be vital in debunking media-driven myths.

A few years ago, a Princeton University economist and public policy analyst named Alan B. Krueger came out with a thin, statistics-laden, yet intriguing volume titled *What Makes a Terrorist*. Krueger's thesis challenged the popular notion that poverty breeds terrorism. Such a linkage seems intuitive and has been invoked by politicians, scholars, analysts, and journalists.[18] Krueger's research showed persuasively, however, that the poverty-terrorism symbiosis is illusory. It is remarkable, he wrote, "that so many prominent, well-intentioned world leaders and scholars would draw this connection without having an empirical basis for it."[19]

The Princeton economist, then, also is a myth-buster, and an implication of his research is that there are, and will be, more media-driven myths to confront and dismantle. By no means do the media myths examined on these pages represent a closed universe. Others surely will assert themselves. They may tell of journalists' great deeds or of their woeful failings. They may well hold appeal across the political spectrum, offering something for almost everyone. They may be about war, or politics, or biomedical research. They may spring from pithy and irresistibly appealing quotations.

Predictably, they will be delicious tales, easy to remember, and perhaps self-congratulatory. They probably will offer vastly simplified accounts of history, and they may be propelled by cinematic treatment. They will be media-driven myths, all rich candidates for debunking.

Notes

PREFACE

1. "Vice President Biden's Remarks at Moscow State University," press release, White House: Office of the Vice President (10 March 2011), www .whitehouse.gov/the-press-office/2011/03/10/vice-president-bidens-remarks-moscow-state-university.

2. "Drive-bys Side with White House, Throw Media Icon Bob Woodward under Bus," transcript, *Rush Limbaugh Show* (28 February 2013), www .rushlimbaugh.com/daily/2013/02/28/drive_bys_side_with_white_house_throw_media_icon_bob_woodward_under_bus.

3. "Sequester Will Be Nothing Compared to the Next Budget Crisis at the End of March," transcript, *Rush Limbaugh Show* (25 February 2013), www .rushlimbaugh.com/daily/2013/02/25/sequester_will_be_nothing_compared _to_the_next_budget_crisis_at_the_end_of_march.

4. Cited in W. Joseph Campbell, "WaPo Move to New Quarters Stirs Retelling of Hero-Journalist Myth," *Media Myth Alert* (blog) (14 December 2015), www.mediamythalert.wordpress.com/2015/12/14/wapo-move-to-new-quarters-stirs-retelling-of-hero-journalist-myth.

5. Cited in W. Joseph Campbell, "Hearst, Garrison Keillor, and 'Furnish the War': Celebrities and Media Myths," *Media Myth Alert* (blog) (29 April 2015),www.mediamythalert.wordpress.com/2015/04/29/hearst-garrison-keillor-and-furnish-the-war-celebrities-and-media-myths.

6. Juan Williams, *Muzzled: The Assault on Honest Speech* (New York: Crown Publishers, 2011), 217.

7. See W. Joseph Campbell, *Yellow Journalism: Puncturing the Myths, Defining the Legacies* (Westport, CT: Praeger, 2001), 123.

8. Dick Cavett, "Will the Vietnam War Ever Go Away?" *New York Times* (24 April 2015), www.nytimes.com/2015/04/25/opinion/will-the-vietnam-war-ever-go-away.html.

9. Robert Reich, "From the Left: Nation's Circus Politics Are a Danger to Us and World," *Dayton Daily News* (19 November 2015): A18.

10. See, for example, "CBS Evening News for October 30, 2013," *CBS Evening News* (30 October 2013), transcript retrieved from www.lexisnexis.com. See also, "This Morning for October 30, 2013," *CBS This Morning* (30 October 2013), transcript retrieved from www.lexisnexis.com.

11. Roget Yu, "Famed Editor Dies at Age 93," *USA Today* (22 October 2014): 1A.

12. Tim Walker, "Ben Bradlee Dead," *London Independent* (22 October 2014), retrieved from www.lexisnexis.com.

13. "Ben Bradlee, John Dean III, and Howard Baker Discuss the 25th Anniversary of the Watergate Break-In," *Meet the Press*, NBC (15 June 1997), transcript retrieved from www.lexisnexis.com.

14. See Max H. Bazerman and Ann E. Tenbrunsel, "Stumbling into Bad Behavior," *New York Times* (21 April 2011): A27. See also, David Brooks, "Let's All Feel Superior," *New York Times* (15 November 2011): A31.

INTRODUCTION

1. Keith J. Kelly, "New York Sun Won't Shine for Long," *New York Post* (4 September 2008): 39.

2. Nicholas Wapshott, "Their 'Historic' Candidate," *New York Sun* (23 July 2008): 6.

3. See Jack Lule, "Myth and Terror on the Editorial Page: The *New York Times* Responds to September 11, 2001," *Journalism and Mass Communication Quarterly* 79, no. 2 (Summer 2002): 277; and S. Elizabeth Bird and Robert W. Dardenne, "Myth, Chronicle, and Story: Exploring the Narrative Qualities of News," in *Media, Myths, and Narratives: Television and the Press*, ed. James W. Carey (Newbury Park, CA: Sage, 1988), 70.

4. David Thorburn, "Television as an Aesthetic Medium," in *Media, Myths, and Narratives*, 56–57.

5. See Norbert Schwarz and others, "Metacognitive Experiences and the Intricacies of Setting People Straight: Implications for Debiasing and Public Information Campaigns," *Advances in Experimental Social Psychology* 39 (2007): 127–161. Schwarz and his colleagues reported that "attempts to inform people that a given claim is false may increase acceptance of the misleading claim" (151). Schwarz's research is discussed in Shankar Vedantam, "Persistence of Myths Could Alter Public Policy Approach," *Washington Post* (4 September 2007): A3.

6. Stephan Lewandowsky, Werner G.K. Stritzke, Klaus Oberauer, and Michael Morales, "Memory for Fact, Fiction, and Misinformation: The Iraq War 2003," *Psychological Science* 16, no. 3 (2005): 194.

7. See Jesse Ellison, "Periscope: The War's First Hero," *Newsweek* (9 June 2008): 13.

8. Brent Staples, "Hollywood: History by Default," *New York Times* (25 December 1991): 30.

9. Max Frankel, "Word and Image: The Facts of Media Life," *New York Times Sunday Magazine* (27 September 1998): 32.

10. Gary Strauss, "'Mythbusters' Hosts Relish Blowing Up Stuff on TV," *USA Today* (6 August 2008): 4D. Strauss wrote that the *Mythbusters* program has tested "the validity of more than 300 urban legends, myths, folklore, sayings and oddities. Can you actually shoot fish in a barrel? (The shock wave from the bullet kills the fish.) Use chili peppers to repel sharks? (Nope.) Find a needle in a haystack? (Possibly.)"

11. Robert E. Bartholomew, *Little Green Men, Meowing Nuns and Head-Hunting Panics: A Study of Mass Psychogenic Illness and Social Delusion* (Jefferson, NC: McFarland, 2001), 217, 218; Michael J. Socolow, "The Hyped Panic over 'War of the Worlds,'" *Chronicle of Higher Education* 55, no. 9 (24 October 2008): B16.

12. See David L. Vancil and Sue D. Pendell, "The Myth of Viewer-Listener Disagreement in the First Kennedy-Nixon Debate," *Central States Speech Journal* 38, no. 1 (Spring 1987): 16–27.

13. David Culbert, "Johnson and the Media," in *Exploring the Johnson Years*, ed. Robert A. Divine (Austin: University of Texas Press, 1981), 214–248.

14. Mariah Blake, "The Damage Done: Crack Babies Talk Back," *Columbia Journalism Review*, September/October 2004: 10.

15. Brian Thevenot, "Myth-Making in New Orleans," *American Journalism Review*, December 2005/January 2006: 30–37.

16. See W. Joseph Campbell, *Yellow Journalism: Puncturing the Myths, Defining the Legacies* (Westport, CT: Praeger, 2001), 71–95.

CHAPTER ONE

1. See James Creelman, *On the Great Highway: The Wanderings and Adventures of a Special Correspondent* (Boston: Lothrop, 1901), 177–178.

2. Charles Krauthammer, "Kidnapped by the Times," *Washington Post* (18 August 2002): B7. Krauthammer wrote, "Not since William Randolph Hearst famously cabled his correspondent in Cuba, 'You furnish the pictures and I'll furnish the war,' has a newspaper so blatantly devoted its front pages to editorializing about a coming American war as has Howell Raines's *New York Times*." Raines was the *Times*'s executive editor.

3. "Off the Wall Street Journal," *American Prospect* (March 2003): 10.

4. See W. Joseph Campbell, *Yellow Journalism: Puncturing the Myths, Defining the Legacies* (Westport, CT: Praeger, 2001), 71–95. See also John D. Stevens, *Sensationalism and the New York Press* (New York: Columbia University Press, 1991), 92; and Kenneth Whyte, *The Uncrowned King: The Sensational Rise of William Randolph Hearst* (Berkeley, CA: Counterpoint, 2009), 300–302.

5. "Remember the Maine? How Governments Manufacture Outrage," *Playboy* 53, no. 5 (1 May 2006): 42. See also Helen Thomas, *Watchdogs of Democracy? The Waning Washington Press Corps and How It Has Failed the Public*

(New York: Lisa Drew/Scribner, 2006), 9; and Willis J. Abbot, *Watching the World Go By* (Boston: Little, Brown, 1933), 217.

6. Quentin Letts, "Fleet Street Uber Alles," *Wall Street Journal* (26 April 2004): A14. Ben Proctor, one of Hearst's biographers, cited the purported vow to "furnish the war" and added, "And that was exactly what Hearst did." See Proctor, *William Randolph Hearst: The Early Years, 1863–1910* (New York: Oxford University Press, 1998), 103. For similar accounts, see Darrell M. West, *The Rise and Fall of the Media Establishment* (Boston: Bedford/St. Martin's, 2001), 45; David Randall, *The Universal Journalist*, 2nd ed. (Sterling, VA: Pluto Press, 2000), 15; James F. Dunnigan, *Dirty Little Secrets of the Twentieth Century* (New York: Morrow, 1999), 50; Donald A. Ritchie, *American Journalists: Getting the Story* (New York: Oxford University Press, 1997), 142; and Philip Seib, *Campaigns and Conscience: The Ethics of Political Journalism* (Westport, CT: Praeger, 1994), 11.

7. See, for example, Philip Seib, *Headline Diplomacy: How News Coverage Affects Foreign Policy* (Westport, CT: Praeger, 1997), 1–14.

8. The cause of the Spanish-American War can be attributed to a three-sided diplomatic standoff that came to a head in early 1898. The Cubans who had rebelled against Spain's colonial rule were determined to win political independence and would settle for nothing less. The Spanish, for domestic economic reasons, would not grant Cuba its independence. And the United States could no longer tolerate the disruptions and human rights abuses created by Spain's failed attempt to put down the Cuban rebellion. See, among others, David F. Trask, *The War with Spain in 1898* (New York: Macmillan, 1981), 58; and Campbell, *Yellow Journalism*, 123.

9. See Tim Harrower, *Inside Reporting: A Practical Guide to the Craft of Journalism* (Boston: McGraw-Hill, 2006), 11; Jane Chapman, *Comparative Media History: An Introduction, 1789 to the Present* (Malden, MA: Polity Press, 2005), 110; Lyn Gorman and David McLean, *Media and Society in the Twentieth Century: A Historical Introduction* (Malden, MA: Blackwell, 2003), 17; and Ray Eldon Hiebert and Sheila Jean Gibbons, *Exploring Mass Media for a Changing World* (Mahwah, NJ: Lawrence Erlbaum Associates, 2000), 151.

10. See Dwayne R. Winsock and Robert M. Pike, *Communication and Empire: Media, Markets, and Globalization, 1860–1930* (Durham, NC: Duke University Press, 2007), 203; Kenneth J. Hagan and Ian J. Bickerton, *Unintended Consequences: The United States at War* (London: Reaktion Books, 2007), 85; Greg McLaughlin, *The War Correspondent* (Sterling, VA: Pluto Press, 2002), 28; Chris Lamb, *Drawn to Extremes: The Use and Abuse of Editorial Cartoons* (New York: Columbia University Press, 2004), 43; Allen Churchill, *Park Row* (New York: Rinehart, 1958), 104; and Seib, *Headline Diplomacy*, 5. See also Peter Langley, "Taxpayers Get Sanitized History at San Simeon," *Contra Costa* [CA] *Times* (27 September 2006): F4.

11. For journalistic examples, see Thomas, *Watchdogs of Democracy?*, 9. See also Dan Bischoff, "Iraq Pornography Makes It America's Dirty War," *Denver Post* (21 May 2004); Michael Powell, "How America Picks Its Fights," *Washington Post* (25 March 2003): C1; Mark Sauer, "It's Taps for the Telegraph," *San Diego Union-Tribune* (14 November 2002): E1; and "Forget the Maine!" *Economist* 346 (3 January 1998): 32. Additionally, the *New York*

Times repeated the anecdote in an article about the centenary of the Spanish-American War in Clifford Krauss, "Remember Yellow Journalism," *New York Times* (15 February 1998): sec. 4, p. 3.

For scholarly examples, see Ted Curtis Smythe, *The Gilded Age Press, 1865–1900* (Westport, CT: Praeger, 2003), 187; and Michael Schudson, *Discovering the News: A Social History of American Newspapers* (New York: Basic Books, 1978), 61–62. See also Hiley H. Ward, *Mainstreams of American Media History: A Narrative and Intellectual History* (Boston: Allyn and Bacon, 1997), 279; and John Tebbel, *The Compact History of the American Newspaper* (New York: Hawthorn Books, 1963), 202.

12. Ben H. Bagdikian, *The New Media Monopoly* (Boston: Beacon, 2004), 88–90; Thomas, *Watchdogs of Democracy?*, 9; Nicholas Lemann, "Paper Tigers," *New Yorker* (13 April 2009), www.newyorker.com/magazine/2009/04/13/paper-tigers; Evan Thomas, *The War Lovers: Roosevelt, Lodge, Hearst, and the Rush to Empire, 1898* (New York: Little, Brown, 2010), 161; ; and David Halberstam, *The Powers That Be* (New York: Dell, 1980), 295. In Lemann's telling, Remington "claimed (without proof, alas) to have received a telegram from Hearst that said, regarding Cuba, 'You furnish the pictures, and I'll furnish the war.'"

13. Such was the appraisal of the U.S. consul-general in Havana, Fitzhugh Lee, a former Confederate cavalry general. See Lee to Secretary of State Richard Olney, 3 February 1897, Richard Olney papers, container 73, Manuscript Division, Library of Congress, Washington, DC.

14. Creelman, *On the Great Highway*, 5, 6.

15. The review in the *Washington Post*, however, said that Creelman's writing was "characterized by an exaggerated sense of self-importance." See "Creelman's New Book," *Washington Post* (3 November 1901): 23.

16. "On the Great Highway by James Creelman," *Saturday Review* supplement of the *New York Journal* (2 November 1901): 402–403.

17. Creelman, *On the Great Highway*, 178.

18. Richard Harding Davis, letter to his mother, 19 December 1896, Richard Harding Davis Collection, Alderman Library of American Literature, University of Virginia, Charlottesville.

19. See "Shipping News," *New York Tribune* (21 January 1897): 12; and "Puerto de la Habana," *Diario de la Marina* [Havana] (19 January 1897): 1.

20. "Cuban War Sketches Gathered in the Field by Frederic Remington; The Gifted Artist, Visiting Cuba Especially for the Journal, Describes with Pen and Pencil Characters That Are Making the War Famous and Infamous," *New York Journal* (24 January 1897): 17.

21. Edmond D. Coblentz, ed., *William Randolph Hearst: A Portrait in His Own Words* (New York: Simon & Schuster, 1952), 58.

22. See Peggy Samuels and Harold Samuels, *Frederic Remington: A Biography* (Garden City, NY: Doubleday, 1982), 249. The Samuels' biography uncritically reiterates Creelman's account of the purported Remington-Hearst exchange.

23. "Cuban War Sketches Gathered in the Field by Frederic Remington," *New York Journal*; "Frederic Remington Sketches a Familiar Incident of the Cuban War," *New York Journal* (29 January 1897): 2.

24. "Frederic Remington's Sketch, from Life," *New York Journal* (24 January 1897): 18.

25. Frederic Remington, letter to the editor, "Frederic Remington Writes to the World about Scovel," [New York] *World* (21 February 1897): 1.

26. Frederic Remington, "Havana, 1899," in *The Reader's Companion to Cuba*, ed. Alan Ryan (San Diego: Harcourt Brace, 1997), 68.

27. James Creelman, "The Real Mr. Hearst," *Pearson's Magazine* (September 1906): 259

28. "The American Press," *Times* [London] (30 September 1907): 5.

29. W. R. Hearst, "Mr. W. R. Hearst on Anglo-American Relations," *Times* [London] (2 November 1907): 5. Years later, Hearst was quoted by his son as denying the purported exchange. See William Randolph Hearst Jr. with Jack Casserly, *The Hearsts: Father and Son* (Niwot, CO: Roberts Rinehart, 1991), 38.

30. See David Nasaw, *The Chief: The Life of William Randolph Hearst* (Boston: Houghton Mifflin, 2000), 509–510.

31. Ibid., 523. Nasaw noted: "It was one thing to 'expose' selected professors, college-age 'sap-heads,' and White House advisers as communistic, but to claim in print that the president was 'Moscow's candidate' was to venture a step too far."

32. Ibid., 524, 521.

33. Joseph E. Wisan, *The Cuban Crisis as Reflected in the New York Press (1895–1898)* (New York: Octagon Books, 1965 [reprint of 1934 ed.]), [v].

34. Ibid., 459.

35. Abbot, *Watching the World Go By*, 217.

36. John Dos Passos, *The Big Money* (New York: New American Library, 1969 [reprint of 1936 ed.]), 473.

37. Ferdinand Lundberg, *Imperial Hearst: A Social Biography* (New York: Equinox Cooperative, 1936), 68–69.

38. See Nasaw, *The Chief*, 567–572.

39. In 1998 and in 2007, the American Film Institute ranked *Citizen Kane* the best motion picture ever. See David Germain, "Welles' 'Kane' Remains Citizen No. 1 among AFI's Greatest Movies," Associated Press (21 June 2007), article retrieved from www.lexisnexis.com.

40. Davis, letter to his mother, 19 December 1896.

41. Ibid.

42. Richard Harding Davis, letter to his mother, 1 January 1897, Davis Collection, Alderman Library, University of Virginia.

43. Richard Harding Davis, telegram to his mother, 30 December 1897, Davis Collection, Alderman Library, University of Virginia.

44. Davis, letter to his mother, 1 January 1897.

45. Richard Harding Davis, letter to his family, 2 January 1897, Davis Collection, Alderman Library, University of Virginia.

46. Richard Harding Davis, letter to his mother, 4 January 1897, Davis Collection, Alderman Library, University of Virginia.

47. Davis, letter to his family, 2 January 1897.

48. Remington, "Havana, 1899," 67.

49. Richard Harding Davis, letter to his mother, 9 January 1897, Davis Collection, Alderman Library, University of Virginia.

50. Richard Harding Davis, letter to his mother, 15 January 1897, Davis Collection, Alderman Library, University of Virginia.

51. Richard Harding Davis, second letter to his mother, 15 January 1897, Davis Collection, Alderman Library, University of Virginia.

52. Richard Harding Davis, letter to his brother, [20?] January 1897, Davis Collection, Alderman Library, University of Virginia.

53. Davis, letter to his mother, 15 January 1897.

54. Richard Harding Davis, letter to his mother, 16 January 1897, Davis Collection, Alderman Library, University of Virginia.

55. "The Press and War," *Fourth Estate* (18 February 1897): 6. The trade journal blamed Spanish censorship for the many vivid but improbable accounts of the rebellion in Cuba that were sent from Key West. "The actual and vital facts are that the censorship at Havana has forced the imaginative Cubans of Key West to invent a series of impossible events to take the place of real news," *Fourth Estate* said.

56. Fitzhugh Lee to Secretary of State Richard Olney, 10 February 1897, Richard Olney papers, container 73, Manuscript Division, Library of Congress.

57. "The Press and War," *Fourth Estate*.

58. "Making War on the Women," *New York Tribune* (19 January 1897): 1. Creelman was familiar with the rigors of Spanish censorship in Havana, having encountered it firsthand on assignment to Cuba in 1896. He boasted in his memoir about outwitting the censor. See Creelman, *On the Great Highway*, 165.

59. Abbot, *Watching the World Go By*, 208.

60. "A New Comer," *Journalist* (26 June 1897): 77. Creelman also was suspected of modifying direct quotations. In 1894, an American diplomat said Creelman had excessively dramatized the content of an interview with the Korean monarch, adding that Creelman "doubtless put into the king's mouth what [Creelman] thought he wished to say." Cited in Jeffery M. Dorwart, "James Creelman, the *New York World* and the Port Arthur Massacre," *Journalism Quarterly* 50, no. 4 (Winter 1973): 698.

61. Edwin Llewellyn Shuman, *Steps into Journalism: Helps and Hints for Young Writers* (Evanston, IL: Correspondence School of Journalism, 1894), 6–7.

62. "The beauty about Creelman," Hearst once was quoted as saying, "is the fact that whatever you give him to do instantly becomes in his mind the most important assignment ever given any writer. Of course, it's a form of egotism. He thinks that the very fact of the job being given him means that it's a task of unsurpassing importance, else it would not have been given to so great a man as he." Quoted in Abbot, *Watching the World Go By*, 208.

63. See Dorwart, "James Creelman," 699.

64. "The Port Arthur 'Outrages,'" *New York Tribune* (20 December 1894): 6.

65. Dorwart, "James Creelman," 699–700.

66. Edwin Dun to Secretary of State W. Q. Gresham, "The Affair of Port Arthur Subsequent to the Capture of That Town by the Japanese Forces,"

20 December 1894, in *Despatches from U.S. Ministers to Japan*, vol. 68, Record Group 59, National Archives, College Park, MD.

67. See "A New Comer's Gossip," *Journalist* (31 July 1897). The "New Comer" columnist declared Creelman "a genuine prig—that is . . . 'stuck on himself.'" See "A New Comer," *Journalist* (11 September 1897).

68. Creelman, *On the Great Highway*, 109.

69. James Creelman, "Famine and Flames: Spain May Destroy, but She Cannot Keep Cuba Even with an Army of 180,000," *New York World* (17 May 1896): 1.

70. Creelman misrepresented the character of the Cuban rebellion. He vastly overstated the size of rebel forces under the command of Máximo Gómez, who, Creelman wrote, "has drilled more men than he has arms for. I am quite certain that with arms and ammunition enough the Cuban Republic can put 100,000 men in the field." See Creelman, "Famine and Flames." The most generous estimates were that the Cuban rebel forces numbered some 40,000 but usually "were deployed in small, mobile detachments engaging in hit-and-run operations." See Trask, *The War with Spain in 1898*, 6.

71. Creelman, *On the Great Highway*, 168–169.

72. James Creelman, "My Experiences at Santiago," *Review of Reviews and World's Work* (November 1898): 545.

73. "A Loud Cry for Creelman," *Washington Post* (28 October 1899): 6. With tongue in cheek, the *Post* also called Creelman "the only real hero" of the battle at El Caney. See "Creelman and His Mule," *Washington Post* (29 March 1899): 6.

74. See *Annual Reports of the War Department for the Fiscal Year Ended June 30, 1898* (Washington, DC: Government Printing Office, 1898), 316, 318, 320, 321. U.S. casualties in the assaults on the blockhouse included 48 soldiers and officers killed and 145 wounded.

75. Nasaw, *The Chief*, 138–139.

76. For a discussion of the "journalism of action," see W. Joseph Campbell, *The Year That Defined American Journalism: 1897 and the Clash of Paradigms* (New York: Routledge, 2006), 5–7.

77. Creelman, *On the Great Highway*, 177.

CHAPTER TWO

1. Michael Kernan, "The Night the Sky Fell In; 50 Years Later, Looking Back on the Panic over 'War of the Worlds,'" *Washington Post* (30 October 1988): G1. *The Night That Panicked America* was the title of a made-for-television movie about the *War of the Worlds* radio dramatization that aired on ABC on Halloween night, 1975.

2. See Richard J. Hand, *Terror on the Air! Horror Radio in America, 1931–1952* (Jefferson, NC: McFarland, 2006), 7.

3. Lawrence M. Fisher, "Orson Welles' '38 Shocker Remade," *New York Times* (29 October 1988): 52.

4. Paul Heyer, "America under Attack I: A Reassessment of Orson Welles' 1938 *War of the Worlds* Broadcast," *Canadian Journal of Communication* 28, no. 2 (March 2003): 154.

5. Performances of the *Mercury Theatre* had been broadcast on CBS since July 1938. The show was placed in the Sunday evening lineup in September 1938. See "Behind the Scenes," *New York Times* (4 September 1938): 108.

6. The *New York Sun*, for example, noted, "Most of those who heard the entire program fail to understand how any one could have been fooled." See "No FCC Action on Mars Scare," *New York Sun* (1 November 1938): 36. Paul Heyer argues in an essay about the program, however, that "the effective pacing of the various segments of the drama made it easy for listeners to suspend disbelief and assume that events in the radio play were transpiring in real time." See Heyer, "America under Attack I," 156.

7. This important point is made by Shearon A. Lowery and Melvin L. DeFleur in *Milestones in Mass Communication Research: Media Effects*, 3rd ed. (White Plains, NY: Longman, 1995), 49. On the implausible pace of events of the *War of the Worlds* program, they noted that, in less than an hour, "the United States had mobilized large bodies of troops; reporters had traveled great distances; government cabinet meetings were held; and savage battles were fought on land and in the air."

8. Many latecomers to the *War of the Worlds* broadcast were engaging in what was called "dialitis," the 1930s equivalent of channel-surfing, in which listeners spun the station dial of their radio in search of more interesting and entertaining programming. The *New York Post* defined dialitis as "a disease of the hand which makes it impossible for some folks to stay with any one program." See Leonard Carlton, "Fuss Is Traced to Dialitis; Radio Listeners Warned," *New York Post* (31 October 1938): 21.

9. See, among others, Hadley Cantril, *The Invasion from Mars* (New York: Harper & Row, 1966 [reprint of 1940 edition]), 76–84.

10. See also "Radio 'War' Scare Probed; 'Invasion' Terrorizes Jersey," *Newark Star-Eagle* (31 October 1938): 1; "Radio 'War' Panic Brings Inquiry," *New York Post* (31 October 1938): 1; "City Terrorized by Radio Drama," *Philadelphia Inquirer* (31 October 1938): 1.

11. Welles was quoted as saying: "Today I had a terrifying mass press interview, and never have I been so bombarded with questions." See R. H. McBride and R. A. Springs Jr., "Orson Welles Calls Broadcast 'Terribly Shocking Experience,'" *Daily Princetonian* (1 November 1938), Box 356, Folder 9, Princeton University Archives, Princeton University Library, Princeton, NJ. Welles was further quoted as saying, "It was a terribly shocking experience to realize that I had caused such widespread terror." He also said, "When you cause pain, you can't laugh about it. Ordinarily I might be indignant with people for their gullibility, but as the unwitting agent of the suffering, I feel a little like one accused of murder."

12. See "FCC to Scan Script of 'War' Broadcast," *New York Times* (1 November 1938): 1, 26. Welles told the clamorous news conference the day after the broadcast, "Despite my deep regret over any misapprehension which our broadcast last night created among some listeners, I am ever the more bewildered over this misunderstanding in the light of an analysis of the broadcast itself." Welles cited four elements which, he said, signaled that the broadcast was a dramatization: the performance was set a year in the future; the broadcast took place during the scheduled program slot of the *Mercury Theatre*; the performance included

three specific disclaimers that it was a dramatization; and Mars and Martians were frequently used as topics for fantasies about adventures in outer space. Not all of those elements were readily apparent, however. Only close listeners would have heard the indirect and passing reference to the program's having been set in 1939. And of the disclaimers, one came at the outset of the program. The other two came during the closing twenty minutes of the program, when the Martian invasion of Earth was well underway.

13. Cited in Orson Welles and Peter Bogdanovich, *This Is Orson Welles* (New York: Da Capo, 1998), 18.

14. Cantril, *Invasion from Mars*, xiii.

15. Ibid., 47. Cantril apparently reached such a conclusion within days of the radio dramatization. According to the *Daily Princetonian* newspaper, Cantril told a psychology class in early November 1938, "People believed that the Martians were here without any particularly benevolent motives. The Martians were mowing down the National Guard and it was only a matter of time before they would kill the individual listener. This increased the feeling of individual desperation." Cited in "'Martian Invasion' Treated by Cantril," *Daily Princetonian* (3 November 1938), Box 356, Folder 9, Princeton University Archives.

16. Lowery and DeFleur, *Milestones in Mass Communication Research*, 66.

17. Cantril, *Invasion from Mars*, 47, 58. Cantril (58) suggested that the number of people frightened by the broadcast exceeded 1.2 million, noting that many people "were probably too ashamed of their gullibility to confess it" in interviews.

18. Robert E. Bartholomew, *Little Green Men, Meowing Nuns and Head-Hunting Panics: A Study of Mass Psychogenic Illness and Social Delusion* (Jefferson, NC: McFarland, 2001), 217, 218.

19. Erich Goode, *Collective Behavior* (Fort Worth: Saunders College Publishing, 1992), 314. Michael J. Socolow, a scholar at the University of Maine, wrote of *The War of the Worlds*, "The panic was neither as widespread nor as serious as many have believed at the time or since." See Socolow, "The Hyped Panic over 'War of the Worlds,'" *Chronicle of Higher Education* 55, no. 9 (24 October 2008): B16. See also Jefferson Pooley and Michael J. Socolow, "The Myth of the *War of the Worlds* Panic," Slate.com (28 October 2013), www.slate.com/articles/arts/history/2013/10/orson_welles_war_of_the_worlds_panic_myth_the_infamous_radio_broadcast_did.html.

20. Jeffrey Sconce, *Haunted Media: Electronic Presence from Telegraphy to Television* (Durham, NC: Duke University, 2000), 116.

21. The thirty-six newspapers examined were: the *Atlanta Journal*, the *Baltimore Sun*, the *Boston Globe*, the *Boston Herald*, the *Brooklyn Eagle*, the *Chicago Herald and Examiner*, the *Chicago Tribune*, the *Cincinnati Enquirer*, the *Cleveland Plain Dealer*, the *Columbus Evening Dispatch*, the *Des Moines Register*, the *Detroit Free Press*, the *Denver Rocky Mountains News*, the *Harrisburg [PA] Patriot*, the *Hartford [CT] Courant*, the *Indianapolis Star*, the *Jacksonville Florida Times-Union*, the *Kansas City Star*, the *Los Angeles Times*, the *New Orleans Times-Picayune*, the *New York Herald Tribune*, the *New York Journal and American*, the *New York Post*, the *New York Sun*, the *New York Times*, the *Newark Evening News*, the *Newark Star-Eagle*, the *Philadelphia*

Inquirer, the *Raleigh* [NC] *News and Observer*, the *Richmond Times-Dispatch*, the *St. Louis Post-Dispatch*, the *San Francisco Chronicle*, the *Seattle Times*, the *Trenton* [NJ] *State Gazette*, the *Washington Post*, and the *Washington Star*.

22. Such stunning claims often appeared in the opening paragraphs of articles about the program but usually were thinly attributed, if attributed at all.

23. The *New York Herald Tribune*, for example, said in an editorial about the broadcast, "At last something has happened which never happened here before." See "Phantasmagoria," *New York Herald Tribune* (1 November 1938): 20.

24. See "Victims of 'Martians,'" *Atlanta Journal* (31 October 1938): 3. A photograph of Cantlon with her left arm in a sling also appeared in the *Los Angeles Times*. See "All-American Bogeyman—Author and One of Victims in Panic Broadcast," *Los Angeles Times* (1 November 1939): 20.

25. "Radio Listeners in Panic," *New York Times* (31 October 1938): 1, 4.

26. All quotations from ibid., 4.

27. "Radio 'War' Scare Probed," *Newark Star-Eagle*.

28. "City Terrorized by Radio Drama," *Philadelphia Inquirer* (31 October 1938): 1.

29. Marshall Andrews, "Monsters of Mars on a Meteor Stampede Radiotic America," *Washington Post* (31 October 1938): 1.

30. A. McK. Griggs, letter to the editor, "Reactions to the Radio Panic," *Washington Post* (3 November 1938): 10.

31. "Quantico Marines Wept and Prayed during 'Invasion,'" *Washington Post* (1 November 1938): 4.

32. "Marines Deny Mars' Monsters Made Them Quail," *Washington Post* (2 November 1938): 4.

33. See, among others, "Prefers Poison," *New York Post* (October 31, 1938): 21.

34. See, among others, "Students Faint," *New York Post* (October 31, 1938): 21.

35. "Radio Listeners in Panic," *New York Times*, 4.

36. Among the newspapers to publish this account were the *Baltimore Sun*, the *Boston Herald*, the *Chicago Herald and Examiner*, the Jacksonville *Florida Times-Union*, the *Hartford Courant*, the *Indianapolis Star*, the *New York Journal and American*, the *Raleigh News and Observer*, and the *San Francisco Chronicle*.

37. See "Radio Listeners in Panic," *New York Times*, 4; "Panicky Calls Swamp Eagle on Mars 'Raid,'" *Brooklyn Eagle* (31 October 1938): 3; and Irving F. Lash, "U.S. May Act to Control Horror Radio Plays after War Scare," *Washington Star* (31 October 1938): 1.

38. "Radio Play Causes Nationwide Panic; Woman Stops Church Service Here," *Indianapolis Star* (31 October 1938): 1; "Radio Story of Mars Raid Causes Panic," *Los Angeles Times* (31 October 1938): 1, 2.

39. "Radio Scare Here Spreads Fear, Anger," *Hartford Courant* (31 October 1938): 1; "Radio Listeners in Panic," *New York Times*, 4; Cantril, *Invasion from Mars*, 47, 58.

40. See "Radio Fiction of 'Invasion' Leaves Scores Panicky," *Harrisburg Patriot* (31 October 1938): 1.

41. Goode, *Collective Behavior*, 314.

42. "Attack from Mars in Radio Play," *New York Herald Tribune* (31 October 1938).

43. One angry caller to the *New York Times* declared, "I've heard a lot of radio programs, but I've never heard anything as rotten as that." See "Radio Listeners in Panic," *New York Times*, 4.

44. See "FCC to Scan Script," *New York Times*, 26.

45. "U.S. May Act to Control Horror Radio Plays," *Washington Star*, 3.

46. See "Radio Listeners in Panic," *New York Times*, 1.

47. See, for example, "F.C.C. Calls for Radio Script of 'Mars Invasion,'" *Newark Evening News* (31 October 1938): 1.

48. Raymond A. Bauer noted in an essay in *Public Opinion Quarterly* that the *War of the Worlds* dramatization "got only a fraction of the population of New Jersey onto the highways to flee a Martian invasion. An enormous traffic jam should not be confused with a unanimous communication effect." See Bauer, "Communication as a Transaction: A Comment on 'On the Concept of Influence,'" *Public Opinion Quarterly* 27, no. 1 (Spring 1963): 85.

49. Cited in Robert J. Brown, *Manipulating the Ether: The Power of Broadcast Radio in Thirties America* (Jefferson, NC: McFarland, 1998), 219.

50. See "Protest Sent to U.S. Commission," *Trenton* [NJ] *State Gazette* (1 November 1938). See also "Radio 'War' Panic Brings Inquiry," *New York Post*, 21. The *Post* reported that "hundreds of . . . New Jersey residents tried to find the meteor and roads around Princeton were jammed for hours."

51. Quoted in "Radio 'War' Panic," *New York Post*.

52. Quotations from "Radio 'War' Scare Probed," *Newark Star-Eagle*.

53. "Attack from Mars in Radio Play," *New York Herald Tribune*, 26, 1.

54. "Radio Listeners in Panic," *New York Times*, 4.

55. "Seeks Sound Truck," *Newark Evening News* (31 October 1938): 8.

56. "F.C.C. Calls for Radio Script of 'Mars Invasion,'" *Newark Evening News*.

57. "Troopers Besieged," *Newark Evening News* (31 October 1938): 8.

58. "F.C.C. Calls for Radio Script of 'Mars Invasion, '" *Newark Evening News*.

59. Cited in Joseph Bulgatz, *Ponzi Schemes, Invaders from Mars and More Extraordinary Popular Delusions and the Madness of Crowds* (New York: Harmony Books, 1992), 123.

60. "Radio Play Causes Nationwide Panic," *Indianapolis Star*.

61. "Many Baltimoreans, near Hysteria, Are Persuaded Not to Flee Homes," *Baltimore Sun* (31 October 1938): 2.

62. "The Editor Says," *New York Journal and American* (1 November 1938): 18. Emphasis in the original.

63. Ibid.

64. "Spankings in Order," [Detroit] *Free Press* (1 November 1938).

65. "That Radio Scare," *Editor and Publisher* (5 November 1938): 20.

66. "Terror by Radio," *New York Times* (1 November 1938): 22.

67. "The Spooks from Mars," *Richmond Times-Dispatch* (1 November 1938): 6.

68. "Terror by Air," *New York Sun* (1 November 1938): 20.

69. "The Gullible Radio Public," *Chicago Tribune* (10 November 1938): 16.

70. "The War of the Worlds," *Cincinnati Enquirer* (1 November 1938): 4.

71. "Newspapers Calm the People," *Harrisburg Patriot* (1 November 1938).

72. See "Phantasmagoria," *New York Herald Tribune*.

73. "'Is It True?,'" *Denver Rocky Mountain News* (1 November 1938): 8.

74. "Radio Irresponsibility," *Chicago Herald and Examiner* (8 November 1938): 14.

75. "This Incredible World," *Hartford Courant* (1 November 1938): 10.

76. Peg Meirer, "The Catastrophe That Wasn't," *Minneapolis Star Tribune* (29 June 2005): 1E; Pamela J. MacLeod, "World Beats Path to Martian Shrine," *Wall Street Journal* (28 October 1988): A11.

77. "Puncturing a Panic," *Wall Street Journal* (18 September 1989), retrieved from www.proquest.com.

CHAPTER THREE

1. See, among others, Jonathan Alter, "The Struggle for the Soul of CBS News," *Newsweek* (15 September 1986): 52; and Robert Goldberg, "See It Again: Murrow TV Documentary," *Wall Street Journal* (6 August 1990): A11.

2. Murrow reportedly was the first journalist to have federal parkland named for him. See "Edward R. Murrow Park to Be Dedicated April 25," *Washington Post* (5 April 1979): DC4.

3. Cited in Mark Leibovich, "Edward R. Murrow, Welcome to the Full-Spin Zone," *Washington Post* (27 March 2005): D1.

4. See Nicholas Lemann, "The Murrow Doctrine: Why the Life and Times of the Broadcast Pioneer Still Matter," *New Yorker* (23 January 2006): 38.

5. Edward Bliss Jr., "Remembering Edward R. Murrow," *Saturday Review* (31 May 1975): 18. Bliss said Murrow's swift rise to fame "was due not only to the quality of Ed Murrow's reporting, but also to the medium itself . . . . Radio was faster, more pervasive, more personal than print [media], so that Murrow was transformed in the public mind, as by magic, from being one of many reporters covering the Battle of Britain to *the* reporter covering that battle."

6. See, for example, Eric Harrison, "Edward R. Murrow: The Epitome of a Newsman," *Houston Chronicle* (14 October 2005), retrieved from www .lexisnexis.com. Harrison wrote that, at the time of Murrow's *See It Now* program, a "backlash was growing against McCarthy's methods and overzealousness. Still, no one dared speak out." See also Jon Carroll, "Bad Times in Afghanistan," *San Francisco Chronicle* (13 July 2010): E8. Carroll wrote that "Murrow's takedown" of McCarthy "was not really news—everybody in Washington knew what was going on, how vile and stupid McCarthy was; the media was just too scared to print it, possibly because politicians were too scared to challenge McCarthy, the ruiner of lives." This theme also is popular in textbooks of journalism and mass communication. See, for example, Jean Folkerts, Stephen Lacy, and Ann Larabee, *The Media in Your Life: An Introduction to Mass Communication* (Boston: Allyn and Bacon, 2008), 263. "Few

people," the authors said about Murrow, "had been willing to do battle with such a powerful senator."

7. See Loren Ghiglione, *CBS's Don Hollenbeck: An Honest Reporter in the Age of McCarthyism* (New York: Columbia University Press, 2008), 196.

8. Alan Chartock, "Shining the Light of Truth," *Berkshire* [MA] *Eagle* (1 October 2005).

9. "They Listened to Murrow," *Broadcasting/Telecasting* (15 March 1954): 132.

10. Cited in "Murrow Calls It 'Reporting,'" *Newsweek* (29 March 1954): 51.

11. Bob Edwards, *Edward R. Murrow and the Birth of Broadcast Journalism* (Hoboken, NJ: Wiley & Sons, 2004), 4.

12. A.M. Sperber, *Murrow: His Life and Times* (New York: Freundlich Books, 1986), 440.

13. Nat Hentoff, "Confronting McCarthy, Then and Now," *Village Voice* (11 December 2007), www.villagevoice.com/news/confronting-joe-mccarthy-then-and-now-6423764.

14. Daniel Schorr, "No Screen Too Big for Murrow," *Christian Science Monitor* (14 October 2005): 9.

15. Joseph Wershba, "Murrow vs. McCarthy: See It Now," *New York Times Sunday Magazine* (4 March 1979): SM12.

16. "Murrow's Unhappy Anniversary," *Broadcasting and Cable* (15 March 2004): 48.

17. "NFL, The League Is Considering a Big Change," *CBS This Morning* (8 March 2014), transcript retrieved from www.lexisnexis.com. The comment was made by Anthony Mason.

18. Marvin Kalb, "Inside Media" program, Newseum, Washington, DC (26 April 2008). Kalb at the time was the Edward R. Murrow Professor of Practice (Emeritus) at Harvard University's Joan Shorenstein Center on the Press, Politics, and Public Policy.

19. Quoted in "Sevareid Recalls How McCarthyism Hurt Journalists," *Broadcast Journalism* 94 (9 January 1978): 48.

20. Data cited here were retrieved from the Gallup Organization's online Gallup Brain database.

21. Jay Nelson Tuck, "What Is Murrow Really Like?" *New York Post* (25 April 1954): 2M.

22. "Murrow Calls It 'Reporting,'" *Newsweek*.

23. Fred W. Friendly, *Due to Circumstances beyond Our Control* (New York: Random House, 1967), 23.

24. "Witticisms Exchanged," *New York Herald Tribune* (10 March 1954): 14.

25. Two subsequent *See It Now* shows were devoted to McCarthy—one on March 16, 1954, which focused on McCarthy's tactics in the Senate hearing room, and another on April 6, 1954, when McCarthy delivered a rambling reply to the charges raised on Murrow's program of March 9.

26. "Murrow's Unhappy Anniversary," *Broadcasting and Cable*.

27. See Stanley Cloud and Lynne Olson, *The Murrow Boys: Pioneers on the Front Lines of Broadcast Journalism* (Boston: Houghton Mifflin, 1996), 307.

28. Andrew Ferguson, "Edward R. Murrow: Infotainment Pioneer," *Weekly Standard* (22 July 1996): 26.

29. Philip Hamburger, "Television: Man from Wisconsin," *New Yorker* (20 March 1954): 71.

30. Gilbert Seldes, "Murrow, McCarthy and the Empty Formula: Giving Equal Time for Reply," *Saturday Review* 37 (24 April 1954): 26.

31. Lemann, "Murrow Doctrine."

32. See Edwin R. Bayley, *Joe McCarthy and the Press* (New York: Pantheon Books, 1981), 26.

33. Thomas Doherty, *Cold War, Cool Medium: Television, McCarthyism, and American Culture* (New York: Columbia University Press, 2003), 14.

34. Doherty, *Cold War, Cool Medium*, 15.

35. The figure was cited by Seldes in "Murrow, McCarthy and the Empty Formula."

36. McCarthy's reply on *See It Now* was broadcast April 6, 1954.

37. Friendly, *Due to Circumstances beyond Our Control*, 41.

38. Jack Gould, "Television in Review: Murrow vs. McCarthy," *New York Times* (11 March 1954): 38.

39. Hamburger, "Man from Wisconsin."

40. Jay Nelson Tuck, "Murrow Rakes McCarthy on TV," *New York Post* (10 March 1954): 5.

41. Friendly, *Due to Circumstances beyond Our Control*, 43.

42. Sperber, *Murrow*, 442–443.

43. Friendly, *Due to Circumstances beyond Our Control*, 43.

44. Cloud and Olson, *Murrow Boys*, 308.

45. Sperber, *Murrow*, 441.

46. Brian Thornton, "Published Reaction When Murrow Battled McCarthy," *Journalism History* 29, no. 3 (Fall 2003): 140. Thornton's newspaper sample included the *New York Times, Washington Post, New York Herald Tribune, Chicago Tribune, Milwaukee Journal, Denver Post, Los Angeles Times,* and *San Francisco Chronicle*. His magazine sample included *Life, Time, Newsweek,* and *U.S. News and World Report*.

47. Ibid., 141, 143.

48. Doherty, *Cold War, Cool Medium* 188.

49. James A. Wechsler, *The Age of Suspicion* (New York: Random House, 1953), 5.

50. Oliver Pilat and William V. Shannon, "The One-Man Mob of Joe McCarthy," *New York Post* (4 September 1951): 3.

51. Ibid.

52. Ibid.

53. Oliver Pilat and William V. Shannon, "Sen. McCarthy: Past Cloudy, Present Windy, Future Foggy," *New York Post* (23 September 1951): 4.

54. Ibid.

55. Ibid.

56. See Wechsler, *Age of Suspicion*, 278.

57. "Excerpts from Testimony of Wechsler before McCarthy Inquiry," *New York Times* (8 May 1953): 14. In his autobiographic account of the hearings,

Wechsler said McCarthy reminded him of "the gangster in a B-movie who faces the unpleasant necessity of rubbing out someone who has gotten in his way: he would really like the victim to feel that there is nothing personal about it and that he rather regrets the exorbitant demands of duty. At no time did I have the feeling that I was confronted by a fanatic." See Wechsler, *Age of Suspicion*, 281.

58. "Excerpts from Testimony of Wechsler," *New York Times*.

59. Cited in Murrey Marder, "Wechsler, McCarthy Exchanges Revealed," *Washington Post* (8 May 1953): 23.

60. "Excerpts from Testimony of Wechsler," *New York Times*.

61. Marder, "Wechsler, McCarthy Exchanges Revealed."

62. "Intimidation," *Washington Post* (9 May 1953): 10.

63. Wechsler, *Age of Suspicion*, 304.

64. "Querulous Quaker," *Time* (13 December 1948).

65. Douglas A. Anderson, *A "Washington Merry-Go-Round" of Libel Actions* (Chicago: Nelson-Hall, 1980), 1.

66. Townsend Hoopes and Douglas Brinkley, *Driven Patriot: The Life and Times of James Forrestal* (Annapolis: Naval Institute Press, 1992), 433.

67. Quoted in Mark Feldstein, "Review: Peace, War, and Politics: An Eyewitness Account," *Washington Monthly* (1 January 2000): 48.

68. Arthur Herman, *Joseph McCarthy: Reexamining the Life and Legacy of America's Most Hated Senator* (New York: Free Press, 2000), 232.

69. "Querulous Quaker," *Time*.

70. See Bayley, *Joe McCarthy*, 57.

71. Drew Pearson, typescript of "Drew Pearson on the Washington Merry-Go-Round" (18 February 1950), Drew Pearson papers, American University, Washington, DC.

72. Ibid.

73. Pearson, typescript of "Drew Pearson on the Washington Merry-Go-Round" (25 February 1950), Pearson papers, American University.

74. Drew Pearson, typescript of "Drew Pearson on the Washington Merry-Go-Round" (14 March 1950), Pearson papers, American University.

75. Ibid.

76. Drew Pearson, typescript of "Drew Pearson on the Washington Merry-Go-Round" (19 April 1950), Pearson papers, American University.

77. Ibid.

78. Tyler Abell, ed., *Drew Pearson Diaries: 1949–1959* (New York: Holt, Rinehart, and Winston, 1974), 121, 122. See also Murrey Marder, "Pearson Says McCarthy Threatened to Maim Him," *Washington Post* (5 October 1951): 18.

79. Marder, "Pearson Says McCarthy Threatened to Maim Him."

80. Mary Van Rensselaer Thayer, "The Sulgrave Outnumbers '400,'" *Washington Post* (13 February 1955): F1.

81. "Battle of the Billygoats," *Time* (25 December 1950), www.time.com/time/printout/0,8816,859062,00.html.

82. Ibid.

83. "McCarthy Admits 'Slapping,' but Not 'Punching' Pearson," *Washington Post* (6 October 1951): 9.

84. "Battle of the Billygoats," *Time*.

85. "McCarthy Prepares to Attack Pearson by Words, Not Deeds," *Washington Evening Star* (15 December 1950): A19.

86. "McCarthy Ascribes Red 'Voice' to Pearson, Who May Sue," *Washington Post* (16 December 1950): 1, 11.

87. Ibid.

88. "Radio Sponsor Plans to Drop Drew Pearson," *Chicago Tribune* (23 December 1950): C4. See also "Adam Hat Explains Dropping Pearson," *New York Times* (31 December 1950): 27. The *Times* account quoted the Adam Hat president, Charles V. Molesworth, as saying the company's decision "not to continue with network radio" advertising had been made in May 1950. Pearson, the official said, was formally notified of this in mid-November 1950.

89. "McCarthyism Becomes a Menace," *Washington Post* (3 March 1951): B13. That installment of the Merry-Go-Round column was written by Pearson's staff. The columnist was traveling in Europe.

90. "McCarthy, Times-Herald, Nine Others Sued by Drew Pearson," *Washington Post* (3 March 1951): 1.

91. Marder, "Pearson Says McCarthy Threatened to Maim Him."

92. Drew Pearson, "Walking Alone Killed McCarthy," *Washington Post* (6 May 1957): B15.

93. Drew Pearson, typescript of "Drew Pearson on the Washington Merry-Go-Round" (14 April 1954), Pearson papers, American University.

94. Abell, *Drew Pearson Diaries*, 302.

95. Lemann, "Murrow Doctrine."

96. Wershba, "Murrow vs. McCarthy."

97. Television sets were in 44.7 percent of American households in 1953 and 55.7 percent in 1954, according to data compiled by Christopher Sterling and John Michael Kittross in appendix C in *Stay Tuned: A History of American Broadcasting*, 3rd ed. (Mahwah, NJ: Lawrence Erlbaum Associates, 2002), 864.

98. See Doherty, *Cold War, Cool Medium*, 174.

99. James Reston, "Washington: The President Plays the Waiting Game," *New York Times* (7 March 1954): E8. Emphasis added.

100. Gary Edgerton, "The Murrow Legend as Metaphor: The Creation, Appropriation, and Usefulness of Edward R. Murrow's Life Story," *Journal of American Culture* 15, no. 1 (Spring 1992): 88. Edgerton perceptively noted, "The most remarkable feature of the Murrow legend is that it flourished so quickly, springing up even as Edward R. Murrow was still alive."

101. "Turn of Tide?" *New York Times* (14 March 1954): E1.

102. Ibid.

103. Quoted in "Smithsonian Sponsors Electronic News Forum," *RTNDA Intercom* 4, no. 2 (February 1987): 2.

104. This point was made in several reviews of *Good Night, and Good Luck*. See, among others, Hugh Anderson, "Yes, Virginia, There Were Reds under the Bed," *Montreal Gazette* (31 October 2005): A25.

105. Michael Sragow, "'Good Night': A Stirring Cautionary Tale," *Baltimore Sun* (March 12, 2006): 10E.

106. Peter Rainer, "The Red Scare, in Black and White," *Christian Science Monitor* (7 October 2005): 14. McCarthy was chair of the Senate Permanent Subcommittee on Investigations. He never served in the House of Representatives.

107. David Carr, "A Ringside Seat for Murrow versus McCarthy," *New York Times* (18 September 2005): sec. 2, p. 12.

108. Roger Ebert, "Good Night, and Good Luck" (20 October 2005), www .rogerebert.com/reviews/good-night-and-good-luck-2005.

109. Edwards, *Edward R. Murrow*, 24.

110. Sperber, *Murrow*, 30.

111. Edwards, *Edward R. Murrow*, 24.

112. Sperber, *Murrow*, 500. Sperber wrote that "Stevenson barely endured" the tutoring, "chiding campaign manager George Ball about the money this was costing the Democrats."

CHAPTER FOUR

1. See Tom Carson, "And the best supporting zinger goes to . . ." *American Prospect* (26 October 2012), www.prospect.org/article/and-best-supporting-zinger -goes.

2. On this point, see Michael Schudson, *The Power of News* (Cambridge, MA: Harvard University Press, 1996), 117. Discussing the presumed effects of television viewing compared to radio listening, Schudson wrote: "On radio, it is assumed, one listens to pure argument; on television, one is distracted by the appearance of things, the superficial look of people rather than the cogency of their arguments."

3. See, among many others, Douglas E. Schoen, *On the Campaign Trail: The Long Road of Presidential Politics, 1860–2004* (New York: Harper Perennial, 2004), 147. Schoen wrote: "Radio listeners thought Nixon has performed at least as well as Kennedy—but the TV audience saw Kennedy as the clear winner."

4. See, for example, Ron Grossman, "The Great Debate that Transformed Politics," *Chicago Tribune* (30 September 2012), www.chicagotribune.com /news/chi-the-great-debate-that-transformed-politics-20140925-story.html . Grossman wrote: "Television viewers experienced a different debate from radio listeners." See also, Christopher Keating, "Social Media Adding to the Debate," *Hartford Courant* (3 October 2012), http://articles.courant.com /2012–10–03/news/hc-debate-social-media-1003–20121001_1_presidential-debate-three-way-debate-democrat-al-gore. Keating wrote: "Famously, those who listened to the radio thought that Nixon had defeated Kennedy in their famous first debate in 1960. By contrast, those watching on television thought that the dapper and cool Kennedy had won."

5. See, for example, Al Neuharth, "How JFK and Nixon Sparked TV Debates," *USA Today* (21 September 2012): 12A. Neuharth, the founder of *USA Today*, wrote in his column that Kennedy "looked relaxed and at ease. Nixon didn't. The hot TV lights appeared to give him a heavy beard. . . . The debate was also broadcast by radio. Listeners generally gave Nixon the nod. But TV viewers strongly favored Kennedy."

6. See Erika Tyner Allen, "The Kennedy-Nixon Presidential Debates, 1960," Museum of Broadcast Communications www.museum.tv/eotv/kennedy-nixon .htm.

7. See "Campaign of 1960," John F. Kennedy Presidential Library and Museum www.jfklibrary.org/JFK/JFK-in-History/Campaign-of-1960.aspx?p=2. In discussing the first presidential debate, the essay said: "Most Americans watching the debates felt that Kennedy had won. (Most radio listeners seemed to give the edge to Nixon.)"

8. The panel reads, in part: "A majority of radio listeners thought Richard Nixon won the debate, but television viewers overwhelmingly thought John Kennedy won."

9. See Karlin Lipson, "Hold Still, Mr. President," New York Times (15 March 2015): sec. LI, p. 10. Lipson wrote: "A video clip from the televised presidential debate between Vice President Nixon and Senator John F. Kennedy in 1960, for instance, seems to show the handsome, youthful Kennedy trouncing a visibly sweating Nixon. (Those who caught the debate on the radio thought Nixon trumped Kennedy.)"

10. See Ken Jennings, U.S. Presidents, Ken Jennings' Junior Genius Guides (New York: Little Simon, 2014), 101. "When Richard Nixon debated John F. Kennedy in the 1960 campaign," the booklet says, "radio listeners thought Nixon won the debate. But TV viewers could see that Kennedy was handsome, while Nixon looked sweaty and unshaven, and they called the debate for Kennedy."

11. The ABC television affiliate in Chicago, WLS, revisited the debate in 2010 in an essay published at its website, stating: "Most of the 70 million people who watched the event on television were convinced Kennedy won, and they voted for him in the presidential election of 1960." See "Ceremony for 50th Anniversary of Kennedy-Nixon Debates," ABC 7 Eyewitness News (26 September 2010),www.abc7chicago.com/archive/7690282/. See also Jeff Labrecque, "Presidential Debates: A History of the Biggest Gaffes and Zingers," Entertainment Weekly (3 October 2012), www.ew.com/article/2012/10/03/presidential-debate-barack-obama-mitt-romney. Labrecque wrote that the "Kennedy-Nixon debates ushered a new era during which television became a defining medium for political discussion."

12. Kayla Webley, "How the Nixon-Kennedy Debate Changed the World," Time (23 September 2010), http://content.time.com/time/printout/0,8816, 2021078,00.html. Webley also wrote: "As the story goes, those who listened to the debate on the radio thought Nixon had won. But those listeners were in the minority. . . . Those that watched the debate on TV thought Kennedy was the clear winner. Many say Kennedy won the election that night."

13. Max Frankel, "Word and Image: Nixon's Last Taunts," New York Times Magazine (23 October 1994): SM30. Frankel's characterization may have been slightly exaggerated for effect.

14. See David L. Vancil and Sue D. Pendell, "The Myth of Viewer-Listener Disagreement in the First Kennedy-Nixon Debate," Central States Speech Journal 38, no. 1 (Spring 1987): 16–27.

15. Vancil and Pendell, " The Myth of Viewer-Listener Disagreement," 18–20.

16. See "Debate Score: Kennedy up, Nixon Down," *Broadcasting* (7 November 1960): 27.

17. Vancil and Pendell, " The Myth of Viewer-Listener Disagreement," 20.

18. Ibid., 21.

19. Ibid.

20. See Larry J. Sabato, *The Kennedy Half-Century: The Presidency, Assassination, and Last Legacy of John F. Kennedy* (New York: Bloomsbury, 2013), 65. Sabato wrote: "According to a survey conducted by Sindlinger and Company, those who saw the debate on TV believed that Kennedy had won the debate; radio listeners arrived at the opposite conclusion." See also Sidney Kraus, "Winners of the First 1960 Televised Presidential Debate between Kennedy and Nixon," *Journal of Communication* 46, no. 4 (Autumn 1996): 78–96. Without offering much new or compelling evidence, Kraus wrote: "I believe the finding that Kennedy won on television while Nixon won on radio is not a myth" (94).

21. Vancil and Pendell, " The Myth of Viewer-Listener Disagreement," 17. Vancil and Pendell also wrote: "Appearance problems, such as Nixon's perspiring brow, *could* have had a negative impact on viewer perceptions, but it is also possible for viewers to be sympathetic to such problems, or to interpret them as evidence of attractive or desirable qualities."

22. Myles Martel wrote: "The logic behind such thinking . . . is decidedly primitive; it assumes that one or a few physical cues constituted sufficient cause for influencing millions of Americans to respond more favorably to Kennedy's performance. Realistically, the debate's outcome was, as is the case with any debate, rooted in an amalgam of physical, vocal, and verbal cues resulting from discrete strategic and tactical plans formulated by each candidate." See Martel, *Political Campaign Debates: Images, Strategies, and Tactics* (New York: Longman, 1983), 4.

23. Schudson wrote: "When I originally published this chapter, I was unaware of a very good paper criticizing the conventional wisdom of the Kennedy-Nixon debate by David L. Vancil and Sue D. Pendell . . . . Vancil and Pendell nicely demonstrate both how pervasive the myth about the Kennedy-Nixon debate is and how meager is the evidence to substantiate it." See Schudson, *Power of News*, 242–243n5.

24. See David Greenberg, "Rewinding the Kennedy-Nixon Debates," *Slate* (24 September 2010), www.slate.com/articles/news_and_politics/history_lesson /2010/09/rewinding_the_kennedynixon_debates.single.html.

25. See Theodore H. White, *The Making of the President, 1960* (New York: Atheneum, 1961), 290.

26. Greenberg, "Rewinding."

27. The thirty-six titles were: *Atlanta Constitution, Atlanta Journal, Baltimore Sun, Boston Globe, Boston Herald, Chicago Daily News, Chicago Sun-Times, Chicago Tribune,* [Cleveland] *Plain Dealer, Cleveland Press, Dallas Morning News, Denver Post, Hartford Courant, Houston Post, Indianapolis Star, Kansas City Times, Los Angeles Times,* [Louisville] *Courier-Journal, Miami Herald, Milwaukee Journal,* [New Orleans] *Times-Picayune, New York Herald Tribune, New York Journal-American, New York Times, New York*

World-Telegram, [Philadelphia] *Evening Bulletin, Philadelphia Inquirer, Pittsburgh Post-Gazette, Pittsburgh Press, St. Louis Post-Dispatch, San Diego Union, San Francisco Chronicle, San Francisco Examiner, Seattle Times,* [Washington] *Evening Star,* and *Washington Post.*

28. See Lawrence Thompson, "TV Debate Was Great Says Joe Smith, But . . ." *Miami Herald* (28 September 1960): 3B. Thompson began his article by stating: "Joe Smith, American, thought the Kennedy-Nixon 'debate' Monday night was a great show—but it didn't do much to change his mind." Thompson explained that "reporters around the country picked up phones and called Joe Smiths listed in the directory. Of the 12 Joe Smiths called, seven were Democrats, four were Republicans; one was independent." The *Boston Globe* said the informal survey of men named Joe Smith was "not a scientific poll but an interesting cross-section of typical Americans' reaction to an important program." The *Globe* account detected what may be termed a faint and partial hint of viewer-listener disparity, noting that Joe Smith in Seattle, a registered Republican, listened to the debate on radio and afterward said: "Yes it changed my opinion. I was neutral before the debate. But it made me feel that Nixon is the superior man of the two. . . . If a vote were cast as a result of tonight's debate, Nixon would get it by a good-sized majority. He won the debate." See "Joe Smith, American, Does Not Change His Mind," *Boston Globe* (27 September 1960): 15.

29. See "10-City Poll Gives Jack Edge in Picking up Votes from the Debate," *Boston Globe* (27 September 1960): 18.

30. See "Debate Audience Yields Wide Range of Reaction," *New York Times* (27 September 1960): 1; and Douglas S. Crockett, "Boys at Bar Get Bored; Nixon Too Agreeable," *Boston Globe* (27 September 1960): 16.

31. See, for example, "Atlanta's Viewers Like Kennedy, 7–5," *Atlanta Constitution* (27 September 1960): 1. The newspaper interviewed fifteen people by telephone, seven of whom preferred Kennedy, and five of whom preferred Nixon. Three rated the debate a draw. See also "How Viewers Sized up First TV Discussion," *Chicago Tribune* (27 September 1960): 1, 11; "Los Angeles Watches and Listens to the Great Debate," *Los Angeles Times* (27 September 1960): sec. 1, p. 3; "Voters Here Comment on the Big Debate, and There's Wide Divergence of Opinion," [Philadelphia] *Evening Bulletin* (27 September 1960): 1, 3; John Haigh, "Most Seattleites Unswayed by Debate," *Seattle Times* (27 September 1960): 1; and Robert C. Albright, "Big Debate Viewed as Dead Heat," *Washington Post* (28 September 1960): A1, A12.

32. Ralph McGill, "Do You See or Hear TV?" *Atlanta Constitution* (28 September 1960): 1. A writer for the *Atlanta Journal* assigned to review the debate reported that he "gave both candidates the closed-eyes test and was surprised to find that Kennedy sounded much like Jimmy Cagney, while Nixon had a voice like Clark Gable. I thought video aided Kennedy, helped me forget his sometimes whining voice, but I would rather have listened to Nixon without video." See "Debate: Low-Key, Electric," *Atlanta Journal* (27 September 1960): 12.

33. Vancil and Pendell discussed McGill's column in their journal article, noting that it did not "meet even the most rudimentary standards for a poll of a national radio audience." See Vancil and Pendell, "The Myth of Viewer-Listener Disagreement," 19.

34. McGill, "Do You See or Hear TV?"

35. "The Great Debate Begins," *Milwaukee Journal* (27 September 1960): 16. The editorial described the debate in enthusiastic terms: "It was exciting. It was unprecedented. Most of all it was informative."

36. "The Nixon-Kennedy TV Debate," *Philadelphia Inquirer* (28 September 1960): 40.

37. "Candidates Face Issues and Public," *San Francisco Chronicle* (28 September 1960): 28.

38. Cited in an Associated Press roundup of editorial reactions and published as "Excerpts from Editorial Comments on Debate," *Los Angeles Times* (28 September 1960): 8. Somewhat less effusive was the *Evening Sun* of Baltimore, also quoted in the roundup, which observed: "The Great Debate wasn't exactly great and it wasn't exactly a debate, but it was the best political program of the year."

39. "No doubt," wrote Harriet Van Horne, a syndicated columnist for the *New York World-Telegram*, "the debate would have gained in drama and excitement had it been staged before a responsive audience in a large hall." See Van Horne, "Popular, Peopleless Politics," *New York World-Telegram* (27 September 1960): 25.

40. See James Reston, "Kennedy on First by a Fielder's Choice," *New York Times* (28 September 1960): 38. Reston also wrote: "The trouble with the first nationwide discussion between Presidential candidates was that they were forced to by the format to deal with a whole catalogue of extremely complicated national issues in a very few minutes. Just when they were coming to grips with the problem of Federal aid to education, the subject was shifted to old-age medical assistance, and precisely when they were getting down to that, somebody wanted to know about economic growth."

41. See Willard Edwards, "Neither Displays Sign of Inner Tension," *Chicago Tribune* (27 September 1960): 1. Edwards wrote: "It was a political television show familiar to many viewers—the usual questions about medical care for the aged, balanced budgets, farm surpluses, and teachers' salaries."

42. "The Debate Wasn't Great," *Hartford Courant* (28 September 1960): 28.

43. Richard Starnes, "No Hits, No Runs, No Errors," *New York World-Telegram* (27 September 1960): 25.

44. John Crosby, "Nixon Better in Prepared Talk, Kennedy Won with His Rebuttal," *Boston Globe* (27 September 1960): 19.

45. See, for example, David Greenberg, "Torchlight Parades for the Television Age: The Presidential Debates as Political Ritual," *Daedalus* 138, no. 2 (Spring 2009): 9. Greenberg wrote that, after the debate, "the press as if by unanimous consent, blamed Nixon's appearance for his loss."

46. "The Debate: Chapter 1," *Washington Post* (28 September 1960): A16.

47. Saul Pett, "Nixon Rates Nod for His TV Folksiness," *Boston Globe* (27 September 1960): 11.

48. Quoted in David Pietrusza, *1960: LBJ vs. JFK vs. Nixon; The Epic Campaign That Forged Three Presidencies* (New York: Union Square Press, 2008), 342.

49. See Russell Baker, *The Good Times* (New York: Penguin Group, 1990), 324. Baker also wrote that his initial impression was off-target and that Kennedy had "won a great victory. . . . I missed it completely because I had been too busy taking notes and writing to get more than fleeting glimpses of what the country was seeing on the screen. Most of the country had been looking, not listening, and what they saw was a frail and exhausted-looking Nixon perspiring nervously under pressure. It was a Nixon catastrophe."

50. Jim Frankel, "Everybody Liked K-N Talks, Happy TV Studios Report," *Cleveland Press* (27 September 1960): 30, suspension points in the original.

51. Van Horne, "Peopleless Politics."

52. "Candidates Define the Issue: How Much Government?" *Chicago Daily News* (27 September 1960): 8.

53. Walter Lippmann, "Today and Tomorrow: The TV Debate," *New York Herald Tribune* (27 September 1960): 22.

54. Gould Lincoln, "First Round of the 'Great Debate,'" [Washington] *Evening Star* (28 September 1960): A22.

55. See "Lists of White House 'Enemies' and Memorandums Relating to Those Named," *New York Times* (28 June 1973): 38.

56. Thomas O'Neill, "So Far, So Good," *Baltimore Sun* (28 September 1960): 14.

57. "Kennedy Armor Shows Chinks," *San Diego Union* (28 September 1960): B2. The newspaper's editorial further stated: "There is another side to Sen. Kennedy's character that was exposed in the cruelty of the spotlight of confrontation. He persistently told us [during the debate] what he personally expected of America; how he personally was dissatisfied with the progress we, the people, are making; and what he personally expected of history. You would think the election was being conducted to bring peace of mind to Sen. Kennedy."

58. "A Slow Fight to a Draw," *Los Angeles Times* (28 September 1960): sec. 3, p. 4. The editorial said that most television viewers "were disappointed because (a) they could not pick a winner and (b) they could not find that any single issue had been sharpened up by the abrasives of debate." It also said, "The election will not turn on the kind of debate the candidates waged" on television.

59. Robert Roth, "Nixon, Kennedy Clash on Domestic Issues," [Philadelphia] *Evening Bulletin* (27 September 1960): 1.

60. See "Candidates Battle to Draw in Nationwide Debate on TV," *Atlanta Journal* (27 September 1960): 1.

61. John Harris, "Foes Slug Hard in TV Bout," *Boston Globe* (27 September 1960): 1.

62. Russell Baker, "Nixon, Kennedy End in Standoff," *Boston Herald* (27 September 1960): 1. The report was distributed by the *New York Times* supplemental news service. The *Herald* slightly modified the report's first paragraph to include the phrase "to what appeared to be a standoff." That wording did not appear in the *Times* account. See Russell Baker, "Nixon and Kennedy Clash in TV Debate on Spending, Farms and Social Issues," *New York Times* (27 September 1960): 1.

63. Roscoe Drummond, "The Debate Was Superb Politics," *Atlanta Constitution* (30 September 1960): 4.

64. Reston, "Kennedy on First." Reston also wrote: "If courage is grace under pressure . . . both [candidates] gained on this score. Both were under extreme pressure."

65. See "10-City Poll," *Boston Globe.*

66. John F. Kennedy, "First Debate, September 26, 1960," transcript in Kraus, *Great Debates,* 349.

67. Kraus, *Great Debates,* 350.

68. This point was made by David Pietrusza in *LBJ vs. JFK vs. Nixon,* 338.

69. Richard M. Nixon, "First Debate, September 26, 1960," transcript in Krauss, *Great Debates,* 350–351.

70. Doris Fleeson, "Diet, Bad Knee Hurt TV Appearance," *Boston Globe* (28 September 1960): 19.

71. Joseph Alsop, "The Great TV Debate Proved Almost Nothing," *Louisville Courier-Journal* (29 September 1960): 10.

72. Pietrusza, *LBJ vs. JFK vs. Nixon,* 336. Pietrusza also argued that Nixon, in the end, did not perform too poorly: "For all of Nixon's blunders and all of Kennedy's patrician grandeur, . . . if one examines the Chicago debate in its totality, balanced point against point, miraculously Nixon ends up doing not too badly" (342).

73. Herbert G. Klein, *Making It Perfectly Clear* (Garden City, NY: Doubleday, 1980), 105.

74. See Krauss, *Great Debates,* 353.

75. Ibid. Pietrusza characterized Nixon's "no comment" as "a stunning nolo contendere," or no-contest plea. See Pietrusza, *LBJ vs. JFK vs. Nixon,* 339.

76. Such a statement would not have been at all far-fetched. On the campaign trail in the run-up to the debate, Nixon had suggested that criticizing American policy was not patriotic and was helpful to the Soviets. See Reston, "Kennedy on First."

77. See James N. Druckman, "The Power of Television Images: The First Kennedy-Nixon Debate Revisited," *Journal of Politics* 65, no. 2 (May 2003): 559–571. Vancil and Pendell conducted a similar experiment in the late 1980s at Colorado State University. The results of their study, which found no support for viewer-listener disagreement, were presented at a conference in Dublin, Ireland, in 1990 but never published. See Sue D. Pendell and David L. Vancil, "An Experimental Study of Viewer-Listener Disagreement in the First Kennedy-Nixon Debate," Fort Collins: Colorado State University, unpublished research paper.

78. Druckman, "The Power of Television Images," 568.

79. Ibid., 568n13.

80. Ibid., 565n6.

81. Ibid., 570.

82. Question wording varied by polling organization. See Elihu Katz and Jacob J. Feldman, "The Debates in the Light of Research: A Survey of Surveys," in *The Great Debates: Kennedy vs. Nixon, 1960,* ed. Sidney Kraus (Bloomington: Indiana University Press, 1977), 196–197, table 11. Three of the seven

surveys were identified as the California Poll, the Gallup Poll, and the Sindlinger Poll, and the four others were conducted separately by Paul Deutschmann of the Communications Research Center at Michigan State University, by the John F. Kraft research firm, by Opinion Research Corporation, and by the Schwerin Research Corporation.

83. George Gallup, "The Gallup Poll: Kennedy Has 49 Pct., Nixon 46," *Washington Post* (12 October 1960): A1.

84. Gallup, "Gallup Poll."

85. On this point, see James A. Stimson, *Tides of Consent: How Public Opinion Shapes American Politics* (New York: Cambridge University Press, 2004), 133.

86. See, for example, "Kennedy in Lead in Final Survey; 15 States Close," *New York Times* (7 November 1960): 1. The *Times* account was published the day before the voting and said: "If all the doubtful [toss-up] states support Senator Kennedy in tomorrow's election, it could result in an electoral landslide for the Massachusetts Senator."

87. Cited in Charles Grutzner, "3 of 4 Major Election Polls Give Kennedy the Edge in Close Vote," *New York Times* (8 November 1960): 18.

88. Or, as James A. Stimson wrote, the 1960 election was so close "it can be said that *anything* could have altered the outcome." See Stimson, *Tides of Consent*, 133.

89. The *Dallas Morning News* hailed Johnson "as the 'political pro' who furnished the victory margin for the Democrats in the national election. By helping to carry Texas and southern states with 108 electoral votes, Johnson is credited . . . by political friends and foes alike with 'making the difference' in the Democrats' successful campaign." See Richard M. Morehead, "LBJ Hailed as Man Who Swung Election," *Dallas Morning News* (10 November 1960): sec. 1, p. 11.

90. White, *Making of the President*, 377.

91. Pietrusza, *LBJ vs. JFK vs. Nixon*, 407.

92. Ibid.

CHAPTER FIVE

1. See Eric Alterman, *Who Speaks for America? Why Democracy Matters in Foreign Policy* (Ithaca, NY: Cornell University Press, 1998), 94.

2. See Edwin Diamond, "Good News, Bad News," *Nieman Reports* (Winter 1978): 13.

3. Neil Hickey, "The Cost of Not Publishing," *Columbia Journalism Review,* November/December 2001: 50.

4. Howard Kurtz, "Piling on the New York Times with a Scoop," *Washington Post* (28 June 2006): C1.

5. Brad Smith, "Leaks Part of Government's Plan for War, Some Say," *Tampa Tribune* (15 August 2002): 4.

6. Philip Gailey, "When Papers Dance to a Terrorist's Tune," *St. Petersburg* [FL] *Times* (24 September 1995): 3D.

7. David K. Shipler, *Freedom of Speech: Mightier Than the Sword* (New York: Knopf, 2015), 138.

8. "F.Y.I.," *Washington Post* (28 February 1977): A22.

9. William O'Rourke, "Media Are Ally, Not Adversary, in War on Terror," *Chicago Sun-Times* (2 July 2002): 29.

10. Pat M. Holt, "The Press—and America's 'Leaky' Government," *Christian Science Monitor* (4 June 1968): 18.

11. "Patriotism and the Press," *New York Times* (28 June 2006): A20.

12. Bill Keller, "The Boy Who Kicked the Hornet's Nest," *New York Times Magazine* (30 January 2011): 39.

13. Tad Szulc, "Anti-Castro Units Trained to Fight at Florida Bases," *New York Times* (7 April 1961): 1.

14. Harrison E. Salisbury, *Without Fear or Favor: The New York Times and Its Times* (New York: Times Books, 1980), 162.

15. Ibid., 148. Szulc's son, Anthony, quarreled with Salisbury's characterization, saying his father favored a 1950s "Miami by the pool" look, with sunglasses and a checkered sport coat. On cold evenings, Anthony Szulc said, his father would wear a black cape, "à la Count of Monte Cristo, with everything but the sword." Anthony Szulc, telephone interview with the author (6 February 2009).

16. Salisbury, *Without Fear or Favor*, 148.

17. Anthony Szulc, telephone interview with the author.

18. Tad Szulc, "The *New York Times* and the Bay of Pigs," in *How I Got That Story*, ed. David Brown and W. Richard Bruner (New York: Dutton, 1967), 316, 317.

19. Tad Szulc, testimony to U.S. Senate Subcommittee on American Republic Affairs, 22 June 1961, in *Executive Sessions of the Senate Foreign Relations Committee*, XIII, part 2 (Washington: Government Printing Office, 1984), 238.

20. Tad Szulc, "*New York Times* and the Bay of Pigs," 318.

21. Anthony Szulc, telephone interview with the author.

22. Ibid.

23. Tad Szulc, "*New York Times* and the Bay of Pigs," 319. See also Salisbury, *Without Fear or Favor*, 153. "They were not in a competitive situation, one reporting for a newspaper and the other for radio," Salisbury wrote of the Szulc-Novins collaboration, "and they were able to intensify their efforts by exchanging impressions and reports."

24. Szulc said he wrote the dispatch "with considerable misgivings about what the United States was about to undertake." See Tad Szulc, "*New York Times* and the Bay of Pigs," 320.

25. Ibid. See also Salisbury, *Without Fear or Favor*, 153. Salisbury wrote, "Szulc and Novins agreed to file their stories for what amounted to simultaneous release" on the evening of April 6, 1961. Szulc's report "would appear in the first edition of *The New York Times*, hitting the street at about 9:45 P.M.," Salisbury said, "and Novins' broadcast would be played at 11 P.M." As it turned out, Novins's report went on the air at 8 P.M.

26. James Reston, *Deadline: A Memoir* (New York: Random House, 1991), 325.

27. Turner Catledge, *My Life and The Times* (New York: Harper & Row, 1971), 261.

28. Ibid.

29. Ibid. The CIA's central role became clear soon after the failed invasion.

30. Ibid., 263.

31. Salisbury, *Without Fear or Favor,* 153. Salisbury also wrote (153–154) that a four-column headline on the front page was "designed to bring the story forcefully to the attention of the ordinary readers of *The Times* and perhaps even more important . . . to the attention of the key figures of the media, the editors, for example, of *Time* and *Newsweek,* of the *Washington Post* and *The Wall Street Journal,* to Walter Cronkite of CBS and, of course, to that special elite of readers, the President of the United States, the Secretary of State, the Prime Minister of England," among others. Reston said in his memoir that he doubted "whether it is the job of a newspaper to make up its front page in such a way as to influence decisions of the president." Reston, *Deadline,* 326. He added (325–326), "If Catledge made any mistake [in handling the Szulc story], it was, I believed, that he didn't make clear . . . that the job of the managing editor was to manage and edit, and that the job of a publisher was not to influence the president but to protect the paper's reputation for accuracy and responsibility."

32. Catledge, *My Life and The Times,* 262.

33. See Tad Szulc, "Anti-Castro Units Trained to Fight at Florida Bases."

34. Dryfoos was the newspaper's president at the time of the Bay of Pigs invasion. He was named publisher later that month. See "Dryfoos Now Publisher, Oakes Editor of Times," *Editor and Publisher* (29 April 1961): 23.

35. Catledge, *My Life and The Times,* 263. According to Clifton Daniel, Catledge's successor as managing editor of the *Times,* Dryfoos "was gravely troubled by the security implications of Szulc's story. He could envision failure of the invasion and he could see The New York Times being blamed for a bloody fiasco." See "Excerpts from Speech on Coverage of Bay of Pigs Buildup," *New York Times* (2 June 1961): 14.

36. Salisbury, *Without Fear or Favor,* 156.

37. Arthur Schlesinger, the historian and Kennedy adviser, claimed that Szulc's story had been "emasculated" by *Times* editors. See "Rebuttal Is Made by Schlesinger," *New York Times* (14 June 1966): 15.

38. Catledge, *My Life and The Times,* 262–263. Salisbury agreed, writing, "*The Times* did publish the Szulc story and the deletions were not so material and the play was big enough to make clear to everyone what was going on." See Salisbury, *Without Fear or Favor,* 161.

39. Some accounts incorrectly state that the article appeared below the fold on the front page. See, for example, James Aronson, *The Press and the Cold War* (Boston: Beacon Press, 1970), 165–166.

40. Tad Szulc, "Anti-Castro Units Trained to Fight at Florida Bases."

41. "Invasion Reported Near," *New York Times* (7 April 1961): 2. The *Los Angeles Times* published on its front page of April 7, 1961, a wire service account of Novins's report. See "Exiles Ready to Invade Cuba, CBS Reports," *Los Angeles Times* (7 April 1961): 1.

42. This point was made by Daniel D. Kennedy in "The Bay of Pigs and the New York *Times:* Another View of What Happened," *Journalism Quarterly* 63, no. 3 (Autumn 1986): 524–529.

43. Tad Szulc, "*New York Times* and the Bay of Pigs," 323.

44. Tad Szulc, testimony to U.S. Senate Subcommittee on American Republic Affairs, 238.

45. David Halberstam, *The Powers That Be* (New York: Dell Publishing, 1979), 624.

46. Peter Wyden, *Bay of Pigs: The Untold Story* (New York: Simon & Schuster, 1979), 154. In a footnote, Wyden added, "It can no longer be determined whether Dryfoos contacted the President or whether Kennedy was told about the story and took the initiative."

47. Stephen Plotkin (reference archivist, John F. Kennedy Presidential Library), email correspondence with Mark Syp, the author's research assistant (29 April 2009).

48. See W.H. Lawrence, "Kennedy and Macmillan Cruise on Potomac Aboard Honey Fitz," *New York Times* (7 April 1961): 4; and "The White House Diary: Appointments for April 6, 1961," John F. Kennedy Library and Presidential Museum, http://whd.jfklibrary.org/Diary.

49. Salisbury, *Without Fear or Favor*, 162–163.

50. Chalmers M. Roberts, *First Rough Draft: A Journalist's Journal of Our Times* (New York: Praeger, 1973), 189.

51. Szulc, however, said that *Times* editors during this period "began doubting that an invasion was really going to occur. . . . In Washington, the Administration pooh-poohed our preinvasion stories. . . . The tone in my editor's voice was one of cold doubt about my tireless forecasts of things to come. It suddenly struck me that my credibility was at stake and that my whole Miami operation was about to be canceled." See Tad Szulc, "*New York Times* and the Bay of Pigs," 324.

52. Sam Pope Brewer, "Castro Foe Says Uprising Is Near," *New York Times* (8 April 1961): 1. The article contained a passage that may have been deliberate misdirection: the Revolutionary Council's president, José Miró Cardona, was quoted as saying that the uprising would be a revolution from within Cuba, not a revolution by invasion.

53. Sam Pope Brewer, "Castro Foes Call Cubans to Arms; Predict Uprising," *New York Times* (9 April 1961): 1.

54. Tad Szulc, "Rivalries Beset Top Cuban Exiles," *New York Times* (9 April 1961): 1.

55. James Reston, "Top U.S. Advisers in Dispute on Aid to Castro's Foes," *New York Times* (11 April 1961): 1. Reston also reported that Kennedy had ruled out deploying U.S. forces to support the exiles in their efforts to topple Castro.

56. James Reston, "Washington: United States and Cuba: The Moral Question—I," *New York Times* (12 April 1961): 40.

57. Tad Szulc, "Castro Foes Map Multiple Forays with Guerrillas," *New York Times* (10 April 1961): 1.

58. Pierre Salinger, *With Kennedy* (Garden City, NY: Doubleday, 1966), 146.

59. Ibid.

60. Douglas Cater and Charles L. Bartlett, "Is All the News Fit to Print?" *The Reporter* (11 May 1961): 23.

61. Joseph Newman, "Report Cuba Invasion On, Rebels Call for Revolt Today," *New York Herald Tribune* (8 April 1961): 1.

62. James Buchanan, "Anti-Fidel Fliers Here Go South," *Miami Herald* (10 April 1961): 1A.

63. James Buchanan, "Here's Cuban Invaders' Timetable," *Miami Herald* (16 April 1961): 2A.

64. "Are We Training Cuban Guerrillas?" *The Nation* (19 November 1960): 378. The *Hispanic-American Report*, which was published by Hinson's institute at Stanford, had carried reports about the training base. So had the Guatemalan newspaper *La Hora*. See Cater and Bartlett, "Is All the News Fit to Print?"

65. "Mystery Strip," *Time* (6 January 1961), www.time.com/time/magazine /article/0,9171,874255,00.html.

66. Paul P. Kennedy, "U.S. Helps Train an Anti-Castro Force at Secret Guatemalan Air-Ground Base," *New York Times* (10 January 1961): 1. The article, however, was largely cast as a precautionary and defensive effort by Guatemalans to thwart "an almost inevitable clash with Cuba." Not until the fifth paragraph did the article support the headline by saying that opposition figures in Guatemala "insisted the preparations are for an offensive against the Cuban regime of Premier Fidel Castro and that they are being planned and directed, and to a great extent being paid for, by the United States."

67. See Peter Kihss, "Anti-Castro Group Is Termed 'Almost Ready' to Invade Cuba," *New York Times* (5 January 1961): 6.

68. James Buchanan, "How Miami's Anti-Castro Airlift Works," *Miami Herald* (11 January 1961): 1A–2A. Buchanan had been expelled from Cuba in late 1959, following his conviction on charges of helping an American national escape custody. A Cuban military court sentenced Buchanan to fourteen years in prison, which was suspended on the condition he leave the island within twenty-four hours. See "Havana Deports Miami Reporter," *New York Times* (24 December 1959): 9.

69. "Herald Held Up Story," *Miami Herald* (11 January 1961): 1A.

70. Quoted in Cater and Bartlett, "Is All the News Fit to Print?," 24.

71. Salisbury, *Without Fear or Favor*, 144.

72. Szulc, testimony to the U.S. Senate Subcommittee on American Republic Affairs, 238, 239. "I was shown a file of 100 photographs of Castro intelligence agents," Szulc testified.

73. "Editors' Decision on Cuba Related," *New York Times* (2 June 1966): 14.

74. See "Excerpts from Speech on Coverage of Bay of Pigs Buildup," *New York Times*.

75. Ibid.

76. Or, as Victor Bernstein and Jesse Gordon wrote in their article, "The Press and the Bay of Pigs," Kennedy "seemed to have been trying to share his monopoly on bad decisions." See Bernstein and Gordon, "The Press and the Bay of Pigs," *Columbia University Forum* 10 (Fall 1967): 10.

77. Reston, *Deadline*, 326. Reston noted that Kennedy insisted on having authority to call off the invasion as late as twenty-four hours before its launch. After publication of the Szulc article of April 7, 1961, Kennedy had ten days to contemplate whether to go ahead with the assault, as Reston observed.

78. Quoted in "Editors' Decision on Cuba Related," 14. Victor Bernstein and Jesse Gordon concurred with Reston in their article, "The Press and the Bay of Pigs." They wrote that "the evidence is strong" that in the weeks immediately before the invasion, "the affair was beyond aborting; planning had reached the point of no return." See Bernstein and Gordon, "The Press and the Bay of Pigs."

79. Quoted in "Excerpts from Speech on Coverage of Bay of Pigs Buildup."

80. Arthur M. Schlesinger Jr., *A Thousand Days: John F. Kennedy in the White House* (Boston: Houghton Mifflin, 1965), 261.

81. Szulc, testimony to U.S. Senate Subcommittee on American Republic Affairs, 238.

82. For example, Alan J. Gould, the general manager of the Associated Press, said on his retirement in 1963: "Occasionally we have withheld stories for a time in the national interest. When the President of the United States calls you in and says this is a matter of vital security, you accept the injunction." Quoted in "Alan Gould Retires to Consultant Role," *Editor and Publisher* (2 February 1963): 12.

83. Szulc, testimony to U.S. Senate Subcommittee on American Republic Affairs, 239–240.

84. Tad Szulc, "*New York Times* and the Bay of Pigs," 328. Szulc added: "I wish, of course, as the President later did, that they had been published in full. But, on the whole, I think we did our job correctly, and if the Administration had wanted to be warned by our reporting of the impending disaster, they could have easily done so. Instead, the official effort was to deny everything we were saying."

CHAPTER SIX

1. Cronkite's trip to Vietnam was not remembered fondly by all war correspondents then in the country. George McArthur, a veteran journalist for the Associated Press, years later recalled Cronkite's visit to the imperial city, Hue, the scene of fierce fighting during the Tet Offensive: "Cronkite is not one of my heroes. When Cronkite broadcast in Hue during the Tet offensive, he arranged to have a shelling of the ridgeline behind him. This was his famous trip when he supposedly changed his mind [about the war]. Baloney. He'd made up his mind before he ever came out there. But the Marines staged a shelling at four in the afternoon, and he was up on top of our [diplomatic] mission building in Hue doing his stand-upper, wearing a bulletproof vest and a tin pot [helmet]. And I was up there [on the same roof] doing my laundry." Quoted in George W. Smith, *The Siege at Hue* (Boulder, CO: Lynne Rienner, 1999), 110.

2. *Reporting Vietnam: Part One; American Journalism, 1959–1969* (New York: Library of America, 1998), 582. Also cited in Peter Braestrup, *Big Story: How the American Press and Television Reported and Interpreted the Crisis of Tet 1968 in Vietnam and Washington* (Boulder, CO: Westview Press, 1977), 188–189.

3. "Walter Cronkite: The Most Trusted Man," *Columbia Journalism Review,* November–December 2001: 64.

4. See David Halberstam, *The Powers That Be* (New York: Dell Publishing, 1979), 716. See also Arnaud de Borchgrave, "A Mini-Tet Offensive?" *Washington Times* (6 April 2004): 21. De Borchgrave wrote, "It was this now famous television news piece that persuaded President Lyndon Johnson six weeks later, on March 31, not to run for re-election." In addition, see Cynthia Littleton, "1968: The Media's Moment," *Variety* (28 April 2008): 1. Littleton wrote that Cronkite's observation "is said to have helped seal President Lyndon B. Johnson's decision to not seek reelection that year."

5. See, among others, James Brian McPherson, *Journalism at the End of the American Century, 1965–Present* (Westport, CT: Praeger, 2006), 6; Steven Rea, "A Primer on Tricks Leading Us into War," *Philadelphia Inquirer* (21 November 2007): E8; and David Smith, "Media: That's the Way It Is Tonight," *Observer* [London] (21 August 2005): 9.

6. James Wolcott, "Round Up the Cattle!" *Vanity Fair* (June 2003): 86.

7. See, broadly, Joe Garner, *Stay Tuned: Television's Unforgettable Moments* (Kansas City: Andrews McMeel, 2002), 74–77. Inevitably, perhaps, the anecdote has crossed language barriers. See, for example, Philipp Gassert, "Die Ohnmacht der Supermacht," *Frankfurter Allgemeine Zeitung* [Frankfurt, Germany] (18 February 1998): 9; and Edouard Launet, "Pentagone, Big Brother," *Libération* [Paris, France] (6 May 2005): 28.

8. See Alessandra Stanley, "A Bomb Detonates, and an Anchorman Tells a Story of the War by Becoming the Story," *New York Times* (30 January 2006): A12. Stanley wrote that Cronkite "shook the nation by declaring the Vietnam War unwinnable."

9. Michael Wolff, "Survivor: The White House Edition; As with Vietnam, So with Iraq," *Vanity Fair* (December 2006): 194.

10. See Deborah Potter, "Anchors Overboard?" *American Journalism Review,* June/July 2005: 76. Potter wrote that Cronkite became "so influential that he's credited with changing the course of history with a single newscast. When he declared that the United States was stalemated in Vietnam, Lyndon Johnson reportedly remarked, 'If I've lost Cronkite, I've lost middle America.'"

11. Halberstam, *Powers That Be,* 716.

12. See James Boyland, "A Raucous Century of Covering Politics," *Columbia Journalism Review,* July/August 1999: 48.

13. Garner, *Stay Tuned,* 77. In his year-study of 1968, Mark Kurlansky identified another consequence of Cronkite's special program on Vietnam, stating that "few broadcasters would ever again wrestle with . . . qualms about a little editorializing." See Kurlansky, *1968: The Year That Rocked the World* (New York: Ballantine Books, 2004), 62.

14. Halberstam, *Powers That Be,* 716.

15. Cited in Frank Rich, "The Weight of an Anchor," *New York Times Magazine* (19 May 2002): E39.

16. See Robert H. Phelps, "President Asks for 'Austerity' to Win the War," *New York Times* (19 March 1968): 1.

17. See R. W. Apple Jr., "Vietnam: The Signs of Stalemate," *New York Times* (7 August 1967): 1.

18. "Former CBS Anchorman Walter Cronkite Talks about His Life, His Career and His New Book, 'A Reporter's Life,'" interview with Tim Russert, CNBC News (12 January 1997), transcript retrieved from www.lexisnexis.com.

19. Walter Cronkite, "What I've Learned," *Esquire* (1 April 2006): 170.

20. See David Culbert, "Johnson and the Media," in *Exploring the Johnson Years*, ed. Robert A. Divine (Austin: University of Texas Press, 1981), 214–248.

21. Noted in "TV Key Previews," *Washington Evening Star* (27 February 1968): A14.

22. "Daily Diary—Feb. 27, 1968," Box 14, Lyndon Baines Johnson Library and Museum, Austin, TX. The timetable says Johnson began his remarks at 10:06 P.M. Another source—*Public Papers of the Presidents: Lyndon B. Johnson, 1968–1969* (Washington, DC: Government Printing Office, 1970)—says Johnson began speaking at 9:54 P.M., which was about the time the Cronkite program was reaching its conclusion.

23. Culbert, "Johnson and the Media," 225.

24. *Public Papers of the Presidents*, 289.

25. See "Pickets Boo Johnson," *New York Times* (28 February 1968): 33.

26. "Daily Diary—Feb. 28, 1968," Box 14, Johnson Library and Museum.

27. Culbert, "Johnson and the Media," 225.

28. Jeffrey Lord, for example, wrote in an article published at the *American Spectator*'s website: "The effect was almost immediate. In the White House, the President of the United States looked grimly at his television and in a remark that would become famous said, 'If I've lost Cronkite, I've lost middle America.'" Lord, "The Limbaugh-Hannity Administration," *American Spectator* (3 February 2009), www.spectator.org/42199_limbaugh-hannity-administration.

29. Kurlansky's book about 1968 quotes Cronkite as saying that he never asked Johnson about the effects of Cronkite's special report on Vietnam. See Kurlansky, *1968*, 61.

30. George Christian, telephone interview with David Culbert (17 September 1979), transcript retrieved from Johnson Library and Museum. Ellipses in the original. Similarly, another aide to president spoke years later of having watched the Cronkite program with Johnson. The aide, Tom Johnson, recalled in an interview with the Newseum: "I will never forget sitting with him as he saw a report from Walter Cronkite [who] had been in Vietnam. And Walter actually gave what many considered an editorial. He stepped out of his correspondent anchor role and gave an editorial saying that this whole policy needed to be considered. And LBJ said approximately this, 'If I've lost Walter Cronkite, I've lost America.' That was tremendous." Tom Johnson did not say when the president viewed the program or whether it was on videotape. See "Newseum. TV: Shelby Coffey Interviews Tom Johnson" (12 December 2001), transcript shared with author.

31. John Wilson, "Cronkite-Tet" file, email correspondence with the author (1 August 2008).

32. For a summary of the 1968 Tet Offensive, see *Reporting Vietnam: Part One*, 790–791.

33. See Roy Reed, "President Urges Firmness on War," *New York Times* (28 February 1968): 33.

34. Ted Sell, "Johnson's Stand: No Viet Retreat," *Los Angeles Times* (28 February 1968): 1.

35. Reed, "President Urges Firmness" *New York Times*, 1.

36. Cited in Ibid., 1, 33.

37. Cited in Sell, "Johnson's Stand," *Los Angeles Times*, 15.

38. Ibid., 1.

39. Rowland Evans and Robert Novak, "Johnson Is More and More the Military Commander," *Los Angeles Times* (28 February 1968): A5.

40. Carroll Kilpatrick, "Johnson Hails U.S. Strength," *Washington Post* (3 March 1968): A1.

41. Quoted in Robert H. Phelps, "U.S. to Put More Men in Vietnam," *New York Times* (17 March 1968): 1, 3.

42. Phelps, "President Asks for 'Austerity.'" Johnson implored his audience to support his war policy and economic austerity measures. The *New York Times* quoted him as saying: "Your President has come here to ask you people, and all the other people of this nation, to join in a total national effort to win the war, to win the peace, and to complete the job that must be done here at home. I ask all of you to join in a program of national austerity to insure that our economy will prosper and that our fiscal position will be sound."

43. Quoted in Carroll Kilpatrick, "Foe's Target Is U.S. Will, Johnson Says," *Washington Post* (20 March 1968): A1, A6.

44. George C. Herring, *LBJ and Vietnam: A Different Kind of War* (Austin: University of Texas Press, 1994), 163.

45. Johnson had never declared his candidacy for reelection to the presidency. See Don Oberdorfer, *Tet!* (Garden City, NY: Doubleday, 1971), 299. Oberdorfer wrote that Johnson "had given clear indication to some of those closest to him that he might not run. Lady Bird [Johnson's wife] was very much opposed to another term, and discussed it with him often . . . . In August of 1967, Johnson confided to Dean Rusk [the secretary of state] that he might not run again and Rusk became convinced he would not."

46. Public opinion may have been a factor in deliberations of the Wise Men, Daniel C. Hallin noted in a study of the news media and the Vietnam War, "but they did not rely . . . on Walter Cronkite to brief them on the military situation in Vietnam." Hallin, *The Uncensored War: The Media and Vietnam* (Berkeley: University of California Press, 1989), 171.

47. Herring, *LBJ and Vietnam*, 163.

48. Don Oberdorfer offers a detailed discussion of the meetings in Washington of the Wise Men. See Oberdorfer, *Tet!*, 308–315. Oberdorfer (308) characterized the meeting of the Wise Men as "a remarkable event, perhaps unique in American history."

49. George Ball, interview with Paige E. Mulhollan (9 July 1971), Lyndon B. Johnson Library and Museum, transcript posted at www.lbjlib.utexas.edu /Johnson/archives.hom/oralhistory.hom/Ball-G/Ball-g2.pdf.

50. See "Summary of Notes [offered by M. Bundy concerning Wise Men's meeting]," (26 March 1968), in *Lyndon B. Johnson's Vietnam Papers: A Documentary Collection*, ed. David M. Barrett (College Station: Texas A&M University Press, 1997): 713.

51. Ball, interview with Mulhollan. President Johnson wrote of his meeting with the Wise Men: "I knew this group had not been reading the detailed reports on Vietnam each day, as I and my principal advisers had, but they were intelligent, experienced men. I had always regarded the majority of them as very steady and balanced. If they had been so deeply influenced by the reports of the Tet offensive, what must the average citizen in the country be thinking?" See Lyndon Baines Johnson, *The Vantage Point: Perspectives of the Presidency, 1963–1969* (New York: Holt, Rinehart, and Winston, 1971), 418.

52. See "Notes of the President's Meeting to Discuss General Wheeler's Trip to Vietnam" (28 February 1968), in *Lyndon B. Johnson's Vietnam Papers, 629–634.*

53. Ibid., 634.

54. Cited in Memorandum from President Johnson to Secretary of State Rusk and Secretary of Defense Clifford (28 February 1968), in *Lyndon B. Johnson's Vietnam Papers,* 635–636. See also William Beecher, "U.S. Reappraising Its Use of Troops in Vietnam War," *New York Times* (29 February 1968): 1.

55. See Tom Wicker, "In the Nation: Agonizing Reappraisal," *New York Times* (10 March 1968): E15. Wicker's column referred to a rancorous debate in the U.S. Senate that "left the impression that not even Senate hawks like John Stennis of Mississippi had much enthusiasm for defending the way the war is being conducted."

56. McCarthy's portion of the primary vote in New Hampshire was about 10 percentage points greater than what Johnson's political advisers had anticipated. See Rowland Evans and Robert Novak, "Johnson's New Hampshire Loss Probably a Gain for Kennedy," *Los Angeles Times* (15 March 1968): A5.

57. Ibid. For further discussion about the reasons for Johnson's change of heart in March 1968, see Bruce E. Altschuler, *LBJ and the Polls* (Gainesville: University of Florida Press, 1990), 58. See also, Michael A. Cohen, *American Maelstrom: The 1968 Election and the Politics of Division* (New York: Oxford University Press, 2016). About the New Hampshire primary, Cohen wrote: "Though [Johnson] had officially won, the result was seen as a clear repudiation of his administration" (98).

58. See John Herbers, "Students Cheer Kennedy in Attack on War Policy," *New York Times* (19 March 1968): 1.

59. Polling data cited here and in the next paragraph are stored at the Roper Center at the University of Connecticut and were retrieved from www.lexisnexis.com.

60. Don Oberdorfer, "The 'Wobble' on the War on Capitol Hill," *New York Times* (17 December 1967): 228.

61. Daniel Hallin, "The Turning Point That Wasn't," *Media Studies Journal* 12, no. 3 (Fall 1998): 6. Hallin also wrote: "It is quite plausible that the changing tone of the news drove home to Johnson and to other political actors how difficult it would be to rally the public for years of additional fighting . . . . But, again, the direction of the policy debate was already well established before Tet" in early 1968.

62. See Greg Mitchell, "What Makes a 'Cronkite Moment'?" Public Eye: CBSNEWS.com (23 December 2005), www.cbsnews.com/news/what-makes-a-

cronkite-moment/. Mitchell suggested that the "Cronkite Moment" was "overblown from its inception."

63. See Kurlansky, *1968*, 61.

64. "The Logic of the Battlefield," *Wall Street Journal* (23 February 1968): 14.

65. Apple, "Signs of Stalemate."

66. See Rowland Evans and Robert Novak, "Inside Report: LBJ's War Frustration," *Washington Post* (27 March 1967): A15.

67. Jack Gould, "TV: Skelton's Pantomime Collides with Slapstick," *New York Times* (28 February 1968): 95.

68. See, for example, James Boylan, "Declarations of Independence," *Columbia Journalism Review,* November/December 1986: 36. Boylan wrote that Cronkite "discarded neutrality for a personal declaration that he believed that the United States must promptly negotiate its way out" of Vietnam.

69. See *Reporting Vietnam: Part One,* 582. Emphasis added.

70. Cited by Jack Gould, "U.S. Is Losing War in Vietnam, N.B.C. Declares," *New York Times* (11 March 1968): 82.

71. One version is "You make the pictures, and I'll make the war." See Oliver Carlson and Ernest Sutherland Bates, *Hearst: Lord of San Simeon* (New York: Viking, 1936), 97. Another variation has Hearst saying, "You provide the pictures, I'll provide the war." According to the original source, Hearst told Remington, "You furnish the pictures, and I'll furnish the war." See James Creelman, *On the Great Highway: The Wanderings and Adventures of a Special Correspondent* (Boston: Lothrop, 1901), 177–178.

72. See, for example, Howard Kurtz, "A Possible Conflict of Panelist," *Washington Post* (23 December 1996): C1; and Judy Rose, "And That's the Way It Is: To No One's Surprise, Walter Cronkite Is a Fine Storyteller," *St. Paul Pioneer Press* (12 January 1997): 8E.

73. David Stout, "George Christian, 75, Aide to President, Dies," *New York Times* (29 November 2002): C6.

74. See, for example, Steven Erlanger, "Israel's 'Mr. TV' Faults Settlements in Documentary," *New York Times* (31 May 2005): A3; and Raymond Carroll, "The Press and Its Influence in Shaping Foreign Policy," *Times Union* [Albany, NY] (23 March 1997): B1.

75. Tom Wicker, "Broadcast News," review of *A Reporter's Life*, by Walter Cronkite, *New York Times Book Review* (26 January 1997): 7.

76. See, for example, Richard L. Strout, "Cronkite Steps Down: That's the Way It Is for America's 'Most Trusted Man,'" *Christian Science Monitor* (5 March 1981): 6; Phil Kloer, "The Anchor Looks Back, Anecdotally but Somewhat Unemotionally, on a Life of News," *Atlanta Journal and Constitution* (8 December 1996): 12K; Phil Kloer, "A Medium's Massive Power," *Atlanta Journal and Constitution* (25 July 1999): 1L; and William McGurn, "Main Street: McCain's Vote Should Trouble Obama," *Wall Street Journal* (17 February 2009): A13. See also Robert Dalleck's biography of Johnson, *Flawed Giant* (New York: Oxford University Press, 1998), 506.

77. Walter Cronkite, *A Reporter's Life* (New York: Knopf, 1997), 258.

78. See, for example, Lon Grahnke, "CBS Tribute Finally Gives Cronkite His Due," *Chicago Sun-Times* (23 May 1996): 40.

79. Martie Zad, "'Cronkite Remembers,' . . . The Way It Was," *Washington Post* (8 June 1997): Y5.

80. See Rupert Cromwell, "My Lai: A Lesson from History," *Independent* [London] (29 May 2006): 21; and "Our Identity Earns Recognition," *Green Bay Press-Gazette* (10 October 2004): 14A.

81. See Hal Boedecker, "War: Journalism's Call to Duty," *Orlando Sentinel* (5 November 2003): E3; and Mike Harden, "Did TV Color How We Viewed Vietnam War?" *Columbus Dispatch* (29 May 2000): 1B.

82. Alan Pergament, "Report from LA: And That's the Way It Is—For Walter Cronkite," *Buffalo News* (19 January 2006): C1.

83. Cited in Glenn Garvin, "Are Evening Network News Broadcasts on the Way Out?" *Miami Herald* (10 December 2004). See also Richard Nilsen, "1968: Slipping into Darkness," *Arizona Republic* (17 February 2008), www.azcentral.com/arizonarepublic/ae/articles/0217sixtyeight0217.html.

84. See Andrew Ryan, "Walter Cronkite: PBS Salutes the Original TV News Anchor on American Masters," *Globe and Mail* [Toronto] (22 July 2006): television sec., p. 4.

85. Hayden wrote: "When Cronkite pronounced Vietnam as 'mired in stalemate,' it is said that Lyndon Johnson went berserk. A few weeks later, Johnson relinquished his presidency." He cited no sources, however. Tom Hayden, "Rachel Maddow Misses Cronkite Moment in Afghanistan," *The Nation* (20 July 2010), www.thenation.com/article/rachel-maddow-walter-cronkite-afghanistan.

86. Trevor Royle, "The Week It All Went Wrong," *Sunday Herald* [Glasgow, Scotland] (28 October 2001): 12.

87. Chester J. Pach Jr., "TV's 1968: War, Politics, and Violence on the Network Evening News," *South Central Review* 16, no. 4 (Winter 1999–Spring 2000): 32.

88. The anecdote about Johnson's supposed reaction was repeated in scores of newspaper articles about Cronkite's death. See, for example, Valerie J. Nelson, "Walter Cronkite, 1916–2009: A Voice the Nation Trusted," *Los Angeles Times* (18 July 2009): A1; and Bart Barnes and Joe Holley, "America's Iconic TV News Anchor Shaped the Medium and the Nation," *Washington Post* (18 July 2009): A1.

89. Cronkite, *Reporter's Life*, 258.

90. "Former CBS Anchorman Walter Cronkite Talks about His Life," interview with Tim Russert.

91. "CNN Newsroom," CNN (9 February 1999), transcript retrieved from www.lexisnexis.com.

92. "Walter Cronkite Talks about His Book 'Around America,'" NBC *Today* show (9 August 2001), transcript retrieved from www.lexisnexis.com.

93. Steve Winn, "A Nation Trusted Him. And He Has Never Betrayed That Trust," *San Francisco Chronicle* (2 March 2004): D1.

94. Pergament, "Report from LA."

95. Cronkite, "What I've Learned," 170.

96. Mike Seccombe, "Still Tacking through Politics: Trusty Walter Cronkite at Age 90," *Vineyard Gazette Online* (29 June 2007), www.vineyardgazette

.com/news/2007/06/28/still-tacking-through-politics-trusty-walter-cronkite-age-90. About the Iraq War, Cronkite was quoted as saying, "I am a little disappointed there were not more of my brethren in the press saying out loud [what they] should have been saying for a long time: We don't belong in the war we are pursuing."

97. "NBC Declares Situation in Iraq Civil War; Why Are Journalists Obsessed with Paris Hilton?" *Reliable Sources* (blog), CNN (3 December 2006), transcript retrieved from www.lexisnexis.com.

98. "The Road Home," *New York Times* (8 July 2007): sec. WK, p. 11. See also Paul Harris, "Business and Media: Media: Call to End War Signals Start of a Media Battle," *London Observer* (15 July 2007): 10.

99. Halberstam, *Powers That Be,* 716.

100. Potter, "Anchors Overboard?," 76.

CHAPTER SEVEN

1. Charlotte Curtis, "Miss America Pageant Is Picketed by 100 Women," *New York Times* (8 September 1968): 81.

2. Judith Duffett, "WLM vs. Miss America," *Voice of the Women's Liberation Movement* (October 1968): 1.

3. Ibid.

4. Cited in Alice Echols, *Daring to Be Bad: Radical Feminism in America, 1967–1975* (Minneapolis: University of Minnesota Press, 1989), 96.

5. Cited in Robin Morgan, *Going Too Far: The Personal Chronicle of a Feminist* (New York: Random House, 1977), 63.

6. See Curtis, "Miss America Pageant Is Picketed."

7. Judith Hole and Ellen Levine wrote in their book, *Rebirth of Feminism,* "The American public learned for the first time there was a new thing called the women's liberation movement." See Hole and Levine, *Rebirth of Feminism* (New York: Quadrangle Books, 1971), 123. See also Bonnie J. Dow, "Feminism, Miss America, and Media Mythology," *Rhetoric and Public Affairs* 6, no. 1 (2003): 135. Dow wrote, "No one could doubt that the Miss America protest had put women's lib on the map."

8. Mark Kurlansky, *1968: The Year That Rocked the World* (New York: Ballantine Books, 2004), 309. Kurlansky added, "In 1920, with the passage of the Nineteenth Amendment, feminism, according to popular belief, had served its purpose, achieved its goal, and ceased to exist."

9. Harriet Van Horne, "Female Firebrands," *New York Post* (9 September 1968): 38.

10. Quoted in David Johnston, "For FBI, Women's Lib Spelled Danger," *Toronto Star* (30 September 1991): B1.

11. Cited in Curtis, "Miss America Pageant Is Picketed."

12. See John L. Boucher, "Bra-Burners Blitz Boardwalk," *Atlantic City Press* (8 September 1968): 4. Robin Morgan, the protest's principal organizer, wrote that the demonstration's "most enduring contribution" may have been the decision "to recognize only newswomen. There was much discussion about this and we finally settled on refusing to speak to male reporters *not* because we were so

naïve as to think that women journalists would automatically give us more sympathetic coverage but rather because the stand made a political statement consistent with our beliefs." See Morgan, *Going Too Far*, 63. Morgan's group, New York Radical Women, sold its newsletter to women for fifty cents; it charged men a dollar. See Howard Smith, "Scenes," *Village Voice* (29 August 1968): 10.

13. Robin Morgan, *Saturday's Child: A Memoir* (New York: Norton, 2001), 260. She also wrote, "The hot September sun and the site gave the event the feel of a day at the beach."

14. Pauline Tai, "Miss America Pageant Chosen as the Latest Target of Protesters," *Wall Street Journal* (6 September 1968): 4.

15. See Curtis, "Miss America Pageant Is Picketed."

16. Discarding brassieres and other items "was meant to serve as a political metaphor for the rejection of all restrictions and limitations in the traditionally accepted definitions of 'the feminine woman,'" Hole and Levine noted in *Rebirth of Feminism*, 229–230.

17. Curtis, "Miss America Pageant Is Picketed."

18. Patricia Bradley wrote that the "press flocked to the protest after Robin Morgan, one of the organizers, hinted at the possibility of a 'bra-burning,' a phrase that was irresistibly euphonic to the headline writers of the time." See Bradley, *Women and the Press: The Struggle for Equality* (Evanston, IL: Northwestern University Press, 2005), 229. See also Echols, *Daring to Be Bad*, 94.

19. Tai, "Miss America Pageant Chosen."

20. "Talent, Curves Help Misses Pageant Awards," *Newark Star-Ledger* (5 September 1968): 12. In 2007, an eighty-two-year-old woman named Jacqui Ceballos was quoted in a Florida newspaper as saying that she participated in the demonstration and that plans were "to burn bras and other items, but it was against the law." See Cloe Cabrera, "No Bras Burned, but They Did Revolt," *Tampa Tribune* (9 October 2007), retrieved from www.lexisnexis.com.

21. Curtis, "Miss America Pageant Is Picketed." Morgan was quoted in the article as saying, "We told [the mayor] we wouldn't do anything dangerous—just a symbolic bra-burning."

22. Ibid.

23. John L. Boucher, "Fire Rips 14 'Walk Shops; Won't Stop Pageant Parade," *Atlantic City Press* (1 September 1968): 1. See also "Big Blaze in Atlantic City," *New York Post* (31 August 1968): 2.

24. Van Horne, "Female Firebrands." Van Horne also wrote: "I didn't happen to see a photograph of these Amazons in action but they're there, fully formed, in my mind's eye. They perfectly match Nina Epton's description of certain English women. 'They look,' she wrote, 'unstroked, uncaressed and emotionally undernourished.'"

25. Buchwald's humor could be irritating at times. J. Edgar Hoover, the longtime FBI director and a not-infrequent target of the columnist's wit, once called Buchwald a "sick comic" and ordered the agency to keep tabs on him. Buchwald's FBI file dated to June 1956, when he received a visa to visit the Soviet Union. See Daniel Carty, "Art Buchwald Couldn't Make This Man Laugh," CBS News (25 June 2008), www.cbsnews.com/news/art-buchwald-couldnt-make-this-man-laugh.

26. Art Buchwald, "The Bra Burners," *New York Post* (12 September 1968): 42.

27. Art Buchwald, "Uptight Dissenters Go Too Far in Burning Their Brassieres," *Washington Post* (12 September 1968): A25.

28. Ibid.

29. Ibid.

30. Buchwald's memoirs make no mention of his improbable role in giving circulation to the bra-burning myth.

31. See "The Price of Protest," *New York Times* (28 September 1968): 25.

32. W. Stewart Pinkerton Jr., "Getting Things off Their Chests—Girls Take to No-Bra Fad," *Wall Street Journal* (11 August 1969): 1.

33. James J. Kilpatrick, "Downhold on the Uplift?" *Los Angeles Times* (26 September 1969): B7.

34. Mary Wiegers, "Beneath Those Charred Bras, Revolution Smolders," *Washington Post* (8 March 1970): G1, G3.

35. Rich Barlow, "Program Forges Feminist Community," *Boston Globe* (26 November 2005): B2.

36. Daphne Merkin, "Are These Women Bullies?" *New York Times* (21 July 1991): sec. 4, p. 17.

37. Shelby Steele, *A Dream Deferred: The Second Betrayal of Black Freedom in America* (New York: HarperCollins, 1998), 174.

38. Riki Anne Wilchins, "What Does It Cost to Tell the Truth?," in *The Transgender Reader*, ed. Susan Stryker and Stephen Whittle (New York: Routledge, 2006), 550.

39. Meg Barone, "A Question of Balance," *Connecticut Post* [Bridgeport] (22 October 2005).

40. Jennifer Steinhauer, "What Becomes a Legend?" *New York Times* (13 February 1998): D1.

41. Wendy Kaminer, "Of Face Lifts and Feminism," *New York Times* (6 September 1988): A23.

42. Tony Chamberlain, "Berman's a Women's Movement unto Herself with Three Official Wins," *Boston Globe* (16 April 2006): C1.

43. Myriam Marquez, "Let Barbie Be Barbie," *The Record* [Bergen County, NJ] (28 November 1997): L13.

44. Sandra Haggerty, "Down with the Four M's," *Los Angeles Times* (27 January 1975): C5.

45. Barbara Olson, *Hell to Pay: The Unfolding Story of Hillary Rodham Clinton* (Washington, DC: Regnery, 2001), 177.

46. Cited in Patricia Sullivan, "Voice of Feminism's 'Second Wave,'" *Washington Post* (5 February 2006): A1.

47. Hole and Levine, *Rebirth of Feminism*, 123. See Morgan, *Going Too Far*, 65.

48. Dow, "Feminism, Miss America, and Media Mythology," 131.

49. Suzanne Braun Levine, "The Truth Was Burned," *Media Studies Journal* 12, no. 3 (Fall 1998): 110.

50. Hole and Levine, *Rebirth of Feminism*, 230.

51. Joanna Foley Martin, "Confessions of a Non-Bra-Burner," *Chicago Journalism Review* 4 (July 1971): 11.

52. Ellen Goodman, "The Trend That Never Was," *Washington Post* (13 January 1981): A15.

53. Susan Faludi, *Backlash: The Undeclared War against American Women* (New York: Crown, 1991), 75.

54. Levine, "The Truth Was Burned."

55. Flora Davis, *Moving the Mountain: The Women's Movement in America since 1960* (New York: Simon & Schuster, 1991), 107.

56. Quoted in Johnston, "For FBI, Women's Lib Spelled Danger." In a memoir published in 2001, Morgan wrote, "No, we never burned bras . . . and Yes, we did crown a live sheep Miss America on the boardwalk." Morgan said the latter bit of street theater was "*not* one of my finest hours: it insulted the contestants and irked the ewe; my animal-rights consciousness had a long way to go" in 1968. See Morgan, *Saturday's Child*, 259.

57. "Watch Fires for Suffrage," *Washington Post* (30 December 1918): 5.

58. "Men in Uniform Rout Suffragists," *New York Times* (2 January 1919): 1.

59. Boucher, "Bra-Burners Blitz Boardwalk."

60. Ibid.

61. "Altman, Hughes Honor Veteran Press Newsman," *Atlantic City Press* (6 June 1964): 1.

62. Jack E. Boucher, telephone interview with the author (July 2007).

63. Jon Katz, telephone interview with the author (30 July 2007).

64. Ibid.

65. Jon Katz, email correspondence with the author (21 July 2007).

66. Ibid.

67. Katz, telephone interview with the author.

68. Jon Katz, "What's Going On? Sightseers Asked," *Atlantic City Press* (8 September 1968): 4.

69. Katz, telephone interview with the author.

70. Carol Newton, email correspondence with author (16 July 2008). Newton also said, "You have finally reached an accurate source!"

71. Curtis, "Miss America Pageant Is Picketed." Interestingly, Curtis was to have been a judge of the Miss America pageant in 1968 but opted to cover the protest instead. See Frank Prendergast, "Pageant Judge Resigns to Report Week's Event," *Atlantic City Press* (5 September 1968): 12. According to Robin Morgan, the protest organizer, Curtis's sympathies ran decidedly with the demonstrators. In her memoir, Morgan recalled that Curtis rode with the demonstrators from New York to Atlantic City. Curtis was "elegantly dressed in black (gloves, pearls, and heels) amid our colorful informality, gamely warbling 'We Shall Overcome' with us as we bounced along in the rattletrap buses. She stayed all day on the hot boardwalk with us, brought us cool drinks, laughed and applauded when we would recognize and respond to women journalists only." That night, some of the demonstrators attended the Miss America pageant and briefly disrupted the event before being arrested. Morgan recalled going "from precinct to precinct in search of where our friends were being held. Finally, at 3 A.M., I learned they'd been released hours earlier on cash bail put up personally by 'some older woman' named Charlotte Curtis. When I phoned the next day to thank her, she asked me to keep it quiet, as 'these dreary grey guys running

the Times' would not be amused." See Morgan, *Saturday's Child*, 261–262. Morgan also recounted the anecdote in a letter to the *New York Times*. See Robin Morgan, "A Lady and a Feminist," *New York Times* (26 September 1999): sec. 7, p. 4. In 1974, Curtis became the first senior female editor at the *Times*. She died in 1987. See Robert D. McFadden, "Charlotte Curtis, a Columnist for the Times, Is Dead at 58," *New York Times* (17 April 1987): B6.

72. Jon Katz, "Shore Top Cop to Take No Lib at Pageant," *Philadelphia Daily News* (11 September 1971). Katz's article mistakenly identified the protest as having taken place in September 1969.

73. Katz, telephone interview with the author.

74. Ibid.

75. Boucher, "Fire Rips 14 'Walk Shops."

76. Pinkerton, "Getting Things off Their Chests."

77. Lindsy Van Gelder, "The Truth about Bra-Burners," *Ms.* 3, no. 2 (September 1992): 80–81. Van Gelder claimed in the *Ms.* article that she was the source of the term "bra-burning," calling herself "the Mother of the Myth of the Maidenform Inferno." Van Gelder said she had written an article for the *New York Post* in 1968 about plans for the Miss America protest, the opening paragraph of which said: "Lighting a match to a draft card or a flag [has] been a standard gambit of protest groups in recent years, but something new is due to go up in flames this Saturday. Would you believe a bra-burning?" Thorough searches at the Library of Congress through microfilmed issues of the *New York Post* of late August and early September 1968 turned up no trace of such an article or of such a passage, however. It is possible that the article Van Gelder described appeared in an edition of the *Post* that was not microfilmed. The microfilm at the Library of Congress is of the first edition of the *Post*. At least one other newspaper, the *Wall Street Journal*, used the term "bra-burning" before the protest at Atlantic City. See Tai, "Miss America Pageant Chosen." Van Gelder told an interviewer, Thomas Lieb, that she did not have a copy of the article. Thomas Lieb, email correspondence with the author (August 2007).

78. The difficulty in setting a brassiere on fire was humorously described in 2001 by a writer for the *Australian* newspaper. "First it refused to ignite," she wrote. "Then it ignited and spluttered out. Then—after countless taunts with a cigarette lighter—it showed impressive self-defence skills by letting off sickening fumes and evil clouds of black smoke. . . . Worst of all, once the experiment was over, I couldn't get the rock-hard remains off my barbecue plate for love, money or steel wool, leaving the Weber [grill] permanently tattooed with the skeletal corpse of a sacrificial undergarment." See Emma Tom, "Women Face the Burning Question," *Weekend Australian* (8 September 2001): 17.

79. Bob Hewitt, telephone interview with the author (19 March 2009).

80. Andrea Billups, "Think Tank Takes Aim at Politically Correct," *Washington Times* (13 April 1999): A1.

CHAPTER EIGHT

1. Nick Ut, oral history interview (August 1997), provided to the author by the Newseum, Washington, D.C. See also Hal Buell, "The Napalm Girl,"

Vietnam 25, no. 1 (June 2012): 36–39. Buell, a former senior Associated Press photo editor, noted that Ut's older brother, an AP photographer named Huynh Thanh My, was killed covering combat in Vietnam in October 1965. "A few weeks later," Buell wrote, "Ut's mother visited the AP bureau in Saigon, seeking a job for Ut. She explained that the family had lost a second soldier-son and was in financial straits. Bureau Chief Ed White and photo boss Horst Faas were reluctant to put another son in harm's way. But White eventually relented and hired Ut on January 1, 1966, as a darkroom assistant. . . . Ut learned photography in the darkroom and started shooting street scenes after work." Henri Huet, an AP photographer in Vietnam, was a mentor to Ut and began calling him "Nic-Nic," a Vietnamese term for a family's youngest child, Buell wrote. "Others picked it up and soon Huynh Cong Ut was—and always would be—Nick Ut" (37).

2. Buell, "Napalm Girl," 37.

3. Denise Chong, *The Girl in the Picture: The Story of Kim Phuc, the Photograph, and the Vietnam War* (New York: Viking, 2000), 90. Kim Phuc's other wounds, Chong wrote, included burns to her right arm, stomach, and buttocks.

4. See Buell, "Napalm Girl," 38. Buell wrote that Ut took Kim Phuc and some of her relatives to a hospital in the town of Cu Chi, where doctors said Kim Phuc's chances of surviving were slim. "Pulling one of the doctor's aside," Buell wrote, "Ut told him that the child had just been photographed and her picture would surely be published around the world in a matter of hours. The doctor ordered Kim's treatment be expedited and care elevated."

5. In late 2015, Kim Phuc began a series of laser treatments intended to soften scar tissue and ease the pain that lingers from the burns. See Jennifer Kay, "Lasers May Ease Pain for 'Napalm Girl' in AP Photograph," Associated Press (24 October 2015), retrieved from www.lexisnexis.com.

6. In an interview on Canadian television in 1999, Kim Phuc explained her decision to defect, saying: "First I prayed and so I talked with him [her husband] and I explained to him that I have no choice, I have to stay in Canada, I want to be free. I explained to him and of course he's shocked but he's understanding." See Dan Matheson, *Canada AM*, CTV Television (18 October 1999), transcript retrieved from www.lexisnexis.com.

7. See "Ten Photographs That Changed the World," *London Daily Telegraph* (8 September 2009), www.telegraph.co.uk/culture/culturepicturegalleries/6152050/Ten-photographs-that-changed-the-world.html. Neither the Saigon execution photograph nor the self-immolation photograph made the roster. The *Telegraph* did not describe the criteria by which the photographs were selected, nor did it explain exactly how the images "changed the world."

8. See Hank Klibanoff, "What the Still Photo Still Does Best," *New York Times* (21 March 2010): WK3. Klibanoff wrote: "The unsettling images from civil rights battlegrounds, followed closely by disturbing images from Vietnam battlefields by Horst Faas, Eddie Adams, and Nick Ut and others, created a golden era for photojournalism."

9. See Buell, "Napalm Girl," 39. Buell wrote that Faas "took one look at the images and ordered them transmitted to Tokyo and New York. Faas then sent a message to New York, alerting AP about the pictures that were on the way."

10. Horst Faas, oral history interview (August 1997), provided to the author by the Newseum, Washington, D.C.

11. Horst Faas, quoted in Chong, *Girl in the Picture,* 364.

12. Philip Kennicott, a critic for the *Washington Post,* wrote in 2007 that *Napalm Girl* "can't possibly be read as anything but a powerful indictment of war." See Kennicott, "Images: Poles and Decades Apart, Two Silent Screams Issue Discomfiting Reverberations," *Washington Post* (30 December 2007): M1.

13. On this point, see David D. Perlmutter, *Photojournalism and Foreign Policy: Icons of Outrage in International Crises* (Westport, CT: Praeger, 1998), 83. Perlmutter persuasively argued that "the aesthetic power" of the famous "Tank Man" image of the lone protester in Tiananmen Square in 1989 "was greater than its political power." He referred to powerful images as "icons of outrage" and wrote that such images "are rarely born great; rather, journalists, academics, and politicians, and only to a very small extent the public, thrust greatness upon them. Furthermore, their significance, their meanings, and their relevance to historical events are not transcendent but are the subject of often bitter political argumentation" (xiv).

14. See, for example, Ian O'Doherty, "Want to Stop Migrant Deaths? Get Tougher Immigration Rules," *Irish Independent* (3 September 2015), www .independent.ie/opinion/columnists/ian-odoherty/want-to-stop-migrant-deaths-get-tougher-immigration-rules-31498657.html. The photograph of the drowned boy, O'Doherty wrote, is "so visceral it stops you in your tracks and could well be the 'napalm girl' moment of our age."

15. Daphne Bramham, "Compassionate Canada Has Lost Its Way," *Vancouver Sun* (4 September 2015): A6.

16. See "Movies: The Birds," *New Yorker* (19 November 2012), www .newyorker.com/goings-on-about-town/movies/the-birds.

17. See Mar Roman, "Women Activists Gather to Fight Gender-Based Violence Worldwide," Associated Press (23 November 2000), retrieved from www .lexisnexis.com.

18. See "Napalm Survivor Becomes Canadian Citizen," Associated Press (3 December 1997), retrieved from www.lexisnexis.com.

19. Lawrence O'Donnell, *The Last Word with Lawrence O'Donnell,* MSNBC (10 September 2013), transcript retrieved from www.lexisnexis.com.

20. See Neal Ascherson, "Bosnia: When the Pictures of War Light a Bonfire of Emotions," *Independent* [London] (15 August 1993): 14.

21. See "Kim Puts Napalm Horror Behind Her," *Sunday Mail* [Queensland] (8 October 1989), article retrieved from www.lexisnexis.com.

22. See "Transcript of Senator McGovern's Speech Offering a Plan for Peace in Indochina," *New York Times* (11 October 1972): 29.

23. McGovern also invoked *Napalm Girl* in a speech in Cleveland in early October 1972, saying: "I really do not understand how any American reared in the traditions of humanity and decency and goodness that we've been taught in this country in our Sunday schools, in our synagogues, taught in all the religious traditions of this country, how we could look at that wirephoto of the little South Vietnamese girl running in pain, screaming, on fire from napalm that has struck her school [*sic*], and literally not have that experience break the heart of

this country." Quoted in William Greider, "M'Govern Calls for Idealism," *Washington Post* (6 October 1972): A1, A17.

24. Fox Butterfield, "South Vietnamese Drop Napalm on Own Troops," *New York Times* (9 June 1972): A9. Butterfield's dispatch anonymously quoted a South Vietnamese soldier who had not been injured in the errant attack as saying, "'Vietnamese pilots Number 10'—which in soldier's slang means the worst." The South Vietnamese air force, known as the VNAF, were not always well-prepared for air support, as Chuyen Van Nguyen, a pilot in 518th Fighter Squadron, the South Vietnamese unit that dropped the napalm at Trang Bang, recalled: "The VNAF tried their best to load Skyraiders with ordinance that fit the need in battlefield, but more often than not, things didn't jive and we had to make our best effort to assist the ground troops." See Chuyen Van Nguyen, "Lt. Chuyen Van Nguyen 518th Fighter Squadron V.N.A.F" (accessed 28 November 2015), www.webring.org/l/rd?ring=ww2;id=1%22%20target=%22_top%22%3E%3Cspan%20class=%22st1ww2%22%20title=%22visit%20World%20War%20II%20WebRing%20member%20sites%22%3ESites%3C/span%3E%3C/a%3E%3C/b%3E%20l%20%3Ca%20href=%22http://A.webring.com/wrman?ring=ww2;url=http%3A%2F%2Fwebspace.webring.com%2Fpeople%2Ffu%2Fum_6608%2FVNAF.html.

25. Donald Kirk, "Innocents Bombed: Napalm Victims in Agony," *Chicago Tribune* (9 June 1972): 1.

26. Christopher Wain, "'The Little Girl Stumbled Forward, Whimpering . . .'" *Indianapolis Star* (9 June 1972): 1. In an interview with a television station in Los Angeles forty years later, Wain recalled that Kim Phuc and the other children fleeing Trang Bang "were absolutely silent" as they ran toward the journalists: "There was no sound from them until they saw us. When they saw us, then they started to cry and shout. But until that point they were, I suppose, in shock." Quoted in David Ono, "'Napalm Girl' Photo from Vietnam War Turns 40," KABC News, Los Angeles (2 June 2012), www.abc7.com/archive/8686842.

27. Wain, "'The Little Girl Stumbled Forward.'"

28. Ibid.

29. Ibid

30. See Nick Thimmesch, "Last 3 Years Have Been Grueling for the Pentagon's Melvin Laird," *Baltimore Sun* (24 October 1972): A17. Thimmesch wrote that "it's questionable that [the napalm bombing was] 'in the name of America,' as Mr. McGovern shouts."

31. Susan Sontag, *On Photography* (New York: Farrar, Straus and Giroux, 1973), 18.

32. Susan Sontag, *Regarding the Pain of Others* (New York: Farrar, Straus, and Giroux, 2002), 57.

33. Nancy K. Miller, "The Girl in the Photograph: The Visual Legacies of War," in *Picturing Atrocity: Photography in Crisis*, ed. Jay Prosser, Geoffrey Batchen, Mick Gidley, and Nancy K. Miller (London: Reaktion Books, 2012), 153.

34. Sylvia Shin Huey Chong, *The Oriental Obscene: Violence and Racial Fantasies in the Vietnam Era* (Durham, NC: Duke University Press, 2011), 116.

Huey Chong further wrote: "If American viewers of the 'Napalm Girl' mistook South Vietnamese bombs for American, the confusion was natural, since not only were American bombers ubiquitous throughout the war, but even South Vietnamese bombers were essentially American in military technological drag" (118).

35. Paul Vitello, "Horst Faas, Vietnam War Photographer, Is Dead at 79," *New York Times* (14 May 2012): A24.

36. Peter Keepnews, email correspondence with the author (22 May 2012).

37. "Corrections: Obituaries," *New York Times* (28 August 2012): A2.

38. See Daphne Bramham, "Truth Is Often a Casualty of Peace," *Vancouver Sun* (17 September 2015): B7.

39. See Peter Pae, "With Forgiveness, a Burden Lifted: Officer Who Ordered Infamous Napalm Attack Makes Peace with Victim," *Washington Post* (6 March 1997): MD6. Plummer was quoted as saying, "The moment I saw the [*Napalm Girl*] picture and read the caption, I knew without a shadow of doubt that was the air strike I had ordered."

40. See Anne Gearan, "A War, a Photograph and a Healing Reunion," Associated Press (12 April 1997), retrieved from www.lexisnexis.com.

41. "John Plummer's Burden," *Nightline*, ABC News (6 June 1997), transcript retrieved from www.lexisnexis.com.

42. Ibid.

43. Tom Bowman, "Veteran's Admission to Napalm Victim a Lie," *Baltimore Sun* (14 December 1997): 1A. Bowman's article also quoted Plummer as saying the napalm bombing at Trang Bang had "ruined" his life for a decade, a period when he "drank heavily and saw two marriages crumble. After marrying for a third time, [Plummer] said, he turned his life around and became more religious, finally leaving a job with a defense contractor for a career" in the Methodist ministry.

44. Tom Bowman, telephone interview with the author (12 May 2015).

45. See Linh Duy Vo, *To America, Love and Gratitude* ([Downey, CA]: Voco Publishing, 2000), 57.

46. Ibid.

47. Ibid.

48. Ibid., 59.

49. Linh Duy Vo, telephone interview with the author (2 July 2015).

50. Chuyen Van Nguyen, telephone interview with the author (28 July 2015).

51. Ibid.

52. Ibid.

53. See Margie Mason, "AP 'Napalm Girl' Photo from Vietnam War Turns 40," *Boston Globe* (2 June 2012), archive.boston.com/news/nation/articles /2012/06/02/ap_napalm_girl_photo_from_vietnam_war_turns_40.

54. Miller, "Girl in the Photograph," 148–149.

55. See David Tattersall, "The *Mail* Tracks Down the Girl Who Helped End the Vietnam War 20 Years Ago Today," *Sunday Mail* [Glasgow] (30 April 1995): 38. Tattersall also wrote that "the unforgettable photograph was credited by many as marking the beginning of the end of America's involvement in

the 13-year conflict. Millions of Americans who saw it were so sickened that they could no longer stomach what was being done in their name."

56. See Bill Hutchinson, "'Napalm Girl' & Little Rich Girl: AP Photog Took Iconic Pix on Same Day, 35 Years Apart," *New York Daily News* (11 June 2012): 37. Hutchinson's article marveled at the coincidence of Nick Ut's having taken a widely published photograph of celebrity Paris Hilton in a police car en route to jail in Los Angeles exactly thirty-five years after he took the *Napalm Girl* image. See also Kennicott, "Poles and Decades Apart."

57. Anne Penketh, "Goya Etchings Centerpiece of Louvre's Disasters of War Exhibition in Lens," *Guardian* (28 May 2014), www.theguardian.com /artanddesign/2014/may/28/goya-etchings-louvre-disasters-of-war-exhibition.

58. David Ono, "Vietnam Marks 40 Years since Fall of Saigon," KABC News, Los Angeles (30 April 2015), www.abc7.com/news/vietnam-marks-40-years-since-fall-of-saigon/690106.

59. See Enid Tsui, "Hong Kong Exhibitions Showcase Artist Yang Jiechang's Mix of Wit and Woe," *48 Hours* (4 June 2015), www.scmp.com/magazines/48-hours/article/1814798/hong-kong-exhibitions-showcase-artist-yang-jiechangs-mix-wit-and.

60. Bramham, "Compassionate Canada."

61. Quoted in Gendy Alimurung, "Nick Ut's *Napalm Girl* Helped End the Vietnam War; Today in L.A., He's Still Shooting," *LA Weekly* (17 July 2014), www.laweekly.com/news/nick-uts-napalm-girl-helped-end-the-vietnam-war-today-in-la-hes-still-shooting-4861747.

62. Nick Ut, video interview with Alessia Glaviano (26 May 2014), www .facebook.com/photo.php?v=472688809528663.

63. Ut, oral history interview (August 1997), Newseum.

64. Quoted in Peter Cheney, "Vietnam Photo Girl Kim Now 'Smiles All the Time'; But She Still Remembers Pain," *Toronto Star* (6 February 1997): A1.

65. For an example of a news article linking the photograph to the peace agreement negotiated in 1973, see Cheney, "Vietnam Photo Girl." Cheney wrote that *Napalm Girl* "is generally believed to have been the final blow to the Vietnam war—the U.S. signed a peace agreement just seven months after it ran."

66. See "Chronology," in *Reporting Vietnam: Part Two: American Journalism, 1969–1975* (New York: Literary Classics of the United States, 1998), 789.

67. "To Meet Troop-Cut Levels but Keep Air-Strike Power, U.S. Reportedly Will Shift Fighter Units to Thailand," *Baltimore Sun* (11 June 1972): A1. See also Malcolm W. Browne, "U.S. Is Disbanding Major Combat Unit in South Vietnam," *New York Times* (17 June 1972): 6.

68. "To Meet Troop-Cut Levels," *Baltimore Sun.*

69. See "Statistical Information about Fatal Casualties of the Vietnam War," National Archives (last updated 29 April 2009), www.archives.gov/research /military/vietnam-war/casualty-statistics.html.

70. The last U.S. troops were withdrawn from Vietnam in March 1973.

71. Quoted in Mike Ahlers, "Nixon's Doubts over 'Napalm Girl' Photo," CNN (28 February 2002), www.edition.cnn.com/2002/WORLD/asiapcf /southeast/02/28/vietnam.nixon. The exchange between Nixon and Haldeman was included in some five hundred hours of taped conversations that the

National Archives and Records Administration released in February 2002. See also "Nixon Tapes Reveal Former President Doubted the Authenticity of Famous War Photo," Associated Press (28 February 2002), retrieved from www.lexisnexis.com.

72. See "War Photo Is Challenged," *Washington Post* (19 January 1986): A3. The article said Westmoreland did not recall who had told him Kim Phuc had been burned in a hibachi accident.

73. Nixon's conversation with Haldeman that day was recorded by the White House taping system and can be heard at "Nixon's 'Smoking Gun,'" History .com (accessed 14 May 2015), www.history.com/speeches/nixons-smoking-gun.

74. The aerial napalm attack at Trang Bang took place during the broader and more intensive U.S. bombing campaign conducted elsewhere in the country; the coincidental timing may help account for the mistaken belief that American warplanes dropped the napalm at Trang Bang.

75. Quoted in "250 Gather to Protest Viet War," *Washington Post* (26 December 1972): B5.

76. Sontag, *On Photography*, 18.

77. George Esper, "A Straw Hut, Old Newspapers and Memories of 'Napalm Girl,'" Associated Press (14 November 1993), retrieved from www.lexisnexis .com.

78. See Samuel G. Freedman, *Letters to a Young Journalist*, The Art of Mentoring (New York: Basic, 2006), 29.

79. Ono, "Napalm Girl." The photograph's "impact," Ono stated, "is immeasurable."

80. See Alimurung, "Ut's *Napalm Girl.*"

81. Soo Youn, "40 Years since Saigon's Fall, Napalm Attack Haunts Woman in Iconic Image," *London Guardian* (30 April 2015), www.theguardian.com /world/2015/apr/30/40-years-since-saigons-fall-napalm-attack-haunts-woman-in-iconic-image.

82. Yasmin Alibhai-Brown, "So David Cameron, Is This Dead Syrian Child One of the 'Swarm' of Migrants You Fear So Much?" *Independent* [London] (2 September 2015), www.independent.co.uk/voices/so-david-cameron-is-this-dead-syrian-child-one-of-the-swarm-of-migrants-you-fear-so-much-10483298.html.

83. "Sometimes an Image Is . . . " *Sun* [London] (6 September 2015): 15.

84. See "Gallup Poll Finds U.S. Divided on Bombing," *New York Times* (26 January 1973): 10.

85. See Frank Newport and Joseph Carroll, "Iraq versus Vietnam: A Comparison of Public Opinion," Gallup News Service (24 August 2005), www.gallup .com/poll/18097/iraq-versus-vietnam-comparison-public-opinion.aspx. By August 1968, a majority of respondents said the Vietnam War had been a mistake, Gallup reported.

86. See William L. Lunch and Peter W. Sperlich, "American Public Opinion and the War in Vietnam," *Western Political Quarterly* 32, no. 1 (March 1979): 29.

87. Quoted in Michael Zhang, "Interview with Nick Ut, the Photojournalist Who Shot the Iconic 'Napalm Girl' Photo," *PetaPixel* (blog) (19 September 2012), www.petapixel.com/2012/09/19/interview-with-nick-ut-the-photojournalist-who-shot-the-iconic-photo-napalm-girl.

88. Washington, D.C., was the theater of an unusual and controversial anti-war protest on June 22, 1972, although it was unrelated to *Napalm Girl*. Led by folk singer Joan Baez, some two thousand women and children linked hands to form a human chain at the Capitol in protest against the war. Some black political leaders in the District of Columbia opposed the protest, saying its cost would be borne principally by African American taxpayers, who represented a majority of Washington's population. See Tom Wells, *The War Within: American's Battle Over Vietnam* (Berkeley: University of California Press, 1994), 550. See also Betty Medsger, "2,000 Women Form a Ring at Capitol," *Washington Post* (23 June 1972): C1, C2. "The women and children at the Capitol were quiet and serious," Medsger reported. "There was little frivolity. And when Joan Baez sang, she usually sang alone, except at the end when she sang the African folk song 'Kum Bah Yah' and substituted the words 'Peace Come by Here'" (C2).

89. Philip Kennicott, "Why Syria's Images of Suffering Haven't Moved Us," *Washington Post* (15 September 2013): B1.

90. Chong, *Girl in the Picture*, 76.

91. See Robert Hariman and John Louis Lucaites, "Public Identity and Collective Memory in U.S. Iconic Photography: The Image of 'Accidental Napalm,'" *Critical Studies in Media Communication* 20, no. 1 (March 2003): 39.

92. See "Photo of the Week: Tragedy in Napalm," *AP Log* (5–11 June 1972): 1.

93. The forty titles were selected for the geographic distribution they collectively represented, and because they were leading mainstream metropolitan dailies. The titles examined were: *Arizona Republic, Atlanta Constitution, Atlanta Journal, Baltimore Sun, Boston Globe, Boston Herald Traveler, Chicago Sun-Times, Chicago Tribune,* [Cleveland] *Plain Dealer, Dallas Morning News, Denver Post, Des Moines Register, Detroit Free Press, Detroit News, Hartford Courant, Honolulu Star-Bulletin, Houston Post, Indianapolis News, Indianapolis Star, Kansas City Star, Los Angeles Herald Examiner, Los Angeles Times, Miami Herald, Newark Star-Ledger, New York Daily News, New York Post, New York Times, Omaha World Herald,* [Philadelphia] *Evening Bulletin, Philadelphia Inquirer, Pittsburgh Post-Gazette, Portland Oregonian, Raleigh News & Observer, St. Louis Post-Dispatch, San Francisco Chronicle, San Francisco Examiner, Seattle Post-Intelligencer, Seattle Times,* [Washington] *Evening Star,* and *Washington Post.*

94. Horst Faas, oral history interview (21 May 2007), Associated Press Corporate Archives, New York.

95. Ibid.

96. Hal Buell, telephone interview with the author (10 June 2015).

97. See "The Fire This Time," *New York Times* (11 June 1972): E3. The commentary revisited the errant napalm strike at Trang Bang and included the observations of Charles Mohr, a correspondent in Vietnam, who wrote: "Unquestionably, civilians were hurt and killed by napalm, but in far smaller numbers than most people in the United States seem to think." Mohr, however, offered no supporting data for that statement.

98. See Donald Kirk, "South Vietnamese Napalm Their Own Village," *Philadelphia Inquirer* (9 June 1972): 1.

99. See "Little Viet Boy Dies of Napalm Burns," *Philadelphia Inquirer* (10 June 1972): 2.

100. See Christopher Wain, "S. Viets Bomb Their Own Side in Error," *Atlanta Constitution* (9 June 1972): 1A.

101. See Thomas W. Lippman, "Foe Disappointed," *Washington Post* (9 June 1972): A1; and George C. Wilson, "Pentagon Optimistic," *Washington Post* (9 June 1972): A1. The *Post* may have placed the photograph below the fold on its front page because the rival *Evening Star* newspaper had published it on its front page the day before, beneath an Associated Press roundup about the fighting in Vietnam. See George Esper, "B52s Again Bomb in North," [Washington] *Evening Star* (8 June 1972): A1.

102. "S. Viets Attack in North; U.S. Raids Mount," *Washington Post* (9 June 1972): A20.

103. "Associated Press Radiophoto," *New York Post* (10 June 1972): 28.

104. Timothy Snyder, "Memoirs of the Murdered," review of *KL: A History of the Nazi Concentration Camps,* by Nikolaus Wachsmann, *Wall Street Journal* (24 April 2015), www.wsj.com/articles/memoirs-of-the-murdered-1429909684.

105. Shelby Steele, *Shame: How America's Past Sins Have Polarized Our Country* (New York, Basic Books: 2015), 16.

106. Kennicott, "Poles and Decades Apart."

CHAPTER NINE

1. See Harry F. Rosenthal, no headline, Associated Press (22 June 1977), retrieved from www.lexisnexis.com.

2. "Nixon's tapes convicted him," Stanley I. Kutler, Watergate's leading historian, has written. See Kutler, ed., *Abuse of Power: The New Nixon Tapes* (New York: Free Press, 1997), xxiii.

3. Gladys Engel Lang and Kurt Lang noted in their study of the press, public opinion, and Watergate that, "since the facts are so quickly forgotten, the folklore is what survives." See Lang and Lang, *The Battle for Public Opinion: The President, the Press, and the Polls during Watergate* (New York: Columbia University Press, 1983), 264.

4. ABC News/*Washington Post* survey, conducted 7–9 June, 2002, retrieved from Polling the Nations database, www.orspub.com.

5. See James McCartney, "The Washington 'Post' and Watergate: How Two Davids Slew Goliath," *Columbia Journalism Review,* July/August 1973: 8. See also David Greenberg, *Nixon's Shadow: The History of an Image* (New York: Norton, 2003), 162.

6. Matt Bai, *All the Truth Is Out: The Week Politics Went Tabloid* (New York: Knopf, 2014), 35.

7. Mencher's textbook recommends that students read *All the President's Men* because "no journalism bibliography would be complete without the book that describes how two young reporters, Bob Woodward and Carl Bernstein, toppled a president." See Melvin Mencher, *Melvin Mencher's News Reporting and Writing,* 11th ed. (Boston: McGraw-Hill, 2008), 33.

8. Shirley Biagi, *Media/Impact: An Introduction to Mass Media,* 8th ed. (Belmont, CA: Thomson Wadsworth, 2007), 248. Biagi wrote of Woodward and Bernstein, "Eventually their reporting led to President Nixon's resignation in 1974."

9. Harrower's textbook says that *All the President's Men* is among five "inspirational books every reporter should read" because it "unravels the threads that lead to Nixon's downfall." See Tim Harrower, *Inside Reporting: A Practical Guide to the Craft of Journalism* (Boston: McGraw-Hill, 2006), 6.

10. O'Neil wrote, "After Bob Woodward and Carl Bernstein brought down the Nixon administration over Watergate, those two quintessential investigators became role models for a generation of budding journalists." See Robert M. O'Neil, *The First Amendment and Civil Liability* (Bloomington: Indiana University Press, 2001), 95.

11. Kosner's memoir refers to Woodward and Bernstein as "the *Washington Post* reporters whose work had toppled Nixon." See Edward Kosner, *It's News to Me: The Making and Unmaking of an Editor* (Cambridge, MA: Da Capo Press, 2007), 173.

12. Carol Pogash, "The Caucus: Meeting Deep Throat," *New York Times* (19 November 2008): A22. See also, Joe Nocera, "Hollywood Catches Journalism's Eye," *New York Times* (3 January 2016): AR 26. Nocera blithely referred in his article to "the investigation by Bob Woodward and Carl Bernstein that led to Richard M. Nixon's resignation."

13. Paul Johnson, *Modern Times: The World from the Twenties to the Nineties,* rev. ed. (New York: HarperCollins, 1991), 649, 653.

14. Michael Schudson, *Watergate in American Memory: How We Remember, Forget, and Reconstruct the Past* (New York: Basic Books, 1992), 124. Somewhat more colorfully, Schudson (125) called Watergate the "exploding supernova in the sky of journalism. . . . Watergate, at least retrospectively, could be widely accepted as a triumph not only of American journalism but of the American system of a free press."

15. Jay Rosen, "Deep Throat, J-School and Newsroom Religion," *PressThink* (blog) (5 June 2005), www.archive.pressthink.org/2005/06/05/wtrg _js.html. Rosen also wrote: "When the press took over the legend of Watergate, the main characters were no longer the bad guys like Richard Nixon [and his corrupt aides] John Mitchell, Bob Haldeman, John Ehrlichman, or Chuck Colson, all of whom broke the law and abused state power. The narrative got turned around. Watergate became a story about heroism at the Washington Post. The protagonists were Woodward and Bernstein."

16. Jay Bookman, a columnist for the *Atlanta Journal-Constitution* raised a similar point in 2005, writing, "Today, if Watergate and Deep Throat are known at all to younger Americans, it's because the media have turned Watergate into a story that's all about the news media." See Bookman, "Deep Throat Myth Better Than Reality," *Atlanta Journal-Constitution* (2 June 2005): 15A. See also Greenberg, *Nixon's Shadow,* 163. "Because of the book and the film," Greenberg wrote in reference to *All the President's Men,* "the Watergate story itself has come to be known from the *Post*'s point of view."

17. From the dust jacket of Carl Bernstein and Bob Woodward, *All the President's Men* (New York: Simon & Schuster, 1974).

18. Adrian Havill, *Deep Truth: The Lives of Bob Woodward and Carl Bernstein* (Secaucus, NJ: Carol Publishing, 1993), 90–91.

19. *All the President's Men* left the top spot on the *Times*'s best-seller list in mid-November 1974. See "Best Seller List," *New York Times* (17 November 1974): 498.

20. Stanley I. Kutler, *The Wars of Watergate: The Last Crisis of Richard Nixon* (New York: Knopf, 1990), 459.

21. See Lawrence A. Armour, "Unraveling the Watergate Grab-Bag," *Wall Street Journal* (10 June 1974): 12.

22. Leonard Garment, *In Search of Deep Throat: The Greatest Political Mystery of Our Time* (New York: Basic Books, 2000), 5.

23. Michael Getler, "'Deep Throat': An Omb's Observations," *Washington Post* (5 June 2005): B6.

24. See Bob Woodward, "How Mark Felt Became 'Deep Throat,'" *Washington Post* (2 June 2005): A1.

25. Bernstein and Woodward, *All the President's Men*, 71. Woodward and Bernstein wrote that a senior *Washington Post* editor, Howard Simons, dubbed the source "Deep Throat," after the title of a 1972 pornographic movie.

26. See Gene Siskel, "Watergate: Big Film behind the Big Story," *Chicago Tribune* (28 March 1976): E2; and "Redford Suggested Watergate Book," *Los Angeles Times* (9 January 1980): B3. See also Alicia Shepard, *Woodward and Bernstein: Life in the Shadow of Watergate* (Hoboken, NJ: Wiley & Sons, 2007), 75. Shepard wrote, "Woodward and Bernstein decided, thanks to Redford, to write a book that only they could write: the story of the road they traveled reporting Watergate."

27. Siskel, "Big Film behind the Big Story."

28. See "Redford Suggested Watergate Book," *Los Angeles Times*.

29. The New York Film Critics Circle and the National Society of Film Critics selected *All the President's Men* as the best motion picture of 1976. See "Critics Pick Best '76 Film: 'All the President's Men,'" *Chicago Tribune* (4 January 1977): 5; and "'All the President's Men' Makes It 2 in a Row," *New York Times* (5 January 1977): 45. Vincent Canby, the movie critic for the *New York Times*, said in his review that *All the President's Men* was "an unequivocal smash-hit— the thinking man's 'Jaws.'" See Canby, "'President's Men,' Spellbinding Film," *New York Times* (8 April 1976): 42.

30. Cited in Mark Feldstein, "Watergate Revisited," *American Journalism Review*, August/September 2004: 62–63.

31. In an online discussion in 2007, Woodward called the film "an incredibly accurate portrait of what happened." See "The Watergate Legacy, 35 Years Later," washingtonpost.com (18 June 2007), www.washingtonpost.com/wp-dyn/content/discussion/2007/06/14/DI2007061400497.html.

32. The point about oversimplification also was made in Robert Brent Toplin, *History by Hollywood: The Use and Abuse of the American Past* (Urbana:

University of Illinois Press, 1996), 180. Toplin wrote, "Like many examples of cinematic history from Hollywood, *All the President's Men* tends to glamorize the achievements of a few individuals and overlook the roles of other people and other causes behind historical developments."

33. Quoted in ibid., 201.

34. Frank Rich, "Will We Need a New 'All the President's Men'?" *New York Times* (17 October 2004): sec. 2, p. 1.

35. David Brooks, "Life Lessons from Watergate," *New York Times* (5 June 2005): sec. 4, p. 14.

36. See, broadly, Chip Heath and Dan Heath, *Made to Stick: Why Some Ideas Survive and Others Die* (New York: Random House, 2007), 8.

37. Jonathan Kirshner, "All the President's Men (1976)," *Film and History* 36, no. 2 (2006): 57.

38. Matthew C. Ehrlich, *Journalism in the Movies* (Urbana: University of Illinois Press, 2004), 120.

39. Other movies about Watergate include *Dick* (1999) and Oliver Stone's *Nixon* (1995). *Dick* is a parody of the Nixon White House that spoofs the "Deep Throat" source and depicts Woodward and Bernstein as petulant incompetents.

40. Havill, *Deep Truth*, 102.

41. Kutler wrote that McCord's charges "led directly to the unraveling of the conspiracy" at the heart of the Watergate scandal. See Kutler, *Wars of Watergate*, 260.

42. Quoted in Feldstein, "Watergate Revisited," 67.

43. "Post 'Didn't Bring Down' the President," in *Watergate: 25 Years Later* (Arlington, VA: Freedom Forum, 1997), 3.

44. Quoted in Feldstein, "Watergate Revisited," 62. Woodward was further quoted as saying, "The press always plays a role, whether by being passive or by being aggressive, but it's a mistake to overemphasize" the impact of the news media's coverage.

45. Getler, "'Deep Throat': An Omb's Observations."

46. McCartney, "Washington 'Post' and Watergate," 8–9.

47. John Dean, White House counsel at the time, later wrote: "I can say without equivocation that *not one story* written by Woodward and Bernstein . . . from the time of the arrest on June 17, 1972, until the election in November 1972, gave anyone in the Nixon White House or the re-election committee the slightest concern that 'Woodstein' was on to the real story of Watergate." See Dean, *Lost Honor* (Los Angeles: Stratford Press, 1982), 271.

48. Quoted in McCartney, "Washington 'Post' and Watergate," 21. Sussman for a time was the *Post* editor who most closely supervised Woodward and Bernstein. He wrote in his book about Watergate, "We had hoped that sources would open up after the election, but instead they got more close-mouthed." See Barry Sussman, *The Great Coverup: Nixon and the Scandal of Watergate* (New York: Crowell, 1974), 135.

49. Quoted in Leonard Downie Jr., *The New Muckrakers* (Washington, DC: New Republic, 1976), 82.

50. Quoted in McCartney, "Washington 'Post' and Watergate," 22.

51. See Bernstein and Woodward, *All the President's Men*, 332.

52. See "Post 'Didn't Bring Down' the President," in *Watergate: 25 Years Later*, 3.

53. Quoted in McCartney, "Washington 'Post' and Watergate," 9.

54. Sussman, *Great Coverup*, 135.

55. See, among others, Shepard, *Woodward and Bernstein*, 58. Shepard wrote that during the second half of 1972, "there was more reporting [about Watergate] going on by other news organizations than is generally acknowledged."

56. See Jack Nelson and Ronald J. Ostrow, "Bugging Witness Tells Inside Story on Incident at Watergate," *Los Angeles Times* (5 October 1972): A1; and Alfred C. Baldwin III, "An Insider's Account of the Watergate Bugging," *Los Angeles Times* (5 October 1972): C7.

57. David Halberstam, *The Powers That Be* (New York: Dell Publishing, 1979), 891.

58. "Time to Come Clean," *New York Times* (14 September 1972): 46. See also "Independent Scrutiny," *New York Times* (28 August 1972): 28.

59. "Independent Scrutiny," *New York Times*.

60. See Seymour M. Hersh, "4 Watergate Defendants Reported Still Being Paid," *New York Times* (14 January 1973): 1. Hersh's report quoted one of the burglars, Frank A. Sturgis, by name and said he was receiving payments of $400 a month.

61. Dean, *Lost Honor*, 272. The exclamation point is Dean's.

62. See Bernard Gwertzman, "G.A.O. Report Asks Justice Inquiry into G.O.P. Funds," *New York Times* (27 August 1972): 1.

63. See James M. Naughton, "McGovern Bars Briefings by Kissinger as Unhelpful," *New York Times* (16 August 1972): 1, 20.

64. Edward Jay Epstein, *Between Fact and Fiction: The Problem of Journalism* (New York: Vintage Books, 1975), 26. See also Martin Schram, "Watergate in Media Legend," *Journal of Commerce* (19 June 1997): 6A. Schram wrote, "Even in the early days [of the Watergate scandal], the Post was not always the Lone Ranger we now remember."

65. Epstein, *Between Fact and Fiction*, 29.

66. See Carl Bernstein and Bob Woodward, "FBI Finds Nixon Aides Sabotaged Democrats," *Washington Post* (10 October 1972): A1, A14.

67. A portion of the memorandum is reproduced in L. Patrick Gray III with Ed Gray, *In Nixon's Web: A Year in the Crosshairs of Watergate* (New York: Times Books, 2008), 128.

68. Epstein, *Between Fact and Fiction*, 29–30.

69. Karen Heller, "He Was the Last Big Secret in a Gabby Age," *Philadelphia Inquirer* (2 June 2005): E1.

70. Shepard, *Woodward and Bernstein*, 109.

71. Stanley I. Kutler, "Watergate Misremembered: The Shallow Debate about Deep Throat," *Slate* (18 June 2002), www.slate.com/id/2067123. Kutler disparaged the guessing game as "endless, pointless."

72. Dennis Farney, "If You Drink Scotch, Smoke and Read, Maybe You're 'Deep Throat,'" *Wall Street Journal* (25 June 1974): 1.

73. See Francine Kiefer, "And the Identity of 'Deep Throat' Is . . . Er . . . Um," *Christian Science Monitor* (18 June 2002): 1.

74. See Kelly Patrick, "Outing Deep Throat: Who Was the Source?" *Globe and Mail* [Toronto] (3 May 2003): A3.

75. Garment, *In Search of Deep Throat.*

76. See Epstein, *Between Fact and Fiction,* 31.

77. Cited in Sara Fritz, "Deep Throat? Still Anybody's Guess," *St. Petersburg* [FL] *Times* (17 June 2002): 1A.

78. Havill, *Deep Truth,* 83.

79. Farney, "If You Drink Scotch."

80. Epstein, *Between Fact and Fiction,* 30–31.

81. See James Mann, "Deep Throat: An Institutional Analysis," *Atlantic Monthly* (May 1992), www.theatlantic.com/doc/199205/mann.

82. Farney, "If You Drink Scotch," 1, 27. The *Wall Street Journal* also reported that Felt said Woodward once asked him "to play a Deep Throat-like role, never volunteering information, just confirming the accuracy of information the reporters obtained elsewhere. Mr. Felt says he refused in the presence of an assistant."

83. Cited in Mann, "Deep Throat."

84. Cited in David Cook and Randy Dotinga, "A Mystery Solved, but 'Deep' Issues Linger," *Christian Science Monitor* (2 June 2005): 2.

85. See Mark Memmott, "'Deep Throat' Revelation Raises New Questions," *USA Today* (2 June 2005): 6A.

86. Max Holland, *Leak: Why Mark Felt Became Deep Throat* (Lawrence: University of Kansas, 2012), 9.

87. See Todd S. Purdum, "'Deep Throat' Unmasks Himself: Ex-No. 2 at F.B.I.," *New York Times* (1 June 2005): 1.

88. Howard Kurtz, "The Source of Whose Troubles? Up to Our Ears in Deep Throats, Parsing the Lessons of the Leak," *Washington Post* (6 June 2005): C1. Kurtz added, though: "Despite the mythology, The Post didn't force Richard Nixon from office—there were also two special prosecutors, a determined judge, bipartisan House and Senate committees, the belated honesty of John Dean and those infamous White House tapes."

89. Heller, "Last Big Secret."

90. Bookman, "Deep Throat Myth."

91. Philip Meyer, "The Lessons of 'Deep Throat' and Watergate," *USA Today* (6 June 2005): 13A.

92. Hank Stuever, "In Dark Times, You Need a Mark Felt in the Shadows," *Washington Post* (20 December 2008): C1.

93. Lee B. Becker and Joseph D. Graf, *Myths and Trends: What the Real Numbers Say about Journalism Education* (Arlington, VA: Freedom Forum, 1995), 3. Becker and Graf further noted (5): "There has been a dramatic growth in the number of bachelor's degrees granted to students in various Communications fields for the last 26 years. The growth is consistent and of significant magnitude—from 3,131 degrees granted in 1966 to 52,799 in 1991."

94. Ibid., 5. Becker and Graf noted an "unusually large jump in communication enrollments between 1970 and 1971"—before Watergate—and said the increase "is best explained by the modification in classification scheme for fields of study between those years."

95. Maxwell E. McCombs, "Testing the Myths: A Statistical Review, 1967–86," *Gannett Center Journal* (Spring 1988): 102.

96. Ben H. Bagdikian, "Woodstein U: Notes on the Mass Production and Questionable Education of Journalists," *Atlantic Monthly* (March 1977): 80–92.

97. Reese Cleghorn, "Getting It Wrong for 16 Years (at Least)," *American Journalism Review,* June 1993: 4.

CHAPTER TEN

1. See, for example, Anna Quindlen, "Hearing the Cries of Crack," *New York Times* (7 October 1990): sec. 4, p. 19. Quindlen described an encounter at a hospital this way: "I am staring deep into the eyes of one baby, having some meeting of the minds, when I idly scratch my chin. The baby jumps in his isolette at the motion, begins to shake uncontrollably, wails an unearthly falsetto wail."

2. Charles Krauthammer, "Children of Cocaine," *Washington Post* (30 July 1989): C7.

3. Courtland Milloy, "A Time Bomb in Cocaine Babies," *Washington Post* (17 September 1989): B4A.

4. Jane E. Brody, "Cocaine: Litany of Fetal Risks Grows," *New York Times* (6 September 1988): C1.

5. Barbara Kantrowtiz, "The Crack Children," *Newsweek* (12 February 1990): 12.

6. Quoted in Jane E. Brody, "Widespread Abuse of Drugs by Pregnant Women Is Found," *New York Times* (30 August 1988): A1.

7. "Crack: A Disaster of Historic Dimension, Still Growing," *New York Times* (28 May 1989): sec. 4, p. 14.

8. See Ellen Goodman, "The Myth of the 'Crack Babies,'" *Boston Globe* (12 January 1992): 69.

9. South Carolina has turned to child-abuse laws to prosecute women who abuse drugs during pregnancy. See Kathy Stevens, "Fetal-Drug Prosecution Ignites Debate in S.C.," *Post and Courier* [Charleston, SC] (23 February 2003): 1A.

10. See Claire D. Coles, "Saying 'Goodbye' to the 'Crack Baby,'" *Neurotoxicology and Teratology* 15, no. 5 (September/October 1993): 290.

11. Mariah Blake, "The Damage Done: Crack Babies Talk Back," *Columbia Journalism Review,* September/October 2004: 10.

12. Susan Okie, "The Epidemic That Wasn't," *New York Times* (27 January 2009): D1. See also Blake, "The Damage Done," 10. The crack baby, Blake declared, turned out to be "a media myth, not a medical reality."

13. Deborah A. Frank, testimony prepared for delivery to the U.S. Sentencing Commission (25 February 2002), www.ussc.gov/sites/default/files/pdf/amendment-process/public-hearings-and-meetings/20020225-26/Frank.pdf. See also Deborah A. Frank, Marilyn Augustyn, Wanda Grant Knight, Tripler Pell, and Barry Zuckerman, "Growth, Development, and Behavior in Early Childhood following Prenatal Cocaine Exposure: A Systematic Review," *Journal of the American Medical Association* 285, no. 12 (28 March 2001): 1614.

14. Quoted in Dahleen Glanton, "Proof Positive of Flawed Data: Chicagoan Overcomes Mother's Addictions and Other Disadvantages to Become a Top Graduate at Morehouse College," *Chicago Tribune* (19 May 2008): C3.

15. Frank et al., "Growth, Development, and Behavior in Early Childhood following Prenatal Cocaine Exposure," 1614. A commentary in the *Journal of the American Medical Association* in 1992 discussed the folly of stigmatizing so-called crack babies, stating: "Labeling and isolating infants and young children because of their prenatal experience are irrational and inhumane actions. Condemning these children with labels of permanent handicap and failure is premature and may lead us to overlook what we have long known about the remediating effects of early intervention." See Linda C. Mayes, Richard H. Granger, Marc H. Bornstein, and Barry Zuckerman, "The Problem of Prenatal Cocaine Exposure: A Rush to Judgment," *Journal of the American Medical Association* 267, no. 3 (15 January 1992): 406.

16. See John L. Doris and others, "Prenatal Cocaine Exposure and Child Welfare Outcomes," *Child Maltreatment* 11, no. 4 (November 2006): 329, 332.

17. See "Research Report Series—Cocaine Abuse and Addiction," National Institute on Drug Abuse (3 May 2006), www.drugabuse.gov/ResearchReports /Cocaine/cocaine4.html#maternal.

18. Frank et al., "Growth, Development, and Behavior in Early Childhood following Prenatal Cocaine Exposure," 1619.

19. Ibid., 1620. The authors wrote, "Many findings once thought to be specific effects on in utero cocaine exposure can be explained in whole or in part by other factors, including prenatal exposure to tobacco, marijuana, or alcohol, and the quality of the child's environment."

20. Cited in Dana Kennedy, "Experts: Children Born Addicted to Crack Rise Above Dire Predictions," Associated Press (6 December 1992), retrieved from www.lexisnexis.com.

21. David J. Jefferson, "America's Most Dangerous Drug," *Newsweek* (8 August 2005): 42, 47. Jefferson (41) described methamphetamine as the "crystalline white drug [that] quickly seduces those who snort, smoke or inject it with a euphoric rush of confidence, hyperalertness and sexiness that last for hours on end. And then it starts destroying lives."

22. Jack Shafer, "Crack Then, Meth Now," Slate.com (23 August 2005), www.slate.com/id/2124885.

23. Kathy Fackelmann, "The Crack-Baby Myth," *City Paper* [Washington, DC] (13 December 1991).

24. See Ira J. Chasnoff, William J. Burns, Sidney H. Schnoll, and Kayreen A. Burns, "Cocaine Use in Pregnancy," *New England Journal of Medicine* 313, no. 11 (12 September 1985): 666–669.

25. Ibid., 668–669.

26. "Cocaine Risk Seen in Pregnancy," *New York Times* (12 September 1985): A20.

27. Andrea Stone, "Drug Epidemic's Tiny Victims: Crack Babies Born to a Life of Suffering," *USA Today* (8 June 1989): 3A.

28. Douglas J. Besharov, "Crack Babies: The Worst Threat Is Mom Herself," *Washington Post* (6 August 1989): B1.

29. Dorothy Gilliam, "The Children of Crack," *Washington Post* (31 July 1989): D3.

30. Michael Isikoff, "Alcohol: The 'Worst' Drug Problem; Officials in Midwest Frustrated by Government Priorities," *Washington Post* (2 April 1990): A1.

31. Ibid.

32. Fackelmann, "Crack-Baby Myth."

33. Goodman, "Myth of the 'Crack Babies.'"

34. Mayes et al., "The Problem of Prenatal Cocaine Exposure," 406, 408.

35. Katharine Greider, "Crackpot Ideas," *Mother Jones*, July/August 1995, www.motherjones.com/politics/1995/07/crackpot-ideas.

36. Susan FitzGerald, "'Crack Baby' Fears May Have Been Overstated," *Washington Post* (16 September 1997): Z10.

37. Sharon Begley, "Hope for 'Snow Babies,'" *Newsweek* (29 September 1997): 62.

38. E. R. Shipp, "Living Down the Label of 'Crack Baby,'" *New York Daily News* (28 March 2004): 48.

39. Kevin Simpson, "A Found Generation: Julius Seawright Is Real-Life Proof That the 'Crack Baby' Fears of the 80s Had Little Basis in Fact," *Denver Post* (6 March 2005): A1.

40. Okie, "The Epidemic That Wasn't."

41. See Greider, "Crackpot Ideas."

42. Ibid. Greider wrote: "The crack-baby myth was so powerful in part because it had something for everyone, whether one's ideological leanings called for enhancing public programs to meet the crisis, or for punishing the drug-addicted mothers seen as responsible. For some, the assertion that crack babies were in dire trouble became a way of begging funds for substance-abusing mothers and their infants."

43. Robert Kaplan, "The Coming Anarchy," *Atlantic*, February 1994, www.theatlantic.com/magazine/archive/1994/02/the-coming-anarchy/304670/. West Africa, Kaplan wrote in his widely discussed essay, "is becoming the symbol of worldwide demographic, environmental, and societal stress, in which criminal anarchy emerges as the real 'strategic' danger. Disease, overpopulation, unprovoked crime, scarcity of resources, refugee migrations, the increasing erosion of nation-states and international borders, and the empowerment of private armies, security firms, and international drug cartels are now most tellingly demonstrated through a West African prism. West Africa provides an appropriate introduction to the issues, often extremely unpleasant to discuss, that will soon confront our civilization."

44. John P. Morgan and Lynn Zimmer, "The Social Pharmacology of Smokeable Cocaine: Not All It's Cracked Up to Be," in *Crack in America: Demon Drugs, Social Justice*, ed. Craig Reinarman and Harry G. Levine (Berkeley: University of California Press, 1997), 151.

45. Ibid.

46. "Science: The Cooling World," *Newsweek* (28 April 1975): 64. On the prospect of global cooling, see also William R. Graham, "Mystery of Climate: Man Tinkers with Survival," *Los Angeles Times* (31 May 1970): L1; and James

Pearre, "Ice Age Coming? Chilling Thought for Humanity," *Chicago Tribune* (2 June 1975): E12.

47. Dorothy Nelkin, "An Uneasy Relationship: The Tensions between Medicine and the Media," *Lancet* 347 (8 June 1996): 1600. Nelkin also writes (1601): "Media constraints of time, brevity, and simplicity preclude the careful documentation, nuanced positions, and precautionary qualifications that scientists feel are necessary to present their work. While scientists are [inclined] to qualify their findings, journalists often see qualification as protective coloration."

48. Ibid., 1601. Nelkin cites the infamous case of cold fusion in 1989, when scientists at the University of Utah called a news conference to announce a purported breakthrough in achieving nuclear fusion at room temperatures, raising hopes that they had developed an inexpensive and limitless source of energy. Other research, however, was unable to duplicate the findings, and the notion of cold fusion soon was discredited. See also David Murray, Joel Schwartz, and S. Robert Lichter, *It Ain't Necessarily So: How Media Make and Unmake the Scientific Picture of Reality* (Lanham, MD: Rowman & Littlefield, 2001), 36.

49. Mayes et al., "The Problem of Prenatal Cocaine Exposure," 406–407.

50. Gideon Koren and others, "Bias against the Null Hypothesis: The Reproductive Hazards of Cocaine," *Lancet* (16 December 1989): 1440, 1441.

51. Coles, "Saying 'Goodbye' to the 'Crack Baby,'" 291.

52. "Top Medical Doctors and Scientists Urge Major Media Outlets to Stop Perpetuating 'Crack Baby' Myth," PR Newswire (25 February 2004), retrieved from www.lexisnexis.com.

53. Ira J. Chasnoff, "Commentary: Missing Pieces of the Puzzle," *Neurotoxicology and Teratology* 15, no. 5 (September/October 1993): 287.

54. "Comedian Bill Cosby and Dr. Alvin F. Poussaint, Co-authors of 'Come On, People: On the Path from Victims to Victors,' Discuss Ideas from Their Book," *Meet the Press*, NBC (14 October 2007), transcript retrieved from www.lexisnexis.com.

55. Colbert I. King, "What They Didn't Do on Their Summer Vacation," *Washington Post* (15 July 2006): A21.

56. DeNeen L. Brown, "Crack, a Rift in Society: Two Decades after Its Arrival, Menacing Drug Shows No Signs of Moving On," *Washington Post* (28 August 2007): C1.

57. "Denise Jackson Prepares for Second 'American Idol' Audition," Associated Press (21 May 2007), retrieved from www.lexisnexis.com.

58. Devin Releford, "Life Gave Me a Script; I Rewrote It," *Atlanta Journal-Constitution* (9 June 2008): 13A.

59. Rebecca English, "Fisticuffs at 3 A.M.? Harry's at It Again," *Daily Mail* [London] (26 March 2007): 10.

60. Jan Moir, "Why We Shouldn't Be Too Hard on Poor Harry," *Daily Telegraph* [London] (28 March 2007): 19.

61. English, "Fisticuffs at 3 A.M.?"

62. Ibid.

63. See "Harry the Crack Baby," *Mail on Sunday* [London] (25 March 2007), retrieved from www.lexisnexis.com.

64. Moir, "Why We Shouldn't Be Too Hard on Poor Harry."

CHAPTER ELEVEN

1. See Rick Bragg, *I Am a Soldier, Too: The Jessica Lynch Story* (New York: Knopf, 2003), 115.

2. Todd S. Purdum, *A Time of Our Choosing: America's War in Iraq* (New York: Times Books, 2003), 132–133.

3. See Bragg, *I Am a Solider, Too*, 120, 155, 160. Lynch said of her injuries: "I've never felt so much pain in my whole, entire life. It was from my foot to my other foot, to my legs, to my arms, to my back, to my head. . . . I seriously thought I was going to be paralyzed for the rest of my life." See "Primetime Live Private Jessica Lynch: An American Story," *Primetime Live*, ABC (11 November 2003), transcript retrieved from www.lexisnexis.com.

4. Susan Schmidt and Vernon Loeb, "'She Was Fighting to the Death,'" *Washington Post* (3 April 2003): A1.

5. Media scholar Christopher Hanson, in a commentary in the *Columbia Journalism Review*, said the *Post*'s account bore an "uncanny resemblance" to the film *Courage under Fire*. See Hanson, "American Idol: The Press Finds the War's True Meaning," *Columbia Journalism Review*, July/August 2003: 59.

6. Milan Simonich and Cindi Lash, "Lynch's Instant Fame Defies Comparison," *Pittsburgh Post-Gazette* (13 April 2003): A1.

7. Jesse Leavenworth, "Army Supply Clerk Joins Legendary War Heroes," *Hartford Courant* (5 April 2003): A9.

8. Bill Lubinger, "Jessica Lynch's Hometown Praises Local Hero," *Plain Dealer* [Cleveland] (13 April 2003): A1.

9. Robin Gerber, "Finally Equalize Sexes in Combat," *USA Today* (23 April 2003): 11A.

10. Melani McAlister, "Saving Private Lynch," *New York Times* (6 April 2003): sec. 4, p. 13.

11. Richard Wallace, "Gulf War 2: Jessica Battled Like a Lion," *Daily Mirror* [London] (4 April 2003): 11.

12. Elaine Monagham, "Jessica Enters the Realms of Bonnie and Clyde," *Times* [London] (4 April 2003): 10.

13. Patrick Anidjar, "Shot and Stabbed: How Jess Kept Fighting," *Daily Telegraph* [Sydney] (4 April 2003): 1.

14. "War with Iraq: New Details in the Rescue of Pfc. Jessica Lynch," *Good Morning America*, ABC (3 April 2003), transcript retrieved from www.lexisnexis.com.

15. "Details are released about how previous POW Jessica Lynch fought the Iraqis until she ran out of ammunition," *Today Show*, NBC (3 April 2005), transcript retrieved from www.lexisnexis.com.

16. "Saving Private Lynch: Jessica Lynch Rescued from Iraqi Hospital," *Dateline*, NBC News Transcripts (6 April 2003), transcript retrieved from www.lexisnexis.com.

17. Cathy Young, a columnist for the *Boston Globe*, noted: "The eagerness to celebrate the prowess of women warriors was undoubtedly one of the reasons the media bought into the vastly exaggerated tale of Jessica Lynch's heroics during her capture by Iraqi troops in 2003." See Young, "Should Women Fight Wars?" *Boston Globe* (30 May 2005): A11.

18. Bragg, *I Am a Soldier, Too,* 71.

19. See ibid., 78. See also Richard S. Lowry, *Marines in the Garden of Eden* (New York: Berkley Caliber, 2006), 134.

20. Richard Keeble, "Information Warfare in an Age of Hyper-Militarism," in *Reporting War: Journalism in Wartime,* ed. Stuart Allan and Barbie Zelizer (London: Routledge, 2004), 44.

21. See David Usborne, "Sisters in Arms," [London] *Independent* (26 January 2013): 34. Referring to Lynch, Usborne wrote that "the Pentagon exaggerated her story as it waged a propaganda war, stating that she had fought back heroically against the enemy when in fact she had never fired her weapon."

22. See, for example, "Where are they now? In 2003, Army Private Jessica Lynch was the center of a dramatic story that grabbed the world," *Today Show,* NBC (17 September 2015), transcript retrieved from www.lexisnexis.com.

23. See, for example, Allison Barker, "Family of POW: She Wasn't Shot, Stabbed," Associated Press (3 April 2003); and "Rescued POW Had No Gunshot, Knife Wounds: Father," Agence France-Presse (3 April 2003). Articles retrieved from www.lexisnexis.com. The wire service reports were distributed the day the *Post* published its "fighting to the death" article. The Associated Press report quoted Lynch's father as saying: "We have heard and seen reports that she had multiple gunshot wounds and a knife stabbing. The doctor has not seen any of this. There's no entry (wounds) whatsoever."

24. Michael Getler, "A Long and Incomplete Correction," *Washington Post* (29 June 2003): B6.

25. As Christopher Hanson wrote in a commentary about the Lynch case, "Journalists are disinclined to puncture 'feel good' stories, especially those that they themselves have sent aloft." See Hanson, "American Idol." See also Jack Shafer, "What Took You So Long?" *Slate* (20 September 2004), www.slate.com/id/2106945. Writing about the reluctance of CBS News to address its flawed report in 2004 about President George W. Bush's military record, Shafer observed: "Once journalists commit themselves to a version of events or to a point of view, they are all too often unwilling to change their minds. . . . Sometimes investigative reporters fall down the rabbit hole and wave off any evidence that disturbs the thrust of their story."

26. Dana Priest, William Booth, and Susan Schmidt, "A Broken Body, a Broken Story, Pieced Together," *Washington Post* (17 June 2003): A1.

27. Hanson, "American Idol."

28. Priest, Booth, and Schmidt, "A Broken Body, a Broken Story," A16.

29. Ibid.

30. A critic of the *Post*'s stunning attempt to shift blame was Bill Sammon, formerly a reporter for the *Washington Times*. In his book, *Misunderestimated,* Sammon said that the *Post*'s attempt at blame shifting represented "a new low, even for the shameless American press." He added: "One of the most influential

newspapers in the nation was now holding the Bush Administration responsible for correcting the paper's own gross journalistic misdeeds. Instead of just coming clean and admitting its initial story was utterly bogus, the *Post* called it 'romanticized,' as if someone other than its own reporters had done the romanticizing." Sammon, *Misunderestimated: The President Battles Terrorism, John Kerry, and the Bush Haters* (New York: Regan Books, 2004), 226.

31. Getler, "A Long and Incomplete Correction."

32. Christopher Coker, *The Warrior Ethos: Military Culture and the War on Terror* (London: Routledge, 2007), 97.

33. Schmidt and Loeb, "'She Was Fighting to the Death.'"

34. See Sammon, *Misunderestimated*, 224.

35. Dave Peyton, "Jessica Lynch Remains a Hero in My Book," *Charleston* [WV] *Daily Mail* (23 March 2007): 4A. See also "Falsity: Military Smokescreen," *Charleston Gazette* (17 July 2008).

36. Richard Cohen, "On Not Admitting Our Mistakes," *Washington Post* (23 May 2003): A25. Cohen's column was very critical of the *Post*'s reporting of the Lynch case. "The original story about Lynch was played on the front page," he wrote. "Later, when it turned out that some of the gripping details in the story were questionable, the 'corrections'—although they were never labeled that—were played inside the paper. You are forgiven, therefore, if you do not have the facts on Jessica Lynch. They were extremely hard to get."

37. "Vernon Loeb, Defense Correspondent with the Washington Post, Tells about His Time Embedded with the U.S. Military in Iraq," *Fresh Air*, National Public Radio (15 December 2003), transcript retrieved from www.lexisnexis .com.

38. Quoted in Mark Bowden, "War and Remembrance: Sometimes Heroism Is a Moving Target," *New York Times* (8 June 2003): sec. 4, p. 1.

39. Quoted in Martha Irvine and David Crary, "American Idol: How Did Jessica Lynch Become a National Hero?" Associated Press (20 June 2003), retrieved from www.lexisnexis.com.

40. "Vernon Loeb, Defense Correspondent with the Washington Post," *Fresh Air*, National Public Radio (15 December 2003). Dana Priest, a veteran journalist who contributed to the *Post*'s hero-warrior story about Lynch, said she obtained information from two sources whom she described as "obscure people . . . not involved with the day-to-day Pentagon press machine." Both sources, she said in an interview, "had seen reports that quoted Iraqis talking to each other . . . saying that there was a woman and she was fighting" during the ambush at Nasiriyah. Priest also said her sources asked "that we cover their tracks" to avoid their being identified. See Esther Scott, "Reporting in the 'Fog of War': The Story of Jessica Lynch," Joan Shorenstein Center on the Press, Politics and Public Policy at the John F. Kennedy School of Government, Harvard University (2004): 8, www.shorensteincenter.org/wp-content/uploads/2012 /03/1773_0_scott.pdf. Scott noted that she had interviewed Priest on 6 March 2004.

41. "Washington Post's Vernon Loeb with Emerging Details of Jessica Lynch's Capture and Rescue," *The News with Brian Williams*, CNBC (3 April 2003), transcript retrieved from www.lexisnexis.com.

42. Alex Neill, "Remains Found at Iraqi Hospital to Be Flown to U.S.," *Military Times* (3 April 2003), posted at http://sctimes.gannettonline.com/gns /iraq/20030403-19986.shtml.

43. Frank Thorp, email to majority staff of Oversight and Government Reform Committee, U.S. House of Representatives (19 April 2007), quoted in "Misleading Information from the Battlefield: The Tillman and Lynch Episodes," Proposed Committee Report of Oversight and Government Reform Committee, U.S. House of Representatives (14 July 2008): 45. Ellipses in the original.

44. Joseph Coleman, "U.S. Military Hospital Says Former POW's Prognosis Is 'Excellent,'" Associated Press (4 April 2003). The French news agency Agence France-Presse quoted Rubenstein as saying, "She was not shot." See "Jessica Lynch 'Doing Well,' Joking, after POW Ordeal in Iraq," Agence France-Press (4 April 2003). The *Post* incorporated a reference to Rubenstein's comment in an article published 6 April 2003. The article said, in part: "Reports in the media, from The Washington Post and elsewhere, that Lynch suffered two entry and exit wounds were contradicted by the commander of the hospital, Col. David Rubenstein, who had said she was not shot or stabbed." The *Post* account muddied matters by quoting a cousin of Lynch as saying that the young woman's injuries were "'consistent with low-velocity, small-caliber rounds,' such as from a small rifle or handgun." See Daniel LeDuc, "Pentagon Identifies 8 Soldiers Killed in Ambush," *Washington Post* (6 April 2003): A14.

45. Bowden, "War and Remembrance."

46. Will Self, "A Tawdry Stunt in a Dirty War," *Evening Standard* [London] (4 April 2003): 13.

47. John Kampfner, "Saving Private Lynch Story 'Flawed,'" BBC News (15 May 2003), http://news.bbc.co.uk/2/hi/programmes/correspondent/3028585.stm.

48. See Jamie McIntyre, "Pentagon Calls BBC's Lynch Allegations 'Ridiculous,'" CNN.com (19 May 2003), http://cnn.com/2003/US/05/19/sprj.irq.bbc .lynch.dod/index.html.

49. Cited in "Hearing of the House Committee on Oversight and Government Reform; Subject: Misleading Information from the Battlefield," Federal News Service (24 April 2007), transcript retrieved from www.lexisnexis.com.

50. "Statement of Mr. Thomas F. Gimble, Acting Inspector General, Department of Defense," House Oversight and Government Reform Committee (24 April 2007).

51. See, for example, Deepa Kumar, "War Propaganda and the (Ab)uses of Women: Media Construction of the Jessica Lynch Story," *Feminist Media Studies* 4, no. 3 (2004): 297–313.

52. "Hyped Tale of Soldier's Rescue Isn't Only War Story in Need of More Digging," *Philadelphia Inquirer* (30 May 2003), retrieved from www .lexisnexis.com.

53. Scheherezade Faramarzi, "Hospital Staff Say Forceful U.S. Rescue Operation of American POW Wasn't Necessary," Associated Press (29 May 2003), retrieved from www.lexisnexis.com.

54. "In such a situation," Michael DeLong, a retired Marine lieutenant general, wrote in a book about the wars in Iraq and Afghanistan, "you always

assume the enemy is there." See DeLong with Noah Lukeman, *Inside CentCom: The Unvarnished Truth about the Wars in Afghanistan and Iraq* (Washington, DC: Regnery, 2004), 111. DeLong, the second-ranking officer in the U.S. Central Command during the first months of the Iraq War, also said of the Lynch rescue (111–112): "From my perspective, as one of the few people on the inside who witnessed the entire rescue op from beginning to end, it was one of the most spectacularly executed rescue operations I'd ever seen. . . . No one was in this operation for publicity—we were in it to save one of our own." Lynch, in an interview on ABC's *Primetime Live* program, called her rescuers "my true fact heroes. They risked their life. They are my heroes." See "Primetime Live Private Jessica Lynch," *Primetime Live.*

55. To have done anything else, wrote Lynch's biographer, "would have been foolish. Americans had been killed by Iraqis in robes and rags—and this hospital was where the guerrilla campaign had been planned and armed." See Bragg, *I Am a Soldier, Too,* 130.

56. Conditions in Nasiriyah "had been so violent and chaotic that the Americans could not be sure what they would find" at the hospital, noted Todd S. Purdum of the *New York Times.* See Purdum, *A Time of Our Choosing,* 170–171.

57. Richard S. Lowry, "The Story of Jessica Lynch: What Really Happened in Nasiriyah," *Weekly Standard* (24 April 2007), www.weeklystandard.com /article/14681.

58. Bragg, *I Am a Soldier, Too,* 119, 133.

59. Philip Smucker, "Chaos Reigns as Armed Looters Steal Drugs in Nasiriyah," *Daily Telegraph* [London] (4 April 2003): 4.

60. See, among others, Charisse Jones, "Lynch's Friends Line Streets," *USA Today* (22 July 2003): 3A.

61. David Lipsky, "Left Behind," *New York Times* (14 December 2003): sec. 7, p. 9.

62. Steve Ritea, "A Little Too Perfect?" *American Journalism Review,* August/September 2003: 10. See also Chris Tomlinson, "AP Impact: Pentagon Boosts Spending on PR," Associated Press (5 February 2009), retrieved from www.lexisnexis.com. Tomlinson wrote flatly that "initial accounts from the military about the rescue of Pvt. Jessica Lynch from Iraqi forces were faked to rally public support."

63. The poll results were reported in Richard Benedetto, "Support for U.S.-Led Invasion Remains Constant," *USA Today* (31 March 2003): 11A.

64. Richard Morin and Claudia Deane, "War Support Persists as Casualties Grow," *Washington Post* (25 March 2003): A22.

65. Richard Morin and Claudia Deane, "Poll: More Say War Justified without Finding Weapons," *Washington Post* (5 April 2003): A26.

66. "The Iraq War: Five Years On," *Observer* [London] (March 16, 2008): 8.

67. "How the US Lied to Itself," *Irish Times* (1 March 2008): 11.

68. The television critic for the *New York Daily News* said of *Saving Jessica Lynch:* "The movie . . . seems to direct its energies at avoiding controversy rather than clarifying conflicting accounts. What's really unfortunate, though, is

that the movie assiduously avoids giving any sense of the misrepresentation—and misinformation—that made Lynch a household name in the first place. Initial news reports of Lynch's story had her bravely emptying her gun, then stabbing her attackers, despite being shot and stabbed herself. That's nowhere in this telemovie. Subsequent disclosures that she was neither shot nor stabbed, but suffered injuries from a collision with a vehicle in her convoy? Not here, either." See David Bianculli, "Facts AWOL in TV Serving of 'Jessica Lynch,'" *Daily News* (7 November 2003): 119.

69. See "Lynch Named West Virginian of Year," Associated Press (28 December 2003), retrieved from www.lexisnexis.com. She was cited "for representing the state with dignity, grace and humility after her capture and rescue in Iraq became a source of inspiration for many and gave her uninvited fame."

70. Gavin McCormick, "A Year Later, Lynch Ponders Survival, Celebrity," Associated Press (1 April 2004), retrieved from www.lexisnexis.com.

71. Ibid.

72. See Eric Deggans, "Hype Only Muddies Lynch's Real Story," *St. Petersburg* [FL] *Times* (13 November 2003): 2B.

73. Wendy Cole, "10 Questions for Jessica Lynch," *Time* (15 August 2005): 6.

74. Arlene Walters, telephone interview with Andrew Knapp, the author's research assistant (4 April 2007).

75. See Lowry, *Marines in the Garden of Eden,* 134.

76. Ibid.

77. Ibid.

78. Ibid., 134–135.

79. Brigadier General Howard B. Bromberg, letter to Mrs. Norman C. Walters, n.d. Copy of letter provided by Mrs. Walters.

80. Lowry, *Marines in the Garden of Eden,* 134. Lowry wrote that Walters "was left in a situation that could have easily turned into the Iraqi radio report."

81. Quoted in "Attempt to Officially Recognize the Actions of Donald Walters, Who Was Killed Trying to Fight Off Iraqi Soldiers," *All Things Considered,* National Public Radio (23 March 2004), transcript retrieved from www.lexisnexis.com.

82. Nicholas D. Kristof, "Unbearable Emptiness," *New York Times* (28 July 2004): A15.

83. Steve Woodward and Paige Parker, "Clearing Up the Record," *Oregonian* (13 November 2003): A1. The *Oregonian* quoted Curtis Campbell, a sergeant in the 507th Maintenance Company as saying about Walters: "Based on the medical reports and the [Army's] investigation, he did everything that Lynch was first given credit for doing." Campbell was further quoted as saying: "He stayed and fought, and he fought heroically. He was the kind of guy who would fight to the last breath."

84. The Associated Press also reported on the case of mistaken identity, asserting that an improperly translated pronoun "helped catapult Pfc. Jessica Lynch to celebrity and left Walters' heroism in the shadows." See Randall Richard, "For Family of Sergeant Killed in Iraq, Clearer Picture of Son's Fate Finally Emerges," Associated Press (5 June 2004), retrieved from www.lexisnexis.com.

85. Norman Walters, telephone interview with the author (7 April 2007).

86. Arlene Walters, telephone interview with the author (7 April 2007).

87. Arlene Walters, telephone interview with Andrew Knapp, the author's research assistant (13 April 2007).

88. Norman Walters, telephone interview with the author.

89. Vernon Loeb, telephone interview with the author (1 October 2008).

90. Josh White, "Panel Vows to Pursue Tillman Case," *Washington Post* (25 April 2007): A4. Emphasis added.

91. Jessica Lynch, "Statement of Jessica Lynch Former Private U.S. Army," House Oversight and Government Reform Committee (24 April 2007), retrieved from www.lexisnexis.com.

92. Ashley Frantz, "For Years, Former POW Jessica Lynch Kept the Hurt Inside," CNN (20 July 2015), www.cnn.com/2015/07/20/us/jessica-lynch-where-is-she-now.

93. See, for example, Tom Vogt, "Symbol of Perseverance," *Columbian* [Vancouver, WA] (6 November 2015): A1.

94. See "Ex-POW Lynch: Rule on Women in Combat 'Good News,'" Associated Press (24 January 2013), article retrieved from www.lexisnexis.com.

95. See "Best Sellers," *New York Times* (30 November 2003): B26.

96. See Joanne Kaufman, "A Publishing Quandary: Do Excerpts Help Sales?" *New York Times* (11 June 2007): C6. A spokesman for Knopf Publishing Group, Paul Bogaards, reported that *I Am a Soldier, Too* sold 175,000 copies in hardcover—about half of what Knopf expected. Bogaards blamed prepublication excerpts that appeared in *Time* magazine, saying, "The excerpt gave away too much—I think people felt they'd had their fill."

97. Jeff Stein, "Jessica Lynch: The Untold Paragraph," *Washington Post* (19 November 2003): C1. Stein also wrote in his review: "There's just no there there. 'I Am a Soldier, Too' is hardly more than a tricked-out People magazine piece, cooked up by hucksters cashing in on her undeserved and mostly unsought fame. Of course, she could've gone on TV and dismissed the whole myth in 15 seconds, but nobody would have gotten paid. Even the public can smell the rot: Reportedly, book buyers are staying away in droves."

CHAPTER TWELVE

1. See, for example, Peter Whoriskey, "Microsoft's Ballmer on Yahoo and the Future," *Washington Post* (5 June 2008): D1; and Jack Shafer, "The Incredible Shrinking Newspaper," *Slate* (24 June 2006), www.slate.com/id/2144201.

2. Rachel Smolkin, "Adapt or Die," *American Journalism Review*, June/July 2006) 17–23.

3. Cited in Lindsey Tanner, "New Katrina Death Tally: Half of Victims 75 and Up," Associated Press (28 August 2008), retrieved from www.lexisnexis .com.

4. See Michael Perlstein, "Copping Out," *Times-Picayune* [New Orleans] (9 April 2006): 1. In all, the newspaper reported, 236 New Orleans police officers were fired for abandoning their posts or failing to report for duty after Katrina swept the city. Of those, 118 appealed their punishment.

5. Brian Thevenot of the *Times-Picayune* offered this vivid description of looting at a Wal-Mart store in New Orleans: "One man smashed the glass tops of jewelry cases, screaming, 'Free samples! Free samples!' Assembly lines ran from the electronics and computer sections to vans waiting outside, clogging the wide boulevard next to the Mississippi River. Cops and firefighters pushed carts alongside looters, who scrambled like coked-up ants through the massive store, slipping and sliding on its soaked and filthy floors. We interviewed looters and cops alike, finding conflicting accounts of how the store had been overrun—and why the authorities now helped loot it. Most cops stuck to the basics—but some joined the free-for-all." Thevenot, "Apocalypse in New Orleans," *American Journalism Review,* October/November 2005: 27.

6. "Editorial: An Open Letter to the President," *Times-Picayune* (4 September 2005): A15.

7. "City of New Orleans Falling Deeper into Chaos and Desperation," *American Morning,* CNN (2 September 2005), transcript retrieved from www .lexisnexis.com.

8. "The FEMA Director Michael Brown's Inexperience Spotlighted," *World News Tonight,* ABC (5 September 2005), transcript retrieved from www .lexisnexis.com.

9. Marc Fisher, "Essential Again," *American Journalism Review,* October/ November 2005: 20.

10. Ibid., 19. Fisher turned to Biblical allusions in praising the traditional media's performance in New Orleans, writing, "The levees broke and the city joined the sea, and the cameras bore witness and the ink-stained scribblers rose up from a vale of troubles to chronicle the days of the fearful and the forgotten."

11. Rem Rieder, "Playing Big: The Media's Impressive Coverage of Hurricane Katrina," *American Journalism Review,* October/November 2005: 6. Rieder wrote: "That the media performed well is hardly a surprise. Journalists live to cover the big story. Acts of nature—what one writer I know calls 'big weather'—have always brought out the best in reporters and news organizations."

12. Howard Kurtz, "Media Notes: At Last, Reporters' Feelings Rise to the Surface," *Washington Post* (5 September 2005): C1, C7.

13. "Tracking Hurricane Rita; Interview with Dan Rather," *Larry King Live,* CNN (20 September 2005), transcript retrieved from www.lexisnexis.com.

14. See House of Representatives, A Failure of Initiative: Final Report of the Select Bipartisan Committee to Investigate the Preparation for and Response to Hurricane Katrina (Washington, DC: U.S. Government Printing Office, 2007), 169.

15. See Beth Gillin, "Katrina Spawned Rumors; Media Ran with Them," *Philadelphia Inquirer* (28 September 2005): A2.

16. The Washington correspondent for Singapore's *Business Times,* Leon Hadar, invoked both analogies in a post-Katrina assessment, writing: "And when you want to imagine how 'solitary, poor, nasty, brutish, and short' life looks like, you will probably recall the scenes of anarchy and 'war of all against all,' in the movie Mad Max or in the book Lord of the Flies or in a television

documentary on Sudan or American-occupied Fallujah or . . . devastated New Orleans. The images of despair and horror that emanated from the battered Louisiana Superdome and the city's Convention Center for several days last week were being watched by television viewers all around the world." See Hadar, "Bush Faces Fight of His Political Life in Katrina," *Business Times* (6 September 2005), retrieved from www.lexisnexis.com. See also Rebecca Solnit, "Four Years On, Katrina Remains Cursed by Rumour, Cliche, Lies and Racism," *Guardian* [London] (26 August 2009),www.guardian.co.uk/commentisfree/2009/aug/26 /katrina-racism-us-media. Solnit said the erroneous and exaggerated news reports of violence in New Orleans in Katrina's aftermath promoted a "belief that a Hobbesian war of all-against-all had broken loose." She added, "Truth, the first casualty of war, is pretty imperilled in disasters, too."

17. Brian Thevenot and Gordon Russell, "Rape. Murder. Gunfights," *Times-Picayune* (26 September 2005): A1.

18. House of Representatives, *Failure of Initiative*, 360.

19. Ibid., 1.

20. Ibid., 249.

21. Ibid., 250. Volunteer medical personnel also were among the "self-deployments" to the stricken areas. See Shantell M. Kirkendoll, "Local Medical Team: Katrina Was 'Chaos,'" *Flint* [MI] *Journal* (16 September 2005): A1.

22. House of Representatives, *Failure of Initiative*, 170, 171.

23. Ibid., 249.

24. Ibid., 248.

25. Quoted in ibid., 361.

26. Jim Dwyer and Christopher Drew, "Fear Exceeded Crime's Reality in New Orleans," *New York Times* (29 September 2005): 1.

27. Christopher Cooper, "Misinformation Slowed Federal Response to Katrina," *Wall Street Journal* (30 September 2005): A4.

28. House of Representatives, *Failure of Initiative*, 248, 249.

29. Ibid., 248.

30. Quoted in Robert E. Pierre and Ann Gerhart, "News of Pandemonium May Have Slowed Aid," *Washington Post* (5 October 2005): A8.

31. Quoted in Matt Welch, "They Shoot Helicopters, Don't They?" *Reason*, December 2005, www.reason.com/news/show/36327.html.

32. House of Representatives, *Failure of Initiative*, 248.

33. Front page headlines posted at www.newseum.org/todaysfrontpages/?tfp _display = archive-date&tfp_archive_id = 090205.

34. Paula Zahn, "Desperation in New Orleans," Paula Zahn Now (CNN) (1 September 2005); transcript retrieved from www.lexisnexis.com.

35. John Burnett, "Looting, Snipers Mar New Orleans evacuation," *All Things Considered* (National Public Radio) (1 September 2005); transcript retrieved from www.lexisnexis.com.

36. David Ovalle, Phil Long, and Martin Merzer, "Death Toll in New Orleans Expected to Swell into Thousands," *Miami Herald* (1 September 2005), retrieved from www.lexisnexis.com.

37. Nicole Body and Corky Siemaszko, "Trapped in a Watery Hell," *New York Daily News* (2 September 2005): 2.

38. Allen G. Breed, "New Orleans in Anarchy with Fights, Rapes," Associated Press (1 September 2005), retrieved from www.lexisnexis.com.

39. "Superdome Evacuation Halted after Shots Are Fired at Helicopters," Associated Press (1 September 2005), retrieved from www.lexisnexis.com.

40. See Ralph Blumenthal, Joseph B. Treaster, and Maria Newman, "New Orleans Slipping toward Anarchy," *New York Times* (2 September 2005): 1.

41. Cited in House of Representatives, *Failure of Initiative*, 247.

42. Mike Madden, "Misery Deepens in New Orleans," Gannett News Service (3 September 2005), retrieved from www.lexisnexis.com.

43. "Death Toll in Louisiana Could Be above 10,000: US Senator," Agence France-Presse (2 September 2005), retrieved from www.lexisnexis.com. See also Gary Younge, "Criticism of Bush Mounts as More Than 10,000 Feared Dead," *Guardian* [London] (3 September 2005): 1.

44. Nagin said that "it wouldn't be unreasonable to have 10,000" Katrina-related fatalities in New Orleans. Quoted in Doug Simpson, "N.O. Mayor Says Death Toll Could Reach 10,000," Associated Press (5 September 2005), retrieved from www.lexisnexis.com.

45. Cited in House of Representatives, *Failure of Initiative*, 248

46. Cited in "In His Words: N.O. Police Superintendent Eddie Compass Was Emotional and Hyperbolic in the Days after Katrina; Many Comments Were Unsubstantiated," *Times-Picayune* (28 September 2005): A1.

47. Cited in House of Representatives, *Failure of Initiative*, 248.

48. Cited in Mike McDaniel, "Visiting Survivors, Oprah Seeks Stories that Haven't Been Told," *Houston Chronicle* (7 September 2005): 7.

49. House of Representatives, *Failure of Initiative*, 248.

50. Quoted in Joseph Channing, "Police Chief Says He Exaggerated Post-Katrina Crime," *New York Sun* (21 August 2006): 5.

51. See Andy Grimm, "Ray Nagin Now Federal Inmate No. 32751–034; 10-Year Sentence Begins in Texas," *Times-Picayune* (9 September 2014): A1.

52. David Carr, "More Horrible Than Truth: News Reports," *New York Times* (19 September 2005): C1.

53. Cited in Brian Thevenot, "Myth-Making in New Orleans," *American Journalism Review*, December 2005/January 2006: 33.

54. Jamie Doward, "After Hurricane Katrina: A Week on, the Scale of This Tragedy Emerges," *Guardian* [London] (4 September 2005): 4.

55. Mary Dejevsky, "When a First World City Is Plunged into the Third," *Independent* [London] (1 September 2005): 27.

56. Tim Reid and Jacqui Goddard, "Survivors Perish as Troops Try to Quell Anarchy," *Times* [London] (2 September 2005), retrieved from www.lexisnexis.com.

57. Giles Whittell, "Separating Fact from Fiction in New Orleans," *Times* [London] (19 September 2005): 20.

58. Ibid.

59. Thevenot and Russell, "Rape. Murder. Gunfights," A1.

60. Ibid., A4.

61. Susannah Rosenblatt and James Rainey, "Katrina Takes a Toll on Truth, News Accuracy," *Los Angeles Times* (27 September 2005), http://articles

.latimes.com/2005/sep/27/nation/na-rumors27. "Hyperbolic reporting spread through much of the media," Rosenblatt and Rainey reported.

62. Dwyer and Drew, "Fear Exceeded Crime's Reality."

63. Gillin, "Katrina Spawned Rumors."

64. Pierre and Gerhart, "News of Pandemonium May Have Slowed Aid."

65. Jennifer Harper, "Media, Blushing, Take a Second Look at Katrina," *Washington Times* (28 September 2005): A1.

66. See, for example, "Urban Myth Fact and Fiction Surrounding Katrina," *Good Morning America*, ABC News Transcripts (28 September 2005), transcript retrieved from www.lexisnexis.com. See also "Katrina Superdome Stories Not True? Blanco Goes to Washington," *Special Report with Brit Hume*, Fox News Network (28 September 2005), transcript retrieved from www.lexisnexis.com.

67. Gillin, "Katrina Spawned Rumors."

68. Thevenot, "Myth-Making in New Orleans," 32.

69. Ibid.

70. Dwyer and Drew, "Fear Exceeded Crime's Reality," 1.

71. Thevenot, "Myth-Making in New Orleans," 32.

72. Ibid.

73. Ibid.

74. Ibid.

75. James Wolcott, "Flooding the Spin Zone," *Vanity Fair*, November 2005: 176.

76. W. Lance Bennett, Regina G. Lawrence, and Steven Livingston, *When the Press Fails: Political Power and the News Media from Iraq to Katrina* (Chicago: University of Chicago Press, 2007), 167.

77. Jeffrey Dvorkin, "The Crisis in American Journalism: Is This the Best We Can Do under the Circumstances?" speech delivered to the 42nd Institute of Ethics in Journalism, sponsored by the Department of Journalism and Mass Communication at Washington & Lee University in Lexington, VA (10 November 2006), transcript at mc-399-228687451.us-east-1.elb.amazonaws.com/ccj/speeches/crisis-american-journalism-best-we-can-do-under-circumstances.

78. A notable exception was Rebecca Solnit's searching commentary published in London's *Guardian* in 2009, at the fourth anniversary of the Katrina disaster. See Solnit, "Four Years On."

79. Jonah Goldberg, "Storm of Malpractice: Katrina Was a Media Disaster," *National Review* (7 September 2007), www.nationalreview.com/article/222019/storm-malpractice-jonah-goldberg.

80. Cited in House of Representatives, *Failure of Initiative*, 361.

81. David Rieff, "Save Us from the Rescuers," *Los Angeles Times* (18 May 2008): M4. Rieff attributed exaggerated casualty estimates to relief organizations that compete "with every other sort of philanthropic cause for the charitable dollar and euro, and thus have to exaggerate to be noticed. It is also because coping with disasters for a living simply makes the worst-case scenario always seem the most credible one, and, honorably enough, relief workers feel they must always be prepared for the worst."

82. Tommy Tomlinson, Lee Hill Kavanaugh, and Martin Merzer, "New Horrors Discovered as Search-and-Recovery Effort Goes On," Knight-Ridder News Service (6 September 2005), retrieved from www.lexisnexis.com.

83. Joseph Scanlon, Suzane Alldred, Al Farrell, and Angela Prawzick, "Coping with the Media in Disasters: Some Predictable Problems," *Public Administration Review* 45 (January 1985): 124.

84. Thevenot, "Myth-Making in New Orleans," 32.

85. Ibid.

86. Ibid, 37.

87. Duncan Campbell, "Media: Reporters to the Rescue," *Guardian* (10 October 2005): 10.

88. Cited in Julie Moos, "Beyond the Headlines: Attribution, Verification and the Time Lapse," Poynter Institute (4 January 2006), www.poynter.org /2006/beyond-the-headlines-attribution-verification-and-the-time-lapse/73032. Libin invoked a well-known cliché in American journalism in stating, "If we believe that when your mama says she loves you, you should check it out, [then] surely what the mayor or police chief or governor says deserves at least some healthy skepticism and verification."

89. House of Representatives, *Failure of Initiative*, 361.

90. See George Melloan, "'I Read the News Today, Oh Boy,'" *Wall Street Journal* (11 October 2005): A17.

91. Thevenot, "Myth-Making in New Orleans," 37.

92. "Urban Myth: Fact and Fiction Surrounding Katrina," *Good Morning America*, ABC (28 September 2005), transcript retrieved from www.lexisnexis .com.

93. Donna Britt, "In Katrina's Wake, Inaccurate Rumors Sullied Victims," *Washington Post* (30 September 2005): B1. See also Anne Applebaum, "The Rumor Mill," *Washington Post* (5 October 2005): A23. Applebaum wrote: "As I am not the first to note, few would have believed that 25,000 white, middle-class suburbanites had reverted to an 'almost animalistic state' within a few days. But then, I'm not sure that 25,000 black middle-class suburbanites would have inspired such stories either, and certainly black officials such as Nagin and Compass wouldn't have repeated them. What I'm guessing the Katrina rumors revealed was not precisely racism but a much deeper fear of the poor, even of poverty itself."

94. Alicia C. Shepard, "Journalism's Prize Culture," *American Journalism Review*, April 2000: 22. Shepard also wrote (24), "In many large newsrooms, there's one person to handle the thankless task of assembling and shipping out dozens and dozens of entries for a proliferating array of journalism contests."

95. Alexander Cockburn, "Viewpoint: When It Comes to Self-Esteem, Journalists Take the Prize," *Wall Street Journal* (19 April 1984): 1.

96. See Dave Walker, "In the Spotlight of the Storm," *Times-Picayune* (1 August 2006). This was due to the station's having a "heavy-duty transmitter structure built on stilts," Walker reported.

97. "Katrina Coverage Earns Reporters Mongerson Prize," U.S. States News (9 May 2006) retrieved from www.lexisnexis.com, also available as a news release at www.northwestern.edu/newscenter/stories/2006/05/mongerson0.html.

CHAPTER THIRTEEN

1. "Some of My Finest Hours Have Been Spent on My Back Veranda, Smoking Hemp . . . (Quotation)," Monticello.org (accessed 12 July 2015), www .monticello.org/site/jefferson/some-my-finest-hours-have-been-spent-my-back-veranda-smoking-hemp-quotation.

2. Anna Berkes (reference librarian at Monticello), telephone interview with the author (14 August 2015).

3. The quotation also corresponds to the erroneous belief that the Declaration of Independence was written on hemp. It wasn't, although the notion persists that it was. See, for example, Frank Armstrong, "High Time Hemp's Bad Image Went up In Smoke," [London] *Sunday Times* (19 October 2014): 17. Carol Simpson, the weekend anchor of ABC's *World News Tonight* program, said of hemp during a program in 1995: "Here's something that was old that is becoming new again. It's a crop that Thomas Jefferson farmed, George Washington's soldiers wore uniforms made from it. The Declaration of Independence was written on it." See "Timothy McVeigh's Attorneys Portray New Image," *World News Sunday,* ABC News (25 June 1995), transcript retrieved from www.lexisnexis.com/.

4. The original, in French, read: "On parle de la conversion de l'eau en vin, à la noce de Cana, comme d'un miracle. Mais cette conversion est faite tous les jours par la bonté de Dieu devant nos yeux. Voilà l'eau qui tombe des cieux sur nos vignobles; là, elle entre les racines des vignes pour être changée en vin; preuve constante que Dieu nous aime, et qu'il aime à nous voir heureux." See Benjamin Franklin, letter to Abbé André Morellet (after 5 July 1779?), accessed 29 November 2015, http://franklinpapers.org/franklin/framedVolumes.jsp.

5. See, for example, Jeff Sommer, "Funny, But I've Heard This Market Song Before," *New York Times* (19 June 2011): BU5. Sommer, a business page columnist for the *New York Times*, demonstrated the quote's irresistible quality in writing: "'History doesn't repeat itself but it often rhymes,' as Mark Twain is often reputed to have said. (I've found no compelling evidence that he ever uttered that nifty aphorism. No matter—the line is too good to resist.)" The aphorism has been attributed to Twain by many other traditional news outlets in recent years, including the tabloid the *New York Post*. See, for example, "Hill Feels the Bern," *New York Post* (15 July 2015): 11; and Michael Goodwin, "Oh Hill No! We're Not for 'stale,'" *New York Post* (12 April 2015): 4.

6. See, for example, Robert S. McElvaine, "Their Party Crashed. Ours May Too," *Washington Post* (28 September 2008): B2. McElvaine began his essay about a near meltdown of the global economy in 2008 by writing: "'History doesn't repeat itself, but it rhymes.' Mark Twain was supposed to have said that, but even if he didn't, there's no denying that we're seeing proof of the adage in today's financial crisis."

7. See Garson O'Toole, "History Does Not Repeat Itself, But It Rhymes," *Quote Investigator* (blog) (12 January 2014), www.quoteinvestigator.com/2014 /01/12/history-rhymes. O'Toole wrote that "there is no substantive support for the Twain ascription."

8. "Quoting famous people and their famous sayings is a favorite trick of essay writers and speechifiers," a writer for the *Washington Post* observed in

2005. "Misquoting them is a close second." See Steven Luxenberg, "A Likely Story . . . and That's Precisely the Problem," *Washington Post* (17 April 2005): B4.

9. Thomas Jefferson to Alexander White (10 September 1797), in *The Works of Thomas Jefferson*, vol. 8 (New York and London, Putnam's Sons, 1904), 341.

10. Ralph Keyes, *"Nice Guys Finish Seventh": False Phrases, Spurious Sayings, and Familiar Misquotations* (New York: HarperCollins, 1992), 12.

11. Louis Menand, "Books: Notable Quotables," *New Yorker* (19 February 2007), www.newyorker.com/magazine/2007/02/19/notable-quotables.

12. Ralph Keyes, *The Quote Verifier: Who Said What, Where, and When* (New York: St. Martin's Griffin, 2006), xviii.

13. Carl M. Cannon, "Putting Words in Mark Twain's Mouth," RealClear-Politics (10 December 2012), www.realclearpolitics.com/articles/2012/12/10/fake_twain_quotes_and_other_hazards_of_twitter_116376.html.

14. See Thomas S. Kidd, "Misquoting Patrick Henry: The Internet and Bogus Sayings of the Founders," *HuffPost Politics* (blog) (1 February 2012), www.huffingtonpost.com/thomas-s-kidd/patrick-henry-quotes_b_1247107 .html.

15. Quoted in Cameron McWhirter, "To Quote Thomas Jefferson, 'I Never Actually Said That,'" *Wall Street Journal* (6 December 2012): A1, A13.

16. Bill Laitner, "Mich. Pot Supporters to Promote Clout Through $2 Bills," *Detroit Free Press* (9 July 2013), retrieved from www.lexisnexis.com.

17. See *Stossel*, Fox Business Network (13 September 2012), transcript retrieved from www.lexisnexis.com.

18. Norbert Cunningham, "Keeping It Real in Debate over Legal Marijuana," *Times-Transcript* [Moncton, New Brunswick] (17 August 2013): D6.

19. See "Quote of the Day," *Prince George Citizen* (9 December 2013): A2.

20. "Is America Going to Pot?" [New Delhi] *Sunday Guardian* (24 November 2012), retrieved from www.lexisnexis.com.

21. See "Editors' Note: November 22, 2014" appended to Joyce Wadler, "I Was Misinformed: Fear of Kim Kardashian's Derrière," *New York Times* (21 November 2014), www.nytimes.com/2014/11/23/style/fear-of-kim-kardashians-derriere.html.

22. Quoted in Erik Wemple, "The Daily Currant Strikes the New York Times over Kardashian-West Butt Comparisons," *Washington Post* (24 November 2014), www.washingtonpost.com/blogs/erik-wemple/wp/2014/11/24/the-daily-currant-strikes-the-new-york-times-over-kardashian-west-butt-comparisons. As Wemple noted, a blogger for the *Washington Post* once treated as factual a *Daily Currant* report that Sarah Palin, the Republican vice presidential candidate in 2008, had joined the Al Jazeera America network. The *Post* said in its correction that its "blogger cited a report on the Daily Currant website as the basis for that information without realizing that the piece was satirical." See "Correction" appended to Suzi Parker, "She the People: Sarah Palin Tries to Stay Relevant," *Washington Post* (12 February 2013), www.washingtonpost .com/blogs/she-the-people/wp/2013/02/12/sarah-palins-when-politics-and-celebrity-meet.

23. Michelle Yee He Lee, "Fact Checker: No, Tom Cotton Did Not Say This Fake Quote," *Washington Post* (23 March 2015), www.washingtonpost.com /blogs/fact-checker/wp/2015/03/23/no-tom-cotton-did-not-say-this-fake-quote.

24. Shane Fitzgerald, "Lazy Journalism Exposed by Online Hoax," *Irish Times* (7 May 2009), www.irishtimes.com/opinion/lazy-journalism-exposed-by-online-hoax-1.760229.

25. See Siobhain Butterworth, "Open Door: The Readers' Editor on . . . Web Hoaxes and the Pitfalls of Quick Journalism," *Guardian* [London] (4 May 2009): 31.

26. See John Riley, "Maurice Jarre: Composer Who Won Three Oscars for His Work with David Lean," *Independent* [London] (31 March 2009): 40.

27. See Shawn Pogatchnik, "Irish Student Hoaxes World's Media with Fake Quote," Associated Press (12 May 2009), retrieved from www.lexisnexis.com/.

28. See the YouTube video of Oliver's comments at "John Oliver (HBO) – Quotations – Last Week Tonight" (18 December 2015), www.youtube.com /watch?v=C_h7vEoflAc.

29. Quoted in Sharman Stein, "Reagan Gives Lincoln Credit That's Not Due," *Chicago Tribune* (19 August 1992), http://articles.chicagotribune.com /1992-08-19/news/9203150694_1_congressional-record-words-private-property. See also Herbert Mitang, "For the Record, Reagan Put Words in Lincoln's Mouth," New York Times (19 August 1992): A13.

30. See Glenn Kessler, "Fact Checker: Gov. Kasich Repeats a Lincoln Whopper," *Washington Post* (27 January 2015), www.washingtonpost.com/blogs /fact-checker/wp/2015/01/27/gov-kasich-repeats-a-lincoln-whopper.

31. See Edward Steers Jr., *Lincoln Legends: Myths, Hoaxes, and Confabulations Associated with Our Greatest President* (Lexington: University of Kentucky, 2007), 91–92. See also Paul F. Boller Jr. and John H. George, *They Never Said It: A Book of Fake Quotes, Misquotes, and Misleading Attributions* (New York: Oxford University, 1989), 83–84.

32. John J. Pitney Jr., "Honest, Mr. President, Abe Never Said It," NPR (25 March 2010), www.npr.org/templates/story/story.php?storyId=125169095.

33. "Remarks by the President to the House Democratic Congress," White House Office of the Press Secretary (20 March 2010), www.whitehouse.gov /the-press-office/remarks-president-house-democratic-congress.

34. See Boller and George, *They Never Said It*, 82. See also McWhirter, "To Quote Thomas Jefferson," A13.

35. See Nancy Badertscher, "PolitiFact: The Roundup," *Atlanta Journal-Constitution* (24 February 2014): 2B.

36. See Kee Malesky, "Follow the Money: On the Trail of Watergate Lore," National Public Radio (16 June 2012), www.npr.org/2012/06/16/154997482 /follow-the-money-on-the-trail-of-watergate-lore.

37. Max Holland, *Leak: Why Mark Felt Became Deep Throat* (Lawrence: University of Kansas, 2012), 86.

38. William Goldman took credit in 2005 for writing the line into the movie. See Frank Rich, "Don't Follow the Money," *New York Times* (12 June 2005): sec. 4, p. 14. Rich quoted Goldman as saying after Felt revealed that he had been the Deep Throat source: "I just want you to remember that I wrote

'Follow the money.'" Goldman's screenplay of *All the President's Men* won an Academy Award for Best Adapted Screenplay. See also Holland, *Leak,* 172.

39. "Follow the money" probably originated as a Hollywood term. An actor named George Hiken invoked the phrased in 1971 in referring to Hollywood stars. Hiken wrote: "I know that stars go through hell to get where they are, but that doesn't make it easier to take their bullying, to sit through their tempers and nerves. To work with them is depressing. In Hollywood, they tell the camera and lights to 'follow the money.' It's the same in New York. I learned to deal with them, to sympathize, and take their acting notes, and the notes from their agents, husbands, or wives." See Hiken, "Don't Give My Regards to Broadway," *New York Times* (22 August 1971): D1.

40. Lawrence E. Pintak, email correspondence with the author (14 February 2011).

41. Paul Mark Wadleigh, email correspondence with the author (14 February 2011).

42. See W. Joseph Campbell, "Suspect Murrow Quote Pulled at Murrow School," *Media Myth Alert* (blog) (17 February 2011), www.mediamythalert. wordpress.com/2011/02/17/suspect-murrow-quote-pulled-at-murrow-school.

43. Harry Reid, then the majority leader of the U.S. Senate, invoked the half-true Murrow quotation in 2006, in urging changes to U.S. policy in Iraq. "Demanding a change of course is not irresponsible, it's not unpatriotic, it is the right thing to do," Reid said, adding, "As Edward R. Murrow once said: 'We must not confuse dissent with disloyalty. When the loyal opposition dies, I think the soul of America dies with it.'" See "U.S. Senator Harry Reid's Remarks on Iraq Policy as Prepared for Delivery on the Senate Floor," Political Transcript Wire (22 June 2006), retrieved from ProQuest database. A book critic for the *Washington Post* included the quotation in a review in 2003, in which he said he was reminded of "Edward R. Murrow's remark half a century ago, at the height of the McCarthy era: 'We must not confuse dissent with disloyalty. When the loyal opposition dies, I think the soul of America dies with it.' Wise words then, wise words now." See Fredrik Logevall, "How It Was," *Washington Post* (1 June 2003): T9.

44. Megan McArdle, "Anatomy of a Fake Quotation," *Atlantic* (3 May 2011), www.theatlantic.com/national/archive/2011/05/anatomy-of-a-fake-quotation/238257. See also Andrew Ferguson, "What Al Wishes Abe Said," *Washington Post* (10 June 2007): B5.

45. See, "Some of My Finest Hours," Monticello.org.

46. Berkes, telephone interview with the author (14 August 2015).

47. See Anna Berkes, "This Is How Bogus Quotes Are Born" (28 March 2009),www.monticello.org/site/blog-and-community/posts/how-bogus-quotes-are-born.

48. Berkes, telephone interview with the author (14 August 2015).

49. See "Growing a Revolution: America's Founding Gardeners," *Science Friday,* National Public Radio (1 July 2011), transcript retrieved from www .lexisnexis.com/.

50. See Michael Karnish, *Flight from Monticello: Thomas Jefferson at War* (London: Oxford University, 2010). Karnish wrote: "The British had chased

Governor Jefferson from the capital of Richmond and they had come within minutes of capturing him in his study at Monticello. Jefferson vacated the governorship, fled his beloved mountaintop [at Monticello], galloped through forests, forded rivers, and climbed through passes to reach the remote fields of his Poplar Forest plantation," where he and his family found refuge (xi). Karnish noted that many Virginians, "not to mention the British, did not know Jefferson owned the property" (295). Jefferson spent the fifth anniversary of the Declaration of Independence in hiding at the plantation.

51. Berkes, telephone interview with the author (14 August 2015).

52. "Some of My Finest Hours," Monticello.org. Robert Deitch, in his book about the history of hemp, claimed that Jefferson "noted in his diary that he smoked hemp for relief from migraine headaches." Deitch provided no citation in support of his claim, however. See Deitch, *Hemp—American History Revisited: The Plant with a Divided History* (New York: Algora Publishing, 2003), 26.

53. See "Peace Is That Brief Glorious Moment in History . . . (Quotation)," Monticello.org (accessed 30 November 2015), www.monticello.org/site/jefferson/peace-brief-glorious-moment-historyquotation.

54. See Jonah Goldberg, "The Left's Illogical Logic of Diversity," *National Review* (28 November 2015), www.nationalreview.com/article/427696/campus-protests-diversity-liberal-illogic.

55. See "Address before the Young Men's Lyceum of Springfield, Illinois" (27 January 1838) in *Collected Works of Abraham Lincoln*, vol. 1, accessed 30 November 2015, http://quod.lib.umich.edu/l/lincoln/lincoln1/1:130?rgn=div1;sort=occur;subview=detail;type=simple;view=fulltext;q1=asia.

56. See "Quotations: Quotations Falsely Attributed," Churchill Centre (accessed 30 November 2015), www.winstonchurchill.org/resources/quotations/135-quotes-falsely-attributed.

57. Keyes, *Quote Verifier*, xvi. "Quotes without citations," Keyes wrote, "should be treated with the utmost suspicion."

58. Ibid., xviii. Most quotation-aggregation sites, Keyes wrote, "simply cut and paste material from each other."

59. Cited in James Jeffrey, "Strewth!" *Australian* (28 November 2015): 24. Jeffrey described the phony quotation as one of "the more concise reminders that there's a lot of misattribution floating around in cyberspace."

CONCLUSION

1. See Denis McQuail, *McQuail's Mass Communication Theory*, 5th ed. (London: Sage, 2005), 65.

2. Robert J. Samuelson, "The Limits of Media Power," *Washington Post* (2 October 2003): A23.

3. McQuail, *Mass Communication Theory*, 456, 457.

4. See, for example, Herbert J. Gans, "Reopening the Black Box: Toward a Limited Effects Theory," *Journal of Communication* 43, no. 4 (Autumn 1993): 33.

5. Ibid.

6. See "Trends in News Consumption: 1991–2012: In Changing News Landscape, Even Televsion Is Vulnerable," Pew Research Center for the People and the Press (27 September 2012), www.people-press.org/files/legacy-pdf/2012%20News%20Consumption%20Report.pdf, p. 10.

7. Ibid. News about crime is a distant second to weather-related news, according to Pew Research. Twenty-eight percent of Americans say they follow crime news "very closely."

8. Mark Bowden, "Sometimes Heroism Is a Moving Target," *New York Times* (8 June 2003): sec. 4, p. 1.

9. See Jay Bookman, "Deep Throat Myth Better Than Reality," *Atlanta Journal-Constitution* (2 June 2005): 15A.

10. Jack Shafer, "Previously Thought to Be True," *Slate* (4 June 2004), www.slate.com/id/2101754.

11. David Murray, Joel Schwartz, and S. Robert Lichter, *It Ain't Necessarily So: How Media Make and Unmake the Scientific Picture of Reality* (Lanham, MD: Rowman & Littlefield, 2001), 36.

12. Amanda Hinnant and Maria Len-Rios, "Tacit Understanding of Health Literacy: Interview and Survey Research with Health Journalists," paper presented at the annual convention of the Association for Education in Journalism and Mass Communication, Chicago, IL (August 2008): 9.

13. Gary Schwitzer, "How Do U.S. Journalists Cover Treatments, Tests, Products, and Procedures? An Evaluation of 500 Stories," *PloS Medicine* 5, no. 5 (27 May 2008), http://journals.plos.org/plosmedicine/article?id = 10.1371/journal.pmed.0050095.

14. Michael Kelly, "The Know-Nothing Media," *Washington Post* (10 November 1999): A39.

15. Thirty-four percent described themselves as "liberal," and 54 percent said they were "moderate." See "How Journalists See Journalists in 2004," report by the Pew Research Center for the People and the Press, in association with the Project for Excellence in Journalism and the Committee of Concerned Journalists (May 2004), 3. See also Jennifer Harper, "Poll Shows Liberal Tilt Escalates in Newsrooms," *Washington Times* (25 May 2004): A4.

16. See "The Web: Alarming, Appealing and a Challenge to Journalistic Values," Pew Research Center for the People and the Press, in association with and the Project for Excellence in Journalism (17 March 2008): 18. The ideological composition reported among national journalists surveyed in 2008 was: 8 percent "conservative," 32 percent "liberal," and 53 percent "moderate."

17. Quoted in Deborah Howell, "Remedying the Bias Perception," *Washington Post* (16 November 2008): B6. Howell, who was the *Post*'s ombudsman, or in-house critic, at the time, wrote: "Journalism naturally draws liberals; we like to change the world. . . . There are centrists at The Post as well. But the conservatives I know here feel so outnumbered that they don't even want to be quoted by name in a memo."

18. See, for example, Thomas Friedman, "Connect the Dots," *New York Times* (25 September 2003): 27. Friedman, an award-winning international affairs columnist for the *Times,* wrote: "Sure, poverty doesn't cause terrorism—no one is killing for a raise. But poverty is great for the terrorism business

because poverty creates humiliation and stifled aspirations and forces many people to leave their traditional farms to join the alienated urban poor in the cities—all conditions that spawn terrorists."

19. Alan B. Krueger, *What Makes a Terrorist: Economics and the Roots of Terrorism* (Princeton, NJ: Princeton University Press, 2007), 13.

Select Bibliography

BOOKS

Abbot, Willis J. *Watching the World Go By*. Boston: Little, Brown, 1933.

Abell, Tyler, ed. *Drew Pearson Diaries: 1949–1959*. New York: Holt, Rinehart, and Winston, 1974.

Aguilar, Luis. *Operation Zapata: The "Ultrasensitive" Report and Testimony of the Board of Inquiry on the Bay of Pigs*. Frederick, MD: University Publications of America, 1981.

Alterman, Eric. *Who Speaks for America? Why Democracy Matters in Foreign Policy*. Ithaca, NY: Cornell University Press, 1998.

Anderson, Douglas A. *A "Washington Merry-Go-Round" of Libel Actions*. Chicago: Nelson-Hall, 1980.

Aronson, James. *The Press and the Cold War*. Boston: Beacon Press, 1970.

Bagdikian, Ben H. *The New Media Monopoly*. Boston: Beacon Press, 2004.

Baker, Russell. *The Good Times*. New York: Penguin Group, 1990.

Bartholomew, Robert E. *Little Green Men, Meowing Nuns and Head-Hunting Panics: A Study of Mass Psychogenic Illness and Social Delusion*. Jefferson, NC: McFarland & Co., 2001.

Bayley, Edwin R. *Joe McCarthy and the Press*. New York: Pantheon Books, 1981.

Bernstein, Carl, and Bob Woodward, *All the President's Men*. New York: Simon & Schuster, 1974.

Bradley, Patricia. *Women and the Press: The Struggle for Equality*. Evanston, IL: Northwestern University Press, 2005.

Bragg, Rick. *I Am a Soldier, Too: The Jessica Lynch Story*. New York: Knopf, 2003.

Brown, Charles H. *The Correspondents' War: Journalists in the Spanish-American War*. New York: Charles Scribner's Sons, 1967.

Brown, Robert J. *Manipulating the Ether: The Power of Broadcast Radio in Thirties America.* Jefferson, NC: McFarland & Co., 1998.

Califano, Joseph A., Jr. *Inside: A Public and Private Life.* New York: Public-Affairs, 2004.

Campbell, W. Joseph. *The Year That Defined American Journalism: 1897 and the Clash of Paradigms.* New York: Routledge, 2006.

———. *Yellow Journalism: Puncturing the Myths, Defining the Legacies.* Westport, CT: Praeger, 2001.

Cantril, Hadley. *The Invasion from Mars.* New York: Harper & Row, 1966.

Carey, James W., ed. *Media, Myths, and Narratives: Television and the Press.* Newbury Park, CA: Sage, 1988.

Carter, William Harding. *The Life of Lieutenant General Chaffee.* Chicago: University of Chicago Press, 1917.

Castro, Fidel, and José Ramón Fernández. *Playa Girón/Bay of Pigs: Washington's First Military Defeat in the Americas.* New York: Pathfinder, 2001.

Chong, Denise. *The Girl in the Picture: The Story of Kim Phuc, the Photograph, and the Vietnam War.* New York: Viking, 2000.

Churchill, Allen. *Park Row.* New York: Rinehart, 1958.

Cloud, Stanley, and Lynne Olson. *The Murrow Boys: Pioneers on the Front Lines of Broadcast Journalism.* New York: Houghton Mifflin, 1996.

Cohen, Michael A. *American Maelstrom: The 1968 Election and the Politics of Division.* New York: Oxford University Press, 2016.

Creelman, James. *On the Great Highway: The Wanderings and Adventures of a Special Correspondent.* Boston: Lothrop, 1901.

Crossen, Cynthia. *Tainted Truth: The Manipulation of Fact in America.* New York: Simon & Schuster, 1994.

Davis, Flora. *Moving the Mountain: The Women's Movement in America since 1960.* New York: Simon & Schuster, 1991.

Dean, John. *Lost Honor.* Los Angeles: Stratford Press, 1982.

Delong, Michael, with Noah Lukeman. *Inside CentCom: The Unvarnished Truth about the Wars in Afghanistan and Iraq.* Washington, DC: Regnery, 2004.

Doherty, Thomas. *Cold War, Cool Medium: Television, McCarthyism, and American Culture.* New York: Columbia University Press, 2003.

Downie, Leonard, Jr. *The New Muckrakers.* Washington, DC: New Republic, 1976.

Echols, Alice. *Daring to Be Bad: Radical Feminism in America, 1967–1975.* Minneapolis: University of Minnesota Press, 1989.

Edwards, Bob. *Edward R. Murrow and the Birth of Broadcast Journalism.* Hoboken, NJ: Wiley & Sons, 2004.

Ehrlich, Matthew C. *Journalism in the Movies.* Urbana: University of Illinois Press, 2004.

Emery, Fred. *Watergate: The Corruption of American Politics and the Fall of Richard Nixon.* New York: Times Books, 1994.

Epstein, Edward Jay. *Between Fact and Fiction: The Problem of Journalism.* New York: Vintage Books, 1975.

Faludi, Susan. *Backlash: The Undeclared War against American Women.* New York: Crown, 1991.

———. *The Terror Dream: What 9/11 Revealed about America.* New York: Metropolitan Books, 2007.

Freedman, Samuel G. *Letters to a Young Journalist.* New York: Basic, 2006.

Friendly, Fred W. *Due to Circumstances beyond Our Control.* New York: Random House, 1967.

Garment, Leonard. *In Search of Deep Throat: The Greatest Political Mystery of Our Time.* New York: Basic Books, 2000.

Garner, Joe. *Stay Tuned: Television's Unforgettable Moments.* Kansas City: Andrews McMeel, 2002.

Goldman, Gerald Jay, and Robert Goldberg. *Anchors: Brokaw, Jennings, Rather, and the Evening News.* Secaucus, NJ: Carol Publishing, 1990.

Goode, Erich. *Collective Behavior.* Fort Worth: Saunders College Publishing, 1992.

Gray, L. Patrick, III, with Ed Gray. *In Nixon's Web: A Year in the Crosshairs of Watergate.* New York: Times Books, 2008.

Greenberg, David. *Nixon's Shadow: The History of an Image.* New York: Norton, 2003.

Griffith, Robert. *The Politics of Fear.* Amherst: University of Massachusetts Press, 1987.

Hallin, Daniel C. *The Uncensored War: The Media and Vietnam.* Berkeley: University of California Press, 1989.

Harrower, Tim. *Inside Reporting: A Practical Guide to the Craft of Journalism.* Boston: McGraw-Hill, 2006.

Havill, Adrian. *Deep Truth: The Lives of Bob Woodward and Carl Bernstein.* Secaucus, NJ: Carol Publishing, 1993.

Herman, Arthur. *Joseph McCarthy: Reexamining the Life and Legacy of America's Most Hated Senator.* New York: Free Press, 2000.

Herring, George C. *LBJ and Vietnam: A Different Kind of War.* Austin: University of Texas Press, 1994.

Hole, Judith, and Ellen Levine. *Rebirth of Feminism.* New York: Quadrangle Books, 1971.

Holland, Max. *Leak: Why Mark Felt Became Deep Throat.* Lawrence: University Press of Kansas, 2012.

Huey Chong, Sylvia Shin. *The Oriental Obscene: Violence and Racial Fantasies in the Vietnam Era.* Durham, NC: Duke University Press, 2011.

Jackaway, Gwenyth L. *Media at War: Radio's Challenge to the Newspapers, 1924–1939.* Westport, CT: Praeger, 1995.

Johnson, Lyndon Baines. *The Vantage Point: Perspectives of the Presidency, 1963–1969.* New York: Holt, Rinehart, and Winston, 1971.

Johnson, Paul. *Modern Times: The World from the Twenties to the Nineties,* rev. ed. New York: HarperCollins, 1991.

Karnish, Michael. *Flight from Monticello: Thomas Jefferson at War.* London: Oxford University, 2010.

Kern, Montague, Patricia Levering, and Ralph Levering. *The Kennedy Crisis: The Press, the Presidency, and Foreign Policy*. Chapel Hill: University of North Carolina Press, 1983.

Keyes, Ralph. *"Nice Guys Finish Seventh": False Phrases, Spurious Sayings, and Familiar Misquotations*. New York: HarperCollins, 1992.

———. *The Quote Verifier: Who Said What, Where, and When*. New York: St. Martin's Griffin, 2006.

Koch, Howard. *The Panic Broadcast*. Boston: Little, Brown, 1970.

Kosner, Edward. *It's News to Me: The Making and Unmaking of an Editor*. Cambridge, MA: Da Capo Press, 2007.

Kranish, Michael. *Flight from Monticello: Thomas Jefferson at War*. London: Oxford University, 2010.

Kraus, Sidney, ed. *The Great Debates: Kennedy v. Nixon, 1960*. Bloomington: Indiana University Press, 1977.

Krueger, Alan B. *What Makes a Terrorist: Economics and the Roots of Terrorism*. Princeton, NJ: Princeton University Press, 2007.

Kurlansky, Mark. *1968: The Year That Rocked the World*. New York: Ballantine Books, 2004.

Kutler, Stanley I., ed. *Abuse of Power: The New Nixon Tapes*. New York: Free Press, 1997.

———. *The Wars of Watergate: The Last Crisis of Richard Nixon*. New York: Knopf, 1990.

Lang, Gladys Engel, and Kurt Lang. *The Battle for Public Opinion: The President, the Press, and the Polls during Watergate*. New York: Columbia University Press, 1983.

Leaming, Barbara. *Orson Welles: A Biography*. New York: Penguin Books, 1985.

Lembcke, Jerry. *The Spitting Image: Myth, Memory, and the Legacy of Vietnam*. New York: New York University Press, 1998.

Lowry, Richard S. *Marines in the Garden of Eden*. New York: Berkley Caliber, 2006.

Lubow, Arthur. *The Reporter Who Would Be King*. New York: Macmillan, 1992.

Marine, Gene. *A Male Guide to Women's Liberation*. New York: Holt, Rhinehart and Winston, 1972.

Martel, Myles. *Political Campaign Debates: Images, Strategies, and Tactics*. New York: Longman, 1983.

McPherson, James Brian. *Journalism at the End of the American Century, 1965–Present*. Westport, CT: Praeger, 2006.

McQuail, Denis. *McQuail's Mass Communication Theory*, 5th ed. London: Sage, 2005.

Mencher, Melvin. *Melvin Mencher's News Reporting and Writing*, 11th ed. Boston: McGraw-Hill, 2008.

Miller, David L. *Introduction to Collective Behavior*. Prospect Heights, IL: Waveland Press, Inc., 1989.

Morgan, Robin. *Going Too Far: The Personal Chronicle of a Feminist*. New York: Random House, 1977.

———. *Saturday's Child: A Memoir.* New York: Norton, 2001.

Murray, David, Joel Schwartz, and S. Robert Lichter. *It Ain't Necessarily So: How Media Make and Unmake the Scientific Picture of Reality.* Lanham, MD: Rowman & Littlefield, 2001.

Nasaw, David. *The Chief: The Life of William Randolph Hearst.* Boston: Houghton Mifflin, 2000.

Oberdorfer, Don. *Tet!* Garden City, NY: Doubleday, 1971.

O'Neil, Robert M. *The First Amendment and Civil Liability.* Bloomington: Indiana University Press, 2001.

Perlmutter, David D. *Photojournalism and Foreign Policy: Icons of Outrage in International Crises.* Westport, CT: Praeger, 1998.

Pietrusza, David. *1960: LBJ vs. JFK vs. Nixon: The Epic Campaign That Forged Three Presidencies.* New York: Union Square Press, 2008.

Purdum, Todd S. *A Time of Our Choosing: America's War in Iraq.* New York: Times Books, 2003.

Pyle, Richard, and Horst Faas. *Lost over Laos: A True Story of Tragedy, Mystery, and Friendship.* Cambridge, MA: Da Capo Press, 2003.

Reston, James. *Deadline: A Memoir.* New York: Random House, 1991.

Roberts, Chalmers M. *First Rough Draft: A Journalist's Journal of Our Times.* New York: Praeger, 1973.

Ryan, Alan, ed. *The Reader's Companion to Cuba.* San Diego: Harcourt Brace, 1997.

Sabato, Larry J. *The Kennedy Half-Century: The Presidency, Assassination, and Last Legacy of John F. Kennedy.* New York: Bloomsbury, 2013.

Salinger, Pierre. *With Kennedy.* Garden City, NY: Doubleday, 1966.

Salisbury, Harrison E., *Without Fear or Favor: The New York Times and Its Times.* New York: Times Books, 1980.

Sammon, Bill. *Misunderestimated: The President Battles Terrorism, John Kerry, and the Bush Haters.* New York: Regan Books, 2004.

Schlesinger, Arthur M., Jr. *A Thousand Days: John F. Kennedy in the White House.* Boston: Houghton Mifflin, 1965.

Schoen, Douglas E. *On the Campaign Trail: The Long Road of Presidential Politics, 1860–2004.* New York: Harper Perennial, 2004.

Schudson, Michael. *Discovering the News: A Social History of American Newspapers.* New York: Basic Books, 1978.

———. *The Power of News.* Cambridge, MA: Harvard University Press, 1996.

———. *Watergate in American Memory: How We Remember, Forget, and Reconstruct the Past.* New York: Basic Books, 1992.

Sconce, Jeffrey. *Haunted Media: Electronic Presence from Telegraphy to Television.* Durham, NC: Duke University, 2000.

Shepard, Alicia. *Woodward and Bernstein: Life in the Shadow of Watergate.* Hoboken, NJ: Wiley & Sons, 2007.

Sherman, Janann. *No Place for a Woman: A Life of Senator Margaret Chase Smith.* New Brunswick, NJ: Rutgers University Press, 2000.

Shipler, David K. *Freedom of Speech: Mightier Than the Sword.* New York: Knopf, 2015.

Shoemaker, Pamela J., ed. *Communication Campaigns about Drugs: Government, Media, and the Public.* Hillsdale, NJ: Lawrence Erlbaum Associates, 1989.

Shuman, Edwin Llewellyn. *Steps into Journalism: Helps and Hints for Young Writers.* Evanston, IL: Correspondence School of Journalism, 1894.

Smith, George W. *The Siege at Hue.* Boulder, CO: Lynne Rienner, 1999.

Smith, Margaret Chase, and William C. Lewis Jr., eds. *Declaration of Conscience.* Garden City, NY: Doubleday, 1972.

Smith, Sally Bedell. *In All His Glory: The Life of William S. Paley, the Legendary Tycoon and His Brilliant Circle.* New York: Simon & Schuster, 1990.

Smythe, Ted Curtis. *The Gilded Age Press, 1865–1900.* Westport, CT: Praeger, 2003.

Sontag, Susan. *On Photography.* New York: Farrar, Straus and Giroux, 1973.

———. *Regarding the Pain of Others.* New York: Farrar, Straus, and Giroux, 2002.

Sperber, A.M. *Murrow: His Life and Times.* New York: Freundlich Books, 1986.

Steel, Ronald. *Walter Lippmann and the American Century.* Boston: Little, Brown, 1980.

Steele, Shelby. *Shame: How America's Past Sins Have Polarized Our Country.* New York, Basic Books: 2015.

Stevens, John D. *Sensationalism and the New York Press.* New York: Columbia University Press, 1991.

Stimson, James A. *Tides of Consent: How Public Opinion Shapes American Politics.* New York: Cambridge University Press, 2004.

Strout, Lawrence N. *Covering McCarthyism: How the Christian Science Monitor Handled Joseph R. McCarthy, 1950–1954.* Westport, CT: Greenwood Press, 1999.

Sussman, Barry. *The Great Coverup: Nixon and the Scandal of Watergate.* New York: Crowell, 1974.

Sweeney, Michael S. *From the Front: The Story of War.* Washington, DC: National Geographic Books, 2002.

Sylvester, Judith. *The Media and Hurricanes Katrina and Rita: Lost and Found.* New York: Palgrave Macmillan, 2008.

Thomas, Evan. *The War Lovers: Roosevelt, Lodge, Hearst, and the Rush to Empire, 1898.* New York: Little, Brown, 2010.

Toplin, Robert Brent. *History by Hollywood: The Use and Abuse of the American Past.* Urbana: University of Illinois Press, 1996.

Trask, David F. *The War with Spain in 1898.* New York: Macmillan, 1981.

Tuchman, Gaye. *Making News: A Study in the Construction of Reality.* New York: Macmillan, 1978.

Vivian, John. *The Media of Mass Communication,* 6th ed. Boston: Allyn and Bacon, 2003.

Wechsler, James A. *The Age of Suspicion.* New York: Random House, 1953.

Weisman, Alan. *Lone Star: The Extraordinary Life and Times of Dan Rather.* Hoboken, NJ: Wiley & Sons, 2006.

Welles, Orson, and Peter Bogdanovich. *This Is Orson Welles.* New York: Da Capo Press, 1998.

White, Theodore H. *The Making of the President, 1960.* New York: Atheneum, 1961.

Whyte, Kenneth. *The Uncrowned King: The Sensational Rise of William Randolph Hearst.* Berkeley, CA: Counterpoint, 2009.

Williams, Juan. *Muzzled: The Assault on Honest Speech.* New York: Crown Publishers, 2011.

Wisan, Joseph E. *The Cuban Crisis as Reflected in the New York Press (1895–1898).* New York: Octagon Books, 1965 (reprint of 1934 ed.).

Woodward, Bob. *The Secret Man: The Story of Watergate's Deep Throat.* New York: Simon & Schuster, 2005.

Wyden, Peter. *Bay of Pigs: The Untold Story.* New York: Simon & Schuster, 1979.

ARTICLES AND BOOK CHAPTERS

Alger, George. "Sensational Journalism and the Law." *Atlantic Monthly* (February 1903): 145–151.

Bagdikian, Ben H. "Woodstein U: Notes on the Mass Production and Questionable Education of Journalists." *Atlantic Monthly* (March 1977): 80–92.

Blake, Mariah. "The Damage Done: Crack Babies Talk Back." *Columbia Journalism Review* (September/October 2004): 10–11.

Chasnoff, Ira J., and others. "Cocaine Use in Pregnancy." *New England Journal of Medicine* 313, no. 11 (12 September 1985): 666–669.

Chiasson, Lloyd, Jr. "McCarthy's Journalism." In *The Press in Times of Crisis,* ed. Lloyd Chiasson Jr. Westport, CT: Praeger, 1995.

Cleghorn, Reese. "Getting It Wrong for 16 Years (at Least)." *American Journalism Review* (June 1993): 4.

Cohen, Jeff. "The Myth of the Media's Role in Vietnam." Fairness and Accuracy in Media (6 May 2001), posted at www.fair.org/index.php?page = 2526.

Coles, Claire D. "Saying 'Goodbye' to the 'Crack Baby.'" *Neurotoxiclogy and Teratology* 15, no. 15 (September/October 1993): 290–292.

Creelman, James. "My Experiences at Santiago." *Review of Reviews and World's Work* (November 1898): 542–546.

———. "The Real Mr. Hearst." *Pearson's Magazine* (September 1906): 249–267.

Culbert, David. "Johnson and the Media." In *Exploring the Johnson Years,* ed. Robert A. Divine. Austin: University of Texas Press, 1981.

Doris, John L., and others. "Prenatal Cocaine Exposure and Child Welfare Outcomes." *Child Maltreatment* 11, no. 4 (November 2006): 326–337.

Dorwart, Jeffery M. "James Creelman, the *New York World* and the Port Arthur Massacre." *Journalism Quarterly* 50, no. 4 (Winter 1973): 697–701.

Dow, Bonnie J. "Feminism, Miss America, and Media Mythology." *Rhetoric and Public Affairs* 6, no. 1 (2003): 127–149.

Druckman, James N. "The Power of Television Images: The First Kennedy-Nixon Debate Revisited." *Journal of Politics* 65, no. 2 (May 2003): 559–571.

Easterbrook, Gregg. "The Sky Is Always Falling." *New Republic* 201, no. 8 (21 August 1989): 21–25.

Edgerton, Gary. "The Murrow Legend as Metaphor: The Creation, Appropriation, and Usefulness of Edward R. Murrow's Life Story." *Journal of American Culture* 15, no. 1 (Spring 1992): 75–91.

Feldstein, Mark. "Watergate Revisited." *American Journalism Review* (August/September 2004): 60–68.

Fisher, Marc. "Essential Again." *American Journalism Review* (October/November 2005): 19–22.

Frank, Deborah A., and others. "Growth, Development, and Behavior in Early Childhood following Prenatal Cocaine Exposure: A Systematic Review." *Journal of the American Medical Association* 285, no. 12 (28 March 2001): 1614–1620.

Greider, Katharine. "Crackpot Ideas." *Mother Jones* (July/August 1995), posted at www.motherjones.com/politics/1995/07/crackpot-ideas.

Hamburger, Philip. "Television: Man from Wisconsin." *New Yorker* (20 March 1954): 71–73.

Hariman, Robert, and John Louis Lucaites. "Public Identity and Collective Memory in U.S. Iconic Photography: The Image of 'Accidental Napalm.'" *Critical Studies in Media Communication* 20, no. 1 (March 2003): 35–56.

Hartman, Donna, and Andrew Golub. "The Social Construction of the Crack Epidemic in Print Media." *Journal of Psychiatric Drugs* 31, no. 4 (October–December 1999): 423–433.

Henry, William A., III. "Reporting the Drug Problem: Have Journalists Overdosed on Print and TV Coverage?" *Time* (6 October 1986): 73.

Heyer, Paul. "America under Attack I: A Reassessment of Orson Welles' 1938 War of the Worlds Broadcast." *Canadian Journal of Communication* 28, no. 2 (March 2003): 149–165.

Keeble, Richard. "Information Warfare in an Age of Hyper-Militarism." In *Reporting War: Journalism in Wartime,* ed. Stuart Allan and Barbie Zelizer. London: Routledge, 2004.

Kennedy, Daniel D. "The Bay of Pigs and the New York *Times:* Another View of What Happened." *Journalism Quarterly* 63, no. 3 (Autumn 1986): 524–529.

Koren, Gideon, and others. "Bias against the Null Hypothesis: The Reproductive Hazards of Cocaine." *Lancet* (16 December 1989): 1440–1442.

Kovach, Bill, and Tom Rosenstiel. "Journalism of Verification." In *Journalism: The Democratic Craft,* ed. G. Stuart Adam and Roy Peter Clark. New York: Oxford University Press, 2006.

Kraus, Sidney. "Winners of the First 1960 Televised Presidential Debate between Kennedy and Nixon." *Journal of Communication* 46, no. 4 (Autumn 1996): 78–96.

Kumar, Deepa. "War Propaganda and the (Ab)uses of Women: Media Constructions of the Jessica Lynch Story." *Feminist Media Studies* 4, no. 3 (2004): 297–313.

Levine, Suzanne Braun. "The Truth Was Burned." *Media Studies Journal* 12, no. 3 (Fall 1998): 110.

Lewandowsky, Stephan, and others. "Memory for Fact, Fiction, and Misinformation: The Iraq War 2003." *Psychological Science* 16, no. 3 (2005): 190–195.

Lunch, William L., and Peter W. Sperlich. "American Public Opinion and the War in Vietnam." *Western Political Quarterly* 32, no. 1 (March 1979): 21–44.

Martin, Joanna Foley. "Confessions of a Non-Bra-Burner." *Chicago Journalism Review* 4 (July 1971): 11–15.

Mayes, Linda C., and others. "The Problem of Prenatal Cocaine Exposure: A Rush to Judgment." *Journal of the American Medical Association*, 267, no. 3 (15 January 1992): 406–408.

McCartney, James. "The 'Washington Post' and Watergate: How Two Davids Slew Goliath." *Columbia Journalism Review* (July/August 1973): 8–22.

McCombs, Maxwell E. "Testing the Myths: A Statistical Review, 1967–86." *Gannett Center Journal* (Spring 1988): 101–108.

Michael, Rudolph D. "History and Criticism of Press-Radio Relationships." *Journalism Quarterly* 15 (Spring 1938): 178–184, 220.

Miller, Nancy K. "The Girl in the Photograph: The Visual Legacies of War." In *Picturing Atrocity: Photography in Crisis*, ed. Jay Prosser, Geoffrey Batchen, Mick Gidley, and Nancy K. Miller. London: Reaktion Books, 2012.

Morgan, John P., and Lynn Zimmer. "The Social Pharmacology of Smokeable Cocaine: Not All It's Cracked Up to Be." In *Crack in America: Demon Drugs and Social Justice*, ed. Craig Reinarman and Harry G. Levine. Berkeley: University of California Press, 1997.

Nelkin, Dorothy. "An Uneasy Relationship: The Tensions between Medicine and the Media." *Lancet* 347 (8 June 1996): 1600–1603.

Remington, Frederic. "Havana, 1899." In *The Reader's Companion to Cuba*, ed. Alan Ryan. San Diego: Harcourt Brace, 1997.

Scanlon, Joseph, and others. "Coping with the Media in Disasters: Some Predictable Problems." *Public Administration Review* 45 (January 1985): 123–133.

Schwarz, Norbert, and others. "Metacognitive Experiences and the Intricacies of Setting People Straight: Implications for Debiasing and Public Information Campaigns." *Advances in Experimental Social Psychology* 39 (2007): 127–161.

Seldes, Gilbert. "Murrow, McCarthy and the Empty Formula: Giving Equal Time for Reply," *Saturday Review* 37 (24 April 1954): 26–27.

"Sevareid Recalls How McCarthyism Hurt Journalists." *Broadcasting* 94 (9 January 1978): 46–48.

Shafer, Jack. "Press Box: Edward R. Movie: *Good Night and Good Luck* and Bad History." Slate.com (5 October 2005), posted at www.slate.com/id/2127595.

Shuchman, Miriam, and Michael S. Wilkes. "Medical Scientists and Health News Reporting: A Case of Miscommunication." *Annals of Internal Medicine* 126, no. 12 (15 June 1997): 976–982.

Sibbison, Jim. "Covering Media 'Breakthroughs'." *Columbia Journalism Review* (July/August 1988): 36–39.

Socolow, Michael J. "The Hyped Panic over 'War of the Worlds'" *Chronicle of Higher Education* 55, no. 9 (24 October 2008): B16.

Szulc, Tad. "*The New York Times* and the Bay of Pigs." In *How I Got That Story*, ed. David Brown and W. Richard Bruner. New York: Dutton, 1967.

Thevenot, Brian. "Myth-Making in New Orleans." *American Journalism Review* (December 2005/January 2006): 30–37.

Thornton, Brian. "Published Reaction when Murrow Battled McCarthy." *Journalism History* 29, no. 3 (Fall 2003): 133–146.

Van Gelder, Lindsy. "The Truth about Bra-Burners." *Ms.* 3, no. 2 (September 1992): 80–81.

Vancil, David L., and Sue D. Pendell. "The Myth of Viewer-Listener Disagreement in the First Kennedy-Nixon Debate." *Central States Speech Journal* 38, no. 1 (Spring 1987): 16–27.

Welch, Matt. "They Shoot Helicopters, Don't They?" *Reason* (December 2005), posted at www.reason.com/news/show/36327.html.

Wershba, Joseph. "Murrow vs. McCarthy: See It Now." *New York Times Sunday Magazine* (4 March 1979): SM12–SM14.

Wiggins, Gene. "Journey to Cuba: The Yellow Crisis." In *The Press in Times of Crisis*, ed. Lloyd Chiasson Jr. Westport, CT: Praeger, 1995.

Wolfe, G. Joseph. "'War of the Worlds' and the Editors." *Journalism Quarterly* 57, no. 1 (Spring 1980): 39–44.

Index

Page numbers in italics indicate photographs.